A. D. Momigliano:
Studies on Modern Scholarship

The publisher gratefully acknowledges the contribution provided by the General Endowment Fund of the Associates of the University of California Press.

A. D. Momigliano

Studies on Modern Scholarship

EDITED BY

G. W. Bowersock and T. J. Cornell

With New Translations by T. J. Cornell

UNIVERSITY OF CALIFORNIA PRESS

Berkeley   Los Angeles   London

University of California Press
Berkeley and Los Angeles, California

University of California Press, Ltd.
London, England

© 1994 by
The Regents of the University of California

Library of Congress Cataloging-in-Publication Data

Momigliano, Arnaldo.
   A. D. Momigliano : studies on modern scholarship / edited by G. W.
Bowersock and T. J. Cornell ; with new translations by T. J. Cornell.
      p.   cm.
   Includes bibliographical references and index.
   ISBN 0-520-07001-1 (cloth). — ISBN 0-520-08545-0 (paper)
   1. Historians — Biography.   2. Historiography.   I. Bowersock,
   G. W. (Glen Warren), 1936–   .   II. Cornell, Tim.   III. Title.
   IV. Title: Studies on modern scholarship.
   D14.M65   1994
   907'.2022 — dc20
   [B]   93-42827
                                                                            CIP

Printed in the United States of America

9 8 7 6 5 4 3 2 1

CONTENTS

INTRODUCTION

From the beginning Arnaldo Momigliano believed that biography was an important means of understanding the past. For him the lives and aspirations of historical figures provided a point of entry into their world, their ideas, and their traditions. Two of Momigliano's earliest books were biographical studies. His influential revisionist study of the Emperor Claudius was first published in 1932 (at the same time as his article on Caligula's personality), and the extended essay on Philip of Macedon appeared just two years later.[1]

Throughout the 1930s Momigliano contributed a vast number of articles to the *Enciclopedia Italiana,* of which the majority were biographical entries. Most of these were on ancient personalities such as Caligula, Corbulo, Demetrius of Phaleron, Phlegon, Nero, Otho, Poppaea, and many others (there are well over two hundred entries).[2] But some, such as the entry on Eduard Meyer, adumbrated Momigliano's later work on modern masters of historical scholarship. This is the work brought together here, including nine pieces published originally in Italian and appearing now in English for the first time. After the war, when Momigliano resumed his contributions to the *Enciclopedia Italiana,* the new direction of his biographical interests is shown by the preponderance of essays on contemporary scholars, such as Frank Adcock, Norman Baynes, Maurice Bowra, Eduard Fraenkel, and others.

The first part of the introduction is the work of G. W. Bowersock, and the second of T. J. Cornell. We are both profoundly indebted to Anne Marie Meyer for her constant support, advice, and correction of error.

References in the introduction to Momigliano's *Contributi alla storia degli studi classici e del mondo antico* are given by volume number and page: for example, VII:171–77 refers to the *Settimo contributo,* pages 171–77.

During the forties and fifties Momigliano undertook the writing of biographical entries for the *Oxford Classical Dictionary* and for the *Encyclopaedia Britannica*. Subsequently he turned with renewed zeal to ancient biography when he delivered the Jackson Lectures at Harvard University in 1968 on *The Development of Greek Biography*. At that time biography was an unfashionable subject in contemporary historiography. It took considerable courage for Momigliano to open up this field when so many historians had abandoned it.

The reaction against biography had been fueled in part by the reaction against prosopography that set in during the late 1950s and early 1960s in the wake of the enormous popularity and influence of Ronald Syme's *Roman Revolution* (1939), which was widely read and imitated after the war, and, subsequently, his *Tacitus* (1958). Both Momigliano and Syme shared a deep interest in the importance of personality, but from an entirely different perspective. Syme himself had virtually no interest in biography as traditionally conceived. Such books as *Tacitus* and *Sallust,* which bear the names of ancient writers as their titles, are in no sense biographies of those figures. Prosopography, for Syme at least, was not a subcategory of biography but rather an analytical method for precise and scientific deductions. When Momigliano once ascribed to Syme a lifelong interest in biography (VIII:392), he was transferring his own predilections to a scholar whom, as we can see from the essay republished here, he never fully understood.

Momigliano's inability to understand Syme reveals, in a positive way, the fundamental characteristics of his own biographical approach. He was perplexed by the lack of personal details about Syme's life—his teachers, his background in New Zealand, and his personal habits. Momigliano wrote with a certain incredulity: "It might even be said that he [Syme] is suspicious of any revealing communication between individuals. His intellectual development is still unclear to me. Even local Oxford gossip has been unable to do anything other than emphasize the more outward and prodigious aspects of his personality: his extraordinary memory and his exceptional linguistic proficiency in both ancient and modern languages. It remains unclear, for example, whether he owes anything personally to that other legendary outsider educated at Oxford, ... Sir Lewis Namier." Momigliano's attempt to find some kind of intellectual and personal pedigree for Syme arose from his belief that no scholar arrives in the world fully trained and independent of the work of others. And obviously he was right.

Syme did indeed try to conceal the forces that had shaped him. In the *Roman Revolution* he paid tribute to Friedrich Münzer, the great German pioneer of prosopography, and yet at the end of his life he denied that he owed much of anything to Münzer. As for Namier, it is hard to say. To the end, Syme claimed that he had never read Namier's work until after the *Roman Revolution* had been published. Yet for Momigliano the *Roman Revo-*

lution was inconceivable as an Oxford product without reference to that eminent Polish exile in Oxford who specialized in prosopography. Toward the end of his life Momigliano became even more emphatic about the need for biography in understanding the past.

The complaint about Syme's reticence was echoed some years later in Momigliano's appreciative but frustrated attitude to the émigré historian Felix Gilbert. In reviewing a volume of Gilbert's essays, Momigliano wrote, "The collection, as a whole, confirms Gilbert's disinclination to speak about himself. . . . There are moments in which something more is really needed — for instance, about the very gifted Jewish wife of Otto Hintze, Hedwig Guggenheimer, a historian in her own right, who left Germany on her own and committed suicide in Holland" (VI:771).

Just a few years before his death Momigliano wrote a striking essay on ancient biography and the study of religion. There he wrote revealingly, "We need personal stories — whether biographical or autobiographical. Personal education, personal religious commitments, punctual relations between social life and personal experience (dreams included) are what we want to know."[3] This astonishing claim reflects the work that Momigliano, in his last years, was doing on ancient religion, for which biography serves as a particularly useful point of access. It is evident that the personal details that he called for were not to be anecdotal or titillating but revelations that would help to explain the thought, presuppositions, and actions of his biographical subjects. The surprising reference to dreams is probably a reflection of Momigliano's study of the famous *Sacred Discourses* of Aelius Aristides in the second century. But not even he had yet turned to the extensive hagiographic literature to pursue this biographical approach to religion. Had he lived, it might have come, and the form of it is perhaps indicated by an essay of the same year as the one on biography and religion, in which Momigliano investigated in detail the life of Saint Macrina by Gregory of Nyssa (VIII:333–47).

The conviction that biography was an important tool for the historian was undoubtedly rooted in Momigliano's abiding concern to work out the tangled fabric of his own life. This is a subject that seems to underlie the work he undertook at the very end of his life on Marcel Mauss and the concept of the person,[4] to say nothing of those remarkably candid revelations about his childhood prepared for the *Pagine ebraiche* in the last months before his death.[5] The relation between his academic career and his scholarship is almost certainly mirrored in his attempts to see the relation between world and scholarship in the great figures whom he studied in the essays presented in this volume. Rostovtzeff, about whom he had first written in the 1930s, became for Momigliano in the 1950s a powerful symbol of the scholarly exile. It was undoubtedly with an eye on himself that Momigliano argued that Rostovtzeff's exile made him in a certain way the

great man that he was. A similar interest in another famous exile can be
seen in Momigliano's consideration of the family of Elias Bikerman ("The
Absence of the Third Bikerman," in Italian, VII:371–75). As a Jew, Bikerman seemed to provide a close parallel to Momigliano; and yet, whenever
he looked for the parallels, they seemed to evaporate.

Perhaps most difficult for Momigliano were his relations with his
teacher, the Catholic historian Gaetano De Sanctis. Momigliano never hesitated to acknowledge his intellectual debt to this formidable man, and yet
there was always a certain tension about their relationship that is now well
documented in the reminiscences published recently by Carlo Dionisotti.[6]
They can easily be felt in the essay on De Sanctis reprinted in this volume.
That essay evidently belongs to the genre of a homage to one's master, but
its beginning is anything but eulogistic: "The man was obstinate, sure of
himself, scornful, and quick to take offense." A little later on Momigliano
says, not without irony, "From the Germans he learned the method which
at that time combined the habit of harsh polemic with a refusal to admit to
the possibility of error." His somewhat critical view of De Sanctis was perhaps Momigliano's way of exorcising his own feelings of uncertainty about
the relations that he had himself maintained with the world of German
scholarship in the middle of the 1930s. He had been the author of a
detailed article on Italian scholarship published in German in a German
periodical, an article that aroused the ire of De Sanctis.[7] This had happened at a time not too many years after De Sanctis had refused to swear
the Fascist oath. The state imposed the oath on all its employees, including
university professors. Momigliano, as we know, did take it when he was
asked to assume the teaching position of none other than De Sanctis
himself.

These are sensitive and perilous topics, and in writing long after the end
of the war on the subject of De Sanctis, Momigliano appeared to be trying
to work them out. He would seem to have rebelled against De Sanctis, with
whom his relations had even been stormy at times. This is probably the
background for the rather harsh judgment that he passed on Mommsen in
the same essay, when he wrote, "It seemed that he [Mommsen] left no room
for other truly independent research, and treated his pupils as involuntary
collaborators in collective enterprises such as the *Corpus inscriptionum* and
the *Monumenta Germaniae*. That Mommsen was impatient of dissent and a
tenacious advocate of collective work directed by himself cannot be
denied."

Momigliano's essay on De Sanctis contains one tiny detail that perhaps
confirms more than anything else the implicitly autobiographical character of this tribute to his teacher. Momigliano wrote, "When he [De Sanctis]
saw me to the door in March 1939 on the eve of my departure for Oxford,
his last words were: 'And remember to write to Salvemini and tell him that

I am always with him in his struggle for liberty.'" But this was not the end of Momigliano's contact with De Sanctis in 1939. Soon after his arrival in Oxford he wanted to get out and move on to the United States. In late May he appealed to De Sanctis in a long and anguished letter in which he begged the great man to assist him in trying to find him some kind of research position in America.[8] He had received a modest award (£250) for research in England, but it was hardly adequate and was only available for a year. Momigliano mentioned to De Sanctis that he had been in contact with Rostovtzeff about a fellowship from an unnamed institution, and he asked De Sanctis to write to Benjamin Meritt at the Institute for Advanced Study in case a vacancy should come up there. He also asked De Sanctis for a general letter for a dossier he was compiling and went on to suggest in considerable detail the items that the master should include in that letter.

Momigliano monitored his own career with the sharp eye of a scholar who had studied closely the careers of others. He was quick to respond to disagreement or polemic, since he knew well from his reading that misinformation, faulty reasoning, and outright error could easily become accepted by a public always willing to believe the last thing to be published. In a personal letter dated 10 November 1980 he confessed that he had perhaps done too little to assure the victory of his views.[9] "I recognize," he wrote, "I committed a mistake in not replying enough to critics." Even so he replied frequently, and some scholars will know that not all of his replies were committed to print.

Although Momigliano's long-standing interest in biography undoubtedly impelled him to look closely at his great scholarly predecessors in the writing of history, the essays he wrote about them are, for the most part, not biographical in form. It was the complex interplay of intellect and personality that particularly attracted Momigliano. His essays are major contributions to intellectual history, and yet personality and character are never far away. The more one reads Momigliano's essays on modern scholars, the more one sees that their exceptionally profound insights into the humanity and thought of their subjects reflect an unceasing struggle on the part of their author to comprehend the counterpoint of thought and action in his own career. The example of his scholarly predecessors was ever present in Momigliano, and he conversed with the luminous dead in the justified conviction that they would consider him an equal.

• • •

The nineteen essays in this volume have been selected from the vast output on the history of historiography which Arnaldo Momigliano produced in the last forty years of his life. Although this output was the result of a lifelong passion, he himself seems to have felt that he was embarking on a new venture around 1946, when he told his Oxford friends, to their evident dismay, that he proposed to devote his future research to the history of historiography.[10]

The first fruit of this research was the essay on F. Creuzer with which the present volume begins. The essay was an appropriately "self-referential" starting point; its purpose was to call attention to the first modern attempt to write a history of Greek historiography. Creuzer saw that the Greek historians could only be studied in relation to a broader conception of historiography in general. For Momigliano Creuzer's work served as a reminder that ancient history and its methods were once exemplary and were considered capable of answering questions of general historical importance. The essay is in fact a programmatic statement, announcing a clear intention to rescue ancient history from the margins of contemporary historical scholarship. One way of doing this, Momigliano suggested, was "quite simply, to regain contact with those writers of the past who treated classical subjects of vital importance to history in general." In accordance with this general aim, he proceeded over the next forty years to publish the great series of studies on individual historians that made him famous among historians and scholars of all periods and disciplines. The present book presents a selection of these studies in chronological order of publication. Momigliano himself would have wanted them to be read with their original dates of publication in mind.

The essays acknowledge the debt we owe to our predecessors in what Momigliano once called our mildly absurd profession. The magnitude of their achievement is constantly stressed. More than once he refers to their lesser known works — monographs, articles, or editions of texts — with the observation that any one of them would be enough to make the reputation of a scholar. To study the work of past historians was for Momigliano an intellectual duty. Edward Shils has described how Momigliano used to begin a lecture by writing on the blackboard a list of the proper names that were going to be referred to, including those of the scholars who had made important contributions to the subject under discussion. When he mentioned one of the names, "he turned towards it deferentially, almost as if its bearer, ancient or modern, were sitting there in a gallery behind him."[11]

Momigliano's studies of past and present historians contain some of his profoundest thoughts about history and historical method. He was writing biography that was, at the same time, intellectual history. One may observe that his study of the Emperor Claudius (1932) deliberately made no mention of Messalina, Agrippina, "and their like."[12] The personal portraits in these essays are drawn with an extreme economy, although the physical appearance, temperament, and drinking habits of the subjects do find their place. Some strong and vivid images emerge, as we are brought face to face with the creative energy of Rostovtzeff, the austere courage of De Sanctis, the melancholy vigor of Beloch, the eccentric genius of Usener, and the human warmth of Eduard Schwartz.

It is equally important to stress that these studies offer more than historiography as it is often understood—that is, as a mildly diverting alternative to serious historical research. It was no doubt this image of historiography as a harmless but worthless activity that caused the dismay of Momigliano's friends in 1946. There was a certain feeling, especially in the English-speaking world,[13] that historians of past generations have little to teach us. This attitude, which demeans the writing of history by regarding it as ephemeral, infuriated Momigliano; in particular, he attacked the practice of treating earlier historians purely as representatives of their own time and without reference to what they themselves studied. He hated all those "dear little dissertations on Baronio, Gibbon, Renan, and Grote by people who would not be able to translate any of the texts which those historians controlled" (VII:54–55).

In Momigliano's view historiography should be centered as much on the object as on the subject under discussion. That is to say, one studies Eduard Meyer in order to understand (or to understand better) the things Meyer wrote about. "History of historiography," he wrote in 1974, "like any other historical research, has the purpose of discriminating between truth and falsehood. As a kind of intellectual history which purports to examine the achievements of an historian, it has to distinguish between solutions of historical problems which fail to convince, and solutions . . . which are worth being restated and developed" (VI:31–32). Great historians of the past are great because they still have much to teach us.

This message is most movingly conveyed in the essay on "New Paths of Classicism in the Nineteenth Century," where we learn how Hermann Usener returned to life during Momigliano's seminar on him in 1982: "We felt that Usener's peculiar use of philology to clarify problems of religion and custom . . . was saying something to us. The old professor of Bonn, who had died in 1905, had suddenly become a real teacher in the Scuola Normale of Pisa."

There is always a danger that a purely subjective treatment of historians, taking no account of the object of their research, will become at its worst the mere retailing of gossip about their personal lives. Research can degenerate into an effort to uncover evidence of their weaknesses and indiscretions. The opening lines of "New Paths of Classicism" are eloquent about this type of production: "In our time there is a great danger that those who talk most readily about historians and scholars may not know too much about history or scholarship. Housman's homosexuality or Wilamowitz's erratic behavior with his father-in-law Mommsen are easier to describe than Housman's achievements as an editor of Manilius or Wilamowitz's understanding of Aeschylus."

Another problem can arise from historicism—that is to say, from the recognition that research is invariably influenced by contemporary circumstances and the personal preoccupations of the historian. If it is too subjective, this approach can lead to relativism and to the production of works "the sole purpose of which is to prove that every historian and any historical problem is historically conditioned—with the additional platitude that even a verdict of this kind by the historian of historiography is historically conditioned" (VI:31).

In Momigliano's view the history of historiography, approached in the proper way, was itself the best defense against relativism and the identification of history as ideology. The proper approach emphasizes the need to examine the evidence and to assess earlier interpretations in the light of it. "No student of the history of historiography does his job properly unless he is capable of telling me whether the historian or historians he has studied used the evidence in a satisfactory way" (VI:54).

As for historicism, Momigliano of course accepted the trite notion that every historical interpretation is the product of a historically conditioned environment and that no one can presume to stand outside the historical process. But as far as he was concerned, this fact gave a positive value to the work of serious historians; it made it possible for them to ask questions that would not otherwise have occurred to them and permitted them to see what others could not see.

Historiography also offers the best defense against ideological or propagandist history. Momigliano frequently came close to identifying intellectual liberty with research, erudition, and respect for the evidence. These are the distinguishing characteristics of the liberal mind, "which is religious in examining the evidence." A determination, like Grote's, "to understand and respect evidence from whatever part it came" provided an antidote to the dishonest misuse of history for ideological and partisan purposes. In Italy in the 1930s, "with Croce as an example, the habit of studying became almost an antifascist habit." Able and intelligent scholars who devoted themselves to propaganda remained able and intelligent, "but they no longer entered a library to discover something new."

Naturally many historians, especially the serious ones, have strong political opinions, religious convictions, and social attitudes, and these are often liable to find expression in their interpretations of the past. Some of the subjects of the present selection of essays had beliefs and opinions that Momigliano did not share and with which he would have had little sympathy. Meyer, Schwartz, and De Sanctis were extremely conservative and nationalistic, Burckhardt was antidemocratic, Freeman flirted with racism, and Beloch was openly anti-Semitic. But such traits do not in themselves make people bad historians, and they do not necessarily have much effect on their personal conduct or their dealings with others. Momigliano noted that even the revered Mommsen had urged Jews to convert but nevertheless continued to count unrepentant Jews, such as Jacob Bernays, among his friends. Momigliano's explanation is that "men are better than their doctrines," a lapidary statement typical of Momigliano.

It follows that the work of a historian should be judged on the strength of its intrinsic merits as an attempt to interpret the evidence, regardless of external considerations. "The fact that Georges Dumézil was, we are told, a supporter of the Action française is not an argument against his theories on Indo-European society. In an age of ideologies, we must be careful to submit scholarly results to the sole legitimate criterion of evaluation, which is the reliability of the evidence." If Momigliano found Dumézil's theories on early Rome wanting, it was not because they were racist but because they did not fit the Roman evidence and did not help to explain the complex development of Rome in the archaic age (III:581–83; VII:382).[14]

For Momigliano what made great historians worthy of admiration was the fact that they all promoted erudition and commitment to research. The subjects of the essays in this volume are as diverse a group of historians as one could imagine, but they are united by a shared commitment to the search for the truth about the past. That commitment, for instance, linked Croce to De Sanctis, "so different in personal physique, manner, and religious outlook, but so similar in their uninterrupted passion for learning and in love of liberty."

A further aspect of Momigliano's view of historicism is the fact that historical circumstances bear not only on the author but also on the reader, and that serious historical research entails a dialogue between the historian and his predecessors. In the history of historiography a difference of viewpoint can lead to a creative dialogue. The study of past historians not only makes us aware of new questions but suggests new lines of research because we tend to ask the questions in the context of our own contemporary needs and preoccupations.

Without a historiographical dimension, historical research can all too easily degenerate into pointless and arbitrary speculation. This was one of the causes of what Momigliano saw as a crisis in the study of Greek history in the postwar period. Part of the solution, he suggested, was to go back to Grote and once again to embrace the principles that Grote had expounded: "Perhaps it is not altogether surprising that our generation should find it increasingly difficult to assess the value of evidence, but the consequence is that idle and misleading speculation is a factor with which the Greek historian has constantly to reckon. Much of the recent work on early Greek traditions is pre-Grotean in character."

Neither intuition nor common sense can replace a critical knowledge of previous interpretations or guarantee that the historian will come to grips with serious historical problems. Historical research is not worth doing unless one can find new questions to ask and the evidence to answer those questions. "Too much historical research," he wrote in 1953, "is being done by people who do not know why they are doing it and without regard to the limits imposed by the evidence" (I:373).

In his papers on the work of individual historians, it is worth asking why Momigliano wrote when he did. In general there are two answers. Some of the essays were occasioned by the death of the historians in question (e.g., Rostovtzeff, De Sanctis), by a centenary (Croce), by the reissue (or translation) of a classic work (Burckhardt, Syme), or by a commission (e.g., for an entry on Beloch in the *Dizionario Biografico degli Italiani*).[15] In these cases his approach is invariably programmatic: the account of the subject is always linked to an assessment of the objective value of his work, how it has influenced subsequent research, why it is still useful, and what it suggests in the way of possible future research.

These concerns are even more evident in the papers belonging to the second broad category, the ones, that is, that Momigliano produced spontaneously on subjects of his own choice. For the most part, these studies arose directly from historical research that he was currently engaged in. In these essays we can see most easily the results of what we have called Momigliano's "creative dialogue" with the historians under examination. By way of example we may mention the case of Fustel de Coulanges; his extraordinary book on the ancient city had a profound influence on Momigliano, who returned to it again and again during the last twenty years of his life.

As far as one can judge, Momigliano's study of Fustel began in earnest during the 1960s and arose from two distinct but connected lines of research: the first was his growing interest in sociology and anthropology and the use of the comparative method in the study of ancient history, and the second was the intensive research he was then doing on the origins of Rome. His first major publication on Fustel appeared in 1970 (chapter 11 of this volume), but some years earlier he and S. C. Humphreys had embarked on a research project which they called "a new *Cité antique*," with explicit reference to Fustel.[16]

At first sight it might seem surprising that Momigliano should have been so stimulated by *The Ancient City*, with its reactionary political outlook, its many fanciful hypotheses, its rather weak control of the ancient evidence, and its deliberate refusal to make use of modern scholarship. Fustel most decidedly did not try to engage in a dialogue with previous historians (although, as Momigliano points out, his professed ignorance of contemporary historical research was disingenuous). But the most uncongenial feature, one would have thought, was Fustel's vision of the ancient city itself.

Nevertheless there was something in Fustel's work that struck a chord in Momigliano. Fustel saw that religion lay at the heart of social institutions.

As time went on Momigliano too gave more and more of his attention to religious belief and the role of religion in history. This ultimately lay behind his admiration for Eduard Meyer and led him to find weaknesses in materialists such as Beloch and Rostovtzeff. There is also a curious parallelism between the religious stance of Fustel de Coulanges and that of Momigliano himself. Fustel was not himself a believer, but he saw the importance of belief and had immense respect for religious tradition. Momigliano alludes to Fustel's will but does not quote the famous clause which stipulated that he should receive a Christian burial because "if one does not think like one's ancestors, one at least respects what they believed." Momigliano said virtually the same thing when he left instructions for his burial in the Jewish cemetery at Cuneo, his home town in Piedmont.

There is much to be learned from Momigliano's studies of past historians. The essays in this volume have been compiled in the belief that they contain instructive material for anyone who wants to see how research on the ancient world can be done. They help to explain why the study of earlier modern historians is important. It would take another Momigliano to do them justice.

Notes

1. *L'opera dell'imperatore Claudio* (1932), translated into English by W. D. Hogarth as *Claudius: The Emperor and his Achievement* (1934). Also in 1932: "La personalità di Caligola," *Annali della Scuola Normale Superiore di Pisa*, 2d ser. I (1932), pp. 205–28, reprinted in IX:191–217. On Philip, *Filippo il Macedone: Saggio sulla storia greca del IV secolo a.C.* (1934; reprint with corrections, a new preface, and a bibliographical appendix, 1987).

2. For a list of the contributions to the *Enciclopedia Italiana*, see IV:721–25.

3. VIII:199. Exactly what "punctual relations" are remains something of a mystery — points of contact, presumably.

4. See G. W. Bowersock, "Momigliano's Quest for the Person," in *The Presence of the Historian: Essays in Memory of Arnaldo Momigliano, History and Theory*, Beiheft 30 (1991), pp. 27–36.

5. A. Momigliano, *Pagine ebraiche* (1987), pp. xxix–xxxi.

6. C. Dionisotti, *Ricordo di Arnaldo Momigliano* (1989), especially pp. 33–46.

7. A. Momigliano, "Studien über griechische Geschichte in Italien von 1913–1933," *Italienische Kulturberichte*, 1 (1934), pp. 163–95 [I:299–326]; G. De Sanctis, *Riv. Fil. Class.*, 14 (1936), pp. 97–99 [*Scritti minori*, VI, pp. 937–40].

8. Letter dated 30 May 1939 from Momigliano to De Sanctis. I (GWB) am grateful to Leandro Polverini for giving me a photocopy of this letter.

9. For the significance of this date, see the perceptive remarks by Dionisotti, *Ricordo* (n. 6 above), pp. 101–2, on the response of Momigliano to the publication of Luciano Canfora's *Ideologie del classicismo* in 1980.

10. See O. Murray, "Arnaldo Momigliano in England," in *The Presence of the Historian,* pp. 53–54, published in Italian in *Riv. St. Ital.,* 100 (1988), p. 427.

11. E. Shils, "The Community of Learning: Arnaldo Dante Momigliano, 1908–1987," *Encounter* 71 (December 1988), pp. 66–71. The story about the blackboard is from the address he gave at the memorial service at the University of Chicago on 22 October 1987.

12. A. Momigliano, *Claudius: The Emperor and his Achievement* (2d English ed., Cambridge, 1961; reprint, Greenwood Press, Westport, Conn., 1981), p. xv. The whole preface makes Momigliano's historical purpose abundantly clear; but *cf.* also his reply to a critic, IX:219–22 (1932).

13. Thus Murray, n. 10 above; but this attitude was not confined to the English-speaking world. In 1959 Momigliano criticized Italian classicists for their "habit of treating the history of historiography as a Sunday pastime, when one is weary of working on real history and has not enough energy to read books, but only to leaf through them" (III:708).

14. Momigliano never made it clear whether he thought that Dumézil's theories were racist. In IV:442 he wrote, "non c'è nulla di deteriormente razzista nel lavoro originale e profondo dello studioso francese" ["There is nothing badly racist in the French scholar's original and profound work"], but there is a double ambiguity in this sentence, since the meaning depends on whether the key words ("deteriormente," "originale e profondo") are restrictive or nonrestrictive. This ambiguity was intentional, as Momigliano confirmed to me (TJC) when I asked him.

15. It is worth noting that Momigliano first wrote about Eduard Meyer and Niebuhr in the *Enciclopedia Italiana* (vols. XXIII and XXIV, 1937); an article on Grote appeared in the *Encyclopaedia Britannica* in 1964.

16. VI:459. Other important contributions on Fustel can be found in VII: 171–77, 179–86; VIII:109–20. In VII:185 he called the *Cité antique* "one of the most stimulating books ever written."

BIBLIOGRAPHICAL REFERENCES

The number at the right in parentheses designates the item number in Momigliano's bibliography, as presented in *Contributi* IV, VI, and VIII.

CHAPTER ONE: "Friedrich Creuzer and Greek Historiography," *Journal of the Warburg and Courtauld Institutes*, 9 (1946), pp. 153–63; *Contributo* (1955), pp. 233–48; *Studies in Historiography* (1966), pp. 75–90. (247)

CHAPTER TWO: "George Grote and the Study of Greek History" (an Inaugural Lecture delivered at University College London on 19 February 1952); Greek translation, *Hê Angloellênikê Epitheôrêsê,* 3 (1953–54), pp. 263–77; *Contributo* (1955), pp. 213–31; *Studies in Historiography* (1966), pp. 56–74; French translation, *Problèmes d'historiographie ancienne et moderne* (1983), pp. 361–82. (288)

CHAPTER THREE: "M. I. Rostovtzeff," *The Cambridge Journal*, 7 (1954), pp. 334–46; *Contributo* (1955), pp. 341–54; *Studies in Historiography* (1966), pp. 91–104; French translation, *Problèmes d'historiographie ancienne et moderne* (1983), pp. 424–40. (300)

CHAPTER FOUR: "Introduzione alla *Griechische Kulturgeschichte* di Jacob Burckhardt" (Italian edition, Florence: Sansoni, 1955); *Secondo contributo* (1960), pp. 283–98; English translation, *Essays in Ancient and Modern Historiography* (1977), pp. 295–305. Translated by Judith Landry; translation revised by T. J. Cornell. (316)

CHAPTER FIVE: "In Memoria di Gaetano De Sanctis (1870–1957)," *Rivista Storica Italiana,* 69 (1957), pp. 177–95; *Secondo contributo* (1960), pp. 299–317. Translated by T. J. Cornell. (332)

CHAPTER SIX: "Introduzione a Ronald Syme, *La rivoluzione romana*" (Italian edition, Turin: Einaudi, 1962), pp. ix–xv; *Terzo contributo* (1966), pp. 729–37. Translated by T. J. Cornell. (395)

CHAPTER SEVEN: "Reconsidering B. Croce (1866–1952)" (a memorial lecture delivered at Durham University in May 1966), *Durham University Journal* (December 1966), pp. 1–12; *Quarto contributo* (1969), pp. 95–115; *Essays in Ancient and Modern Historiography* (1977), pp. 345–63. (448)

CHAPTER EIGHT: "Giulio Beloch," *Dizionario Biografico degli Italiani* (1966), vol. VIII, pp. 32–45; *Terzo contributo* (1966), pp. 239–65. Translated by T. J. Cornell. (450)

CHAPTER NINE: "Jacob Bernays," *Mededelingen der Koninklijke Neder-landse Akademie van Wetenschappen*, Afd. Letterkunde, Nieuwe Reeks, Deel 32, no. 5 (1969), pp. 151–78; *Quinto contributo* (1975), pp. 127–58; French translation, *Problèmes d'historiographie ancienne et moderne* (1983), pp. 441–74; Italian translation, *Pagine ebraiche* (1987), pp. 157–80. (490)

CHAPTER TEN: "J. G. Droysen between Greeks and Jews," *History and Theory*, 9 (1970), pp. 139–53; *Quinto contributo* (1975), pp. 109–26; *Essays in Ancient and Modern Historiography* (1977), pp. 307–23; French translation, *Problèmes d'historiographie ancienne et moderne* (1983), pp. 383–401; Italian translation, *Tra storia e storicismo* (1985), pp. 211–31; German translation, *Wege in die Alte Welt* (1991), pp. 177–91. (501)

CHAPTER ELEVEN: "La città antica di Fustel de Coulanges," *Rivista Storica Italiana*, 82 (1970), pp. 81–98; *Quinto contributo* (1975), pp. 159–78; English translation, *Essays in Ancient and Modern Historiography* (1977), pp. 325–43; French translation, *Problèmes d'historiographie ancienne et mo-derne* (1983), pp. 402–23; German translation, *Wege in die Alte Welt* (1991), pp. 192–208. Translated by Judith Landry; translation revised by T. J. Cornell. (503)

CHAPTER TWELVE: "Premesse per una discussione su Karl Reinhardt," *Rivista Storica Italiana* 87 (1975), pp. 311–18; *Annali della Scuola Normale Superiore di Pisa*, 3d ser., V, fasc. 4 (1975), pp. 1309–17; *Sesto contributo* (1980), pp. 351–59. Translated by T. J. Cornell. (561)

CHAPTER THIRTEEN: "Premesse per una discussione su Eduard Schwartz" (introduction to a seminar at the Scuola Normale Superiore in Pisa, February 1978), *Rivista Storica Italiana*, 90 (1978), pp. 617–26; *Annali della Scuola Normale Superiore di Pisa*, 3d ser., IX, fasc. 4 (1979), pp. 999–1011; *Settimo contributo* (1984), pp. 233–44. Translated by T. J. Cornell. (600)

CHAPTER FOURTEEN: "Uno storico liberale fautore del Sacro Romano Impero: E. A. Freeman" (introduction to a seminar at the Scuola Normale

Superiore in Pisa, February 1981), *Rivista Storica Italiana,* 92 (1980), pp. 152–63; with slight variations, *Annali della Scuola Normale Superiore di Pisa,* 3d ser., XI, fasc. 2 (1981), pp. 309–22; *Settimo contributo* (1984), pp. 187– 200 [the later version translated here]. Translated by T. J. Cornell.   (642)

CHAPTER FIFTEEN: "Premesse per una discussione su Eduard Meyer" (introduction to a seminar at the Scuola Normale Superiore in Pisa, February 1981), *Rivista Storica Italiana,* 93 (1981), pp. 384–98; *Settimo contributo* (1984), pp. 215–31. Translated by T. J. Cornell.   (637)

CHAPTER SIXTEEN: *New Paths of Classicism in the Nineteenth Century, History and Theory,* Beiheft 21 (1982), 64 pp.; Italian translation, *Tra storia e storicismo* (1985), pp. 99–192; German translation, *Wege in die Alte Welt* (1991), pp. 108–76.   (647)

CHAPTER SEVENTEEN: "Premesse per una discussione su Georges Dumézil" (introduction to a seminar at the Scuola Normale Superiore in Pisa, January 1983), *Opus: Rivista internazionale per la storia economica e sociale dell'antichità,* 2 (1983), pp. 329–42; *Rivista Storica Italiana,* 95 (1983), pp. 245–61. Translated by T. J. Cornell.   (658)

CHAPTER EIGHTEEN: "Un 'Ritorno' alla etruscheria settecentesca: K. O. Müller," *L'Età dei Lumi: Studi storici sul Settecento europeo in onore di Franco Venturi* (1985), vol. II, pp. 653–68; *Ottavo contributo* (1987), pp. 45–58, and see *Nono Contributo* (1992), p. 635. Translated by T. J. Cornell.   (675)

CHAPTER NINETEEN: "From Bachofen to Cumont," Italian translation, *Saggi di storia della religione romana* (1988), pp. 135–49; English original in *Nono contributo* (1992), pp. 593–607.   (725)

ONE

Friedrich Creuzer
and Greek Historiography

Alla cara memoria di Leone Ginzburg morto nelle carceri di Roma il 5.II.1944.

The name of Professor Friedrich Creuzer of Heidelberg University is associated with two of the most typical episodes of the Romantic period. His
reluctance to throw in his lot with the gifted Caroline von Günderode led
to her suicide (1806)—and to the vindictive remarks by Caroline's friend
and champion, Bettina Brentano: "Creuzer came to visit Savigny in Marburg. Repulsive as he was, it was inconceivable that he could interest a
woman."[1] His *Symbolik und Mythologie der alten Völker* (1810–12) was an attempt to give a scientific basis to the Neoplatonic interpretation of Greek
mythology.[2] Though soon dismissed by responsible philologists, it was
greeted with enthusiasm by philosophers like Schelling,[3] lastingly influenced the erratic genius of Bachofen,[4] and altogether played a very important part in the development of mythological studies.

We do not propose to offer any contribution to the discussion of these
two episodes. There is another aspect of Creuzer which is much less known
and deserves attention: his study of Greek historiography. It belongs to the
early phase of his life, before Caroline von Günderode and the *Symbolik*
appeared on his horizon. Indeed, it belongs to those years around 1800
which mark the beginning of a new era for historical studies in Europe and
can still offer much inspiration. What was done in ancient history was then
immediately relevant to history in general. The methods of Greek and Roman history were still exemplary. The results thus obtained were of general
interest. Ancient history has now become a provincial branch of history. It
can recover its lost prestige only if it proves again capable of offering results
affecting the whole of our historical outlook. One of the ways is, quite simply, to regain contact with those writers of the past who treated classical

"Friedrich Creuzer and Greek Historiography," *Journal of the Warburg and Courtauld Institutes,*
9 (1946), pp. 153–63; *Contributo* (1955), pp. 233–48; *Studies in Historiography* (1966), pp. 75–90.

subjects of vital importance to history in general. Creuzer produced a book of this kind. In writing his *Historische Kunst der Griechen* he was fully aware that the Greeks invented what we admit to be true historiography and that any understanding of Greek historiography is not possible without a firm grasp of the principles of historiography at large.

Friedrich Creuzer's *Die historische Kunst der Griechen in ihrer Entstehung und Fortbildung* is now read in the second edition of 1845—twelve years later than H. Ulrici's *Charakteristik der antiken Historiographie* (1833). Inevitably, one forgets that the book had first appeared in 1803. A recent comparison between the two editions confirmed my suspicion that the second edition, though it was increased by almost two hundred pages of *Nachträge* and enriched with bibliographical notes, did not introduce any change into the text. What one reads in the text of pages 1–252 of the second edition[5] is what Creuzer had already published in 1803.[6] The impression one may get from the notes of the second edition that Creuzer was indebted to some books later than 1803, and especially to the *Entwurf einer Theorie der Geschichte* by W. Wachsmuth,[7] published at Halle in 1820, is therefore misleading. Wachsmuth, who dedicated his book to Creuzer, was certainly his friend, and Creuzer liked to mention him in his notes to the second edition, but the text was in no way affected by him or by any of the other writers later than 1803 who are listed in a note on pages 2–3. Creuzer's book is nothing more nor less than the first modern history of Greek historiography, as the contemporary review in the *Göttingische Gelehrte Anzeigen* immediately recognized:[8] an epoch-making book, though it receives no mention in the *Geschichte der Philologie* by Wilamowitz and is barely referred to in Sandys's *Classical Scholarship*. Creuzer's *Symbolik* has remained famous and is again enjoying a revival of popularity in the train of the fashionable interest in symbols and symbolism.[9] Its refutation by Lobeck's *Aglaophamus* is, indeed, a part of its prestige. But the *Historische Kunst der Griechen*, which was a healthy inspiration, is relegated to the dubious obscurity of books which are assumed to be superseded. Only O. Regenbogen, in writing his remarkable essay on Herodotus,[10] was struck by the fact that he had been anticipated by Creuzer and acknowledged it in eloquent words. Yet his characterization of Creuzer's personality—"rationalistische Polyhistorie und romantische Einfühlungsfähigkeit"—is, as I hope to show, neither exhaustive nor correct.[11]

Vossius was still, at the end of the eighteenth century, *the* book on Greek historiography.[12] He was far from being a mere antiquarian. Both his *Historici Graeci* and his *Historici Latini*[13] have their complement in his *Ars Historica* (1623), the hero of which is Polybius. But his interest in historiography was to discover principles, not to describe a development. Theory

provided criteria by which to judge the ancient practice, and ancient practice gave illustrative material to the *Ars Historica*. That was only a particular
case of the general relation between history and philosophy: "Est enim
historia, ut non semel dictum, philosophia exemplis constans. Haec
philosophiae et historiae affinitas ac coniunctio facit, ut philosopho
praecepta sua liceat historicorum exemplis illustrare, et vicissim historicus
possit facta quaedam ad philosophorum praecepta expendere" (*Ars Hist.*,
chap. 18).

It is hardly necessary to add that this approach was everywhere crum-
bling long before Creuzer's appearance on the scene. In the second part of
the eighteenth century one could read scores of dissertations inspired by
the principle that historians are the voice of their times and must be examined in relation to what was called the genius of their age. The authority of
Herodotus and Thucydides was steadily growing. Indeed Herodotus —
naïve, cosmopolitan, "historien des moeurs," and an imitator of Homer —
was becoming very popular.[14] Thucydides also was better appreciated as a
student of politics.[15] It remained true, however, that Vossius's *Historici
Graeci* had not been replaced as a whole by a more modern history of Greek
historiography. Besides, Creuzer was entitled to ask himself whether the
reaction against Vossius had gone far enough. In 1797, when he wrote his
first essay on Herodotus and Thucydides,[16] he had been a pupil of Schiller
in Jena,[17] was well acquainted with Herder's work and had just been reading the new little book *Die Griechen und Römer* by F. Schlegel.[18] The Romantic wind was blowing around him. Other inspiration in the same sense,
though not pointing so clearly in the new direction, was to be found in
some students of the history of philosophy whom he had known well in his
undergraduate years, for instance D. Tiedemann.[19] The preface to *Herodotus und Thukydides* declares that the ancient historians had not yet been
"philosophically" studied to such good purpose as the most ancient Greek
poets. It also says that a complete understanding of Herodotus will be possible only after the successful completion of the research still in progress on
the epic poems: the allusion to F. A. Wolf (and to F. Schlegel?) is obvious.
Many other allusions in this essay and in the following dissertation *De
Xenophonte historico* (1799) leave no doubt that Creuzer was already thinking
of a new and up-to-date history of Greek historiography.

Examined in itself, the pamphlet on Herodotus and Thucydides cannot
be said to be more than an acute and pointed restatement of current contemporary opinions. It was Creuzer's aim to prove that Herodotus and
Thucydides had different conceptions of history for reasons depending
partly on the times in which they lived and partly on the subjects they chose.
Thucydides had the advantage of a stricter ideal of truth. Herodotus was
superior in the depth and variety of human interests. As in many contemporary studies, the difference between Herodotus and Thucydides is no

longer examined in the abstract, but in relation to their historical environ-
ments. The historical perspective does not lead to complete relativism, but
helps to attribute a value of his own to each historian. The special value of
Herodotus is found in his wider humanity, according to a famous passage
of Herder's *Briefe zur Beförderung der Humanität*.[20]

The dissertation *De Xenophonte historico* seems to me to represent a definite step forward. The survival of more traditional patterns of judgment is
evident in the Latin form and academic purpose of the booklet. But the
sharp differentiation between the pragmatism of Polybius and that of the
early Greek historians, the analysis of the differences between Xenophon's
and Herodotus' religion, and the conclusion that Xenophon marks the
beginning of the decline of Greek historiography because he is more subjective and superstitious, show that Creuzer was getting into shape the idea
of a new history of historiography.

What was really only rudimentary in these first essays was the interest in
the relation between poetry and history, insofar as it could help to define
both the specific quality of Greek historiography and the nature of historiography in general. On these points Chr. Gottl. Heyne, F. Schlegel—and
the intense philosophic discussion of the beginning of the new century
which proceeded through the Schlegels to Fichte and Schelling—were decisive. Heyne's *Historiae scribendae inter Graecos primordia* was printed in
1799. F. Schlegel's *Geschichte der Poesie der Griechen und Römer* appeared in
1798. The *Athenaeum* was started in the same year, and Schelling's *System des
transcendentalen Idealismus* was published in 1800. As we have said, *Die
historische Kunst der Griechen* was first edited in 1803.

It was Creuzer's opinion, when he wrote his *Historische Kunst,* that no one
could talk of Greek historiography without having a clear notion of what
historiography was. Thus, he inserted a brief theory of historiography for
which, as he says, he had "die Ansicht der Neueren vor Augen gehabt"
(p. 187). This theory was not to be considered an external criterion
imposed upon Greek historiography, but a hermeneutic hypothesis to be
checked on the Greek texts (p. 175). Historiography, according to Creuzer,
tries to discover the unity ("übersinnliche Einheit") and meaning of empirical facts by the application of critical research and of an artistic process of
synthesis. The task of the student of historiography is to find out the critical
methods and the artistic proceedings whereby historians establish the facts
in their individuality and formulate the ideas which are behind the facts.
So far as Greek historiography is concerned, one has to examine two problems: (a) the origin of Greek historical thought; (b) its development from
Herodotus onwards.

The origin of Greek historiography is to be found in epic poetry. The
evolution happened in four stages: (1) Homeric poems; (2) epic cycle;

(3) *logographoi;* (4) Herodotus. Each of these stages must be analyzed from the point of view of (a) style; (b) method of ascertaining the facts; (c) disposition of the facts, in order to see how the Greeks became increasingly aware of the difference between fine artistic creation and the recounting of facts. Only Homer and Herodotus present their facts, not in a superficial order, but in a real artistic unity. The traditional opinion that Herodotus was an imitator of Homer is given a deeper meaning.[21] The fact that Herodotus, like the poets, read his historical compositions to the Greek public is taken to confirm the theory that history developed from poetry. In the analysis of the unity of Herodotus, Creuzer writes his most impressive pages. They are almost a hymn to the birth of history.

The second part of the book on the development of Greek historiography is simpler and shorter. Creuzer does not go beyond Xenophon. The rest is decay because the artistic element of historiography was suffocated by narrow didactic preoccupations. Herodotus, Thucydides, and Xenophon had method in ascertaining facts; they had also art. Herodotus was inspired by a religious-national idea; Thucydides by a political idea — though, according to Creuzer, more in his description of single events than in the general annalistic plan of his work — whereas Xenophon's inspiration is clearly ethical and is accompanied by a nice sense for harmony. All these forms of historiography are legitimate because their ideas are not personal reflections of the writer, like the ideas of Polybius, but objective patterns. Creuzer cannot help regretting that Thucydides had to miss the freshness of Herodotus ("jener Reiz der jugendlichen Historie," p. 224), but realizes that a political historian could not do otherwise. On the other hand pragmatic history with a view to utility, as in Polybius, is little less than the great enemy of sound historical thought. Insofar as modern historians are influenced by Polybius rather than by Herodotus or Thucydides — not a little, one understands, being Vossius's personal fault — ancient historiography of the severe style is superior to modern historiography. Modern historiography, admittedly, is often better in one of the elements which contribute to the writing of history, namely critical research, but harmony between facts and ideas is lacking in it. With the modern, what is not pragmatic is aprioristic. In the modern world the alternative to pragmatic historiography is philosophy of history "nach welcher der Geist, statt sich in religiöser Betrachtung über die Natur zu erheben, aus stolzer Willkür sich eine Natur erschuf" (p. 201). Only the new history by Johannes Müller may be compared with Herodotus (p. 197) — good German prose, "gemütlich," better than the professorial style or than French frivolity.

It is obvious that the brothers Schlegel were the most profound influence on the author of the *Historische Kunst der Griechen.* Even Herder, Lessing, and F. A. Wolf were, at least in part, seen by the young Creuzer through the eyes of the two Schlegels. Many years later, in a review which appeared in the *Heidelberger Jahrbücher,* (XVIII, 1825), Creuzer proclaimed the great debt of his generation to them.[22] From F. Schlegel he borrowed the idea of the origin of Greek historiography from the epic cycle[23] and through Schlegel assimilated the Wolfian conception of the Greek world as a spiritual unity. On the other side it is probable that A. Wilhelm Schlegel sharpened his eye for style. Generally, the atmosphere of Creuzer's book is that of the brothers Schlegel: the same deep concern with poetry and language, the same underlying assumption that the study of Greek literature will illuminate the nature of the human mind or, to put it in a way which the brothers Schlegel would not have rejected, that if one wants to understand a thing one must follow up its historical origin.

This influence, however, has clear limits. The more speculative work of the two brothers on methodology of history and philology was not known to Creuzer because it was confined either to unpublished lectures (A. W. Schlegel) or to unpublished drafts (Friedrich). Neither wrote a specific history of historiography, and Friedrich, the nearer to Creuzer, seems to have thought in his early phase that history of historiography could be treated as pure literary history—an idea against which Creuzer felt that he still had to protest twenty years later in the review in the *Heidelberger Jahrbücher* quoted above.[24] In those years Friedrich Schlegel, though so emphatic on the necessity of history for *"Selbstkenntniss,"* was much more directly concerned with the problem of the philosophy of philology which would form a fit prelude to the higher synthesis of poetry and philosophy. Even if it were true that his philosophy of philology, if developed, would have been a full philosophy of history, it is at least certain that Creuzer was not aware of it.[25] Creuzer was not specifically interested in the problem of hermeneutic, but in that of historiography. The extension of research to a field which the two brothers had left almost untouched implied a somewhat different attitude towards the problem of history.

In this situation Heyne's memoir on the origin of Greek historiography in the Göttingen *Commentationes* of 1799 (vol. XIV) was providential. What young F. Schlegel had suggested in a few words—the origin of Greek historiography from the epos—was independently demonstrated by the veteran master at great length and in a sober scholastic Latin. Creuzer, who was after all an academic scholar, could find in it solid ground on which to build his book. F. Schlegel provided the inspiration, Heyne the foundation.

I should not care to commit myself on the relation of the *Historische Kunst* to the great contemporary systems of philosophy. Creuzer, in his old days, when he had entirely lost faith in his juvenile attempt at writing theory and history of historiography together, spoke of it as "ein Kantisch-Fichtescher Lappen."[26] Direct or indirect echoes from Kant and Fichte are easy to catch in his pages. His conception of art as freedom and of historical events as nature can perhaps be described as approximately Kantian. But Kant and Fichte (at least until 1813) both deprecated empirical history (and historiography) as a mere "rhapsody" of facts and, whatever their special points, were agreed that the only history which made sense was the history *a priori* of human liberty.[27] It seems clear that Creuzer was proceeding in a different direction. In his modest way he was busy, together with many of the very best of his generation, in reestablishing the value of empirical history within the frame of the new idealism. Though I should not be able to say how much Schelling meant to Creuzer in those years, a glance at Schelling, the main motive force of this reaction, can, better than anything else, remind us of what was happening. By Schelling, Herder was vindicated and Schiller's conception of art was "erected into the principle of knowledge and existence" (to echo Hegel's solemn words).

In his essay on the philosophy of history (1798)[28] Schelling denied the possibility of history *a priori,* indeed of any philosophy of history, and attributed to the field of history those events which are neither periodical nor otherwise bound by necessary laws. "Was a priori zu berechnen ist, was nach notwendigen Gesetzen geschieht, ist nicht Objekt der Geschichte." The historian was also said to be a poet (*Dichter*) without much explanation. The *System des transcendentalen Idealismus* (1800) strongly reaffirms that "die Willkür ist . . . die Göttin der Geschichte" and that what is necessary cannot be historical. The new analysis of necessity and liberty, however, shows that a line is to be drawn between pragmatic history (historiography) and universal history, the latter aiming at the real object of human life: "Das allmähliche Entstehen der weltbürgerlichen Verfassung." Only such a history, which admits liberty and necessity together, is directly connected with (indeed absorbed into) the supreme sphere of art. The practical conclusion which Schelling himself derived in 1802 in his *Vorlesungen über die Methode des academischen Studiums* (published in 1803 and therefore probably not known to Creuzer before he finished his book) was not far from Creuzer in the general attitude to the historians of the past. Herodotus and Thucydides were opposed to Polybius and Tacitus as the authentic historians to the pragmatic ones. Modern historians were depreciated with the partial exception of Gibbon and the more complete exceptions of Machiavelli and J. Müller. Sound historiography was described as a synthesis of reality and ideality obtained by art.[29] As the *Vorlesungen über die Methode* show a great change in many points of Schelling's thought, it may be emphasized that in the matter of history the continuity is patent.

That the times were ripe for this conception is confirmed by A. W. Schlegel's expression of analogous ideas in lectures which were not published during his life and therefore probably did not affect Creuzer. In the *Vorlesungen über schöne Litteratur und Kunst* of 1801–2 the conception of an empirical history based on universal ideas is neatly formulated.[30] In the

Vorlesungen über Enzyklopädie of 1803, which were written under the influence of Schelling's new book *Vorlesungen über die Methode*, the artistic character of historiography was defined in an impressive formula: history was called "Poesie der Wahrheit." It goes without saying that pragmatic historiography was attacked, and Johannes Müller praised as the really great historian of the age.[31]

Thus, what makes it legitimate to relate Creuzer to Schelling is the common conception that art is *the* instrument whereby empirical history is possible. Creuzer's formulations are very brief and somewhat superficial, and it would be both unfair and grotesque to press them or to measure them by the standards of compact systems. Creuzer never drew a rigorous distinction between pragmatic and universal history and never tackled the problem of the transcendental unity of necessity and liberty which was basic for Schelling. What, to my mind, makes the interest of Creuzer's pages is that he did not simply theorize as to what historiography ought to be, but showed in a history of historiography what historiography is. Being chiefly interested in history of historiography, he came to defend the autonomy of empirical history by writing history of historiography. On the other hand, his theory of historiography proved to be a very sensitive instrument for the analysis of Greek historiography. No other student of Greek historiography has ever made better remarks on the artistic unity of Herodotus, Thucydides, and Xenophon. A history of modern historiography did not appear, so far as I know, until 1812; it was the *Geschichte der historischen Wissenschaften* by L. Wachler. And Wachler, though of an admirable erudition, cannot be compared with Creuzer in grasp of ideas.

The broader issues can only be hinted at. The conception that historiography is the discovery of ideas by an artistic process combined with a critical method is to be found again in Schleiermacher and W. von Humboldt and may be taken as typical of the first phase of the so-called *Historismus*,[32] by which first phase we mean the defense of empirical history against the theory of a history *a priori* whether in the dualistic form of Kant and Fichte or in the monistic one of Hegel. The determining influence of Schelling's philosophy in this movement is proved by its relevance to Schleiermacher, Humboldt, and Boeckh.[33] Furthermore, because of the dependence of Ranke, Gervinus, Boeckh, and Droysen on Humboldt, much of the historical research of the nineteenth century appears to be founded on those presuppositions. All that is claimed here is that the *Historische Kunst der Griechen* is on the same lines and deserves attention for its early date, for the unusual emphasis on the history of historiography, and for its solid contribution to the knowledge of Greek historiography.

As was only natural, Creuzer had meantime been made aware by his studies that a collection of the surviving fragments of ancient historians was needed. He planned such a collection and in 1806 published the first part of the *Historicorum Graecorum Antiquissimorum Fragmenta* including Hecataeus, Charon, and Xanthus. This collection of fragments, though taken over by others, was never completed.[34] Creuzer, under the influence of Frau von Günderode and Görres, was proceeding towards the *Symbolik* in a direction nearly parallel to that chosen by F. Schlegel and Schelling. Yet he and his pupils prepared much of the material for the other, more successful collection we still have on our shelves, Müller's *Fragmenta historicorum Graecorum* (1841) — a modest confirmation of the truth that even a collection of fragments can arise only out of problems.

The *Historische Kunst der Griechen* had other early recognitions besides the review in the *Göttingische Anzeigen*. F. A. Wolf described it to Goethe as a good book,[35] and in the famous report to the French Institute on learning in Germany by Charles Villers, Creuzer obtained a very honorable place.[36] Echoes of the book are to be found everywhere in the following years.[37] The first serious attack on the method of the book appeared in the life of Herodotus published by F. C. Dahlmann in 1823. The very concept of logographoi was denied, the epic style of Herodotus qualified, his religion taken as a negative element: Herodotus was no longer the poet of history, but the brilliant, competent political historian of the type which Dahlmann himself was going to be.[38] It was already significant that a *life* of Herodotus should be presented as an *essay* on Herodotus. From a different angle, the criticism of H. Ulrici in his *Charakteristik der antiken Historiographie* (1833) was not less radical. Intensely religious, Ulrici thought that the task of the historian was to give "das Bild des göttlichen Gedankens und Willens." For lack of true religion no Greek or Roman could do that. They were too much tied to the sensible world to be able to grasp pure ideas. The Christian idea of mankind was inevitably alien to them: a true universal history was impossible for them: their historical art was a substitute for historical science. Insofar as Polybius in his universalism and Tacitus in his moralism are nearer to Christianity, they are greater historians than Herodotus and Thucydides. If Thucydides is superior to Herodotus because his irreligion goes deeper into human nature than Herodotus's traditional piety or superstition, Polybius's universalism (if I understand Ulrici right) implies a deeper conception of humanity than that of Thucydides. Without a real knowledge of Providence, ancient historiography was also without a proper knowledge of the development of arts and science. Only modern historiography is scientific — or philosophic.

If Dahlmann brought home the new realistic trends of political historiography after the Romantic orgy, Ulrici showed the evolution of Romantic philosophy itself from its early humanistic phase to the religious one. He spoke of the necessity of taking Christianity into account in a history of historiography. One may add that Ulrici had an admirable mastery of all

Greek and Roman historiography and a shrewd capacity for pointed formulations which make his book much better reading than Creuzer's. His
pages on the religion of Xenophon, for instance, are still the best on the
subject.

Nearer to Creuzer in advocating the perennial value of Greek historiography and the need of artistic intuition in history was W. Roscher in his
juvenile book on Thucydides (1842). A pupil both of Humboldt and of
Ranke, he found in Thucydides his congenial spirit. Yet, in Roscher again,
it is possible to see the growing detachment from Creuzer. Roscher studied
Thucydides as a guide to political realities, whereas Creuzer was concerned
with the relation between history and art.

Ulrici became a pure philosopher, Roscher turned out a great economist and student of politics, Dahlmann became a politician and modern
historian: none of them in his maturity had either time or inclination to
carry on research on Greek historiography. Here are some of the forces
which led the following generation to neglect the study of Greek historiography. The Greek historians were no longer asked to answer problems of
importance. They were left to useful, yet brutal, erudition until towards the
end of the century when Eduard Meyer expounded his historical method
by an analysis of Thucydides.[39] But E. Meyer remained an exception. Few
classical scholars are seriously interested in problems of historical method.
This fact, rather than Creuzer's connection with the *Symbolik,* explains why
(as far as my knowledge goes) his *Historische Kunst der Griechen* has never
been critically reexamined.[40]

Notes

1. *Goethes Briefwechsel mit einem Kinde,* 2d ed. (1837) I, p. 110. From a letter, An
Goethes Mutter, pp. 80–126. Later Bettina Brentano devoted a whole novel to the
idealization of her friend, *Die Günderode* (1840). *Cf.* also her husband, A. von
Arnim's novel *Isabella* (1812). We need not enter into Bettina's peculiar methods of
literary composition.

2. Creuzer did most valuable work as an editor of Neoplatonic texts; Proclus
and Olympiodorus (Frankfurt 1820–22), Plotinus (Oxford 1835).

3. *Einleitung in die Philosophie der Mythologie,* in *Sämmtl. Werke,* II, 1, p. 89.

4. *Versuch über die Gräbersymbolik der Alten* (1859).

5. F. Creuzer's *Deutsche Schriften,* neue und verbesserte Auflage, III. Abtheil.
(1845). The quotations in the text are from this edition.

6. I used the copy of the first edition in the possession of Trinity College, Cambridge. The book is in the British Museum.

7. I hope to write on this work in connection with Gervinus's and Droysen's
Historik.

8. In the 33rd issue, 27 February 1804, p. 321, an installment almost entirely devoted to Creuzer's book. The obscurity of the style was, however, reprimanded: "Ist es die Terminologie einer neueren Schule, welche diese Dunkelheit verursacht, oder lag sie in den Ideen des Verfassers?" The reviewer was almost certainly Chr. Gottl. Heyne (*cf.* F. Creuzer, "Aus dem Leben eines alten Professors," in *Deutsche Schriften*, V, 1 (1848) p. 26).

9. E. Cassirer, *Philosophie der symbolischen Formen*, II, p. 21; A. Baeumler in J.J. Bachofen, *Der Mythus von Orient und Occident* (1926) pp. civ ff.; E. Howald, *Der Kampf um Creuzers Symbolik, Eine Auswahl von Dokumenten* (1926), etc. For a highly significant recent debate *cf.* F. Cumont, *Recherches sur le symbolisme funéraire des Romains* (1942) (on Creuzer p. 13) and A. D. Nock, "Sarcophagi and Symbolism," in *Amer. Journ. Arch.*, 50 (1946) p. 340.

10. *Die Antike*, 6 (1930) p. 203. *Cf.* also the same author's "Thukydides als politischer Denker," in *Das humanistische Gymnasium* (1933) pp. 2 ff. Regenbogen echoes E. Rohde's judgment (see following note).

11. Creuzer was born in Marburg in 1771. He studied in Marburg and Jena (where he was in 1790) but got his doctorate in Tübingen in 1799. Professor *extraordinarius* in Marburg in 1800, *ordinarius* in 1802, he passed to Heidelberg in 1804 and remained there to the end of his life (1858), except for a brief period of residence in Leyden (1809) after Frau von Günderode's suicide — *cf.* Guigniaut, *Notice historique sur la vie et les travaux de George-Frédéric Creuzer* (Institut Impérial de France, séance publique annuelle du 31 juillet, 1863), 1864; K. B. Stark, *Vorträge und Aufsätze* (1880) pp. 390–408 and 480–507 with some important letters by Creuzer; C. Bursian, *Gesch. d. class. Philologie in Deutschland* (1883) p. 562; W. Rehm, *Griechentum und Goethezeit* (1936) p. 322; and the article in *Allgem. Deutsche Biographie*. The often uninspiring literature on Frau von Günderode must be consulted: *cf.* especially E. Rohde's well-known essay *F. C. und K. v. G.* (1896); K. Preisendanz, *Die Liebe der Günderode: F. Creuzer's Briefe an C. v. G.* (1912); R. Wilhelm, *Die Günderode: Dichtung und Schicksal* (1938) pp. 114 ff. The best on the subject is still Bettina Brentano.

12. *De historicis graecis libri tres* (1624) (2d ed., 1650). They were still useful enough in the nineteenth century to be reedited "auctiores et emendatiores" by A. Westermann in 1838. D. Wyttenbach's *Selecta Principum Historicorum* (Amsterdam 1794) is an anthology showing a marked preference for Polybius's pragmatism.

13. *De historicis latinis* (1627) (2d ed., 1651).

14. *Cf.* for instance Abbé Geinoz, "Défense d'Hérodote," *Mém. Acad. Inscr.*, XXIII (1756) p. 101; M. de Rochefort, "Sur la morale d'Hérodote," ibid., XXXIX (1777) p. 1; Voltaire, *Le Pyrrhonisme de l'Histoire* (1768) in *Oeuvres complètes*, XXXIX (1825) p. 334; C. A. Böttiger, *De Herodoti historia ad carminis epici indolem propius accedente*, I–II (1792–93).

15. *Cf.* J. D. Heilmann, "Krit. Gedanken von dem Charakter und der Schreibart des Thucydides," (1758), in *Opuscula*, II (1778) pp. 87–208; Abbé de Mably, *De la manière d'écrire l'histoire* (ed. London, 1789, *Oeuvres*, XII) p. 340 and the significant judgment in J.J. Barthélemy's *Voyage du jeune Anacharsis*, 3d ed. (Paris 1790) V, p. 413 (1st ed., 1787): "Hérodote, Thucydide et Xénophon seront sans doute regardés à l'avenir comme les principaux de nos historiens, quoiqu'ils diffèrent essentiellement par le style ... Hérodote voit partout une divinité jalouse. ... Thucydide ne

découvre dans les revers que les fautes des chefs de l'administration ou de l'armée: Xénophon attribue presque toujours à la faveur ou à la colère des dieux les bons ou les mauvais succès." It is only fair to add that the most famous apology for Thucydides belongs to the late seventeenth century: Père Rapin, *Les comparaisons des grands hommes: La comparaison de Thucydide et de Tite-Live,* II (Paris 1684) pp. 65–162 (Engl. transl. Oxford 1694), but *cf.* the remarks by A. Dain, "Thucydide au XVIIᵉ siècle," in *Congrès de Strasbourg de l' Ass.* Budé, *1938* (Paris 1939) pp. 95–96.

16. Republished in *Deutsche Schriften,* III, 2, pp. 591 ff. Reviewed in *Gött. Gelehrte Anz.* (1798) no. 122, pp. 215–16 ("Manche brauchbare Materialien zu einer Geschichte der historischen Kunst unter den Griechen, woran es uns bisher noch fehlt").

17. Schiller's *Was heisst und zu welchem Ende studiert man Universalgeschichte* had been written a year before (1789) Creuzer's residence in Jena. *Cf.* also *Ueber die aesthetische Erziehung* (1795), 25. Brief; B. Mugdan, *Die theoretischen Grundlagen der Schillerschen Philosophie* (1910) (*Kantstudien,* Erg.-H. 19); F. Meinecke, *Sch. und der Individualitätsgedanke* (1937). I regret that I have been unable to find anywhere a short essay published by the Tübingen poet and professor K. Ph. Conz—known especially for his connections with Schiller and Hölderlin—which has the title "Einige Bemerkungen über die historische Kunst der Alten" and was published in the short-lived *Museum für die Griechische und Römische Litteratur* (1795). Creuzer knew and appreciated it. (*Cf.* G. Cless, *Der schwäbische Dichter K. Ph. Conz 1762–1827* (Tübingen 1913). The article was not reprinted in Conz's three volumes of *Kleine prosaische Schriften,* published in Tübingen, 1821–22 (2 vols.) and Ulm, 1825. For an idea of the teaching of history of historiography in German universities at that time, *cf.* M. Fülleborn, *Encyclopaedia philologica* (1798) (2d ed. 1800) which, as is well known, summarizes F. A. Wolf's lectures (*cf.* also F. A. Wolf's "Darstellung der Altertumswissenschaft," in *Museum d. Alterumsw.,* I (1807) p. 61).

18. Reprinted in *Prosaische Jugendschriften,* ed. Minor, I (1882) (2d ed. 1906).

19. *Cf.* especially D. Tiedemann, *Geist der speculativen Philosophie* (1791). Creuzer wrote the official obituary of Tiedemann in 1803; *Opuscula selecta* (1854) p. 163. Also Reinhold's *Ueber den Begriff der Geschichte der Philosophie,* in Fülleborn's *Beyträge zur Geschichte der Philosophie,* I (1791) pp. 5–35, was almost certainly well known to Creuzer. Reinhold was a professor in Jena. The classic formulation of the principles of a history of philosophy was given in 1798 by W. G. Tennemann's *Gesch. d. Philosophie.*

20. "Also bleibt der Geschichte einzig und ewig Nichts als der Geist ihres ältesten Schreibers, Herodots: der unangestrengte milde Sinn der Menschheit," 121. Brief.

21. "Erst aus der inneren Einheit einer grossen Weltbegebenheit, welche der homerische Sinn und der gebildete Geist des Herodotos aufzufassen wussten, konnte die volkommnere Organisation einer Historie aufblühen" (p. 122).

22. *Deutsche Schriften,* III, 2, pp. 7 ff.

23. *Geschichte der Poesie der Griechen und Römer,* ed. Minor, I, p. 342.

24. *Deutsche Schriften,* III, 2, p. 20. The passage by F. Schlegel referred to is in *Die Griechen und Römer,* ed. Minor, I, p. 77.

25. On F. Schlegel and philology compare especially C. Enders, *F. Schlegel: Die Quellen seines Wesens und Werdens* (1913) p. 351; J. Körner, *Romantiker und Klassiker* (1924); K. Börries, *Die Romantik und die Geschichte* (1925); F. Imle, *F. v. Schlegel's*

Entwicklung von Kant zum Katholizismus (1927); J. Körner, "F. Schl.'s *Philosophie der Philologie* mit einer Einleitung herausgegeben," *Logos,* XVII (1928) pp. 1–72; Idem, Introd. to F. Schlegel's *Philosophische Schriften* (1935); F. Gundolf, *Romantiker* (1930) pp. 9 ff.; V. Santoli, "Filologia, Storia e Filosofia nel pensiero di F. Schlegel," *Civiltà moderna,* 2 (1930) p. 117; Idem, Introd. to F. Schlegel's *Frammenti critici e scritti di estetica* (1936); A. Emmersleben, *Die Antike in der romantischen Theorie: Die Gebrüder Schlegel und die Antike* (1937). A. Schlagdenhauffen's big work, *F. Schlegel et son groupe: La doctrine de l'Athenaeum, 1798–1800* (1934) must be consulted, but is superficial. On F. Schlegel in general see also V. Grönbech, "F. Schlegel i Aarene 1791–1808," *Det Kgl. Danske Vidensk. Selskab* 22 (1935); O. Mann, *Der junge Schlegel* (1936); L. Wirz, *F. Schlegel's philos. Entwicklung* (1939) (*Grenzfragen z. Theol. u. Phil.,* 13).

   26. "Aus dem Leben eines alten Professors," in *Deutsche Schriften,* V, 1 (1848) p. 26. *Cf.* also the very important review of Schöll's *Geschichte der griechischen Literatur* in *Wiener Jahrbücher der Literatur,* LXI (1833) pp. 164–210 = *Deutsche Schriften,* III, 2, pp. 28 ff. It may here be noted that the insistence of Lessing on the distinction between dramatic truth and historical truth (for instance *Hamburgische Dramaturgie,* 11. Stück, ed. Reclam, p. 49) was important to Creuzer: *Hist. Kunst,* 2d ed., pp. 162, 192, etc.

   27. *Cf.* for instance F. Medicus, "Kants Philosophie der Geschichte," *Kantstudien,* 7 (1902) pp. 1–22, 171–229 (*cf.* also 4 (1900) pp. 61–67); E. Lask, *Fichtes Idealismus und die Geschichte* (1902); K. R. Brotherus, *I. Kants Philosophie der Geschichte* (Helsingfors 1905); W. G. Herbst, *J. G. Fichtes Geschichtsphilosophie nach den Prinzipien der Wissenschaftslehre* (1913); and in general X. Léon, *Fichte et son temps* (1922–27); M. Gueroult, *L'Évolution et la structure de la doctrine de la science chez Fichte* (1930). I do not know W. Steinbeck, *Das Bild des Menschen in d. Philosophie J. G. Fichtes* (1939). See also below n. 32 and De Ruggiero and Collingwood quoted in the following note.

   28. *Sämmtl. Werke,* I, 1 (1856) p. 461. On Schelling and history *cf.* G. Mehlis, *Schellings Geschichtsphilosophie in den Jahren 1799 bis 1804* (1906); A. Pötzsch, *Studien zur frühromantischen Politik und Geschichtsauffassung* (1907); H. Knittermeyer, *Schelling und die romantische Schule* (1929); and the monographs by L. Noack (1859); E. v. Hartmann (1869); E. Bréhier (1912); and N. Hartmann (*Die Philosophie des deutschen Idealismus,* I (1923). Also G. De Ruggiero, *Storia della filosofia,* IV, 4, 2d ed. (1946) p. 337 and R. G. Collingwood, *The Idea of History* (1946) p. 111.

   29. *Vorlesungen,* 2d ed. (1813) p. 221 (10. Vorlesung) "Auch die wahre Historie beruht auf einer Synthesis des Gegebenen und Wirklichen mit dem Idealen, aber nicht durch Philosophie, da diese die Wirklichkeit vielmehr aufhebt und ganz ideal ist: Historie aber ganz in jener und doch zugleich ideal sein soll. Dieses ist nirgends als in der Kunst möglich...." In K. Chr. F. Krause, *Grundriss der historischen Logik* (1803) "historisch" means simply "empirisch": Krause does not discuss historiography.

   30. *Deutsche Literaturdenkmale,* XVII (1884) p. 14.

   31. The *Vorlesungen über Enzyklopädie* are, as far as I know, still unpublished. There is a summary in R. Haym, *Die Romantische Schule,* 5th ed. (1928) pp. 911–12. On J. Müller *cf.* P. Requadt, *J. v. M. und der Frühhistorismus* (1929). Two typical formulations of Müller's ideas will be found in *Sämmtliche Werke,* VIII (1810) pp. 412–14 (on Tacitus); XI, pp. 330–41 (on historical style).

32. It is perhaps evident that F. Meinecke, *Entstehung des Historismus* (1936), though of great importance for the historiography of the eighteenth century, does not describe the "Entstehung des Historismus" which is to be found in philosophers and philologists whom Meinecke does not consider. More relevant is his later book of essays, *Vom geschichtlichen Sinn und vom Sinn der Geschichte* (1939) (*cf.* especially his chapter on Schleiermacher). For discussions on Meinecke *cf.* E. Seeberg, *Hist. Zeitschrift,* 157 (1938) p. 241; C. Antoni, *Dallo storicismo alla sociologia* (1940) ch. 3; B. Croce, *La storia come pensiero e come azione* (1938) p. 51. C. Antoni has given an invaluable introduction to the problem in *La lotta contro la ragione* (1942). *Cf.* also his *Considerazioni su Hegel e Marx* (1946). A. Korff, *Geist der Goethezeit,* III (1940) (*Frühromantik*), is unfortunately known to me only indirectly; *cf.* De Ruggiero, *Storia della filosofia,* IV, 4 (1946) pp. 424 ff. For earlier discussions: R. Fester, *Rousseau und die deutsche Geschichtsphilosophie* (1890); I. Goldfriedrich, *Die historische Ideenlehre in Deutschland* (1902); W. Dilthey, *Der Aufbau der geschichtlichen Welt in den Geisteswissenschaften* (1920); E. Troeltsch, *Der Historismus und seine Probleme* (1922). For a discussion of J. Thyssen, *Geschichte der Geschichtsphilosophie* (1936), *cf.* C. Antoni, *Considerazioni su Hegel e Marx,* p. 156.

33. On Schleiermacher and Schelling, H. Süskind, *Der Einfluss Schellings auf die Entwicklung von Schleiermachers System* (1909); Idem, *Christentum und Geschichte bei Schleiermacher* (1911); G. Wehrung, *Schleiermacher in der Zeit seines Werdens* (1927). More generally: R. B. Brandt, *The Philosophy of Schleiermacher* (1941). On Humboldt and Schelling *cf.* E. Spranger, *Hist. Zeitschrift,* 100 (1907) p. 541. On Boeckh, J. Wach, *Das Verstehen,* I (1926) p. 168. On Droysen, H. Astholz, *Das Problem "Geschichte" untersucht bei J. G. D.* (1933); E. Rothacker, *Hist. Zeitschrift,* 161 (1940) p. 84; C. Antoni, *Considerazioni su Hegel e Marx,* pp. 118–25.

34. Ctesias and Ephorus were edited respectively by another Heidelberg professor, Chr. F. Bähr (Frankfurt, 1824) and by M. Marx (Karlsruhe 1815), the second with Creuzer's preface. The edition of Philistus and Timaeus by Fr. Göller (Leipzig 1818) was also, perhaps, indirectly inspired by him: see K. B. Stark, *Vorträge und Aufsätze* (1880) p. 483. Hellanicus's fragments had already been collected by F. G. Sturz in 1787: his *Pherecydes* appeared in 1789. Bähr also finished a commentary on Herodotus which Creuzer had started.

35. *F. A. Wolf. Ein Leben in Briefen* . . . besorgt . . . durch S. Reiter, I (1935) p. 358 (letter of 30 January 1804).

36. *Cf.* the English translation of the report in *The Classical Journal,* IV (1811) p. 143.

37. For instance in Wachler, mentioned in the text, or in Chr. D. Beck, *Nonnulla de iudicio artis historicae classicorum scriptorum* (1805).

38. F. C. Dahlmann, "Herodot, aus seinem Buche sein Leben," *Forschungen auf dem Gebiete der Geschichte,* II, 1 (1823). Against Creuzer: p. 213 (*cf.* p. 109). Dahlmann, typically, tried to prove that Herodotus never made public recitations of his history.

39. *Forschungen zur alten Geschichte,* II (1899) pp. 269–436.

40. I am indebted to Mrs. M. I. Henderson, Dr. F. Jacoby, Professor H. M. Last, and Dr. R. Pfeiffer for discussion. My friends V. Santoli and C. Antoni could not contribute when this paper was written (1944).

TWO

George Grote
and the Study of Greek History

To Anna Laura

It was about twenty-five years ago that the name of Gower Street first impressed itself on my mind. I was reading Mrs. Grote's biography of her husband. Some of you may remember how Grote is described as returning "from the meetings of Council quite over-wearied, taking a shilling fare of hackney coach from Gower Street to Highbury Barn, and walking thence across the field-path to his house in Paradise Place."[1]

Thus, in my admittedly rather imperfect map of a mythical London, the Gower Street of George Grote had its place beside the Baker Street of Sherlock Holmes and the George Street of Giuseppe Mazzini, near the Euston Road. The transition from myth to reality is always complicated. Yet for once the reality was not inferior to the myth. Because the first member of University College I ever met personally was Norman Baynes, that great historian who typifies so much of what is best in the tradition of the College.

To teach Ancient History in the College of George Grote and Norman Baynes must have seemed a severe responsibility to my predecessors Professor Cary and Professor Jones. For me the responsibility is even more serious because my predecessors fulfilled their task with distinction, setting high standards both of teaching and research. Yet two considerations give me courage. First of all, like the Stoic emperor, I can thank the gods for having given me good teachers and having made me acquainted with many good men. Secondly, when as a special lecturer in 1946 I was so cordially introduced to the life of University College by the present master of Birkbeck,

"George Grote and the Study of Greek History" (an Inaugural Lecture delivered at University College London on 19 February 1952); Greek translation, *Hê Angloellênikê Epitheôrêsê*, 3 (1953–54), pp. 263–77; *Contributo* (1955), pp. 213–31; *Studies in Historiography* (1966), pp. 56–74; French translation, *Problèmes d'historiographie ancienne et moderne* (1983), pp. 361–82.

I soon came to appreciate the propitious atmosphere of this institution born in liberty for liberty. The earliest days of the college provide the example of the first Italian professor, Antonio Panizzi, who combined to good effect love for the country in which he was born with love for the country which had given him sanctuary in his hour of need.

It is the tradition of this college that the professor of Ancient History takes responsibility for Oriental, Greek, and Roman history. This is certainly a wise provision, even if it is not necessarily compatible with the mortal nature of a mere historian. Today it is Greek history that presents most difficulties both to the teacher and to the researcher. Oriental history is still in that happy stage in which the almost vertiginous increase of evidence lends plausibility to the convention that thinking is a work of supererogation for the historian. As for Roman history, it was put solidly on its feet a hundred years ago by Theodor Mommsen, and nobody has yet succeeded in turning it upside down; it is still safe to assume that he who does not know Roman law does not know Roman history. But all students of ancient history know in their heart that Greek history is passing through a crisis, and in order to clarify the nature of this crisis I now ask you to reconsider with me Grote's contribution to the study of Greek history against the background of the work of his predecessors and successors.

May I remind you that it is uncertain whether Greek history was invented in England or in Scotland? The two claimants are the Englishman William Mitford, who published the first volume of his *History of Greece* in 1784 but did not finish his work until 1810, and the Royal Historiographer of Scotland, John Gillies, who in 1786 published a complete Greek history in two volumes in quarto and by 1778 had already published a discourse "on the history, manners, and character of the Greeks from the conclusion of the Peloponnesian War to the battle of Chaeronea."

Between the Scot and the Sassenach I shall of course maintain strict neutrality. We continentals never knew of such a thing as Greek History with capital letters until the end of the eighteenth century or the beginning of the nineteenth century when it became generally known that Greek history was being taken as seriously in *ultima Thule* as Roman history was on the Continent. This was the important point. In the eighteenth century handbooks of Greek history were not uncommon on the Continent, some of the most popular books being in fact vulgarizations translated from English into French, German, and Italian. Diderot translated into French the *Grecian History* of Temple Stanyan in 1743, and the rather low-level compilation by Oliver Goldsmith enjoyed popularity on the Continent as long as it did in England.[2] What was really new was, however, political discussion embodied in a Greek history, such as one could read in Mitford and Gillies.

The priority of Mitford and Gillies in the study of ancient Greek politics seems to be well established. But it has not yet been noticed that Mitford and Gillies themselves were stimulated by a discussion on the decline of Greece in the fourth century B.C. which started in France and continued in Ireland before passing to England — or Scotland. In the age of enlightened despotism Philip of Macedon would naturally arouse more sympathy than Demosthenes. Philip had been a patron of historians and philosophers exactly as the historians and philosophers of the eighteenth century expected their kings to be. The first to raise Philip to a research subject in the seventeenth century was Pufendorf, the great international lawyer,[3] but the first full-scale apologetic biography was written about 1736 by the French gentleman Claude Mathieu Olivier.[4] L'Abbé de Mably, another conspicuous name, followed with his *Observations sur les Grecs* on the same line in 1749. Then the subject was taken up in two stately volumes by Thomas Leland, Fellow of Trinity College, Dublin.[5] The curious poetical preface of this book explicitly says that Leland had Frederick of Prussia in mind while writing on Philip of Macedon. The date of publication, significantly enough, was 1758, the year of the treaty between England and Prussia.

The comparison of Philip of Macedon with Frederick the Great, once made, was unlikely to be forgotten, since it carried conviction. Both kings gave an unexpected turn to history by a singular combination of military abilities, intellectual interests, and ruthless cunning which made them well suited to their role as leaders of nations which were expanding while their more civilized neighbors were declining. John Gillies took up the comparison at great length in his *View of the Reign of Frederick II with a Parallel between that Prince and Philip II of Macedon* published in 1789. It must be added that Gillies traveled in Prussia and met Frederick several times. But he had already written in 1778 that discourse on the Greek history of the fourth century B.C. which considered even wider issues of contemporary life — nothing less than the consequences of the American Revolution. In his eyes the Athenian democrats were forerunners of the American rebels:

> If that turbulent form of government [namely republics] should be established in a new hemisphere, and if popular assemblies and senates should be there entrusted with the right to exercise power, why might they not abuse it as shamefully as before? Why might not the ancient barbarities be renewed, the manners of men be again tainted with a savage ferocity?[6]

The savage ferocity of which Gillies was afraid was apparently that of the Athens of Demosthenes.

Gillies was not, however, the fool that an isolated quotation can make him look. He had the sweep of imagination of the true historian and was the first to realize that Lysias and Isocrates could be made to contribute to a history of Athens. Uncritical about the early ages to the point of accepting literally the story of Helen of Troy, he introduced new and interesting ideas into the political history of Greece. Later, in 1807, he performed a feat for which nobody has yet given him credit. He was the first to write *in extenso* the history of the Greco-Macedonian states from the death of Alexander to the reign of Augustus.[7] Here again I suspect, though I am not certain, that he was inspired by contemporary events. His Romans conquering the Greek states are not unlike the French conquering Europe under Napoleon.

However that may be, the simple facts I have stated compel us to revise ideas on the development of historiography in the nineteenth century. It is commonly believed—and I have said so myself—that Niebuhr was chiefly responsible for starting the discussion on Demosthenes and Philip in Germany during the Napoleonic wars and that Droysen discovered the analogy between Macedon and Prussia. Droysen is also credited with the original idea of a history of the period intervening between Alexander and Augustus.[8] It now appears that the discussion of the fourth century in terms of modern political principles—and even of Prussia—had started almost a century before Droysen. Though Droysen's penetrating vision of the Hellenistic age as the age of transition between paganism and Christianity cannot be compared with Gillies's limited political interests, it is undeniable that he had a predecessor in this respect too.

As an antidemocratic historian of Greece, Gillies was soon superseded by Mitford, chiefly because the latter's *History of Greece* was richer and more reliable in scholarly details. Yet as August Boeckh, a good judge, remarked, Mitford had more information and less political judgment than Gillies. During most of his working life Mitford had before him the experience of both the American and French revolutions. A determined supporter of the rights of kings, he was admired by his political friends of the *Quarterly Review* and respectfully hated by Byron and by the young Macaulay.[9] When the Philosophic Radicals decided to intervene in the study of ancient history, it was inevitable that Mitford's work, already in its fourth edition, should become their chief target.

We associate the Philosophic Radicals with population and taxation problems, with the pleasures and pains of self-interest, and with the refusal to mention good taste. But when John Arthur Roebuck visited the Utilitarian Society for the first time he found its members in "a low, half-furnished, desolate sort of room" discussing "a critique for some review of an edition of a Greek author."[10] The importance that the Utilitarians attributed to Greek history can be illustrated by a sentence of John Stuart Mill:

> The battle of Marathon, even as an event in English history, is more important than the battle of Hastings. If the issue of that day had been different, the Britons and the Saxons might still have been wandering in the woods.[11]

About 1822 it was settled that Grote would make Greece his province. In later years Mrs. Grote, who seldom underrated her husband, and never herself, claimed to have inspired the idea of the Greek history in the autumn of 1823. Chronology seems to be against her claim.[12] In October 1823 she herself wrote to G. Warde Norman:

> The Grecian History prospers, and G[rote] is more absorbed in it than ever. He has nearly concluded the account of the Greek colonies. Into this part of the work he has infused some useful doctrines both as to political economy and the principle of population.

In the printed text, Greek colonization occupies chapter 22 and the following in the second part. Even if the first draft was shorter, it is clear that the work had already been progressing for some time.

Roman history was not yet apportioned. Warde Norman and John Stuart Mill, then little more than seventeen years old, were both thinking of writing it. Mill, precise as always, had decided to start it when he reached the age of twenty. Both projects fell through. The only book on Roman history inspired by the radical school, the *Inquiry into the Credibility of the Early Roman History* by Sir George Cornewall Lewis, another lifelong friend of Grote, appeared in 1855.

In 1826 Grote felt sure enough of himself to launch a major attack on his predecessor Mitford. It filled fifty pages of the *Westminster Review* and was ostensibly a discussion of Clinton's *Fasti Hellenici*.[13] Clinton of course drops out after the first page. This article is still the best introduction to the thought of Grote. Already he shows that sympathy for small states which led him later to make a close study of the politics of Switzerland. He exalts the "unparalleled stimulus to the development of individual talent" provided by Greek society, and finally he interprets Greek democracy as the form of government coinciding not with the interests of the poor, but with the interests of society as a whole.

Whether by accident or design the *Quarterly Review* published a defense of Mitford and an attack on the Greek Courts of Justice at about the same time.[14] The Radicals replied in the *Westminster Review* of 1827, but this time the anonymous article was written by Charles Austin. Mitford and the *Quarterly* were castigated for forty pages.[15] This vigorous start was followed by delays. Grote's banking business and his election to Parliament retarded the progress of the work. There was an interruption of ten years between 1831 and 1841. When Grote picked up the thread of his book he had to decide whether he could compete with his old schoolfellow Connop Thirlwall, whose *Greek History* had begun to appear in 1835.[16]

The society of Trinity College, Cambridge, where Thirlwall developed into a historian, was strikingly different from that of Threadneedle Street, where Grote convoked his friends in the early morning before his banking business started. Yet the two groups had much in common. Hurrell Froude's description of those wonderful Cambridge fellows who "know everything, examine everything, and dogmatize about everything"[17] might as easily apply to Grote's society. Both societies disliked Mitford, read German, and were attacked by the *Quarterly Review*.[18] Both aimed at a liberalization of English political and intellectual habits and wanted them to be founded on firm philosophical principles. These similarities between the "apostles" of Trinity College and the radicals of Threadneedle Street explain why the stories of Thirlwall and Grote have so many qualities in common and why ultimately Thirlwall's was superseded by Grote's.

This is not to deny the importance of the differences between the two schools. According to Thirlwall and his friend Julius Charles Hare, Niebuhr and Schleiermacher were giving more than what Grote called the inestimable aid of German erudition; they were providing a philosophy of history, a theological system—in a word, a faith. Thirlwall introduced Schleiermacher's theology to the English, and Hare put into his volume *Guesses at Truth* as much German romantic philosophy of history as the English language was capable of taking. The radical philosophers of London were unsympathetic to Schleiermacher's theology, though not to his Platonic studies, and followed Niebuhr only up to a point. This became evident when Sir George Lewis published his *Inquiry into the Credibility of the Early Roman History* which criticized Niebuhr's historical method as too subjective. Grote showed a large measure of agreement with his friend in an article in the *Edinburgh Review* which is his only contribution to Roman studies.[19] Later he wrote privately to him about another of his books: "I wish I could think that it would be successful in repressing the German license of conjecture."[20]

Furthermore, the two Trinity men and their associates, including Arnold of Rugby, were fighting within the walls of the old universities for a reform of the prevailing methods of teaching the classics. They wanted the empirical knowledge of the classical languages characteristic of the English school to be replaced by scientific investigation of the classical literatures as pursued in German universities. Grote was less directly interested in this reform and probably less anxious at heart to have it brought about.

There cannot be two opinions on Thirlwall's intellectual qualities. His scholarship was fine, his judgment sure; his straightforward and incisive style was better suited to historical writing than that of Grote. But he could not put his whole heart and mind into a Greek history as Grote could. Neither his theology of German origin nor the gentle worldly wisdom which we can see in his letters was necessarily drawing him to scenes of the Persian wars or to the Athenian marketplace. Grote, on the contrary, found all that he wanted in ancient Greece: the origins of democratic government and the principles of freedom of thought and of rational enquiry. His major discovery in the field of Greek thought—the revaluation of the Sophists—was the result of his search into the relations between Greek democracy and intellectual progress. Thirlwall really loved Germany; Grote loved Athens. He loved Athens without any romantic nostalgia as a state which was formed for the sake of the good life. He saw a parallel between the education imparted by the Sophists and Socrates and that imparted in modern universities.

And there is a further point. Nothing was more important to the Philosophic Radical than the careful examination of evidence. His voice became particularly solemn when he spoke of the "law respecting sufficiency of the evidence." Bentham, the two Mills, Sir George Lewis, Grote, and John Austin, our great professor of jurisprudence whose lectures were so good that only John Stuart Mill understood them, were all engaged in examining the laws of evidence. When a proper study of the contribution of this group to English historiography is made, it will probably show that the importance of Sir George Lewis and his influence on his friends have not yet been properly appreciated. Lewis is well remembered as the prodigious man who succeeded in being at different stages of his career a student of the Romance languages and of ancient astronomy, an editor of Greek texts, a critic of Comte and Niebuhr, a translator of Boeckh and Karl Otfried Müller, an investigator of English law and administration, the author of *An Essay on the Influence of Authority in Matters of Opinion* and of *A Treatise on the Methods of Observation and Reasoning in Politics*—not to speak of his public offices. What really unifies his activity—as Walter Bagehot came near to seeing—is his passion for rigorous examination of the evidence.[21] This passion Grote shared, and he brought to its support an immense capacity for minute work.

I have often wondered whether John Stuart Mill's famous letter on Grote written to Carlyle in 1833 must be taken seriously. A letter to Carlyle was by definition an embarrassed letter, and a letter by John Stuart Mill to Carlyle was the least likely to be the exception. But let us suppose that Mill was perfectly sincere when he wrote to Carlyle:

> [Grote] is a man of good, but not first-rate intellect, hard and mechanical, not at all quick; with less subtlety than any able and instructed man I ever knew.... After all I had said of him you will be surprised to learn that he reads German.[22]

The answer to Mill is surely contained in Mr. Garrod's remark about Scaliger and Bentley: "Learning, consummate learning, is a thing a good deal more rare than genius."[23]

Respect for the law of evidence brought Grote to what was then the revolutionary conclusion that Greek history had to be divided into two neatly separated compartments: legendary Greece, historical Greece. Grote never denied that the legends on early Greece might contain a good deal of history. He simply confessed his inability to separate history from myth without "collateral evidence and without possibility of verification."[24] Thus he broke with K. O. Müller and his English admirers. It is easy for us made wise by the discoveries of Mycenae, Crete, Troy, and Boghaz-Keui to react against Grote's skepticism. He could justly reply that Mycenae, Crete, Troy, and Boghaz-Keui have provided the collateral evidence that he lacked.

What gives Grote's *History* its almost unique distinction is this combination of passionate moral and political interests, vast learning, and respect for the evidence.

The natives of Europe used to be civilized in the nineteenth century, and these qualities of Grote were immediately recognized by almost everyone. John Stuart Mill, notwithstanding his grudges against Grote and their temperamental differences, commented with admiration in the *Spectator* and in the *Edinburgh Review* upon the volumes of the *Greek History* which appeared from 1846 onwards. He greeted them as the first attempt at a philosophic history of Greece.[25] Not less admiring was the *Revue des Deux Mondes,* in which the first volumes were discussed by Prosper Mérimée.[26] Even the *Quarterly* was swept off its feet. It forgot to protest against the rehabilitation of Cleon and only made a very mild reservation about the Sophists: indeed it celebrated "the strict attention to the laws of evidence" and "the high moral tone which breathes through the whole work."[27] The only notable exception was Richard Shilleto, the distinguished Cambridge don, who wrote a pamphlet entitled *Thucydides or Grote?* He was candid: "I cannot refrain from saying . . . that I am thankful that [Mr. Grote] is not a member of either of the old universities of our land." Mr. Shilleto was answered by another Cambridge man who happened to be George Grote's brother, and nothing more was heard of him in this connection.[28]

It would be pleasant to follow in greater detail than is possible here the steps of the *Greek History* towards popularity and authority. There is for instance a letter by Auguste Comte promising to read it in order to find confirmation of his own theories, though in obedience to mental hygiene he was no longer reading books.[29]

As I have mentioned, the study of Greek history had been almost unknown to the Continent before the end of the eighteenth century. In the first half of the nineteenth century insofar as research on detail was concerned the situation was reversed by the industry of the German universities. Three or four epoch-making works emerged, such as K. O. Müller's books on the Dorians and on mythology, Boeckh's *Public Economy of Athens,* and Droysen's *History of Hellenism.* With the exception of Droysen, whose importance was not recognized until much later, these works were immediately influential. But the general histories of Greece (such as those by Graff, Plass, and Roth) remained poor compilations. Only Duncker's *History of Antiquity* which included Greek history to 479 B.C. had some independent value for its clear presentation of the archaic age and for its interpretation of Themistocles' personality; it was later translated into English. No distinguished Greek history appeared in France either until 1851. Victor Duruy who published one in that year had to rewrite it ten years later under the impact of Thirlwall and Grote.[30]

In fact Grote's history set new standards and gave new impulse to the writing of Greek history. Under Grote's archonship a new era started. His work, either in the original or in its French and German translations, traveled everywhere and impressed every classical student by its approach to the legends, by its revaluation of Greek political life, and above all by its insistence on the close connection between political and intellectual history. Grote utilized in full the results of German scholarship and assessed their value with independent judgment. His twelve volumes were neatly planned and consistently readable. In England, Freeman was inspired to write the *History of Federal Government* to cover an aspect which Grote had almost overlooked, in part for chronological reasons.[31] In the next generation the restless and fertile mind of Bury wrestled continuously with problems that Grote suggested to him.[32] In France, Grote influenced a long series of researches on social and constitutional history, especially of Athens.

But it was in the German world that Grote created the greatest commotion. The German professors could hardly believe their ears when they heard that he was a banker. But they took his challenge seriously. All the German studies on Greek history of the last fifty years of the nineteenth century are either for or against Grote. The German scholars produced their famous series of Greek histories in answer to Grote: Kortüm (1854), Curtius (1857), Busolt (1885), Holm (1886), Beloch (1893), to which the *History of Antiquity* by E. Meyer (vol. II, 1893) must be added. Two of the most penetrating researches on special periods of Greek history—the study of Demosthenes and his age by A. Schaefer (1856) and the history of Athenian politics after Pericles by Beloch (1884)—were directly inspired by Thirlwall and Grote. In 1854 the veteran scholar Schömann thought it necessary to devote a whole book to the discussion of Grote's opinions on the Athenian constitution.[33] In 1873 Hermann Müller-Strübing, an extravagant but learned German scholar who lived in London, wrote what amounted to a pamphlet of 735 pages against the German adversaries of Grote.[34] Later Theodor Gomperz took pride in acknowledging how much his *Greek Thinkers* owed to Grote, whom he knew personally.[35] I suspect that Gomperz was in fact Grote's greatest pupil. The reputation of the English historian spread outside the circle of the specialists. Karl Lehrs has left a description of how Heinrich Theodor von Schön, the Prussian Minister, anxiously awaited the appearance of each new volume of the *History*.[36] Johann Jacoby, the democratic leader, made extracts from Grote for political propaganda.[37] In 1890 Pöhlmann wrote one of the first examinations of Greek democracy from a quasi-Marxist point of view to refute Grote.[38] In 1893 Wilamowitz-Moellendorff concluded his survey of the studies of Greek history with Grote, and a very significant page it was. Wilamowitz wanted to replace the unpleasant political discussions on Cleon and Demosthenes inspired by Grote with sober study of Greek constitutional law. We shall soon see the consequences.[39]

In Italy, Grote was not unknown. His theories on Greek legends were mentioned a few months after their publication in the *Rivista Europea* of 1847.[40] When Grote died, Pasquale Villari, already famous as a student of Savonarola, wrote to J. S. Mill deploring the loss.[41] But in the first seventy years of the nineteenth century the Italians seem to have accepted too literally Lodovico Antonio Muratori's invitation to leave the Greeks and Romans and devote themselves to medieval history, which was at the roots of their present troubles. When I consider how little was apparently written on Greek history in Italy at that time, I sometimes wonder whether by strange chance some such work has not eluded me. Anyway the Italian universities recognized the need of importing teachers of Greek history from Germany. Holm and Beloch wrote their histories of Greece as professors in Italian universities. The results of this infusion of German scholarship were soon evident and almost spectacular. In 1898 Gaetano De Sanctis, a pupil of Beloch, produced at the age of twenty-eight a history of Athens which put Italian studies in the forefront and which is still unsurpassed. Both Beloch and De Sanctis were keen students of Grote; at their schools of Rome and Turin Grote has been discussed by three generations of students who are now teachers in their turn.[42]

After 1900 the decline of creative work on Greek history became evident. The age in which practical politicians and moralists were interested in Greek was ushered out by Wilamowitz on the one hand and by John Ruskin on the other. As Ruskin's once-famous words on Grote are no longer well remembered, I may perhaps quote them:

> Grote's History of Greece.... There is probably no commercial establishment between Charing Cross and the Bank, whose head clerk could not write a better one, if he had the vanity to waste his time on it.[43]

While Greek history was taught more and more in old and new universities everywhere, few important books, either on archaic or on classical Greece, were published. In Germany, E. Meyer never finished the Greek section of his *History of Antiquity,* and Wilamowitz gave priority to literary studies in what was perhaps the least clearly directed period of his extraordinary activity. In Italy, De Sanctis devoted himself chiefly for many years to the study of Roman history. The general level of production sank rapidly.

It is true that the history of the Hellenistic states was attracting the attention of some of the best men—Tarn in Great Britain, Wilcken in Germany, Holleaux in France, Rostovtzeff in Russia and then in America, Cardinali in Italy. But it would be naïve to suggest that the history of Greece proper is an exhausted field. The opposite is true. Never before have so many fundamental discoveries challenged the historian.

With the discovery of inscriptions and papyri, the written evidence has been increased in the last seventy or eighty years as it had not been since the end of the sixteenth century. The amount of lyric poetry has been almost doubled, filling gaps in the most obscure periods of Greek history. Pindar is no longer alone, Menander can speak for himself, the study of Athenian constitutional history has been transformed by the discovery of the *Atheniensium res publica,* and the history of the Athenian empire has been made possible by inscriptions. Greek elements have been found in Jewish, Indian, Arabic, and perhaps Hittite sources.

Archaeology has been no less generous with help and problems. It has extended the evidence for Greek history which used to begin with Homer any moment after 1000 B.C. to about 2000 B.C.; it has added two new periods, the Minoan and the Mycenaean, and has given us the possibility of seeing the Greek cities and sanctuaries as they were. We are apt to forget that seventy or eighty years ago Cnossus, Mycenae, Delphi, Olympia, Smyrna, Priene, and Olynthus did not exist for historical purposes. Nor were the museums organized to provide direct evidence for the historical evolution of ancient Greece. A few months ago I was walking through the rooms of the Museum of Syracuse—that monument to the genius and patience of Paolo Orsi. It was natural to ask oneself what K. O. Müller or George Grote would have given for such an orderly collection of the evidence showing all the stages through which the Greeks passed in Sicily from the first contacts with the natives to the not inglorious Byzantine end.

Finally, archaeology combined with comparative philology has broken forever the isolation of Greek history. The Indo-European invasion of Greece, once a wonder in itself, has become a part of a vast chain of events in the eastern Mediterranean. The study of Hellenization has been extended to the Indus, that of Orientalization to the Pillars of Hercules. We know what Greek art and religion became in Etruscan, Celtic, and Scythian hands—indeed in Roman hands.

If evidence in itself were a source of inspiration, what could be more inspiring than all this evidence of which Grote and his generation knew practically nothing?

It is to be admitted that between the two wars the interest in Greek political and cultural history was again on the increase, perhaps more in Germany and in Italy than elsewhere. In the tense atmosphere of the Weimar Republic Wilamowitz returned to greatness, producing the unbroken chain of masterpieces of his old age from the book on Pindar to *Der Glaube der Hellenen*. We are proud to have here among us Dr. V. Ehrenberg, who has contributed so much to revising Greek constitutional history. In Italy official emphasis on Roman imperialism persuaded the honest to return to Greek history. The grand old man of ancient history, as Professor Cary called De Sanctis,[44] produced in 1939 what is perhaps the only Greek history of this half century bearing the imprint of a strong personality. Also, much work was done in Italy towards a reinterpretation of the fourth century B.C. More recently one has noticed a new interest in Greek constitutional history in the United States, chiefly due to Professor Larsen of Chicago; and Professor Gomme has revived the study of Thucydides in this country. Perhaps, though it is not devoted to political history, one should not omit a book by the Regius Professor of Greek at Oxford — *The Greeks and the Irrational* — which opens such wide perspectives on the achievements and failures of classical Greece. But even if some of these developments had not been disturbed in the way we know they were, they could not represent more than the symptoms of a possible change for the better in a situation which is frankly critical. The most important aspects of this crisis appear to me to be the following four.

First, we are increasingly interested in social and economic history, but the available evidence is as yet insufficient to provide those statistics without which no proper social and economic history of Greece can be written. Furthermore the evidence, such as it is, is almost invariably archaeological and therefore can be used only after classification by highly specialized methods. The technical difficulties are such and the rewards in results are so problematic that no serious economic and social historian of ancient Greece has yet appeared.

Secondly, the prevailing approaches to history — Marxism, psychoanalysis in its different varieties, sociology in its different varieties, the neo-Spenglerism of the first Toynbee and the neo-Augustinianism of the second — have the merits and demerits which everybody knows or should know. But in any case they are unilateral approaches, ill-suited to be applied without integration and correction, as they usually are, to the eminently many-sided history of Greece. The trouble is that people who do not accept unilateral approaches too often have no approach at all.

Thirdly, Fustel de Coulanges prophesied as long ago as 1872 that historical evidence would be distorted more and more for partisan purposes.[45] But what nobody seems to have expected is that evidence would be distorted for no purpose at all, simply because of lack of common sense. Yet this is what has been happening with alarming frequency in recent years. Perhaps it is not altogether surprising that our generation should find it increasingly difficult to assess the value of evidence, but the consequence is that idle and misleading speculation is a factor with which the Greek historian has constantly to reckon. Much of the recent work on early Greek traditions is pre-Grotean in character.

Fourthly, the study of Greek political ideas has become increasingly divorced from the study of political events and institutions. Nobody can speak without admiration of Professor Jaeger's *Paideia*—one of the most influential books of our time in the classical field, original in its outlook, subtle in its analysis. Yet, it is necessary to repeat that it is written with insufficient reference to the political and social history of Greece.

I hope I have not put an undue amount of self-righteousness into my last paragraphs. As Benedetto Croce once remarked, intellectual failures are collective phenomena from which no contemporary can presume to escape. We all partake of the cruel dullness of our age. But it seems to me that we shall never be able to talk about Greek history without embarrassment until we return to first principles. The first principles were stated by Grote: Greek history is essential to the formation of the liberal mind, but in its turn the liberal mind is religious in examining the evidence. A hundred years after its appearance, the limits and shortcomings of Grote's *History* are only too obvious. We need not quarrel about Cleon. It will be enough to say that, when Grote committed his most notorious mistake by identifying the Athenian liberty of the fifth century with absolute liberty, he overlooked the warning already given many years before by Benjamin Constant in his classic essay on the differences between ancient and modern ideas of liberty.

If we agree with Grote that so much of our intellectual patrimony has its origins in Greece and that it is our duty to assess it with careful analysis of the evidence, then we can see better what is worth studying in Greek history. We want to explain how the Greeks emerged from the north to get in touch with the great empires of the second millennium B.C., how they founded their big states, how they survived the crisis of the beginnings of the Iron Age, how the new centers of civilization developed that Homer and Hesiod knew, and how the Greek mind created the new politics, philosophy, art, and poetry of the sixth and fifth centuries. We want also to know how the Greeks came to attribute universal validity to their conceptions and proceeded to hellenize both the West and the East and what happened in these encounters. Athens must remain the center of a Greek history. But beyond the borders of classical Greece we expect to perfect our knowledge of southern Italy, where Greek and Roman civilization cannot be disentangled, of Syria where Christianity was born, and of Egypt where Christianity and Greek philosophy were fused and monasticism was invented. Finally, we must know what Greece contributed to the creation of the new Rome,

Constantinople, and how she impressed her mark on the Moslem civilization from Baghdad to Toledo.

If this is the history of Greece that we would like to know, it is also easy
to mention the parts of it we know least. We have no up-to-date history of
archaic Ionia, of the Athenian empire, of Magna Graecia in the fifth and
fourth centuries B.C., of the Seleucid empire, of the province of Achaea
under the Roman empire. The studies of Greek private law are deplorably
behindhand, and those of public law can be improved. There is no history
of Greek agriculture or of Greek coinage, and that of Greek trade is out of
date. Finally, a history of Greek political theories after Aristotle and of
historiography after Thucydides is still to be written. The continuity in
political and historical thought has often been postulated; it has never been
described. On these subjects the Roman and the Greek historian become
one, and the Byzantine historian is the indispensable collaborator. Felix
Jacoby's masterly collection of the fragments of the Greek historians, a
unique achievement in the philological field, has made the task possible, if
not easy.

These, to my mind, are the fields of research in which we can usefully
engage ourselves and our pupils, atomic bombs permitting. I trust that in
so doing we shall be acting in the spirit of George Grote. He may or may
not be classified as a Whig historian, and the Whig historian may or may
not have committed all the sins that Professor Butterfield has visited upon
him so thoroughly. When all is said, it remains true that Grote possessed
the all-redeeming virtue of the liberal mind. He was determined to understand and respect evidence from whatever part it came; he recognized freedom of speech, tolerance, and compromise as the conditions of civilization; he respected sentiment, but admired reason. One can take some pride
in being a teacher or a pupil in the College which for more than forty years
provided so many joys and so many tribulations for George Grote.[46]

Notes

1. Mrs. Grote, *The Personal Life of George Grote* (1873) p. 57.

2. French translation in 1802; Italian translation, Florence, 1807; Greek translation, Vienna, 1806; German translation, Leipzig, 1792; Spanish translation,
Madrid, 1822. Some of these are from the abridgement.

3. "De rebus gestis Philippi Amyntae F.," *Dissertationes Academicae Selectiores*
(Lund, 1675) pp. 109–95: Pufendorf discusses constitutional points.

4. *Histoire de Philippe* (Paris 1740–60) I, p. li: "C'est l'histoire d'un Prince habile et
heureux, qui n'est heureux que parce qu'il est habile."

5. *The History of the Life and Reign of Philip, King of Macedon* (1758); the poetical
preface is by Samuel Madden.

6. *The Orations of Lysias and Isocrates translated from the Greek with some account of their lives, and a discourse on the history, manners, and character of the Greeks from the conclusion of the Peloponnesian War to the Battle of Chaeronea* (1778) p. lxiii.

7. *The History of the World from the Reign of Alexander to that of Augustus* (1807); *cf.* also J. Gast, *The History of Greece from the accession of Alexander till its final subjection to the Roman Power* (1782); A. Boeckh, *Encyklopädie und Methodologie* (1877) p. 346.

8. *Cf.* Momigliano, *Filippo il Macedone* (Firenze 1934); "Genesi storica e funzione attuale del concetto di Ellenismo," *Giorn. Crit. Filos. Ital.*, 16 (1935) and papers there quoted.

9. Byron, *Don Juan,* Canto XII, 19 and note; Macaulay, *Miscellaneous Essays,* in *Works,* VII (1866) ed. Lady Trevelyan, pp. 683–703 (written in 1824).

10. *Life and Letters* (London and New York, 1897) p. 27; *cf.* for what follows, G. L. Nesbitt, *Benthamite Reviewing: The First Twelve Years of The Westminster Review* (New York 1934).

11. *Early Grecian History and Legend,* reprinted in *Dissertations and Discussions,* II (1859) p. 283. J. S. Mill's early interest in Roman and Greek history is well known: *Autobiography,* ed. H. J. Laski, pp. 10–11.

12. Mrs. Grote, *The Personal Life of George Grote,* p. 49, compared with [Mrs. Grote], *The Philosophical Radicals of 1832* (1866) p. 65, and above all G. Grote, *Posthumous Papers* (1874) p. 26.

13. *The Westminster Review,* V (1826) pp. 269–331.

14. *The Quarterly Review,* XXXIII (1826) pp. 332–56.

15. *The Westminster Review,* VII (1827) pp. 227–68.

16. For an impressive testimonial on Grote, *cf.* Thirlwall's *Letters to a Friend* (1882), ed. A. P. Stanley, p. 323.

17. *Remains of Hurrell Froude* I (1838), p. 310, already quoted by J. Thirlwall, *John Connop Thirlwall, Historian and Theologian* (1936) p. 62.

18. J. C. Hare, *A Vindication of Niebuhr's History of Rome from the Charges of the Quarterly Review* (Cambridge 1829). The useful account of this period of English historiography by K. Dockhorn, *Der deutsche Historismus in England* (Göttingen 1950) is discussed by me in *Rivista Storica Italiana,* 63 (1951) p. 592. *Cf.* now D. Forbes, *The Liberal Anglican Idea of History* (Cambridge 1952).

19. *Minor Works,* pp. 205–36.

20. *Life of G. Grote,* p. 264.

21. *Cf.* W. Bagehot, in *Biographical Studies* (1895) ed. R. H. Hutton, pp. 223, 357; L. Stephen, *The English Utilitarians,* III (1900) p. 334, and my essay, "G. C. Lewis, Niebuhr e la critica delle fonti," *Rivista Storica Italiana* (1952). See also Lewis's *Letters* (1870), which contain much about his friendship with Grote. The *Treatise on the Methods of Observation and Reasoning in Politics* has a section "On the Treatment of Political History," I, pp. 181–323. A review of Grote's *History* by Lewis, in *Edinburgh Review,* XCI (1850) pp. 118–52. *Cf.* Mrs. Grote's *Life,* p. 195.

22. *The Letters of J. S. Mill,* I (1910) p. 58.

23. H. W. Garrod, *Scholarship: Its Meaning and Value* (Cambridge 1946) p. 10.

24. *Cf.* his essay "Grecian Legends and Early History" (1843) in *Minor Works,* p. 75.

25. *Spectator* of 4 April 1846. The most important reviews of Grote's books by Mill are collected in *Dissertations and Discussions,* II (1859) pp. 283–334, 510–54; III (1867) pp. 275–379; IV (1875) pp. 188–230.

26. *Revue des Deux Mondes*, XVIII (1847) pp. 52–69; *cf.* also Kortüm's review in *Heidelberger Jahrbücher* (1846) pp. 641–52, for an instructive account of the Greek studies in Germany.

27. *The Quarterly Review*, LXXVIII (1846) pp. 113–44; LXXXVI (1850) pp. 384–415; LXXXVIII (1850) pp. 41–69; XCIX (1856) pp. 60–105. The last article was written by Dr. William Smith, the lexicographer. As Mrs. Grote says, "It was an additional pleasure on the part of the Historian to find, in his unknown critic and eulogist, a pupil of his own cherished institution, University College." *Life,* p. 231.

28. J. G[rote], *A few remarks on a pamphlet by Mr Shilleto entitled 'Thucydides or Grote?'* (Cambridge 1851). The respect which soon surrounded Grote's name is shown by the pamphlet by E. M. Cope, *Plato's Theaetetus and Mr Grote's criticisms* (Cambridge 1866).

29. "Quoique, par régime cérébral, je ne lise presque rien, il me tarde de m'assurer directement si le jugement que ma grande théorie historique m'a conduit à formuler sur cette civilisation se trouve suffisamment conforme à votre profonde appréciation spéciale." Grote, *Posthumous Papers*, p. 90.

30. Compare J. P. Mahaffy's remarks in his introduction to the English translation of V. Duruy (1898) and see also W. Vischer, "Ueber die neueren Bearbeitungen der griechischen Geschichte" (1861) in *Kleine Schriften,* I (1878) pp. 511–33.

31. *Cf.* Freeman's reviews of Grote, now in *Historical Essays,* II (1873).

32. The importance of Bury's *History of Greece* is perhaps underrated by N. H. Baynes in his classic memoir of Bury (1929); *cf.* also Baynes and H. M. Last in *Dict. Nat. Biogr.,* suppl. 1922–30, s.v. J. B. Bury.

33. English translation by B. Bosanquet (Oxford 1878).

34. *Aristophanes und die historische Kritik* (Leipzig 1873).

35. Th. Gomperz, *Essays und Erinnerungen* (1905) pp. 33, 184–96. *Cf.* his son's biography, H. Gomperz, *Th. Gomperz,* I (Vienna 1936) index s.v. G. Grote.

36. K. Lehrs, *Populäre Aufsätze aus dem Altertum,* 2d ed. (1875) p. 478. See also J. von Döllinger, *Akademische Vorträge,* II (1889) pp. 174–76 (written in 1872).

37. J. Jacoby, *Geist der Griechischen Geschichte: Auszug aus Grote's Geschichte Griechenlands,* nach dessen Tode hrsg. von F. Rühl (Berlin 1884).

38. Published in *Deutsche Zeitschrift für Geschichtswissenschaft* and republished in *Aus Altertum und Gegenwart* (München 1895) pp. 315–42. Pöhlmann has acute remarks on Ricardo's influence on Grote; *cf.* his speech *Griechische Geschichte im 19. Jahrhundert,* Festrede der Münchener Akademie (1902), in *Aus Altertum und Gegenwart,* Neue Folge (1911) pp. 277–322. Grote's influence on German historiography is ignored by H. von Srbik, *Geist und Geschichte vom deutschen Humanismus bis zur Gegenwart,* II (1951).

39. *Aristoteles und Athen,* I (1893) pp. 375–81. But see also J. G. Droysen, *Briefwechsel,* II, p. 442 (written in 1857).

40. G. Rosa, "Dei miti greci e latini," *Rivista Europea* (1847) p. 432: but Rosa calls Grote "Gregorio" and must know him indirectly through reviews. An Italian translation of Grote, which began to appear in Naples in 1855, was discontinued after three volumes.

41. J. S. Mill, *Letters,* II, p. 332.

42. See my account in C. Antoni and R. Mattioli, *Cinquant'anni di vita intellettuale italiana. Scritti in onore di B. Croce,* I (1950) pp. 85–106; *cf.* A. Ferrabino, *La dissoluzione della libertà nella Grecia antica,* 2d ed. (Padua 1937) p. 44.

43. J. Ruskin, *Arrows of the Chace* (1886) in *Works,* ed. Cook and Wedderburn, XXXIV, p. 586. In a letter of 1864 Ruskin says, "The only two works of value on Rome and Greece are by a polished infidel, Gibbon, and a vulgar materialist, Grote." *Works,* XVIII, p. xxxiv.

44. *Journ. Hellen. Studies,* LIX (1939) p. 296.

45. "De la manière d'écrire l'histoire en France et en Allemagne depuis cinquante ans," *Revue des Deux Mondes,* CI (1872) pp. 241–51.

46. I am indebted to H. M. Last, G. Pugliese Carratelli, and P. Sraffa for information.

THREE

M. I. Rostovtzeff

The *Social and Economic History of the Roman Empire* by M. Rostovtzeff appeared in 1926 when I was an undergraduate. Soon I was given the book to read by my teachers, and I have not yet forgotten the impression it made on me.

All seemed, and indeed was, extraordinary in the book. Even the external appearance was unusual. We were accustomed to books on ancient history where the archaeological evidence, if used at all, was never presented and explained to the reader. Here a lavish series of plates introduced us directly to the archaeological evidence, and the caption of each plate really made us understand what one could learn from apparently insignificant items. The notes were something unusual too. Learning we knew, but here was overwhelming learning on out-of-the-way subjects. And, of course, the main novelty was the text itself. Some other contemporary historians with whom we were well acquainted — De Sanctis, Beloch, Ed. Meyer, Tarn — were great men, not less great than Rostovtzeff. Even as undergraduates we could see that some of our teachers (such as Beloch and De Sanctis) analyzed the ancient sources with a surer touch than Rostovtzeff. But Rostovtzeff delighted and surprised us by what seemed to us his uncanny gift of calling things ancient to life. He guided us through the streets of Rome, Pompeii, Nîmes, and Trèves and showed how the ancients had lived.

It was little we knew of the man who was giving us such a thrill. But what we heard was in keeping with the impression made by the book. We were told that Rostovtzeff was a Russian liberal who had taught in the University of St. Petersburg until 1918 and had become an exile when the Bolsheviks

"M. I. Rostovtzeff," *The Cambridge Journal*, 7 (1954), pp. 334–46; *Contributo* (1955), pp. 341–54; *Studies in Historiography* (1966), pp. 91–104; French translation, *Problèmes d'historiographie ancienne et moderne* (1983), pp. 424–40.

seized power. We also knew that he was a man of great physical strength and exceptional memory, passionate and egotistic, capable of lecturing in six different languages and of quarreling in as many. De Sanctis, who had been his friend for thirty years, told us with a smile that one night in Athens he had had some difficulty in saving a Greek cabman from the wrath of Rostovtzeff, who had underestimated (or perhaps fully appreciated) the powers of Greek wine. A German archaeologist had another story about Rostovtzeff. On the eve of his departure from Germany Rostovtzeff had been invited to visit the cellars of a famous wine producer of the Rhine valley. The next Rostovtzeff knew was that he was approaching the station of Vienna: the railway ticket had been carefully tied to his buttonhole by his German host.

A few years later, in the early thirties, one had plenty of opportunities of meeting Rostovtzeff in Rome. Short, tough, with strange, forbidding, and yet sad blue eyes, he lived up to his reputation without any difficulty. These were the years of the excavation of Dura-Europos, and he would lecture in five languages on his work there without needing a note. He was in his sixties, but his energy seemed unspent. He could still pass from an intense season of excavations at Dura to another not less exacting season of research in the wonderful library of the German Archaeological Institute in Rome. He was perhaps less aggressive than in his younger days. Nobody disputed his greatness. Yale University surrounded him with unique respect and gave him all the means for his work. Though he was still bitter about Russia, one felt that America had really become his home. Perhaps the quality most noticeable in him was his love for street life. The streets, the gardens, the manifold out-of-door activities of a Mediterranean city appealed to him immediately. One could see that his love for classical history was inspired by his intimate acquaintance with and his great love of modern southern life—whether in the Mediterranean or in Anatolia. Pompeii had been his favorite city since his youth. Later he fell in love with Ostia and Leptis Magna. The recovery of another city, Dura on the Euphrates, was one of the great achievements of his life.

So much for a first impression. But Rostovtzeff poses very difficult questions to the students of historiography who want to know something more precise about him. He left Russia when he was forty-eight. We shall see that it would be wrong to assume that he had reached intellectual maturity before leaving Russia. Rostovtzeff was one of the very rare men who are capable of developing until old age. The crisis of the exile gave new impetus to his mind. It is safe to assume that the exile made Rostovtzeff the great man he was. However, the first forty-eight years of his life count for something. We are all doing him a great injustice in speaking about him without a proper knowledge of his Russian background, but this knowledge I found very hard to obtain. As far as I know, Rostovtzeff did not write an autobiography, and none of the studies on Rostovtzeff known to me—not even that by the American critic Meyer Reinhold, which appeared in *Science and Society* in 1946—contributed anything of importance to the knowledge of the first part of his life. The obituaries which came to my notice are disappointing in this respect. Strange as it may seem, not even the Russian teachers of Rostovtzeff are mentioned.[1]

To explain this situation, two facts should be borne in mind. Russian is a language normally unknown to ancient historians, and Rostovtzeff, even before his exile, had to write much of his work in Italian, French, and above all German in order to be understood by his colleagues. Furthermore he translated or had translated into English, Italian, French, and German much of the work he originally published in Russian. Thus he became widely known among people who neither cared for nor thought of his Russian background. On the other hand, in Russia it has become impossible to speak freely about Rostovtzeff. In the first years after the revolution things were perhaps easier. Anyway in 1925 the Soviet authorities published a manuscript on the ethnography and history of southern Russia which Rostovtzeff had left behind while escaping. The first to be surprised about the publication was Rostovtzeff himself, who of course was not asked to see the book through the press. But later, as far as I can judge on limited evidence, talk on Rostovtzeff was either discouraged or controlled. The work by B. Buzeskul on *Universal History and Its Representatives in Russia in the Nineteenth Century and at the Beginning of the Twentieth Century* which was published posthumously in 1931, does not consider Rostovtzeff's activity after 1914 and gives little more than a summary of his earlier work.[2] The bibliography on Russian historians published by Madame Švedova in 1941 contains the name of Rostovtzeff in the index of names, but not in the text;[3] the section on Rostovtzeff seems to have been suppressed in manuscript or proofs. The much discussed history of Russian historiography by N. I. Rubinstein, which appeared in Moscow in 1941, devotes a few insignificant lines to Rostovtzeff and does not examine his activity after 1918.[4] More recent books such as that by Maškin on Augustus[5] and that by Ranovič on the eastern provinces of the Roman Empire,[6] both published in 1949, discuss Rostovtzeff briefly as a typical representative of un-Russian, bourgeois historiography, though one of them refers to a review by Mr. Last in the *Journal of Roman Studies* to prove that Rostovtzeff did not even please his bourgeois colleagues.

So the Russian background is not studied by Western scholars because they know little about Russian historiography, nor by Russian scholars because the name of Rostovtzeff is unpleasant. One hopes that Rostovtzeff's Russian pupil Elias Bickerman, now a professor at Columbia University and a great historian himself, will sometime write about his master. He is the only one who can do it properly, having known Rostovtzeff before 1918.

The fact that until 1914 Rostovtzeff worked in close collaboration with German scholars and was one of the few foreigners they respected is both significant and deceptive. No doubt Rostovtzeff joined the new school of research on Hellenistic and Roman history that developed in Germany towards the end of the last century. This school emphasized the importance of regional administrative and agrarian history, invented the new science of papyrology, and rewrote the history of Hellenistic and Roman Egypt. Ulrich Wilcken was the leader of the school, but Max Weber, later to become the greatest German sociologist, was behind the new interest in agrarian history, and two first-class students of Roman law, Mitteis and Partsch, were soon won to the study of Romano-Egyptian law. Old Mommsen and the younger yet very authoritative Hirschfeld approved and encouraged the new trend, though it was a reform of their method. Mommsen and Hirschfeld, with their keen legal minds and their perfect command of literary sources and inscriptions, studied the organization of the Roman Empire from the center. Wilcken chose to study that province of the Roman Empire, Egypt, that was least typical of the Roman Empire as a whole. He proved that the Roman province of Egypt preserved much of the social and administrative structure of the former Hellenistic kingdom. Wilcken and his friends emphasized the Hellenistic influences on the Roman Empire and made people aware that Roman law and Roman administration looked quite different if seen at work in a remote province. The discovery of thousands of documents on papyri made it possible to apply the methods of modern sociological research to ancient history. Quantitative analysis was applied to fields where only vague conjectures had been possible. For many years Rostovtzeff studied Hellenistic history and the Roman provinces of the East on the evidence of papyri and legal texts. He wrote a book on tax-farming and another, more important, on the history of the Roman Colonate in its relations to Hellenistic land-tenure. The history of the Roman Colonate was published by Wilcken in a special supplement to his *Archiv für Papyrusforschung* and made Rostovtzeff's reputation. His juvenile studies on the so-called Roman *Tesserae* were clearly modeled on the epoch-making study of Wilcken on Ostraca.

Yet the activity of Rostovtzeff was not confined to these researches, nor were these researches as similar to those of Wilcken as might seem at first. While writing books on administration and land-tenure, Rostovtzeff made himself a master of Hellenistic and Roman archaeology. He traveled widely, taking notes on monuments having a bearing on social life. He studied Pompeii with special care and produced a monograph on Hellenistic landscape painting which was a contribution to social studies. Though he knew how to use his eyes, he was never an art critic. His interest in style was always less than his interest in subject matter. He saw that landscape painting reflected contemporary life and was important evidence for housing, agriculture, trade, not to speak of religion. Furthermore, he applied his knowledge of Hellenistic art to the study of the archaeology of southern Russia. Russian prehistory was developing fast under the guidance of men like N. P. Kondakov, B. V. Farmakovskij, and V. A. Gorodcov, whose *Prehistoric Archaeology* is said to have made a deep impression when it appeared in 1908. The tombs of southern Russia yielded treasures which now fill the Museum of the Hermitage and showed that during the Hellenistic period nomadic tribes of Iranian origin played an important part in the composite civilization of the Black Sea region. Rostovtzeff, who already knew the Hellenistic side of this civilization, soon proved to be an authority on Scythians and Sarmatians as well. In following up his nomads, he reached the borders of China and tackled problems of Chinese art whenever they could throw light on the Iranian elements of southern Russia. In addition to his many contributions to journals, he produced (in 1914) the standard work on wall-painting in southern Russia. At the same time, he prepared a work on the Scythians in southern Russia which, as I have already said, was first published by the Soviet authorities in 1925 and was then reelaborated in the German translation supervised by Rostovtzeff himself in 1931. A third book on Iranians and Greeks in southern Russia appeared first in Russian and then in an English version published at Oxford in 1922.

I have no qualification to judge this work on southern Russia. But it is highly appreciated by the few students of this subject, for instance Sir Ellis Minns. What a classical scholar can say is that it was something more than pioneer research on the fringes of the Classical world. Classical scholars too often forget that Greek and Roman civilizations themselves were precarious, though glorious achievements at the fringes of a well-developed world of nomadic or semi-nomadic tribes. It was the business of the Hellenistic kingdoms and of the Roman Empire to contain the nomads and enlarge the fringe of cities. But ultimately the nomads broke through, and this was the end of the Roman Empire. For obvious reasons Celts and Germans have always been kept under observation by students of the Classical world. But their forms of life and sources of strength can be fully understood only if seen against the background of the wider semi-nomadic world to which they belonged. The southern Russian tribes transmitted to the West impulses which came from as far as China. It was Rostovtzeff who brought home to classical scholars what the nomads had meant. Later Alföldi and Altheim developed the theme and enlarged the scope of research by calling in Huns and Turks, but in doing so they were no more than Rostovtzeff's pupils, whose judgment is perhaps less sound than their teacher's. It is not surprising that a Russian should have been the first to recognize the importance of the nomads for classical history. He himself lived beyond the classical fringe of Mediterranean cities. And here we begin to perceive what Rostovtzeff owed to his Russian origins.

Nor is that all. We noticed Rostovtzeff's interest in agrarian history, in Hellenistic planned economy, and in the city life of the middle class. All these three elements play an important part in Russian historiography of the late nineteenth and early twentieth centuries.

Roman agrarian history had, of course, been made fashionable by Max Weber, but agrarian history in general was a speciality of Russian historians. In a country where agrarian problems were both archaic in form and contemporary in substance, the study of the peasantry could hardly escape attention. Perhaps because the analysis of Russian agrarian problems might easily get one into trouble—Semevskij was banned from teaching for his work on the peasant question in Russian—many distinguished Russian historians studied the agrarian history of other countries. Kareev and Lučickij studied the French peasantry, and P. Vinogradoff wrote his epoch-making book on English villeinage before being called to the Oxford chair of Jurisprudence. The study of Roman Colonate was introduced into Russia as early as 1886 by an enthusiastic admirer of Fustel de Coulanges, I. M. Grevs; and the subject became quite fashionable. It is easy, indeed perhaps too easy, to account in this way also for the Russian interest in the economic organization of Hellenistic Egypt. Living under the Czars, the Russian professors could understand the complicated regulations of the Ptolemies more readily than could their Western colleagues living in the pre-1914 world of free competition. Rostovtzeff's most distinguished predecessor in this field was Michael Chvostov, who also did some work on land ownership in France before the revolution. After having written papers on the agrarian problems of archaic Athens and Sparta, Chvostov published in 1907 his *History of the Eastern Trade of Greco-Roman Egypt*. Later he published a study of the textile industry in Egypt in which he went into its technical aspects. Chvostov, who died in 1920, was two years younger than Rostovtzeff but developed more quickly and influenced him. The Russians had an obvious interest in Hellenistic and Byzantine history. Thus Rostovtzeff also found in Russia many good students of the later Greek world as a whole: it will be enough to mention the two epigraphists, V. V. Latyšev and A. V. Nikitskij, and the historian of Hellenistic Athens, S. A. Žebelev. Rostovtzeff later proved to have learnt from all of them.

Finally, Rostovtzeff found in Russia a keen interest in ancient and medieval city life. In this case contrast rather than similarity provided the motive. Russia is proverbially lacking in cities with a history comparable to those of Italy, ancient Greece, and Germany—the lands of city-states *par excellence*—or even of France, Spain, and Great Britain. A friend of mine was an attaché to the Italian Embassy in Moscow a few years ago when the Russians celebrated the eight-hundredth anniversary of their capital. A Russian woman asked him rather defiantly: "Have you got in Italy eight-hundred-year-old cities like Moscow?" My friend had to think a little before he could

find an Italian city less than a thousand years old: finally he produced it—
Alessandria della Paglia. Czarist Russia had its peasants and was very often
inclined to idealize them, but it had very little of the active and prosperous
bourgeoisie which built, beautified, and ruled the Western cities. *Bourgeoisie*
may seem a vague and misleading term to us, but obviously was not to the
Russian liberals who deplored the absence in their country of the merchants
of London, Ghent, and Florence. Here again it is no chance that one of the
most sensitive studies of French and Italian medieval cities was produced by
N. Ottokar, then a professor in the University of Perm and now the professor of medieval history in the University of Florence. It was as a Russian
liberal, longing for the creative *bourgeois* society of the Western world, that
Rostovtzeff traveled to discover the cities of the Mediterranean fringe.

These are simple indications of the complexity of the currents of ideas that
fertilized the mind of Rostovtzeff before the tragedy of exile fell upon him.
For tragedy it was. And the tragedy was made worse perhaps by an
unhappy period spent in Oxford. Rostovtzeff, who had no mean opinion of
himself, was made even more aggressive by the upheaval of exile, and probably did not realize that the average Oxford don knew Greek and Latin
much better than he did. He antagonized and in some cases offended his
hosts, but many of these seem to have failed to perceive his rapid progress
towards absolute greatness. The consequence was that Rostovtzeff was lost
to Europe. He left England and taught in the American University of Wis-
consin for a few years before finding a permanent and happy home at Yale
in 1925.

Whoever goes through the gigantic output of Rostovtzeff in the period
1918–26 has some idea of the crisis through which he passed. It was a fever-
ish production, lacking formal perfection, often marred by vulgar mistakes
in detail, but exceptional in originality, relevance to contemporary life,
and variety. The giant had been hit, but was hitting back. Rostovtzeff was
trying both to conclude all the work he had been accumulating before his
exile and to meet the challenge of exile by tackling new problems. He still
had much to say on his old themes of southern Russia, Hellenistic land tenure, landscape painting, Asiatic animal style. But he was also maturing the
twin masterpieces of the economic and social histories of the Roman
Empire and of the Hellenistic world. A first sketch of the main thesis of the
Hellenistic work appeared in the *Journal of Egyptian Archaeology* in 1920; a
first formulation of the basic theory of his Roman volume was published in
the *Musée Belge* in 1923. Before 1918 Rostovtzeff had been a man of exceptional learning in the archaeological and papyrological field and of conspicuous originality in any theme he treated but had given no precise
sign of becoming a great historian. He had reached the age of forty-eight
without finding the great theme—the inspiration—which could unify his

knowledge and mature his mind. Exile provided the shock that transformed him. The Russian liberal rapidly became a great liberal historian. He joined the line that from Guizot and Grote to Marc Bloch and the Hammonds has proved to be singularly capable of a comprehensive view of human nature and the only one seriously interested in the social consequences of intellectual liberty. A liberal faith was Rostovtzeff's inspiration, and the ancient bourgeoisie was made the theme of the two works which were to occupy their author for the next twenty years.

As it happened, the *Economic and Social History of the Roman Empire* was finished first and appeared fifteen years before the Hellenistic history. The differences between the two works are conspicuous, but they should not make one forget that the basic inspiration is the same. When Alexander destroyed the Persian empire, he opened the gates of the East to Greek soldiers, traders, farmers, sailors, teachers, doctors, engineers. These people built cities in the Greek way and spread the Greek language and Greek customs. Centuries later the Romans took over the Hellenistic monarchies of the East and established their rule over the tribal communities of Spain, Gaul, and Africa. History repeated itself. A new enterprising minority Romanized the West and revitalized the declining bourgeoisie of the East by an infusion of new men and ultimately of social security. The Hellenization of the East and the Romanization of the West were not planned, strictly speaking, by any government. They were the result of the work of people who firmly believed in their way of life and attracted to it the upper class of their subjects. The Roman and Greek cities spreading from Gibraltar to the Euphrates and beyond were the results of this activity. They told a story of adventure, work, prosperity which appealed to Rostovtzeff and made him forget the darker sides of the efforts whereby Greeks and Romans built their cities. Born in a country where the bourgeoisie was hard to find, be came to idealize the Hellenistic and Roman bourgeoisie. He loved Rhodes more than any other Hellenistic state because no other was ruled so completely and successfully by its bourgeoisie. He was equally appreciative of the *petit bourgeois* who boasted of his trade on his tombstone and of the wealthy financier who built theaters and gymnasia for his own city. Slaves and peasants attracted Rostovtzeff's attention only insofar as they helped, or interfered with, the activity of the city builders. Agrarian history, to which Rostovtzeff had devoted so much important research when he was in Russia and in the first years of his exile, played only a secondary part in the two great histories. This is serious enough, and we shall come back to it, as it is essential to the understanding of Rostovtzeff. He is not the historian of Roman and Hellenistic society as a whole. He is primarily the historian of their traders, gentlemen farmers, and professionals. He is never so good as when he can show how they extended the range of their activity and spread prosperity and comfort where they stepped in.

Yet it is evident that the triumph of the Hellenistic and of the Roman bourgeoisie was comparatively short and incomplete. In the second century B.C. the Hellenistic middle class was already declining. In the third century A.D. the city life of the empire was vitally affected by inflation, wars, and military tyranny. Twice Rostovtzeff was faced by the problem of explaining the decline of city life. In respect of the Hellenistic bourgeoisie he never hesitated. He fastened the responsibility for its fall on both the Hellenistic kings and the Roman invaders. The kings paralyzed the middle class by their planning and regulations and wars: the Romans completed the work of destruction since they destroyed cities, increased taxation, disorganized traffic, and terrorized individuals before being persuaded by Augustus that it was in their interest to give security to the Eastern middle class.

In the case of the Roman Empire, Rostovtzeff was not so certain of himself. Under the impact of the Russian Revolution he thought he had discovered the clue to the decline of Rome in the conflict between the bourgeoisie and the peasantry. According to the theory he first made public in the *Musée Belge* (1923) the peasants remained outside the civilization of the Roman Empire. They hated the bourgeoisie and found an opportunity for revenge when they became more numerous in the Roman army. Helped by emperors who sympathized with them, they rebelled against the cities and spread disorder. The Red Army of the third century ruined the Roman state of the Caesars, just as the Red Army of the twentieth century ruined the Russian state of the Czars. This is the famous theory that has provoked so much discussion. Norman Baynes among others found no difficulty in proving that in the third century A.D. the peasants were not less terrorized by the army than the city dwellers.[7] These criticisms certainly affected Rostovtzeff, but in any case he was bound to see things differently as soon as he became less preoccupied with Russian affairs. Already in the book of 1926 he leaves space for the alternative explanation that the Roman bourgeoisie was weakened by state intervention and barbarian attacks just as the Hellenistic bourgeoisie had been weakened by state intervention and Roman attacks. Later, in the German edition of his book (1929), he deleted all explicit mention of the Red Army of peasants. Finally in an article in the *Economic History Review* (1930) he emphasized state intervention only as the cause of the Roman decline and dropped his theory of the peasant rebellion.

One easily sees that the *Social and Economic History of the Roman Empire* is a book not very clearly and coherently thought out. It was written much more quickly and with much less thorough knowledge of the evidence than the later book on Hellenistic history. It was also emotionally disturbed by his impressions of the Russian Revolution. The image of a Red peasant army for which there was really no evidence took hold of Rostovtzeff against his better judgment. He was unable to combine it with the other explanation that state control progressively cut the roots of free initiative and prosperity. But without his painful experience of the Russian Revolution Rostovtzeff would probably not have described the bourgeoisie of the Roman Empire with such loving care. Though his theory of the alliance between peasants and army proved to be delusive, we know that there were peasant rebellions in the empire and we know also that peasant discontent occasionally allied itself with religious movements. The part played by the peasantry in the history of the third to the fifth centuries A.D. has still to be assessed fairly.

When Rostovtzeff turned to the completion of the *Social and Economic History of the Hellenistic World* he was peacefully established in America. I was perhaps not the only reader to miss in the Hellenistic history the generous impatience, the emotional intensity of the book on Rome. Something of the old fire had gone out, but the new history was a much more careful piece of research. Rostovtzeff had learned to examine the evidence more prudently and patiently. He had in the meantime returned to field archaeology, and the excavation of Dura-Europos with all the work of interpretation it implied had been a wonderful discipline both for himself and for the American pupils he trained there.

Not much can be said here about the rediscovery of Dura, except insofar as it is relevant to Rostovtzeff's interpretation of Hellenistic and Roman civilization. The story is better read in Rostovtzeff's little book *Dura and Its Art* which appeared in 1938. Dura was a mere name until its site was identified by chance after the First World War and soon attracted the attention of the great Franz Cumont. Cumont excavated there on behalf of a French academy and published his results in 1926. This encouraged Yale University and Rostovtzeff to take over the excavations (about 1928) when it became clear that the French did not intend to go on. Dura was first a Macedonian colony on the border of the Euphrates, then it became a Parthian city and included large sections of population of Iranian and Semitic origin. Later it was occupied by the Romans and received a garrison. It was finally destroyed in the third century, and its ruins were slowly buried in the desert. The new Pompeii suited Rostovtzeff well and confirmed his ideas about the composite character of Hellenistic civilization. He analyzed admirably the various elements that went to make the history of Dura. Never dogmatic because of his liberal education, he proved also to be much more discriminating, much more patient in interpreting the ruins of Dura, than one would have expected from his earlier work. The volumes of the reports on the excavations, though written to a great extent by his collaborators and pupils, were the results of their common study under his direction and represented his third great life work—which alone would suffice to make the glory of a historian.

In the *Social and Economic History of the Hellenistic World* there is not so evident a hiatus as that between the two interpretations of the decline of the empire which one can discover in the Roman book. But there is a more subtle conflict of points of view. Elsewhere I have tried to explain that the Hellenistic history is the result of the superimposition of two books.[8] One analyzes the causes of the decline of Hellenistic social life under the impact of state intervention and Roman invasion. The other is an inventory of the main achievements of Hellenism in the economic and social field. What unifies the two books to a certain extent is the emphasis on the creative work of the Hellenistic bourgeoisie. The bourgeoisie deserves the credit for the achievements of the Hellenistic civilization, and the Hellenistic kings and the Roman generals are responsible for its shortcomings. But Rostovtzeff did not succeed in fusing together the two themes of his book. Something separates the main section on the consequences of state intervention and Roman invasion from the final section on the achievements of Hellenistic civilization, though I should be embarrassed to say what it is.

A critical evaluation of Rostovtzeff should therefore start from the prominent position he assigns to the bourgeoisie in his Hellenistic and Roman histories. In my opinion, Rostovtzeff is essentially correct in assuming that both the Hellenization and the Romanization of the territories of the Roman Empire resulted from the activities of the urban middle class. But four rather obvious remarks come to my mind:

1. Rostovtzeff did not make a close enough study of the problem of political liberty in the ancient world. He overestimated the importance of economic liberalism in comparison with political freedom. This is evident in his study of the Roman Empire, with the result that he hardly grasped the meaning of the political opposition to the Emperors and the importance of the senatorial class as a political elite.

2. Rostovtzeff oversimplified the economic structure both of the Hellenistic and of the Roman period and never defined the term *bourgeoisie*. He never examined the means by which the cities governed themselves nor asked the question, who governed them? He was not much interested in taxation and inflation, which are the main indications of changes in the social structure. He was lucky in being born early enough to escape the present ridiculous adoration of so-called prosopography (which, as we all know, claims to have irrefutably established the previously unknown phenomenon of family ties). But it may be regretted that he did not pay more attention to the general problem of the formation of the ruling classes.

3. Rostovtzeff, as we have said, gave peasants and slaves sometimes less than their due, not because he ignored them, but because he focused his attention on middle-class urban activities.

4. Rostovtzeff, although he studied ancient religion, can hardly be said to have been aware of the profound impact that the religious needs of man have had upon his development. He never examined the implications of the fact that Christianity ultimately made its appeal to people of all classes. He assumed the fatality of the clash between the educated city-dweller and the less educated peasant, but Christianity did embrace both peasants and citizens and made them work together.

Perhaps other objections can be made to Rostovtzeff. One, obvious enough, is that he was more intuitive than logical (as Russians often are) and therefore seldom thought his theories out clearly. But he must be measured by his achievements, not by his shortcomings. He was a liberal man who loved life in his creative moments and had the gift of calling things back to life. His learning was enormous, but he cannot be confused with those people who know all about a thing without knowing the thing. He fought for the ideas in which he believed and was never quite at peace with the surrounding world, though America gave him his best years. At last, the Second World War and old age coming together were too much for him: he sank into melancholia and was never himself again. Those who have known him have known greatness. They will always cherish the memory of a courageous and honest historian to whom civilization meant creative liberty.

Notes

ADDITIONAL NOTE: When I wrote this paper I was not acquainted with the biographical sketch (with bibliography) published by G. V. Vernadskij in *Seminarium Kondakovianum*, IV (Prague 1931) pp. 239–52. Vernadskij gives many details about Rostovtzeff's family (his father was a student of Virgil) and makes it clear that Kondakov was the main influence in his intellectual formation. Later (1895–96) R. studied in Vienna with Bormann and Benndorf.

1. *Cf.* C. Bradford Welles, *Gnomon* (1953) pp. 140–44.

2. *Vseobščaja istorija i ee predstaviteli v Rossii v xix i načale xx veka*, čast' vtoraja (Leningrad 1931) pp. 172–74; 184; 207–10.

3. O. I. Švedova, *Istoriki SSSR* (Moscow 1941) p. 147.

4. *Russkaja Istoriografija* (1941) pp. 492–93.

5. N. A. Maškin, *Principat Avgusta* (Moscow 1949) p. 375 (cf. pp. 355–56).

6. A. Ranovič, *Vostočnye Provincii Rimskoj Imperii v I–III vv.* (Moscow-Leningrad 1949) p. 33 (*cf.* pp. 5–6).

7. *Journal of Roman Studies*, 19 (1929) p. 229; *cf.* H. M. Last, ibid., 16 (1926) p. 126.

8. *Journal of Hellenic Studies*, 63 (1943) p. 116.

FOUR

Introduction to the
Griechische Kulturgeschichte
by Jacob Burckhardt

Mir als Geschichtsdozenten ist ein ganz merkwürdiges Phänomen klargeworden:
die plötzliche Entwertung aller blossen "Ereignisse" der Vergangenheit.
BURCKHARDT TO F. VON PREEN, 1870

An inspired teacher with a natural aptitude for collecting together his re-searches and reflections and presenting them clearly and calmly, Burckhardt was able, as were few other historians, to express his ideas in courses of lectures. This is particularly true of the *Griechische Kulturgeschichte*, a course of lectures given repeatedly between 1872 and 1885, which he had already started to think about shortly after 1860. Although he prepared it and even partly drafted it for future publication, he never considered it ready for the press, and in the end, in about 1880, he decided finally to abandon his attempt to turn it into a book. Whatever the reasons for this decision, the reader must remember that he has before him an unfinished work, indeed a course of lectures never approved by the author for publication.[1]

Inevitably most courses of lectures aim at more than one end. In the case of the *Griechische Kulturgeschichte* it is easy to distinguish two tenden-cies. Burckhardt intended to offer his listeners a course in Greek history and antiquities that would be more satisfactory in method than those he had him-self attended as a young man. At the same time he was communicating cer-tain reflections on the nature of Greek civilization — reflections clearly connected with the course of lectures on the "study of history" which he gave three times (in 1868–69, 1870–71, and 1872–73) and which were later pub-lished posthumously with the title *Weltgeschichtliche Betrachtungen*.

Burckhardt decided in 1868 to arrange his course on Greek culture in systematic, not chronological, order. He was not alone in these years in preferring the descriptive approach in historiography to the evolutionary

"Introduzione alla *Griechische Kulturgeschichte* di Jacob Burckhardt" (Italian edition, Florence: Sansoni, 1955); *Secondo contributo* (1960), pp. 283–98; English translation, *Essays in Ancient and Modern Historiography* (1977), pp. 295–305. Translated by Judith Landry; translation revised by T. J. Cornell.

scheme. In 1871 Mommsen published the first volume of his *Römisches Staats-recht*, possibly the greatest descriptive work of modern historiography. Mommsen never really returned to evolutionary historiography: even the fifth volume of the *History of Rome*, which came out subsequently in 1885, is structurally descriptive and systematic.

Chronological order and systematic order have alternated in historical works since the fifth century B.C. At least from Varro onwards the two methods of arrangement have corresponded to two kinds of historiography, the one concerned with describing institutions and customs, the other with narrating events: the *Antiquitates* in systematic order went side by side with the *Annales* and *Historiae* in chronological order. But in the eighteenth century antiquarian research fell into disrepute with the majority of philosophically trained historians, and in the nineteenth century this disrepute was combined with a feeling of doubt as to whether such research could rightfully exist alongside narrative history. In the century of evolution it was easy to observe that even institutions and customs undergo evolution and should be studied in chronological order. Without wishing to simplify a complex situation, it is perhaps legitimate to assert that about 1870 antiquarianism was at best admitted as an inferior form of historiography.[2]

It is to some degree surprising that just at that time Mommsen and Burckhardt should have had recourse to the systematic form typical of the study of antiquities. Both believed it necessary for their interpretations, and from different points of view they hoped for greater advantages from it than from the chronological form. Naturally neither intended to relapse into the antiquarian genre as such. While the traditional *Antiquitates* described all aspects of ancient life without attempting to look into their meaning, Burckhardt aimed at describing the Greek spirit as it emerged from an analysis of the institutions and forms of life in Greece. Furthermore, though systematic, he did not aim to review every aspect of Greek life; as is well known, he always claimed the right to a subjective choice of interesting details.

In the introduction to the course Burckhardt himself explains the advantages he attributes to his own method. Historiography in chronological order blurs the essential with the particular, the permanent with the changing, the typical with the accidental; furthermore, it must inevitably involve endless discussion of the authenticity and chronological sequence of documents. In a *Kulturgeschichte* in systematic order a document stands on its own, as evidence of a state of mind, quite apart from the objective truth of the facts attested in it and its exact chronological position. The return to the systematic form therefore has the virtue not only of making possible an understanding of the spirit of the Greek world, but also of dispelling the doubts introduced by historical criticism concerning the value of the ancient sources.

Similarly, Mommsen's aim was to describe the essential principles of the Roman state, the lasting ones, without losing himself in details; and in the coherence of his description, echoing the organic unity of the Roman state, he found the best remedy against the proliferation of conjectures. While Burckhardt was establishing a correlation between the systematic form and the presence of the Greek spirit, Mommsen was justifying the same form by adducing the organic nature of the state. Both wanted to avoid the consequences of the destructive criticism at which the successors of Niebuhr excelled. In short, in both of them a descriptive and systematic historiography reaffirmed its right to exist—a type of historiography which was in danger, since it offended the evolutionary principle so widely accepted in the nineteenth century. The new antiquarianism of the nineteenth century, like that of the seventeenth and eighteenth centuries, was an answer to Pyrrhonism, but unlike the earlier antiquarianism it claimed to be able to penetrate beyond phenomena into the spirit of a people and the structure of a political organization. It was a study of antiquity revised in accordance with romantic notions of national character and the organic state, which in its turn paved the way for the sociological investigation of the ancient world introduced by Max Weber.

But the notion of the Greek spirit (like that of a political organization) is not in fact so simple and definite as to justify the abandoning of chronological order with no further discussion. And the solution of taking the evidence on its own, out of time, is at best only a partial reply to skeptical criticism. It is still necessary to decide if the historian is lying or mistaken about himself or things which happen during his lifetime. The method of *Kulturgeschichte* favored by Burckhardt might make it possible to avoid the problem of whether Herodotus was well-informed about Gyges, but it does not free one from the task of deciding whether his picture of contemporary society corresponds to the facts or whether it is the product of his imagination. There is clearly a difference between a description of customs based on Herodotus or Tacitus and one based on unreliable writers such as Ctesias or the *Scriptores Historiae Augustae*. However, Burckhardt did not want completely to eliminate chronological order, and, like some earlier antiquarians and archaeologists—including Winckelmann and K. O. Müller—and later Mommsen, he arrived at a rather cloudy compromise between systematic order and chronological order. For example, in the last volume he discussed the evolution of Greek man; but the types and characteristics were at least partly the same as those he had described in the preceding volumes without reference to their chronological context.[3]

In abandoning chronological order Burckhardt laid himself open to the accusation immediately leveled against him by Wilamowitz, E. Meyer, and J. Beloch of lacking critical sense in the examination of evidence.[4] The accusation was all the more easily made in that, unlike Mommsen, Burckhardt did not keep abreast of the progress made in classical studies after his youth (let us say, roughly speaking, after 1850) and for this reason often appeared out of date in the matter of details. But more serious still was his uncritical acceptance of the notion of the Greek spirit, even though this had been traditional in German historiography from Winckelmann onwards and was therefore far less irritating to Burckhardt's critics, who took no account of the fact that one of his reasons for adopting an atemporal form was that it corresponded to an atemporal Greek spirit. There is clearly no way of deciding *a priori* if those who understood one another by talking or writing one of the many varieties of the language we call Greek had mental habits and characteristics in common which could be designated a Greek "spirit" or "character." Only a piece of research extending over the centuries and various regions of the Greek world could establish whether Homer and Tzetzes, the Arcadian peasant of the fourth century B.C. and the Alexandrian intellectual of the sixth century A.D. reveal common mental characteristics, or whether on the other hand what is called the Greek spirit was the sum of intellectual qualities restricted to a Greek-speaking group found in a particular chronological, geographical, and social situation. Burckhardt and his predecessors were wrong not because they admitted the existence of the Greek spirit, but because they presupposed it. Far from justifying a nonchronological exposition, the question of the Greek spirit demands research in strictly chronological order. Even some more recent works inspired by Burckhardt or written in this same nonchronological order (such as *Der hellenische Mensch* by M. Pohlenz and *Die Götter Griechenlands* by W. F. Otto) arbitrarily extend observations and reflections which are or could be true only of a limited section of the Greek-speaking peoples: their margin of error is directly proportional to the extension of the generalization. The question of the existence of the Greek spirit is open, because it has not yet been critically approached.

Insofar as he offered a systematic description of the Greek spirit, Burckhardt satisfied a deeply felt need of the whole of nineteenth-century German culture. It is certain that he was strongly influenced by Boeckh; he not only attended Boeckh's lectures on Greek antiquities in 1839–40, but also probably knew of his plan (which was never realized) for a *Culturgeschichte* of the Greeks with the title *Hellen*.[5]

The section on the Greeks in Hegel's *History of Philosophy* was also a *Griechische Kulturgeschichte* in embryo. But the fact that Burckhardt was the first to present an extensive analysis of the Greek spirit shows that although the idea had been in the air for a century, it was difficult to realize: it required a breadth of reading and a constructive ability that are rarely found. In this sense the *Kulturgeschichte* of Burckhardt is a monument to the Romantic spirit he had absorbed before 1848, a monument if not actually anachronistic, at least certainly created when the main German historians of the Greek world could no longer fail to see its defects.

There is, however, another aspect in which Burckhardt shows himself to be far more original, though here too it is possible to sense traces of Boeckh's teaching. The publication in 1905 of the *Weltgeschichtliche Betrachtungen* revealed the thorough revision of values undertaken by Burckhardt in the years preceding and following the foundation of the German empire. The letters of this period (particularly those to F. von Preen), the text of certain lectures, and the recollections of his pupils confirm that Burckhardt not only cut himself off from Bismarck's Germany, but showed a greater appreciation of Catholicism and modified his own ideas on the Middle Ages and Counter-Reformation. Religion appeared to him, at least in some cases, as a bulwark of the individual against the state; one such case was naturally the resistance of the Catholics in the *Kulturkampf.*

The *Weltgeschichtliche Betrachtungen* attempted to unravel the thread of an historical process in which democracy kills liberalism, the national state strangles the small regional and civic units, and the desire for power grows in inverse proportion to education in truth and beauty. But his pessimism in the face of the immediate future was tempered by his radical pessimism about all human history, since Burckhardt recognized that the historical forces regulating the present had also operated in the past, from which everything beautiful, good, and true in the world had come. Though the state and religion could devitalize culture, culture would not exist without religion and the state. Precisely because he had no illusions about the cost of culture, Burckhardt was ready to recognize the conditions upon which culture depended. The analysis does not end in relativism. Two decisive chapters discuss historic "greatness" and the question of what constitutes a favorable outcome (*Glück*) in history. The first, while it makes concessions to the relativity of points of view, reaffirms the possibility of an objective judgment on the greatness of individuals. The second calls for the replacement of the approximative and optimistic notion of the providential by that of the evil which cannot be eliminated from history: the only consolation is knowledge.

Burckhardt saw that Greek civilization had experienced the same conflicts that were to be found in modern civilization — those between material power and spiritual culture, between masses and individuals, between religious subjection (and inspiration) and humanistic independence. He developed a sharp eye for the failings of the Greek world, but an awareness of the fragility of every culture also sharpened his perception of the greatness and variety of Greek culture. A tenderness, a warmth, a new intimacy in the contemplation of the Greek miracle were combined with a merciless analysis of those forces with which and against which Greek culture developed. Realism and pessimism color Burckhardt's exposition: it is possible to recognize the roots of both of these in Boeckh's teaching at Berlin.[6] Burckhardt established a new solidarity between Greek culture and modern culture on the basis of their common difficulties and common conflicts. He explicitly repudiated the interpretation diffused by Schiller and later by E. Curtius of the Greek world as a serene and beautiful world, undisturbed by anxieties about what lay beyond.[7] Less explicitly, Burckhardt also opposed the interpretation of G. Grote and the other radicals for whom Greek democracy and sophistics were the height of Greek civilization.

In both these points (as in his scant respect for the *viri eruditissimi*) Burckhardt naturally agreed with Nietzsche. In those years of friendship between 1869 and 1872, Burckhardt and his young colleague must have said more to one another than has been documented. But the letters that Nietzsche, who was less reticent than Burckhardt, wrote to Rohde are sufficient proof that fellow-feeling never actually amounted to collaboration. Nietzsche and Burckhardt, though encouraging and possibly inspiring one another, proceeded independently. There are few traces of Nietzsche in Burckhardt's work. Even the chapter on tragedy bears his mark only slightly. Dionysiac elation, let alone rebellion against morality, attracted Burckhardt little, being as he was cautious by nature and by now over fifty years old.[8]

Burckhardt turned to the Greeks because they too derived a basically pessimistic conclusion about life from their own conflicts. His most telling pages concern Greek pessimism, and of these the ones dealing with the propensity to suicide, which are also particularly fully documented, are especially striking: the most carefully drawn figure, almost a self-portrait, is that of the pagan ascetic Diogenes the Cynic, *der heitere Pessimist*. Burckhardt was fully aware of the debt which Greek art and poetry owed to religion, but at the same time he believed that Greek religion was more a matter of imagination than moral energy. It was not in the myths but in the pessimism of their ethics and their praxis that Burckhardt saw and loved the essential seriousness of the Greeks, and here his Calvinist heritage came to the fore. It is pointless to speculate on what would have been his reaction to the new trend which was started in the studies on Greek religion by E. Rohde and the Scandinavian school, if he had ever known about it. Burckhardt knew only the interpretation of Greek religion as the religion of an artistic people and accepted it as an indication that the moral strength of the Greek people was to be sought elsewhere.

Burckhardt appreciated Greek myth as an immediate apprehension and purification of reality, as a fruit of beauty, but believed that there was a tension between myth and the precepts of morality and reason. Among the Greeks pessimism was the complement of the mythical imagination; it sustained their moral life and made possible the coexistence of imagination and rational effort. Greek pessimism was therefore liberating and creative; it expressed itself in terms of knowledge and beauty and was thus inseparable from the Greek vocation for dispassionate contemplation. Prepared for death, the Greeks were also prepared for life. Unafflicted by a priestly religion, they could easily transform religious experience into a source of aesthetic pleasure. They had in fact to struggle not against the church, but against the state. The basic conflict of the Greek world was between state and culture, not between religion and culture.

Burckhardt's antipathy to democracy explodes in the famous chapter in which the paradoxical thesis is expounded that the Greek culture of the fifth century was the product not of a golden age but of the resistance of the spirit to an age of iron. On the other hand, admiration for Greek aristocracies led him to the definition of the agonistic, individualistic phase of Greek culture which, even if exaggerated by later scholars, is one of Burckhardt's genuine discoveries.[9] In the world of archaic Greece the historian of the Renaissance found himself at home once more. He is not really praising the aristocratic state, but an aristocracy which lives according to its own rules of honor and its own artistic tastes. There is therefore no contradiction if subsequently he extends his sympathy to the apolitical individual of the Hellenistic period. Other extremely powerful passages examine the position of sculptors, painters, and architects in a society which equated art with manual labor, but for this very reason left it undisturbed, while it tended to exert control over poetry, philosophy, and science.

Chiefly concerned with religion, state, and culture, Burckhardt's exposition leaves out of account, for instance, law, finances, the art of war, education, family life, friendship, and love. Comparison with Boeckh's *Encyclopedia* and K. F. Hermann's *Lehrbuch der griechischen Antiquitäten* is instructive in connection with these limitations.

But the fact remains that much of the *Griechische Kulturgeschichte* was written not to analyze the conflicts of Greek civilization, but to provide a systematic treatment of Greek art, politics, religion, and poetry. To express the conflicts between religion, state, and culture, a representation of Greek civilization in movement would have been necessary, yet the antiquarian treatment is static. The result is uneven. The two tendencies hamper one another, and certain of the author's prejudices and shortcomings become more evident because of the work's lack of proportions. For example, the one-sidedness of the judgment on Greek democracy would be less offensive if Burckhardt had not taken upon himself the task of describing Greek democracy.

Although it was badly received on publication by historians and philologists, Burckhardt's book soon gained the favor of German philosophers and aesthetes.[10] The prestige of the work grew between the two world wars.[11] Burckhardt became fashionable in Germany because he was anti-democratic, pessimistic, sophisticated, and wise, and because many of his judgments could easily be translated into the sociological language current at the time. The specialists themselves ended by accepting the judgment of the educated public and were won over to admiration for Burckhardt. Some of his ideas, such as those of Greek pessimism and of the competitive spirit, became common property. But it would be inaccurate to say that Burckhardt had a deep effect on Greek studies between 1919 and 1939. Burckhardt moved in an area of problems concerning the conflicts between state, culture, and religion which were of little interest to the German classical philologists locked in the blind alley of the third humanism. The warning of the *Weltgeschichtliche Betrachtungen* was as little heeded as that of F. Meinecke's *Idee der Staatsräson*. Burckhardt had rather the negative effect of causing many philologists to persist in the uncritical acceptance of the postulate of the Greek spirit.

Anyone wanting to develop Burckhardt's ideas must have a clear knowledge of the difficulties inherent in his thought. His *Kulturgeschichte* belongs to two historical periods. As an analysis of the Greek spirit it is rooted in German Romanticism and inherits the laziness with regard to chronology, as well as a certain indifference to source criticism, of some representatives of German Romantic thought (Creuzer, Schelling, Hegel). As an examination of the complex and contradictory roots of Greek culture it is an anti-Romantic and revolutionary book, comparable with Nietzsche's *Die Geburt der Tragödie,* but, although sharing many of its prejudices, far more realistic and sincerely humane. Burckhardt's novelty lies in the intense, pessimistic concern with the position of a free culture vis-à-vis politics and religion. His *Griechische Kulturgeschichte* should therefore bear fruit in historians of a liberal turn of mind who read it together with Grote's *History of Greece* and are able to benefit from the pessimism combined with awareness of the good things of life which is the distinctive characteristic of Burckhardt.

Notes

1. The material on the origins of *Griechische Kulturgeschichte* is quoted by F. Stähelin in the introduction to the new edition in *Gesamtausgabe*, VIII, p. xvi. Here one should note particularly the letter to O. Ribbeck of 10 July 1864: "Ich bin doch einigermassen infiziert von jener Idee, welche einst beim Bier in der Wirtschaft gegenüber vom badischen Bahnhof zur Sprache kam: einmal auf meine kuriose und wildgewachsene Manier das Hellenentum zu durchstreifen und zu sehen, was da herauskommt, freilich gewiss nicht für ein Buch, sondern für einen akademischen Kurs 'Vom Geist der Griechen'" (*Briefe,* ed. Kaphan, 1935, p. 282). But one should also bear in mind what Burckhardt wrote to H. Schreiber in October 1842 (Kaphan, p. 65; *Briefe,* Vollst. Ausg., ed. M. Burckhardt, I, p. 218): "Ist es nicht ein Jammer, dass nach drei Jahrhunderten einer tyrannisch behaupteten klassischen Bildung doch noch immer keine vernünftige Geschichte Griechenlands existiert?"

And to G. Kinkel in February 1843 (Kaphan, p. 72; M. Burckhardt, I, p. 234): "Die Philologie beweist ihren geistigen Bankerott immer mehr dadurch, dass sie noch nicht eine gute Darstellung des Altertums hervorgebracht hat.—Niebuhr ist bloss zum Studieren;—zum Lesen scheusslich. Ueber Griechenland existiert noch nichts; Ottfried Müller hatte bloss gelehrte Zwecke. Man wird noch den Triumph erleben, dass die erste lesbare alte Geschichte ohne Zutun der Philologen ans Tageslicht treten wird.—Die Philologie ist jetzt nur noch eine Wissenschaft zweiten Ranges, so grosse Airs sie sich auch gibt. . . ."

2. *Cf.* my *Contributo alla storia degli studi classici,* pp. 95, 395, and elsewhere. G. von Below, *Die deutsche Geschichtschreibung,* 2d ed., Munich, 1924, p. 71, rightly says of Burckhardt, "Man möchte ihn fast mehr einen Antiquar nennen . . . als einen Historiker."

3. It should be noted that Burckhardt valued Greek historiography (and especially Herodotus) because it was true as far as the typical was concerned, even if it was mistaken about the individual.

4. Wilamowitz, *Griechische Tragödien,* II, 1899, p. 7: ". . . würde ich es für feige halten, wenn ich es hier nicht aussprächе, dass die Griechische Kulturgeschichte von J.B. . . . für die Wissenschaft nicht existiert . . . dass dies Buch weder von griechischer Religion noch vom griechischen Staate zu sagen weiss, was Gehör verdiente, einfach, weil es ignoriert, was die Wissenschaft der letzten fünfzig Jahre an Urkunden, Thatsachen, Methoden und Gesichtspunkten gewonnen hat. Das Griechentum Burckhardts hat ebensowenig existiert wie das der klassicistischen Ästhetik gegen das er vor fünfzig Jahren mit Recht polemisiert haben mag." Another negative judgment by Wilamowitz in this same tone in *Kleine Schriften,* V, 2, p. 185, from *Deutsche Literaturz.,* 1899, col. 15. For an opinion of Mommsen ("Diese Griechen hat es nie gegeben"), see H. Wölfflin, *Gedanken zur Kunstgeschichte,* 2d ed., 1941, p. 135. For E. Meyer, see *Geschichte des Altertums,* III, 1901, p. 291, in a passage (IV, p. 273, in H. E. Stier's edition) which also attacks Ranke's *World History.* For J. Beloch, Gercke-Norden, *Einleitung in die Altertumsw.,* 2d ed., III, 1914, p. 150; *Griech. Geschichte,* 2d ed., I, 2, 1926, p. 18. The anonymous review in *Liter. Centralbl.,* 1899, pp. 197–98, is worth bearing in mind: "die Zeugnisse versteht er gar nicht zu benutzen. Ohne es selbst zu wissen und zu ahnen (das ist das Allerschlimmste) ist er ihnen gegenüber einfach hülflos." With a different orientation and therefore more appreciative, A. Holm, *Berl. Phil. Woch.,* 1899, pp. 686–95, 717–24; J. Kaerst, *Die Geschichte des Altertums im Zusammenhange der allgemeinen Entwicklung der modernen historischen Forschung,* 1902, now in *Universalgeschichte,* ed. J. Vogt, Stuttgart, 1930, pp. 58–60, and *Geschichte des hellenistischen Zeitalters,* I, 1st ed., 1901, p. v (missing from the *Geschichte des Hellenismus,* 1927). But for an immediate recognition of Burckhardt's position in Greek historical studies *cf.* above all the vigorous pages of R. Pöhlmann, *Griechische Geschichte im neunzehnten Jahrhundert,* Munich, 1902, pp. 18–23, reprinted in *Aus Altertum und Gegenwart,* II, Munich, 1911, pp. 297–301.

5. *Cf. Allgem. Deutsche Biographie,* s.v. A. Boeckh, p. 774 (the idea of the *Hellen* goes back to 1810). Apart from the first volume of Kaegi's biography, *cf.* also his "Jacob Burckhardt und seine Berliner Lehrer," *Schweizer Beiträge zur allgemeinen Geschichte,* 7, 1949, pp. 101–16.

6. Thanks to Burckhardt, A. Boeckh's saying in *Staatshaushaltung der Athener,* 3d ed., I, p. 710, has become famous: "Die Hellenen waren im Glanze der Kunst und in der Blüthe der Freiheit unglücklicher als die Meisten glauben." A mine of information on this interpretation and in general on all Burckhardt's predecessors can be found in G. Billeter, *Die Anschauungen vom Wesen des Griechentums,* Leipzig and Berlin, 1911.

7. C. Neumann, *Jacob Burckhardt,* Munich, 1927, p. 175, has rightly noted that Burckhardt engaged in implicit controversy with Curtius in attributing little importance to the Persian Wars and in defining the trophies of Delphi as a document of hatred between the Greeks.

8. The facts are examined with exemplary intelligence by K. Löwith, *Jacob Burckhardt,* Lucerne, 1936, pp. 11–61.

9. *Cf.* V. Ehrenberg, "Das Agonale," in *Ost und West,* Prague, 1935, pp. 63–96, which has the essential bibliography.

10. A history of Burckhardt's reputation up to 1935 is traced (not in chronological order) by E. Colmi, *Wandlungen in der Auffassung von J.B.,* diss., Köln, Emsdetten, 1936.

11. This is reflected in discussions of the history of Greek culture. *Cf.* for instance W. Otto, *Kulturgeschichte des Altertums,* Munich, 1925, pp. 89–91; the preface by T. von Scheffer to *Die Kultur der Griechen,* Phaidon-Verlag, 1935; E. Howald, *Kultur der Antike,* 1938, 2d revised ed., Zürich, 1948, p. 11, with the criticism of W. Otto, "Antike Kulturgeschichte," *Sitz. Bayer. Akad.,* no. 6, 1940. More recently B. Knauss, *Staat und Mensch in Hellas,* Berlin, 1940, and W. Kranz, *Die Kultur der Griechen,* Leipzig, 1943. Here it may be as well to bear in mind two of the most independent assessments of the German Third Humanism: R. Pfeiffer, *Die griechische Dichtung und die griechische Kultur,* Munich, 1932, and K. Reinhardt, "Die klassische Philologie und das Klassische," in *Von Werken und Formen,* Godesberg, 1948, pp. 419–57. On postwar works A. Heuss, "Kulturgeschichte des Altertums," *Archiv f. Kulturg.,* 36, 1954, pp. 78–95.

FIVE

In Memory of Gaetano De Sanctis (1870–1957)

The man was obstinate, sure of himself, scornful, and quick to take offense. He had a fragile appearance but had acquired an almost infinite resistance to fatigue and physical suffering. He did not know what fear was. He once confessed that he had difficulty in thinking of fear as an important factor in history—and he was a historian of battles. It gave him pleasure to oppose, to provoke, and to challenge. He moved, as he had always done, along a path of his own, and he was solitary even in the company of others. But he never lost contact with others when he was alone. The emotions of love and hate held him in their grip, and sometimes exploded; he was faithful in friendship and unrelenting in enmity. Solitude, courage, loyalty, and clarity of purpose made him a born leader. If he had not become the head of a historical school, he could have led a band of irregulars in any war he liked; and inevitably there were wars that he liked.

The intrinsic value of taking an active part in things was instilled in him by his intellectual and religious background. He was born into one of the blackest papal families in Rome and inherited from it a devotion to the Catholic church and in particular to the person of the Pope. His father, formerly an official of the Vatican police, had refused to swear allegiance to the king of Italy. The son was reminded of his father's decision when the Fascist government ordered him to swear an oath of loyalty. But he quickly dissociated himself from clerical circles in Rome. On his own admission he even found it difficult to live with his parents. At the University of Rome, Enea Piccolomini first drew him to the study of Greek manuscripts. Then— a change that was prompted in part by the first signs of trouble with his eyesight—he was irrevocably converted to ancient history by K. J. Beloch.

"In Memoria di Gaetano De Sanctis (1870–1957)," *Rivista Storica Italiana*, 69 (1957), pp. 177–95; *Secondo contributo* (1960), pp. 299–317. Translated by T. J. Cornell.

Beloch's pupil retained to the end a warm and reverent devotion to his teacher; but as his wife Emilia once remarked, in her playful, affectionate voice, "You two were always squabbling." The contrast between the materialist German and the Catholic Roman was never suppressed.

Beloch introduced De Sanctis to the world of German *Altertumswissenschaft*. De Sanctis always remembered with a certain pride that even as a young man he had been the only Italian to be accepted as an equal by the heads of the German Archaeological Institute. From the Germans he learned the "method" which at that time went together with the habit of harsh polemic and a refusal to admit the possibility of error. Even among these learned men, however, De Sanctis sensed that he was working on his own. I do not think he ever formed personal friendships with German historians. The one he most admired, Eduard Meyer, he never knew personally—or, if he did, it was only superficially.

Nevertheless, he had friends in other parts of the world: M. Rostovtzeff in Russia (later in America), A. J. Reinach, who died so young, in France, Pio Franchi de Cavalieri in the Vatican. Among centers of research he especially valued the institute of the Bollandists; Père Delehaye was the embodiment of his ideal of dispassionate research, albeit within the boundaries of the Church. The modernist movement, which included men he counted as friends, such as Padre Semeria and Buonaiuti himself, touched him lightly but did not sway him. On the other hand, if I am not mistaken, he later turned down a chance to become professor at the Catholic University of Milan. It was inevitable that in politics as in everything else, he was unable to submit to rigid party discipline. He played a part in the formation of the Popular Party in the belief that Catholics had something decisive to offer in the postwar crisis. He later continued to be a loyal friend of Don Sturzo and of De Gasperi. But his political activity in the pre-Fascist period resulted in nothing more than election as city councillor in Turin, an election that was annulled shortly afterwards; typically, in twenty years of residence, he had forgotten to put his name on the electoral register. It was equally inevitable that he could feel nothing but abhorrence for Fascism and Nazism; for him life itself was liberty. But from his early years he was convinced that colonial expansion would bring together the interests of Catholicism and the interests of Italy. For that reason, just as he had supported the Libyan War, so too he approved of the campaign in Abyssinia and later inclined more towards Germany than towards England in the Second World War. His need for isolation, and his unwillingness to allow his loyalties to be dictated by circumstances carried him dangerously close to those who were his own worst enemies as well as enemies of humanity. Appointed senator for life on the nomination of L. Einaudi, he sat as an independent.

Once he had decided to recognize the Italian state and become regius professor, his career was easy. At the age of thirty he became full professor (*ordinario*) at Turin, after an earlier contest that had gone in his favor had been annulled. Anyone who saw him conversing with university colleagues, or in the National Library in Turin, seated in the room reserved for professors as if no one else were there, has a visible reminder of how detached he was even in academic life. Among the irascible Piedmontese De Sanctis's tetchiness did not go down too badly. In Turin, in the period before the First World War, he spent the happiest years of his life. Among his colleagues were men whose esteem he could return without effort. The names of Carlo Cipolla, of "Renier bonus," and above all of Arturo Graf and of Giuseppe Fraccaroli, were never mentioned by him without perceptible warmth in his voice.

His own disciples where the only group for whom he acknowledged responsibility. Large classes were never his forte. His seminar, even for those of us who later attended famous seminars like those of E. Fraenkel and F. Jacoby, remains a model. De Sanctis's qualities as a teacher were a unique combination of precision without pedantry, instant perception of solutions, and a capacity to transform the solution into a detailed piece of history. His precision was most evident in language. His command of ancient and modern languages was not especially conspicuous; only in French did he display a certain elegance. But De Sanctis never committed a linguistic error, and I have known no other Italian, apart from Pasquali, of whom that could be said. He also had a mastery of English and of modern Greek unusual among men of his generation. He was thus a skillful interpreter of difficult inscriptions. He himself published and commented on many in articles that remain fundamental, and he was unstinting in his assistance of those who, like Gaspare Oliviero and Margherita Guarducci, sought his help as a matter of course. The work of the Italian epigraphists at Cyrene and on Crete is inextricably connected with his name.

In his seminars and in private conversation it was remarkable how quickly De Sanctis was able to perceive the solution to a problem. Sometimes his theories were sensationally confirmed. His interpretations of the decree of Cn. Pompeius Strabo (*Atti Accad. Torino*, 1910–11) and of the Volubilis inscription (*Riv. Fil. Class.*, 1925), and his supposition that Ephorus-Diodorus drew upon the so-called *Hellenica Oxyrhynchia*, were confirmed, against eminent critics, by new discoveries. It is worth recalling two typical examples that are less well known. During the discussion in a teaching seminar of the trilingual decree of Ptolemy IV Philopator (the "Rosetta Stone"), with W. Spiegelberg's translation of the demotic section in front of him, De Sanctis suddenly noticed that a phrase was missing from the translation "through the fault of either the stonecutter or the translator." A few months later we discovered that Spiegelberg (*Abh. Akad. München*, 34, 1, 1828, p. 81 n. 2) had inadvertently missed the translation of a sentence. To many of us the article on "Callimachus and Horatius Cocles" (*Riv. Fil. Class.*,

1935) seemed one of De Sanctis's less happy efforts. He connected the name of Horatius Cocles with a war against the Peucetii, in spite of the fact that it was in none of the sources known at that time. But a few years later it was observed that the connection already existed in a passage of the *Stromata* of Clement of Alexandria (R. Pfeiffer, *Callimachus*, II, p. 114).

Bold in matters of detail, De Sanctis was cautious in his broader interpretations. Familiarity with the ancient world and a good knowledge of history in general prevented him from drawing conclusions that were too big for their premises, and his innate realism made him yet more careful in his choices. But he never hesitated to draw conclusions. Anyone who has read the essays he wrote between 1923 and 1933, almost all of them concerning matters he had discussed with his students, will know what kind of light he could throw on individuals (Aristagoras, Perdiccas), on single documents or events (the letter of Claudius to the Alexandrians, the Athenian expedition to Sicily), or on entire historical works (Herodotus, Thucydides, Xenophon).

These same qualities — exactitude, rapidity of decision, historical realism — he naturally encouraged in the work of his pupils. Few teachers have been as scrupulous as De Sanctis in their respect for the individuality of their followers. Indeed, his tact prevented him from drawing sufficiently to the attention of his students the weak points in their technical equipment. Men and women, Christians and Jews, rabbis and priests, modernists and traditionalists, atheists and mystics, fascists and antifascists — all came together to learn at the feet of a teacher who never sought to influence anyone's personal convictions.

It is in the nature of a school, however, that neither the teacher nor the pupils are ever wholly subsumed by it. An element of the artificial surrounded De Sanctis in his school. His polemical temperament encouraged the idea of a "method" that was better, in an abstract sense, than that of other schools. His disagreements with Pais and Bonfante were implanted almost unconsciously in his followers even before the reasons for the differences were clear, and the teacher became the standard-bearer for truth against error.

De Sanctis, in order to be himself, had to be left alone: at prayer, doing good (by stealth, and with the utmost generosity), and studying in his immense library. On rare occasions he opened up, sometimes with a practical joke, an expression of his eternal youthfulness of spirit, sometimes with the seriousness and tenderness of a father who has discovered that his son has become an equal. In earnest late-night conversations his turbulent soul was calmed. Enemies were treated with the same understanding and sympathy as friends. Plagued as he was by so many misfortunes, he never forgot the misfortunes of others. The famous dedication of volume IV of the *Storia dei Romani*, some of his articles, and certain pages of the *Storia dei Greci*, particularly the final chapter on Socrates, give an idea of this state of mind. When he saw me to the door in March 1939 on the eve of my departure for Oxford, his last words were, "And remember to write to Salvemini and tell him that I am always with him in his struggle for liberty."

What kind of relationship he established between prayer and study I could not say. I would not even find it easy to define the relationship between his insatiable hunger for knowledge and his published works. He read about anything and everything for as long as his eyesight held out. When his eyes finally gave up, he continued to have works of all kinds read to him. He does not seem to have felt the need for music. But the figurative arts — particularly classical art — interested him to the end. He acquired a vast knowledge of ancient and modern literature, even if his choice was not very refined. Of history, of all periods and places, he could never get enough. Without these encyclopedic interests he would not have become the ideal director of the section on antiquity of the *Enciclopedia Italiana,* nor have found in this work a partial compensation for the loss of his school between 1932 and 1945.

"I am well; what ails me is, among other things, the fact that the reconstruction of my volume of the *Storia dei Romani* is proceeding so slowly. But what can I do? A teacher's first responsibility is always to his school, and although I can work from morning to night without interruption, I cannot prolong the day as Joshua did (or rather failed to do)." Thus he wrote at the age of eighty after twenty years of blindness, political persecution, the misery and hunger of the war years, the theft of the irreplaceable manuscript of two new volumes of the *Storia dei Romani,* and finally the long agony and death from cancer of his wife, Emilia Rosmini, his beloved companion for forty years. He lived on for another seven years, increasingly detached from contacts with the outside world. Even his pupils were unable to visit him any longer. But he continued to work on the reconstruction of the lost volumes of the *Storia* (one volume has been published, the other is in proof).[1] And he continued to have books and articles read to him on a variety of topics, taking a particular interest in studies of the New Testament and of hagiography, about which he had always been well informed. Beside his deathbed there lay open the last book that he had been working on a few days before, the *Saggi linguistici* of B. Migliorini.

On the last page of his obituary of Julius Beloch (1929), De Sanctis recalled that the old master had responded to a schoolboy, who in a moment of youthful dejection had asked for a word of advice, with a reply in Greek: ζήτει ἀληθείην, ἡ γὰρ θεός ἐστι μεγίστη. "Seek the truth: She is the highest divinity." The word was made flesh in Gaetano De Sanctis: it explains his solitude, his love of liberty. Like Marc Bloch, he could go on saying, until the moment of his death: *Dilexi veritatem.*

II

In 1892, while still a student, De Sanctis published his first paper, "Studi sull' Ἀθηναίων πολιτεία attribuita ad Aristotele" ("Studies on the 'Constitution of the Athenians' Attributed to Aristotle"). This was followed a year later by an article on "La battaglia dell'Eurimedonte in Diodoro" ("The Battle of the Eurymedon in Diodorus"), and by his graduation thesis (*tesi di laurea*), which Beloch published in his *Studi di Storia Antica* (II, 1893, pp. 3–32), with the title "Contributi alla storia ateniese dalla guerra lamiaca alla guerra cremonidea" ("Contributions to the History of Athens between the Lamian War and the Chremonidean War").

The 1892 article was naturally prompted by the discovery a year earlier of Aristotle's "Constitution of the Athenians." De Sanctis saw the essential point immediately: Aristotle had made use of fourth-century antiquarians and political propagandists who were not necessarily to be preferred *a priori* to already known historical sources such as Herodotus, Thucydides, and Xenophon. The contrary view was upheld a year later by Wilamowitz in his *Aristoteles und Athen* and continued to prevail in Germany until 1949, when F. Jacoby demolished its principal support, demonstrating that in Athens in the sixth and fifth centuries B.C. there was no annalistic chronicle upon which Aristotle's predecessors could have drawn. In the article on the Battle of the Eurymedon De Sanctis, following a suggestion of Beloch, showed that a misinterpretation of an epigram had led Diodorus's source to a false reconstruction of the battle. The same conclusion was reached seven years later by E. Meyer, in the second volume of the *Forschungen,* in ignorance of the work of the Italian student. The graduation thesis was immediately recognized as a substantially correct reconstruction of political events in Athens in the first half of the third century B.C. The reconstruction had been established by putting together a number of epigraphic and literary fragments for the worst-documented period of Greek history. It survived (and it was exceptional in this) the discovery, made in 1898 by W. S. Ferguson, of the cycle of secretaries, which made it possible to date the Athenian archons with new precision (in 1911 Ferguson registered at the beginning of his *Hellenistic Athens* an acknowledgment of the debt he owed De Sanctis). Three years later (1896) De Sanctis published an article on the *Historia Augusta,* in which he discussed the question of forgery that had been raised in 1889 by H. Dessau and had subsequently been debated by the best German philologists. De Sanctis's article, which rejected forgery and upheld the Diocletianic-Constantinian date of the compilation, was still recognized in 1926, by an adversary of the quality of N. H. Baynes, as the best exposition of the traditional view; it demonstrated among other things that De Sanctis, while he was working on Greek history (and was in the process of publishing articles on various subjects such as Homer, Solon, Aeschines, Agathocles, and the social reforms of the third century B.C.), had made himself master of the institutional history of the late empire and its sources.

When one considers that they were the work of a very young man, these first articles of De Sanctis have something miraculous about them. To keep this miracle in proportion it is naturally important to remember that four young teachers like E. Piccolomini, J. Beloch, F. Halbherr (epigraphy), and E. Loewy (archaeology) were infusing their teaching at Rome with a rigor that can only be compared to that being given to philological matters by Rajna and Vitelli in contemporary Florence; and that from Florence the robust and calm intelligence of Comparetti was spreading all over Italy. But what is perhaps more important is that De Sanctis embarked on his research at a time which saw the publication of many fundamental and innovative works in the field of Greek history.

The discovery of Aristotle's Constitution of Athens coincided with the appearance of a series of other fundamental advances and discoveries. In 1892 E. Meyer published the first volume of his *Forschungen zur alten Geschichte,* followed the next year by the second volume of the *Geschichte des Altertums,* which contained the first historical evaluation of the Greek "Middle Ages" after the discovery of the Mycenaean civilization and included all of archaic Greek history. The same year saw the publication of K. J. Beloch's *Griechische Geschichte,* audacious in its criticism of the tradition, but especially original in its treatment of political and social history. Other works published around 1893 included E. Rohde's *Psyche*—which revealed the part played by problems of the soul and immortality in the thought of the Greeks—and the first volume of the *Geschichte des antiken Kommunismus und Sozialismus* by R. Pöhlmann, the official acknowledgment of the contribution of Marxism to the understanding of the ancient world. Meanwhile, in 1891 D. Comparetti had widened the study of epic with his work on the Kalevala, which finally disposed of the notion that the Homeric poems had been formed by the accretion of isolated songs. In 1893 Comparetti was also finishing his researches on the laws of Gortyn, which revealed a whole new aspect of archaic Greek society. Finally 1893 was the year of Wilamowitz's *Aristoteles und Athen,* which, even if it was architectonically less robust than the other works mentioned, included in every chapter a revision of the historiographical tradition and the political and social history of Athens which even now remains unrivaled in its depth and acumen. Three years later, in 1896, the *Götternamen* of Usener appeared, dedicated to Wilhelm and Karl Dilthey.

Men with original minds and realistic vision, interested in fundamental problems of religion, law, economy, and anthropology, and at the same time committed to refined techniques in the editing and interpretation of texts, were taking charge of Greek history. The contrast with the textbook compilations and mechanical source-analysis of the preceding decades is striking. Burckhardt had spoken about Greek civilization only to a restricted public in Basel, and it is interesting to note that when the *Griechische Kultur-geschichte* was printed (beginning in 1898), it was to be greeted with more hostility than approval by a new generation which, at least in some directions (source criticism and the study of religion), had gone considerably further than Burckhardt himself.

What the publication of this series of major works meant for the young De Sanctis is evident from what he did after graduation. In 1894 he explored the field of social history in an article "Questioni politiche e riforme sociali, Saggio su trent'anni di storia greca 258-28" ("Political Issues and Social Reforms: Essay on Thirty Years of Greek History, 258-228 B.C."). In 1896 and 1897 two penetrating Homeric papers, "La divinità omerica e la sua funzione sociale" and "L'anima e l'oltretomba secondo Omero" ("Divinity in Homer and Its Social Function"; "The Soul and the Afterlife According to Homer"), entered the debate that was then going on between E. Meyer and Rohde about the place of the cult of the soul in Greek religion. The decision to side with Meyer rather than Rohde was a real gain for the intellectual development of De Sanctis; and the critical tone against Usener should not be ignored.

The year 1898 (when the Thessalian Inscriptions published by the Lincei confirmed his maturity as an epigraphist) saw the appearance of *Atthis: Storia della repubblica ateniese dalle origini alle riforme di Clistene,* a true work of history.

Like Beloch, Meyer, and Wilamowitz, De Sanctis accepted the notion formulated by Boeckh of a science of antiquity that embraced all aspects of the ancient world. But, like his older contemporaries, he introduced his own more personal interests in a conception which now could no longer be justified, as it had been justified for Boeckh, by postulating that every aspect of the life of a nation reflected its national character, and which for that reason ran the risk of becoming purely encyclopedic. Their reinterpretations of Boeckh's science of antiquity made evident both the affinities and the differences between Wilamowitz, Meyer, Beloch, and De Sanctis. Wilamowitz made use of Boeckh's conception to exploit the grammatical interpretation of texts in the study of the history of language and style, of institutions and customs, of philosophical theories and of religious emotions; in fact, in the footsteps of Usener, he became the most complete interpreter of Greek texts there has ever been. Meyer, extending Boeckh's ideal to the East, gave it a new content: he established new relationships between classical and oriental civilizations and viewed the histories of Egypt and Israel in the way that had become traditional for Athens and Rome. The revolution was especially remarkable in the field of Jewish history, which Wellhausen had torn from the hands of the theologians but had not yet been able to immerse in the mainstream of ancient political and social history. Apart from that Meyer exhibited particular subtlety in studying the evolution of the political and religious institutions of individual states. For Beloch the essential task was to destroy the tradition with the weapons of logic and statistics, and to replace it with a few essential outlines, realistic and quantitatively precise, drawn if possible from geography, from comparison with modern conditions, from inscriptions, and from coins. In De Sanctis (as *Atthis,* the *Storia della repubblica ateniese,* indicated) the major concern was with the emergence of the city-state from preexisting tribal structures and with the concurrent juridical, religious, military, and cultural developments. This evolution satisfied the religious sense of one who saw in history the veiled hand of Providence, but who equally believed that individuals took an active part in its work. Later he would be pleased to identify his conception of the course of historical events with the philosophy of Henri Bergson.

The reconstruction, episode by episode, institution by institution, of the emergence of Athens from a tribal state to the polis model was certainly closer to the spirit of E. Meyer than to that of the other historians referred to — whatever the differences resulting from different religious convictions and from the absence of direct experience of oriental studies (an absence which was perhaps not unconnected with those religious convictions). Beloch's influence can be detected in minor and perhaps erroneous theories which De Sanctis continued to uphold even later (e.g., regarding the date of Cylon's attempted coup). But Beloch had no doubt about the significance of the work. De Sanctis recalled that he accepted a copy with the words, "It's not bad, but your graduation thesis was better." And Wilamowitz (again according to De Sanctis) let him know that he had not reviewed it because he esteemed the author and had high hopes for his future work. Revised in 1912 and enriched with new chapters on the period down to Pericles, the *Storia della repubblica ateniese* is still today, sixty years after its first publication, fresh and uncorroded.

III

After the completion of the *Atthis* and his appointment to a chair at Turin (1900), De Sanctis continued to maintain contact with the study of Greek history. He taught it in alternate years, and he guided his pupils towards Greek historical studies (one of the results was the unfinished *Storia di Sparta arcaica* by L. Pareti). He himself wrote articles prompted by new discoveries in archaeology, epigraphy, and papyrology, but also for polemical reasons. These articles, when inspired by inscriptions, are invariably of the greatest importance. Those concerning literary sources vary. An article on a new papyrus of Philistus (1905) is fundamental. Three Homeric studies, two of them in direct polemic against G. Fraccaroli's *L'irrazionale nella letter-*

atura, represent a weak offshoot of earlier research. The attempt to make the Atthidographer Androtion the author of the so-called *Hellenica Oxyrhynchia,* which were published in 1908, was clearly mistaken. I am obliged to point this out, because I myself accepted the theory in a youthful article and sought to confirm it. We did not take account (as H. Bloch pointed out to us) of the fact that the annalistic form of Androtion's *Atthis* was different from that of the *Hellenica Oxyrhynchia.*

But these Greek studies were now only minor parentheses in the activity of De Sanctis, who from 1900 to 1923 devoted himself to the history of monarchic and republican Rome with a concentration of energy and an examination of detail that are little short of miraculous. The five volumes of the *Storia dei Romani* contain more than 2500 pages, not one of which is superfluous. In its conception, the history entailed a study of the prehistory of the Indo-European peoples, a detailed investigation of Italian prehistory, a critical examination of the archaeological, epigraphic, and literary material for regal and republican Rome, and finally research on the history of the enemies of Rome, especially Carthage. Writers of perfectly well-informed handbooks were naturally to be found in Germany (though not for the history of Rome). What was new in De Sanctis, and what distinguished his work from Busolt's *Greek History* or Schürer's *History of the Jewish People in the Time of Jesus Christ,* to name the best two handbooks I can think of, was that it combined a comprehensive grasp of the material with the independence and the broad perspective of a true historian. The appendices on the sources for the Punic Wars in volume III, for example, constitute the most accurate and concise analysis of the annalistic tradition in existence. Not for nothing does the *Storia dei Romani* still dominate the field, even after the publication of collective works like the *Cambridge Ancient History,* in which a group of specialists has redone what De Sanctis did on his own.

De Sanctis's transition from Greek history to Roman history coincided with a situation that was coming to a head around 1900, this time in Italy rather than in Germany. Whereas in Greek history a new impulse had arisen from a buildup of intellectual forces in Germany around 1890, Roman history was evidently becoming stagnant. Only Mommsen went on, until his death in 1903, with a creativity that showed no signs of exhaustion. But it seemed that he left no room for other truly independent research, and he treated his pupils as involuntary collaborators in collective enterprises such as the *Corpus inscriptionum* and the *Monumenta Germaniae.* That Mommsen was impatient of dissent and a tenacious advocate of collective work directed by himself cannot be denied. When Beloch with *Der italische Bund* in 1890 introduced new insights from statistics and geography into the study of Roman Italy, he found himself immediately under attack from Mommsen: "Kaum ist je . . . eine Fahrt ins Blaue der Wissenschaft mit gleich leichtem Gepäck angetreten worden" ("Rarely has ... an expedition been undertaken into unexplored areas of scholarship with so little equipment").[2] After this there could be no question of Beloch pursuing an academic career in Germany. But as we now know from the study of the letters of Mommsen that have so far been published and from so many other aspects of his personality that have come to light, in these negative judgments he was not giving expression to his true self. One recalls the constant support given to a man of such different religious ideas and interests as A. Harnack; one recalls also how he recognized the genius of the young Max Weber. The loss of interest in Roman history is a problem in the history of contemporary German thought that cannot be resolved merely by reference to the predominance of Mommsen. In fact, Max Weber's admiration of Mommsen is an indication that the sociological systematism of the former and the juridical systematism of the latter were related, and that classical philologists were not equipped with a sufficient command of law and sociology for an effective continuation of Mommsen's true work. Besides, one cannot overlook the fact that Mommsen's best collaborators (Hirschfeld, Dessau, etc.) were Jews, as were those who renewed the study, if not of Roman history, at least of Roman literature and law in the generation after Mommsen (Leo, Traube, Norden, Lenel, Gradenwitz, etc.). It was nationalism that detached the Germans from Roman history.

Restlessness over the state of Roman studies emerged in France with a pupil of Mommsen who had become a fanatical French nationalist, Camille Jullian. But the reaction was even stronger in Italy on the part of Ettore Pais, who like Jullian was both a pupil of Mommsen and a nationalist, and on the part of certain young Marxists (C. Barbagallo, G. Ferrero, E. Ciccotti). The dissatisfaction extended to the study of Roman law, in which P. Bonfante vigorously sought new paths with the help of ethnographic comparisons. A pupil of Beloch and an admirer of Meyer like De Sanctis inevitably took part in this movement of reaction against the juridical formalism of Mommsen; nor was he free of nationalistic sentiments. Apart from this it was clear that, in the time since Mommsen had written his history of Rome, an accumulation of nearly fifty years of intense archaeological, linguistic, and literary research was waiting to be put in order. But a work in the company of Pais, or Bonfante, or the young Marxists, was naturally unthinkable for De Sanctis. Indeed it is probable that irritation with the first volumes of Pais's *History* (1898) and of Ferrero's *Grandezza e decadenza* (1902) confirmed his decision to move from Greek to Roman studies. He was offended by the anti-Catholicism of all those named, and he despised their methods of work even more.

Today it is generally agreed that Bonfante tended to create sociological schemes (like that of the family-state) that were just as rigid as those of traditional pandectism; that Pais combined his arbitrary skepticism towards the tradition with an equally arbitrary faith in his own conjectures; that Barbagallo, Ciccotti, and Ferrero were hasty and rather journalistic in their intelligent and original attempts to modernize the history of Rome. There is therefore a certain justification in the polemic begun by De Sanctis in reviews, continued in the preface and the notes of the first two volumes of the *Storia dei Romani* (1907), and culminating in the hundreds of virulent pages of *Per la Scienza dell'Antichità* (1909). But one might equally ask whether this polemic, which occupied him in the ten decisive years of his maturity and continued beyond 1925, did not have negative aspects, albeit ones that he eventually overcame.

First of all, with a little more tolerance of others whose opinions differed from his, De Sanctis might perhaps have been less ready to adopt a rigid posture in defense of certain basic hypotheses in the first volumes of the *Storia dei Romani*. The continuity between the culture of the Terramaricoli, the Villanovan, the Etruscans, and Rome had already been put in doubt by archaeologists like Brizio and Patroni, and De Sanctis would perhaps have been less ready to follow Pigorini in a theory which Säflund's later revision proved to be without foundation. Equally, the theory made famous by Niebuhr, that the annalists had drawn upon banquet songs as sources for the most ancient Roman history, had already been the object of well-founded criticism; it could not be revived with any assurance.

Nor was there any lack of historians in Italy who could have interpreted more soundly the part played by the Etruscans in the archaic culture of Italy; and it seems clear that De Sanctis's whole reconstruction of the later monarchic period is fragile. But above all there arises the suspicion that his constant preoccupation with telling his opponents how they should be working and his persistent refusal to look more closely at how they did work have impoverished the first three volumes of the *Storia dei Romani*. Consistent technical perfection does not amount to unity of inspiration. Undoubtedly the *Storia dei Romani,* like the *Atthis,* was dominated by an interest in the evolution of the state from tribe to metropolis. But the encyclopedic tendency that had been repressed in the *Atthis* reemerged more strongly in the *Storia dei Romani.* The reader admires the command of the sources, the soundness of judgment, the capacity for solid construction of individual chapters, but the work does not succeed in asserting itself, by the overturning of a thesis or by the force of its exposition, in the way that the histories of Mommsen or Rostovtzeff do, or even as E. Meyer's *Entstehung des Judentums* does. Not only De Sanctis's older studies on the Homeric poems, but also the academic address of 1904 on "War and Peace in Antiquity" had shown that he was capable of grasping the subtleties of a complicated spiritual process. This ability to penetrate shadowy areas is less marked in the first three volumes of the *Storia dei Romani.* Here the style is clear and precise, and in the third volume there is a conscious dignity that reflects a new familiarity with the Italian classics of the cinquecento, but what is still lacking is the calm force of truth touched by the hand that characterizes De Sanctis's best essays of the postwar period.

In the field of Roman history it was easy at that time to concentrate one's attention on work done in Italy. Only with Rostovtzeff's *Studien zur Geschichte des römischen Kolonats* (1910), Warde Fowler's *The Religious Experience of the Roman People* (1911), M. Gelzer's *Die Nobilität der römischen Republik,* and A. Rosenberg's *Der Staat der alten Italiker* (1913) did truly new voices make themselves heard outside Italy. But the fact is that these works did appear outside Italy, and when they appeared they signaled the end of the brief period of Italian primacy in the study of Roman history. The deeper understanding of the pre-Roman world, of the social structure of the Roman republic, of the agrarian and religious history of the Hellenistic-Roman world presupposed a different orientation of historical thinking, an interpretative method, a sociological training, and a subtlety in handling religious problems, of which there had certainly been some signs in Italy (witness the works of the said Marxists, of Bonfante, of Pais in his better moments; one thinks besides of Trombetti, Minocchi, Salvioli, etc.), but no serious and systematic development.

Transferred to Greek history this lack of vigor in social and religious studies and the low level of interpretative ability explain why no Italian work made use of the new possibilities offered by papyrology, folklore, and anthropology for a thoroughgoing study of classical and Hellenistic Greek society and thought.

IV

These things can now be spoken of with detachment. The First World War, the postwar crisis, then Fascism, then personal and national calamities, gradually eliminated the old causes of dispute and destroyed the basic roots of nineteenth-century encyclopedism in the field of antiquity. De Sanctis himself, when reissuing on the eve of his death the first volume of the *Storia dei Romani,* wanted to omit the preface, which took the form of a letter to Beloch and which was such a vivid expression of the polemical emotions of fifty years earlier. It fell to me to assist in an exchange of letters between G. Ferrero and De Sanctis in which two men of noble character recognized each other's merits and their common concern for shattered liberty. In this impending crisis for the whole structure of pre-1914 culture it would be impossible to determine precisely how De Sanctis was influenced by the authority of B. Croce, by discussion with his pupils (especially with A. Ferrabino, who nervously sought an independent line) and up to a point by the recognition of Croce's greatness as a historian, which came not from German scholarship but from Oxford and Cambridge.

Already in the third volume of the *Storia dei Romani* De Sanctis had been faced with the problem of Roman imperialism, and in a rather ingenuous way his response had been to condemn it. The ruins of Carthage and Corinth could not be forgotten; the hero of the third century was the Semite who defended the liberty of his country, Hannibal — and the shade of another Semite, St. Paul, was invoked to pacify conquerors and conquered. Indo-European prejudice, which had never been reconciled with Christian faith, vanished into thin air. Then in the fourth volume (1923) the encyclopedic structure was itself abandoned. De Sanctis devoted himself to the study of the political consequences of the great conquests. In articles in 1920 and 1921 in *Atene e Roma* on "The Postwar Period in Antiquity" ("Dopoguerra antico I e II," in *A. e R.*, n.s., 1, 1920, pp. 3–14, 73–89) and on "Revolution and Reaction in the Age of the Gracchi" ("Rivoluzione e reazione nell'età dei Gracchi," n.s., 2, 1921, pp. 209–37), he gave an idea of what a continuation would have been like: the very titles are indicative.

But could there have been a continuation of the *Storia dei Romani?*

De Sanctis always answered in the affirmative, but for years he worked on other things. In 1923, when he became director of the *Rivista di Filologia,* he fashioned an instrument for the rapid diffusion of his ideas through articles and reviews, and by means of these articles and reviews he put himself in contact with new currents and renewed his own culture. For a decade or more, thanks to the collaboration of De Sanctis and Rostagni, the *Rivista di Filologia* was the most vital journal of classical philology in Europe. In articles published there and elsewhere and in reviews, De Sanctis also discovered a new style, with less malice, more variety, and greater serenity than the one that had become habitual. He refined his perennial interest in the history of historiography. Even if inclined to exaggerate the possibility of reconstructing the phases of a historian's development (which had also been the starting point for Wilamowitz and Schwartz), he was able to seize upon the decisive moments in Hecataeus, Herodotus, Thucydides, Xenophon, and Livy.

The series of articles that came out in those years, of which only a small selection is collected in the two volumes *Problemi di storia antica* (1932) and *Studi di storia della storiografia greca* (1951), represents, in the variety and importance of its themes and in its clarity of execution, De Sanctis's most mature and complex work. Some of the reviews were statements of principle addressed by one great historian to another. The review in 1926 of Rostovtzeff's *Social and Economic History* remains especially memorable. Only Eduard Meyer produced *Kleine Schriften* of comparable importance.

Gradually this activity, suggested sometimes by new documents, sometimes by disputes with teachers (Beloch), colleagues, and pupils, and sometimes by sudden flashes of inspiration (as in the case of the classic article on Herodotus), led to the formation of a new project. Once again it was Hellas that aroused a love that had never been extinguished in De Sanctis, Hellas the mother of free inquiry and of political liberty, which between the seventh and the fifth century had acquired a consciousness of itself as a nation and had separated itself from the oriental world, had faced it without hatred in battle and won, and had associated national liberty with free discussion in assemblies and with the freedom to criticize its own religious and historical tradition. De Sanctis therefore found the Miletus of Aristagoras and Hecataeus even more congenial than the Athens of Pericles. But naturally Thucydides, who with a steady hand measured the depth of the conflict into which Athens was plunged by her own imperialism, and Socrates, who appealed over the laws of the polis to the laws of his own conscience, came equally to life on the pages of De Sanctis. The Crocean history of those years, the ethical-political history of liberty, also fired his imagination. His education had been encyclopedic, and this new activity, which culminated in the *Storia dei Greci fino a Socrate* ("History of the Greeks Down to Socrates") of 1939, once again has many encyclopedic aspects; heavy and sometimes dead pages are not lacking. We should also note that he was soon prevented from exploiting the contribution that direct use of archaeological material and close examination of epigraphic sources could make to a history of Greece. Blindness, which had threatened in 1929 and became total in 1931, compelled De Sanctis to have all the ancient texts read to him; political persecution deprived him of the use of university libraries. That explains why the *Storia dei Greci* has no footnotes. It was also natural that in this work a historian who was nearly seventy should no longer be willing to revise his own ideas on doubtful points like the Dorian invasion or the constitution of Lycurgus. But on the whole De Sanctis overcame blindness, sufferings, and the weight of old age, and succeeded in giving us an original, lively, and thoroughly informed history of Greece; in Italy it entered the consciousness of the educated public as none of his other works has done.

A companion to the Greek history was the volume on Pericles (1944), in which, without offering much that was substantially new, De Sanctis elaborated his thesis that Pericles, by converting the Athenian democracy into imperialism, made the Peloponnesian War inevitable and for that reason also threatened the future of democracy not only in Athens but in the Greek world in general.[3]

After 1940 De Sanctis devoted the majority of the energies he still possessed to the completion of the fourth volume of the *Storia dei Romani,* the first part of which had appeared in 1923. The manuscript was ready around 1946 in a single copy which, after it had been sent to the publisher, was stolen and never recovered. On the basis of notes and rough drafts De Sanctis applied himself to the task of reconstructing it; but in these years not only was his physical strength growing ever weaker, but he had been given the responsibility of directing the *Enciclopedia Italiana* and, having been restored as professor for life at the University of Rome, he refused to consider his chair a sinecure, resumed his teaching, and continued to hold classes for as long as he was able. The reconstruction of the lost manuscript was still going on when death overtook him; one volume, as has been said, was published in 1953, and another is in the press.

De Sanctis was not a man to have illusions about himself. He knew that at his age and with his blindness he could no longer write volumes of the *Storia dei Romani* comparable in wealth of information and vigor of research to the earlier volumes, but he knew just the same that he could still offer a reasoned and well-informed reconstruction of various aspects of Latin culture in the age of the great conquests. This he has done. Our culture has no surfeit of well-considered syntheses. The chapters on art and on religion and the one (still in proof) on law are exemplary, in their light reactionary tone, for solidity and clarity. The chapter on law is perhaps also something more. Given the persistent dogmatism of handbooks of private law, it could well become the point of departure for a historical treatment of Roman law in the third and second centuries B.C.

It is hard to escape the analogy between the development of De Sanctis and that of Croce. Both matured in relative solitude towards the end of the nineteenth century, absorbing the best of contemporary culture in their respective fields of activity and reacting to it with independence. In the first decades of the twentieth century they both divided their energies between systematic works of broad scope and a tough battle for the renewal of the Italian culture that surrounded them. In this polemical activity both were inclined to steel themselves with certain elements—by now archaic—of the German culture they had assimilated (the Hegelian encyclopedia for Croce, the Boeckhian encyclopedia for De Sanctis). For that reason they undervalued new currents of semantic, social, and religious research that, notwithstanding their initial crudeness, were later to contribute to a renewal of European historiography. In the decisive years of his maturity De Sanctis no less than Croce lacked the corrective that, in cultures richer and more articulate than ours, like those of France and Germany, offers a plurality of vigorous currents of thought that mutually reinforce one another. From the crisis of the postwar years and of Fascism both emerged changed and, in revising their earlier points of view, produced in old age works of great importance and fertility. But as they were works of old age they naturally could no longer include the mass of research that had characterized the output of their younger years. Like the *Storia di Europa*, so too the *Storia dei Greci* was no longer based on detailed work of analysis. At this point revision had its limits.

Corresponding to the analogy of the development of their long lives is something more essential. Behind their works we see once again the two men just as they appeared to us at the entrance of the National Library in Turin, around 1928: two figures so different in personal physique, manner, and religious attitude, but so similar in their uninterrupted passion for learning and in love of liberty, in the sovereign intelligence that lit up their eyes.

Bibliographical Note

Throughout this paper knowledge is assumed of the bibliography of De Sanctis's writings to 1950 which was prepared by P. Künzle and which forms an appendix to the *Studi di storia della storiografia greca* (Florence: La Nuova Italia, 1951): there are some small additions in the review of G. Tibiletti, *Riv. St. Ital.*, 63, 1951, p. 402. Two papers of mine about Italian historiography on ancient history, which already include pages on De Sanctis, respectively of 1945 and 1934, are now reprinted in *Contributo alla storia degli studi classici* (Rome: Edizioni di Storia e Letteratura, 1955), pp. 275–97, 299–326. On the 1934 essay, *cf.* De Sanctis's polemical note in *Riv. Fil. Class.*, 64, 1936, pp. 97–99. In my 1945 essay I have indicated some of the more important critical assessments of the work of De Sanctis and of his adversaries. The article by P. Fraccaro, *Riv. St. Ital.*, 1924, is now reprinted in *Opuscula*, 2, 1957, pp. 5–18. Other papers on (or rather against) the *Storia dei Romani* are cited and discussed by De Sanctis himself in *Per la Scienza dell'Antichità* (Turin: Bocca, 1909), especially pp. 231–531. Among the essays not mentioned by me in 1945 is that of Adolphe Reinach, *Atthis: Les Origines de l'état Athénien* (Paris: Publications de la *Revue de Synthèse Historique*, 1912) pp. 85 ff., which, coming as it does from a friend of De Sanctis and from a foreign scholar well versed in Italian studies, has particular interest. But the present essay has no pretensions to bibliographical — or, indeed, biographical — completeness, and is intended as a simple testimony among the many which have been prompted by the death of De Sanctis. A more thorough study would require a review of the historiography of the ancient world during the past half century. For a more precise idea of De Sanctis's political and religious ideas his correspondence will be indispensable — and the evidence of those who knew him before 1925 will also be important. For the present, notice only the article of G. Levi della Vida in *Il Mondo*, 30 April 1957, p. 8. I owe to conversations with G. Levi della Vida and with A. Ferrabino the confirmation of my impressions and assessments of De Sanctis.[4]

[ADDITIONAL NOTE: From the article by P. Treves in *L'Osservatore politico letterario* 3, no. 6, 1957, pp. 49–65, I learn that before 1930 De Sanctis wrote memoirs, which it is to be hoped may soon be published, if his will does not prove a hindrance.]

June 1957

Notes

1. TRANSLATOR'S NOTE: At the time ADM was writing, one volume had appeared in 1953; a second appeared in 1957 (the year of the article, hence the reference to proof). A third volume was published in 1964.

2. *Hermes,* 18, 1883, p. 208; reprinted in *Ges. Schriften* V, p. 249.

3. The book makes political allusions (p. 265 n. 18) which provoked the severe review by A. Omodeo, *Quaderni della Critica,* no. 3, 1945, pp. 84–89 = *Il senso della storia,* 2d ed. (1955), pp. 511–18.

4. *Cf.* the articles by P. Treves, *Itinerari,* 5, 1957, pp. 174–82; A. Ferrabino, *Economia e Storia,* 4, 1957, pp. 199–203; S. Accame, *Humanitas,* 12, 1957, pp. 431–46; I. Lana, *Convivium,* n.s., 3, 1957, pp. 339–42; A. M. Ghisalberti, *Rassegna Storica del Risorgimento,* 44, 1957, pp. iii–ix; G. Giannelli, *Atene e Roma,* n.s., 3, 1958, pp. 77–81; A. Ferrabino, *Accademia dei Lincei,* quaderno 43, 1958. G. Levi della Vida's article is reprinted in *Aneddoti e Svaghi Arabi e non Arabi* (1959), pp. 362–66.

SIX

Introduction to R. Syme,
The Roman Revolution

I

Syme's *Roman Revolution* appeared in the summer of 1939. I remember read-ing the copy given to me by the author at a time when war had already been declared and the nights were getting longer in an Oxford plunged in gloom. The book was gripping to read: it established an immediate rapport between the ancient March on Rome and its modern counterpart, between Augustus's seizure of power and Mussolini's coup d'état and perhaps Hitler's as well.[1] The incisive vividness with which it represented the men and events of ancient Rome was a reflection of the experience of the times through which we were then living. The effect was never contrived: the ancient texts spoke directly. It was also obvious that an author who wrote like this had achieved clarity of vision through a personal act of liberation. It was enough to have read the chapters on Augustus in the *Cambridge Ancient History* ("made in Cambridge, but written at Oxford"), which had appeared in 1934, to realize that in England the usual assessment of the gov-ernment of Augustus was, by contrast, one of sympathy and assent. Other works by authoritative English scholars, such as the British Academy Raleigh Lecture of 1937, *The Virtues of a Roman Emperor: Propaganda and the Creation of Belief,* by M. P. Charlesworth, pushed this consensus to the point of accepting the "noble lies" of ideological propaganda as both inevitable and useful. Syme's style, which consciously took up the themes and lan-guage of Tacitus — not without a pinch of Gibbon — was the outward sign of the break with the academic conventions adopted by his colleagues at Oxford and elsewhere.

"Introduzione a Ronald Syme, *La rivoluzione romana*" (Italian edition, Turin: Einaudi, 1962), pp. ix–xv; *Terzo contributo* (1966), pp. 729–37. Translated by T. J. Cornell.

Up to this point everything was clear, even to the present writer, who had arrived only a few months previously as a newcomer to the world of Oxford. But here the difficulties began; difficulties of interpretation and evaluation, which for me have still not been resolved after twenty-two years of living in England and as many years of continuing friendship with my colleague R. Syme. The first reason for these difficulties is simply that between 1938, when the book was finished, and 1939, when it was published, the situation had changed so much that an imbalance had developed between the mind of the writer and the mind of the reader. What in 1938 had manifestly been the implacable wish to see clearly what the intentions of the dictators were, as against the illusions of the appeasers, was now inadequate as a point of view in a war from which—for good or ill—a new society was bound to emerge. Syme's book, which in its taut and penetrating style sought to grasp the essence of events, was itself overtaken by them. Other difficulties are by their nature more personal. Now that Syme has published his two books of 1958, on Tacitus and on *Colonial Elites*, it has become easier to understand the link between him and the *"parentes et patria"* (New Zealand) to which he dedicated *The Roman Revolution*. His attachment to New Zealand goes together with his lack of sympathy for the Anglican and Anglo-Catholic circles of Oxford, where he studied and where he has taught continuously since 1929, apart from the interruption of the war. The fact still remains, however, that Syme is a historian chary of making theoretical pronouncements and autobiographical utterances and is for that reason not inclined to explain himself. It might even be said that he is suspicious of any revealing communication between individuals. His intellectual development is still unclear to me. Even local Oxford gossip has been unable to do anything other than emphasize the more outward and prodigious aspects of his personality: his extraordinary memory and his exceptional linguistic proficiency in both ancient and modern languages. It remains unclear, for example, whether he owes anything personally to that other legendary outsider educated at Oxford, Ludwik Bernstein Niemirowski, who was to become famous as Sir Lewis Namier. There is no doubt that with *The Structure of Politics at the Accession of George III* (1929) Namier created in England an intellectual atmosphere that would make it possible for *The Roman Revolution* to be accepted ten years later. Syme "namierized" the constitution of Augustus. But when Syme arrived as a student, Namier had long since left Oxford for good, and Syme has never hinted, as far as I know, at a debt to Namier. And one should not overlook a certain intrinsic difference between Namier's effort to discover the key to English constitutional mechanisms in a relatively stable social group and Syme's attempt to analyze the groups that bore Augustus to power in a revolutionary situation. Marx, Pareto, and Max Weber, whom Namier knew so well, do not seem ever to have interested Syme—but who can be certain about this? And if Mussolini is ever-present in his book, it is more difficult to see in it the Spanish Civil War, which also created deep divisions in Oxford as elsewhere.

In 1939 inquiry and investigation could have clarified some elements of the cultural atmosphere of Oxford in the preceding ten years. But in 1939 there were many obstacles, not just linguistic ones, in the way of communication between Oxford dons and us refugees who were arriving one after another shortly before the island put up the shutters for a heroic defense. This is not the place for a consideration of this issue. Suffice it to say that the interpretation of this book is for me—and I'm sure not only for me— inextricably bound up with the outbreak of the Second World War.

II

But if we return to what seems to me unquestionably clear in the book, enough can be said about it to establish its place in contemporary historiography about the Roman world. Between 1918 and 1938 two lines were followed in interpreting the period between the Gracchi and Augustus. One perhaps went back to Mommsen, but was taken up and refashioned by E. Meyer, precisely at the end of the First World War, in *Caesars Monarchie und das Prinzipat des Pompeius*. The principal aim was to define the constitutional form of the Augustan regime and its antecedents in the political tradition of the Republic. E. Meyer maintained that Augustus, the heir of Caesar, actually bound himself to Pompey, and thus appropriated the Ciceronian program of the *princeps*. Similarly Carcopino set out to study the "unfulfilled monarchy" of Sulla and the failed monarchy of Caesar. In Italy, with P. de Francisci and M. A. Levi, the discussion turned on the characterization of the form of the Augustan regime, even if Levi, in his aim (which before the war was only half-complete) of tracing the evolution from Octavian the party boss (1932) to Augustus the Princeps, showed that he had an interest in the political struggle as such.

In 1936, from his Chair at Berlin, W. Weber presented an Augustus with the charismatic features of a Princeps-Führer and transformed the sober prose of the *Res Gestae* into a manifesto of imperial mysticism. Thus the interpretation of the principate was converted into a reconstruction of an abstract political program and easily gave way to idealization along fascist lines.[2] The Augustus portrayed in the tenth volume of the *Cambridge Ancient History* (1934) is infinitely more humane and moderate than, for example, the one created by W. Weber and is less encumbered by theoretical formulations; but he is none the less burdened with the mission of saving a morally decadent world.[3]

On the other hand increasing attention was being paid to the work of the German-Jewish scholar F. Muenzer on the history of the Roman aristocracy. Family ties, clienteles, and alliances between rival groups had been patiently analyzed by Muenzer, one by one and in alphabetical order, in his articles on the Roman *gentes* in the Pauly-Wissowa encyclopedia. His work of synthesis, with the programmatic title *Römische Adelsparteien und Adelsfamilien* (1920), was already a classic. It had reinforced and taken further the conclusions of M. Gelzer's youthful and more abstract sociological study *Die Nobilität der römischen Republik;* and Gelzer had continued to work in the same direction both in articles in Pauly-Wissowa and in penetrating monographs on Caesar and Pompey. It is not an accident that the appearance of Syme's book coincided almost exactly with the posthumous publication of a vast academic treatise by A. von Premerstein which sought to define the character of Augustus' clientele (*Vom Werden und Wesen des Prinzipats, Abh. Bayer. Akad.,* XV). In other words, what mattered to Premerstein was the form not of Augustus's government but of his personal following. True enough, it was still a piece of structural research, but one that took account of the importance of *clientela,* which had been emphasized in Republican history in the work of Gelzer and still more in that of Muenzer.

Now Syme proceeded to give substance to the notion of *clientela* in the political conflicts from 60 to 27 B.C.; he made use of the material accumulated by Gelzer and Muenzer and of that furnished by his own immense knowledge of the sources, and one by one he described the principal clients of Augustus. These clients were not just individuals but members of communities, mostly Italian municipalities; they were predominantly landowners of good family, hitherto confined to the obscurity of their home towns but now emerging in glory and new wealth in the train of Augustus. Syme evidently identified a continuous line of development from the Social War, which had extended the Roman citizenship to most of Italy, to the civil wars of the Caesarian and post-Caesarian periods, in which the wealthy elites of the Italian communities, together with a modest number of similarly placed provincials, bestirred themselves for the seizure of power. Horace, Virgil, and Livy became spokesmen for an Italian bourgeoisie that was increasingly satisfied by the new regime. But Syme did not end his account at this point. He continued it through the various phases of adjustment and dissatisfaction during the reign of Augustus down to the creation of a party of Tiberius.

There can be no doubt that Syme brought about the victory of the second tendency, the interpretation of Augustan politics not in constitutional or ideological terms but in terms of clienteles and rival aristocratic families. At the same time he followed in the footsteps of Muenzer by identifying the origin of these clienteles and their significance for the displacement of the Roman governing class.

It was possible to challenge Syme's interpretation in matters of detail. For example G. Tibiletti had no difficulty in showing that the idea of a party of Tiberius was mistaken.[4] But there could be no turning back. Syme had created a new way of looking at the nascent principate. That explains why the only important general book on Augustus since *The Roman Revolution*, M. A. Levi's *Il tempo di Augusto,* published at a time when wartime conditions had still not allowed Syme's findings to be sufficiently assimilated (1951), appeared as a compromise and did not have the capacity to arouse much discussion.[5]

III

The first criticisms of Syme arose implicitly from the emergence of new evidence which showed that he had underestimated the importance of constitutional reforms in Augustan politics. The discovery of the so-called Tabula Hebana, authoritatively published by U. Coli around 1948, indicated that in A.D. 5 Augustus had reformed the elections for the magistracies by giving a decisive vote to ten mixed centuries of certain knights and of senators (which implicitly ensured that the knights would have the predominant voice in elections).[6] This once again drew attention to the fact, also attested in other sources, that Augustus never managed to gain complete and permanent control of the *comitia.* Another epigraphic publication, less important but still significant, seems to show that Augustus in 27 B.C. made use of consular powers to control the provinces—and consequently casts doubt on the now dominant view that the basis of Augustus' position in 27 B.C. was the proconsular power.[7] On the other hand there had been a steady accumulation of new finds and new interpretations of old documents which showed that even the problems of ideological propaganda needed to be reexamined. For example, at Arles a replica was discovered of the *clipeus virtutis* which Augustus boasted in the *Res Gestae* had been conferred on him in 27 B.C.; evidently this emblem had been widely distributed throughout the provinces.[8] The unfortunate restoration of the Ara Pacis for the Augustan bimillenary opened a discussion on the interpretation of the monument which has now entered a new phase with the daring suggestion of S. Weinstock, who frankly maintains that the monument in question is not the Ara Pacis at all.[9] A series of publications on the Augustan writers, above all that of E. Fraenkel on Horace, has taken up from various angles the question of the relationship between Augustus and the culture of his time—which was certainly not, as P. Fraccaro has observed with particular acuteness in the case of Livy,[10] a mere vehicle for Augustan propaganda.[11]

But like all great books *The Roman Revolution* contains within itself the seeds of the most telling future criticism, precisely because it demands new research. Today one cannot avoid asking what was the social structure of the different parts of Italy at the end of the first century B.C. Syme does not describe this structure, but rather presupposes it. In truth the epigraphic and archaeological evidence that is presently available is inadequate and needs to be supplemented; but one of the urgent tasks of Italian archaeology is to examine more thoroughly the social and economic life of Roman Italy. Documents can be discovered if one looks for them. Another question that arises from the heart of Syme's book is that of the active and passive participation of the provinces in the "revolution," which after all was largely contested, and certainly decided, outside Italy. Syme has offered a timely reassessment of the moral persona of Antony in comparison with that of Augustus, but he has neglected to examine the situation of the provinces. Only if the provinces are given the attention they deserve can the Augustan edifice come to be properly appreciated in terms of an international civilization which undoubtedly satisfied a broad constituency, but which also gave rise to discontents, expressed now in revolts by provinces or armies, now in homilies directed against tyranny. It is childish to deny the existence of a problem of liberty under the empire.[12] What is more, in Judaea there developed a radical opposition of civilization against civilization, of faith against faith, which under the name of Christianity became a problem for the empire within fifty years. The Dead Sea finds now allow us to glimpse new aspects of this revolt and also to gain a better idea of its political aspects. Once again the discovery of new documents has served to call attention to the limitations of Syme's vision. He undoubtedly tends to underestimate both the lasting results and the enduring conflicts that the Augustan revolution brought with it.[13] His attention is concentrated on the passions and immediate ambitions of men. Hence the impression of a world without hope and without ideals which already puzzled me when I read the book for the first time in 1939.

Syme himself has not stopped with his *Roman Revolution*. The long experience of serving abroad as a political and cultural representative of Great Britain during and after the war has not been useless, to borrow Gibbon's phrase, to the historian of the Roman Empire. The two volumes on Tacitus are a vast description of the society of the empire in the first century as it presented itself to the eyes of its foremost historian—whose judgment is accepted as valid and not reduced to ideology.[14] The valuable little book on *Colonial Elites* foreshadows some of the results of a huge inquiry presently under way into the relationship between the provincial aristocracies and the central government of the empire. A volume in press on Sallust in the Sather Classical Lectures will contain—one can safely predict—an analysis of Roman society in the first century B.C.[15] Other studies can be expected with confidence from the mature historian at the height of his powers. *The Roman Revolution* was evidently a point of departure for Syme himself.

It must also remain a point of departure for historians of the Roman Empire. In Italy in 1939–40 a translation of this book was unthinkable; it was not possible even to review it. It is a good sign—and it is not too late—

that it has now been translated. The translation is also a mark of gratitude to a historian who has opened new horizons on the ancient history of our country.

November 1961

Notes

1. *Cf.* my review in *Journal of Roman Studies* 30, 1940, pp. 75–80; now republished in *Secondo contributo alla storia degli studi classici* (Rome, 1960).

2. *Cf.* Syme's important review of the last product of this prewar juridical-ideological interpretation: H. Siber, "Das Führeramt des Augustus" (*Abh. Sächs. Akad.*, 1940), in *Journal of Roman Studies*, 36, 1946, pp. 149–58.

3. *Cf.* my review in *Journal of Roman Studies*, 34, 1944, pp. 109–16.

4. *Principe e magistrati repubblicani* (Rome, 1953), p. 239; to be noted in connection with everything that follows.

5. For M. A. Levi's judgment of Syme, *cf. Il tempo di Augusto,* pp. 399 and 462. On Levi's book I find myself in agreement with the remarks of J. Reynolds in *Journal of Roman Studies*, 46, 1956, p. 171.

6. Among discussions of this issue notice A. H. M. Jones, in *Journal of Roman Studies,* 45, 1955, pp. 9–21; reprinted in *Studies in Roman Government and Law* (Oxford, 1960), pp. 24–50. Jones appreciates the constitutional problems better than Syme, *Tacitus,* II, 1958, p. 756. *Cf.* P. A. Brunt, in *Journal of Roman Studies,* 51, 1961, pp. 71–83; also J. Béranger, in *Museum Helveticum,* 14, 1957, pp. 216–40.

7. H. W. Pleket, *The Greek Inscriptions in the Rijksmuseum van Oudheden at Leyden* (1958), p. 49; but *cf.* J. Reynolds, *Journal of Roman Studies,* 50, 1960, p. 207, and K. M. T. Atkinson, *Rev. Intern. Droits Antiq.,* 7, 1960, pp. 227–72. Among recent studies of the Augustan constitution in general, see e.g., A. H. M. Jones, in *Journal of Roman Studies,* 41, 1951, pp. 112–19, reprinted in *Studies in Roman Government and Law,* pp. 1–17; J. Béranger, *Recherches sur l'aspect idéologique du principat* (Basel, 1953); P. Grenade, *Essai sur les origines du principat* (Paris, 1961). Notice also the survey by G. E. Chilver in *Historia,* 1, 1950, p. 408; the article "Princeps" by L. Wickert in Pauly–Wissowa, *Real-Encyclopädie der classischen Altertumswissenschaft,* XXII (1954); P. Sattler, *Augustus und der Senat* (Göttingen, 1960) and W. Kunkel, "Ueber das Wesen des augusteischen Prinzipats," in *Gymnasium,* 68, 1961, pp. 353–69.

8. W. Seston, *C.R. Acad. Inscr.,* 1954, pp. 287–97, which should, however, be read with caution. The copy from Arles is dated to 26 B.C.

9. *Cf. Journal of Roman Studies,* 50, 1960, pp. 44–58, and the criticisms of J. Toynbee in *Journal of Roman Studies,* 51, 1961, pp. 153–56. Among various studies of imperial mystique notice above all those of A. Alföldi, in *Museum Helveticum,* 7–10, 1950–53, and the recent note by E. Bickerman, "Filius Maiae," in *Parola del Passato,* 76, 1961, pp. 1–19.

10. *Opuscula,* I (1942), pp. 81–101.

11. H. D. Meyer's recent and acute *Die Aussenpolitik des Augustus und die Augusteische Dichtung* (Graz, 1961) perhaps goes too far in the other direction in finding a contrast between the defensive policy of Augustus and the aggressive aspirations expressed by his poets. *Cf.* also A. La Penna, "La lirica civile di Orazio

e l'ideologia del principato" in *Maia*, 13, 1961, pp. 83–123, 209–45 [Idem, *Orazio e l'ideologia del principato* (1963)].

12. On this point H. Fuchs, *Der geistige Widerstand gegen das Römertum* (Berlin, 1938) and Ch. Wirszubski, *Libertas* (Cambridge, 1950) remain fundamental. But *cf.* L. Wickert, "Princeps," in Pauly-Wissowa, *Real-Encyclopädie der classischen Altertumswissenschaft*, XXII, p. 2080; J. Palm, *Rom, Römertum und Imperium in der griechischen Literatur der Kaiserzeit* (Lund, 1959); J. H. Oliver, *Demokratia, the Gods and the Free World* (Baltimore, 1960), p. 158; also the article by R. F. Rossi, "Libertas," in De Ruggiero's *Dizionario Epigrafico* (1958).

13. These points are all taken into account in the complex and wonderfully rich analysis by S. Mazzarino, *Trattato di storia romana*, II (Rome, 1956). The nonspecialist reader needs to be warned, however, that many of Mazzarino's interpretations are more ingenious than true: this applies particularly to what he has to say about Augustus (for example on the "evangels" of Augustus, p. 100, and on the Tabula Hebana, p. 555). Attention should also be given to the important, but unfortunately not annotated, *Römische Geschichte* of A. Heuss (Braunschweig, 1960).

14. *Cf.* my review in *Gnomon*, 1961, pp. 55–58 [reprinted in *Terzo contributo*, p. 739].

15. [The volume appeared in 1964.]

SEVEN

Reconsidering B. Croce
(1866–1952)

To the memory of Eugenio Colorni

I have found myself wondering how Croce would have taken his own cente-nary. After all he came rather near it. Croce was entirely without vanity, but cared for anniversaries and was a prudent administrator of his own reputa-tion. Honors and ceremonies he considered part of that reality which no-body can presume to escape. But he always tried to turn anniversaries into opportunities for useful work. When he was fifty he wrote his autobiogra-phy; when he was sixty he concluded forty years of studies on the Italian Seicento with his *Storia dell'età barocca* (it appeared in 1929). When he was seventy the few friends Fascism had left him published in his honor a re-print of Baumgarten's *Aesthetica;* but he added a quite characteristic celebra-tion of his own: he wrote the book on *La Poesia* which was by implication the most searching criticism both of Baumgarten's *Aesthetica* and of his own previous *Estetica.* When he was eighty he founded an institute for historical studies in his own house in Naples and gave himself a last lease of creative life in the company of the gifted young historians who were just emerging from the ruins of Fascism. I suspect that, faced by his own centenary, Croce would have got up two hours earlier than usual, as he is said to have done when he became a minister in the Giolitti cabinet (1920) and wanted to have a little time for his private work. He would have gone through ceremonies and interviews with that mixture of impatience and old-fashioned courtesy which was his own—and at the end of the year he would have produced the only useful book inspired by his own centenary.

To say that Croce remains something of an enigma even to those who knew him personally may seem a paradox. He wrote perhaps more than any

"Reconsidering B. Croce (1866–1952)" (a memorial lecture delivered at Durham University in May 1966), *Durham University Journal* (December 1966), pp. 1–12; *Quarto contributo* (1969), pp. 95–115; *Essays in Ancient and Modern Historiography* (1977), pp. 345–63.

other writer of the twentieth century. The eighty-odd volumes of his works in the characteristic Laterza edition are full of personal recollections and anecdotes.[1] We have his autobiography,[2] the recollections of his eldest daughter[3] and of some of his intimate friends—to begin with, Fausto Nicolini.[4] Though his correspondence with Giovanni Gentile is still unpublished, for perfectly valid reasons—those who have seen it speak of it as a document of great importance—the correspondence with K. Vossler is available.[5] There are enough other letters both by Croce and his correspondents (for instance Georges Sorel[6] and Antonio Labriola[7]) to give an idea of Croce's relations with his contemporaries. I single out for its interest the publication of some letters by Croce to Emilio Cecchi which comment on Cecchi's articles about Croce.[8] The autobiographical and biographical evidence about him is as plentiful as one can wish for any contemporary. Yet the basic riddle of Croce's personality is perhaps only increased by the abundance, ease, and elegance of his writing—and by the observations of his friends.

Part of the difficulty in understanding Croce lies in the variety of the historical situations in which he operated during his very long life. At least six periods can be distinguished in his own activity, and each of them corresponds to a well-defined period in the history of modern Italy. The apprenticeship years ended in 1900, when Italy was shaken by the murder of King Umberto. The creative years of collaboration with Giovanni Gentile, the years in which he wrote all his systematic philosophy, ended approximately with the war in Libya (1911). In the Libyan War and even more in the First World War Croce found himself isolated and he deeply modified his ideas. In the postwar years 1919–24 he collaborated for all practical purposes with Christian democrats, nationalists, and Fascists—even if he maintained his distance from them in theory. Then for nineteen years (1925–43) he was not only the moral leader of Italian anti-Fascism, but also the constant term of reference for all the intellectual activities of the Fascists themselves. Finally in the last decade of his life the old thinker had to realize that the new generations were going their own way, but it would be rash to infer that his influence became negligible or his own writing merely repetitive.

In comparison with the majority of Italian intellectuals, Croce grew up slowly. He published his first original considerations on *La storia ridotta sotto il concetto generale dell'arte* when he was twenty-seven and he took another nine years to develop his theory in the *Estetica* of 1902. For about eighteen years between 1882 and 1900 he devoted the greater part of his time to the local history of Naples (where he had B. Capasso as a guide) and to literary criticism (where F. De Sanctis was his model). A contemporary described Croce as he appeared in 1891: "Questo giovane imberbe, che ha tutte la apparenze di un fanciullo e che rivolgendovi la parola ha nello sguardo l'espressione più sincera della sua naturale timidità, questo lavoratore silenzioso e taciturno, che la fortuna fece nascere molto ricco. . . . "[9] For a few years between 1895 and 1900 Croce also intensively studied in an original manner the economic and social ideas of Karl Marx and made himself the editor of the writings on historical materialism by his former teacher Antonio Labriola. The combination of pure erudition and Marxism was unusual: even Labriola was suspicious. As a matter of fact, Croce remained outside the circles of both academic *érudits* and militant socialists. Italian culture was then a culture of professors. Poets were professors too. One of the points which distinguished Croce and D'Annunzio from the surrounding world was that neither had cared to get a university degree and both maintained an ambivalent attitude towards academic respectability. On the other hand, Croce's friendship with Labriola and Georges Sorel was that of a thinker with thinkers. The study of Marx was of permanent importance for Croce: he learned from it that legal systems reflect an economic and social order and that political history is a struggle for power. Marx — rather than Francesco De Sanctis — led Croce to the rediscovery of Hegel and Machiavelli and perhaps even of the Neapolitan Vico. But Croce had no intention or desire to subvert the social order to which he owed his affluence and consequently his freedom to study what he liked; even less did he care to overthrow the moral order he instinctively recognized as his own, though he had abandoned the religious beliefs which had created it.[10]

In 1900 he gave up the study of economics, and much to the disgust of Labriola he concentrated his reflections on the nature of beauty and on the relations between poetry and ordinary language.[11] De Sanctis had first proposed these problems for his attention many years before, but now he made a careful study of Vico and mastered the rest of the relevant literature. By claiming to be the continuator of Vico and De Sanctis, he gave retrospectively a new meaning to all the time he had spent studying Neapolitan history and could feel that he was the restorer of a native tradition of philosophic thought.

Outside Naples, however, the appearance of Croce's *Estetica* had a different meaning. By 1902 D'Annunzio was replacing Carducci as the fashionable poet for younger Italians. His appeal was a mixture of well-digested sensuality and half-digested Nietzsche. In later years Croce was right in reminding his younger readers that his own generation had been *carducciana*, not *dannunziana:* Carducci remained to the end his favorite modern poet. Croce was not the man to indulge in aesthetic refinements: if anything is obvious from his work as a literary critic in the decade 1900–1910 it is the unadventurous, even provincial, character of his taste. The fact, however, remains that Croce came out of his isolation, found followers and admirers — and was soon recognized as an intellectual power to be reckoned with — when he offered to the Italians a philosophy which proclaimed the centrality and amorality of art. Many followed Croce because they thought that Croce had left Marx for D'Annunzio. As Marx was commonly taken to be a democrat, and Croce showed no sympathy for democracy, it was inferred that Croce was for the advent of the Superman.

Croce started his own journal, *La Critica*, in the same year 1903 in which Enrico Corradini began to publish *Il Regno* and Papini and Prezzolini set up their *Leonardo*. In the following year G. A. Borgese began to print *Hermes*. The four journals were closely associated. Borgese, then a protégé of Croce, was both a full-blown follower of D'Annunzio and a nationalist. The *Regno* — a nursery of the future Fascist intelligentsia from L. Federzoni to R. Forges Davanzati — was committed to the same antipositivistic, antidemocratic creed. Papini and Prezzolini, though less predictable, joined forces in attacking the conventional ideas of academic circles.[12]

The contrast between Croce and his younger allies was certainly marked, so marked as to become almost symbolic of the differences between two generations. Croce, as we have observed, was by nature slow in forming his opinions and correspondingly slow in changing them. All the noise around him never distracted him from his rigid routine of scholarly work which, supported as it was by an exceptional memory, made him one of the greatest *érudits* of any time. In 1906 he began to make a daily list of his reading in order to check whether he had wasted time. The companion he had chosen for his work in *La Critica*, Giovanni Gentile, though younger by nine years, shared his scholarly habits and discipline. With the help of Gentile, Croce transformed a small southern publishing house — Laterza of Bari — into the most important in Italy and dictated its editorial policy. The younger intellectuals, born between 1880 and 1890, had exactly the opposite characteristics. Precocity and lack of method were the norm. A few were of rare intellectual distinction. These died young. Carlo Michelstaedter, an original, perhaps a great, philosopher, committed suicide at twenty-three.[13] Renato Serra, the literary critic, was killed at thirty in the war he had chosen to fight after a searching self-examination.[14] Others — most conspicuously Borgese, Papini, and Prezzolini — were self-appointed geniuses, quick to learn and even quicker to forget. Papini and Prezzolini, with their hotchpotch of pragmatism, Bergsonianism, and mysticism *à la* Novalis, considered themselves capable of doing the things which Croce was too much of a bourgeois to attempt. In 1905 Prezzolini could write to Papini in all seriousness: "La nostra amicizia . . . potrà durare ora che tu sai e che io so che *non posso diventare Dio?*" In their uneasy alliance with Croce there was a great deal of cold calculation: "Di quell'uomo bisogna essere in ogni modo alleati," Papini wrote to Prezzolini in 1907. But they were in good faith when they took Croce's message as an invitation to revolt. Croce's first *Logica*, which appeared in 1905 as a continuation of the *Estetica*, seemed even more to encourage contempt for natural sciences and intolerance of errors.[15]

The confusion and equivocations which ensued were not all on the side of the young. Croce deluded himself in hoping for a quick intellectual revolution of national, or perhaps international, importance. The equivocation extended to what in a way was the most pleasant and solid aspect of *La Critica*, the steady collaboration between Croce and Gentile. If Croce loved poetry and history and correspondingly distrusted metaphysics, Gentile was a born metaphysician and, like many other metaphysicians, kept a nice balance between mysticism and rhetoric. Both Croce and Gentile must have known from the start how different they were, but they were friends and they thought that they complemented each other. They compromised, Croce perhaps more than Gentile. Croce accepted many Hegelian assumptions which were really more appropriate to Gentile. Under the influence of Gentile he came to identify history and philosophy in plain contradiction to the structure of his own system and involved himself in insuperable difficulties.[16] Gentile consented to cooperate in a routine of reviewing books and writing short monographic articles which were probably outside his real interests and often remained superficial.

Time slowly dissolved some of these alliances. When the third volume of Croce's philosophic system, the *Filosofia della pratica*, appeared in 1909, it ended on an austere note of religious resignation which was not calculated to please the followers of D'Annunzio and Barrès. The first big quarrels coincided with the colonial war of 1911–12, which was the first success of the Italian nationalists. Borgese used Croce's book on Vico, which had just appeared (1911), as an occasion for a frontal attack.[17] Papini abandoned in wrath the journal *La Voce*, which since its inception in 1908 had supported Croce.[18] Prezzolini himself, who remained for a while the editor of *La Voce* after Papini's departure, gave increasing space to those pupils of Gentile who, with varying degrees of condescension, treated Croce as "superseded" — *superato*. The opinion that Croce was out of touch with the new generation was often repeated. On the eve of the First World War, in February 1914, Giuseppe De Robertis defined Francesco De Sanctis and Croce as obstacles to be overcome, "e c'è tra i giovani qualcuno ardimentoso e adatto al compito."[19] One of the young men he had in mind, Renato Serra, echoed him: "D'Annunzio e Croce cominciano oggi a essere messi da parte."[20] Curiously enough, these young people were to follow D'Annunzio against Croce a few months later. "Giovinezza, giovinezza" was repeated only too frequently in those years, though not yet with musical accompaniment.

The First World War left Croce in marked isolation. What Croce disliked was not really the war — he was no pacifist — but the rhetoric which accompanied it. He hated the idealization of war and imperialism. He knew the difference between search for truth and propaganda and despised those who mistook the latter for the former. He never changed his attitude on this point—which explains his later hostility towards the Fascist regime. He defined the world war as the war of "historical materialism"; the definition has stuck.[21] In this isolation he reexamined himself and explored new fields. He studied the great European poetry of Dante, Ariosto, Shakespeare, and Corneille and found a congenial spirit in the greatest poet of the enemy country—Goethe. This study led him to revise his judgment about the nature of poetry and to emphasize its inherent morality; he even saw in it an equivalent to religious experience (1917). At the same time he studied the great historians of the past and reflected on historical method. Though he had previously claimed that all is history, the historical work he had so far done had been confined to episodes of Neapolitan history. He had educated a new generation of literary critics which included Tommaso Parodi, Renato Serra, Eugenio Donadoni, Attilio Momigliano, Luigi Russo, but he had hardly influenced historians. The only historian of considerable merit who had so far contributed to *La Critica*, Gioacchino Volpe, was in basic disagreement with him. The other leading historian of the time, Gaetano Salvemini, never disguised his total lack of sympathy for Croce's philosophical opinions. The situation was changed by the appearance of the *Teoria e storia della storiografia* in 1915, and of the *Storia della storiografia italiana nel secolo decimonono* in 1918. Croce began to interest young historians in his ideas and prepared himself for that kind of "storia etico-politica" he exemplified in *Storia del regno di Napoli* (1924); *Storia d'Italia dal 1871 al 1915* (1928); *Storia dell'età barocca in Italia* (1929); *Storia d'Europa nel secolo decimonono* (1932). But between the new theory and the new practice of historiography Fascism intervened.

In the first years after the Great War Croce's ambiguous position on the contemporary Italian scene had merely been confirmed. Old Italian socialists owed traditional allegiance to the positivist philosophy of Roberto Ardigò. But the younger Marxists of the postwar period were ready to start from Croce, who himself had started from Marx. Still during the war, in 1917, Antonio Gramsci declared Croce "il più grande pensatore dell'Europa in questo momento." After the war, another of the young leaders of the left, Piero Gobetti, emphatically repeated that whoever was against Croce was against moral integrity.[22] Croce liked Gobetti and did not dislike Gramsci, but personally became a steady supporter of, and contributor to, the nationalist journal *Politica*.[23] He approved, as a senator and as a minister, of Giolitti's implicit support of Fascism. While in 1915 he had refused to accept the *coup d'état* which led to the declaration of war, in 1922 he sympathized with the Fascists. He went on voting for Mussolini in the Senate even after Matteotti's murder. A problem which only the publication of their correspondence will solve is the political influence of Gentile on Croce in the years between 1919 and 1924. They had continued to collaborate during the war, though Gentile was much more favorable to it than Croce. After the war it became apparent that philosophically their ways would part. Gentile started a philosophical journal of his own in 1920, and his pupils were more than ever convinced that Croce was *superato*. But paradoxically Croce and Gentile became much closer to each other in political matters. Under Gentile's influence Croce, as a minister of education in 1920, introduced religious instruction—that is, the Catholic catechism—into the state elementary schools.[24] The appointment of Gentile as a minister in the first Mussolini cabinet was commonly interpreted as a sign of Croce's willingness to collaborate with the new regime. In 1923–24 Croce supported Gentile's reform of education against all the attacks by liberals and socialists.

It is difficult now to realize how suddenly the situation changed in Italy in 1925. After Mussolini's speech of 3 January 1925, no illusion was possible as to the character of the new regime. In a matter of months, Amendola and Gobetti had been beaten to death, Salvemini had to run for his life, Gramsci was sent to a slow death in jail. In April 1925 Gentile discredited himself with his "Manifesto degli intellettuali fascisti," and Croce became almost overnight the leader of the anti-Fascist intelligentsia by drafting the answer to it.[25] The change resulted from the new situation; it was also the sign that Mussolini had really managed to kill, jail, or banish the majority of his active opponents. The very success of Mussolini's political dictatorship made Croce the virtual dictator of Italian culture. The most obvious feature of the Fascist regime was that it discouraged intelligent men from doing research. G. Gentile, G. Volpe, G. Q. Giglioli, F. Ercole, P. De Francisci, and so many other leading scholars remained under Fascism the intelligent men they had always been, but they no longer entered a library to discover something new. There was also plenty of intelligence among the young men who led the new "corporativist" movement, but they never learned enough economics to face a Cambridge economist—or even old-fashioned Einaudi. Croce went on studying, discovering new facts—even forgotten poets—and writing books full of learning. Some of these books were extremely relevant to the political situation. Such were not only the histories of Italy and Europe, but also the biographies of Italian heretics who looked so much like anti-Fascists of previous ages. Other books, such as *Poesia popolare e poesia d'arte* and *La poesia,* kept alive peculiar interests of his own and modified his former theories on the relation between poetry and literature. With Croce as an example, the habit of studying became almost an anti-Fascist habit. Croce himself was fond of saying that Papini and Prezzolini had been much more intelligent than he, but had done nothing good because they had not worked hard enough. Only members of religious orders or the professed Catholics who had their center in the Università del Sacro Cuore in Milan competed in studious habits with Croce's group.[26] Though the philosophic disputes of the time were mainly between Neo-Thomists and pupils of Gentile (the so-called *attualisti*), we may well wonder whether the most serious intellectual conflicts did not pass above the heads of Gentile, Volpe, Bottai and were really between the Catholics and Croce's group. The school of Gentile was going to pieces. Some of his pupils returned to traditional Catholicism, others became crypto-Communists or pragmatists or even open racialists. The two most authoritative — Adolfo Omodeo and Guido de Ruggiero — went over to Croce and contributed to *La Critica*. Gentile himself remained more important as an organizer and patron than as a thinker.

Croce's activity during the Fascist regime was clearly conditioned by certain unwritten rules. He was allowed by Mussolini to go on with *La Critica*, provided that no direct political attack on the Fascist government was published. Mussolini, who read Croce's books and articles with attention, found it convenient to keep alive an anti-Communist, anticlerical, and, after 1933, anti-Nazi journal. Some of these unwritten rules suited Croce's temperament perfectly well, others of course less well. Indefatigable as he was in introducing new and old foreign books to his Italian readers, he naturally chose those which best conformed to his conservative taste. We must recognize that the selection had its negative effects in a situation of virtual monopoly. This situation was made even more static by the circumstance that any criticism of Croce automatically became support for Fascism. When in 1937 Giorgio Pasquali, the great classical scholar, made some intrinsically harmless remarks on Croce's opinions about Greek and Latin writers, we knew it was the price Pasquali — a former anti-Fascist — had to pay to become an Accademico d'Italia.[27]

The liberalism Croce now put before his readers was that of Constant, Guizot, and Cavour; his economic thought never went beyond Henri De Man; his literary sympathies went as far as G. M. Hopkins — and that was already a remarkable discovery.[28] Of Wittgenstein, Freud, Husserl, neo-Marxism, American sociology we were to hear little, and what we heard was not encouraging. Perhaps one should add in fairness to Croce that Guido de Ruggiero, who was mainly responsible for these subjects in *La Critica*, was singularly narrow in his taste. Even the contemporary foreign historians to whom we were introduced look very odd now. That old-fashioned book, H. A. L. Fisher's *History of Europe*, because it was translated under Croce's auspices, was impounded by the police. Croce saw himself as a Thrasea Paetus or a Boethius in a time of tyranny and barbarism. He expected the end of Fascism to come not from the hands of men, but from mysterious Providence. Though what the Fascists and even more the Nazis had done compelled him to admit that certain historical periods represent an authentic regress, his resigned attitude towards the world remained the same. His notion of history as the history of liberty was essentially fatalistic: it relied on Providence.[29]

Thus Croce was not able to indicate a way out of Fascism. If he had been, Mussolini would not have allowed him to speak. But the liberty Croce spoke about there was not just a philosophic notion. It was the liberty our fathers had won for themselves in the revolutions and on the battlefields of the Risorgimento. Croce represented a constant reproach to Fascism, a constant reminder of what we had lost—freedom and honesty of thought, especially in matters of religion, of social questions and of foreign policy, tolerance, representative government, fair trials, respect for other nations and consequently self-respect. He spoke for Italian civilization, and his speech was the more moving because he might so easily have become a Fascist. He was the living link with the Risorgimento.[30] When Nazism came to add its own brutality, his protests became more radical, his famous jokes bitter. His remark that the word "Aryan" was in danger of becoming synonymous with "imbecile" has not been forgotten.[31] By its very nature the precise importance of Croce in the years 1925–39 is very difficult to assess, but anyone who lived in Italy in those years will probably agree that Croce prevented Fascism from becoming a respectable ideology in the eyes of educated Italians. The active anti-Fascism of those years is inseparable from Croce's teaching.

I was not in Italy when the Second World War broke out, but in retrospect it seems clear that about 1940 Croce must have lost his position of moral leader of the anti-Fascist intelligentsia. The fact that philosophers now turned to existentialism and to phenomenology under the guidance of N. Abbagnano and especially of A. Banfi is perhaps not very significant. Italian professional philosophers were never much under Croce's spell. But existentialism percolated among the young; it affected literary taste. Even in the traditional preserves of Crocean orthodoxy—literary criticism and political historiography—one heard new voices. Gianfranco Contini turned to linguistic and stylistic analysis, Delio Cantimori, more significantly, to the Jacobins.

With the end of the war and the reestablishment of freedom of speech (which meant return to the free circulation of ideas on an international level), the obsolete and reactionary aspects of Croce's attitude to life inevitably came to the forefront. In 1949, the posthumous publication of Gramsci's notes on Croce produced results which Gramsci had certainly not foreseen and probably had not wanted. His acute epigrammatic remarks on Croce's attitudes—his *ateismo da signori,* his *papato laico*—circulated widely, while it was less noticed that Gramsci's basic indifference to natural sciences, anthropology, even economics, was a direct result of Croce's teaching.[32] The dominating preoccupation of Croce's last years—which was to fight Communism—formalized the opposition between Croce and Marx. Croce himself seemed to encourage his pupil Carlo Antoni to present a new version of his own philosophy in which the principle of dialectic opposition — hitherto the most obvious connection between Croce and Marx — was carefully deleted.[33]

What is surprising is not that Croce found himself so distant from men who were fifty or sixty years younger than himself. What is surprising is that he still maintained contact with them, especially through the Historical Institute he had established in Naples. Indeed his influence on professional historians remained stronger than his influence on literary critics. The director of the Naples Institute, Federico Chabod, wrote on Crocean lines the most important historical book of the postwar years — the prolegomena to a history of Italian foreign policy after 1870. Even more surprisingly Croce developed ideas on the elementary conditions of spiritual life — what he called *vitalità* — which interested the Italian existentialists and seemed to introduce a new meaning into his old distinction between economics and ethics.[34] When he died at eighty-seven he left the impression that he had not yet said all he wanted to say.

Nobody can foresee whether Croce's philosophy will be a point of departure for future philosophers. It has few followers in Italy at the moment; and perhaps none abroad. Collingwood had already ceased to be a disciple of Croce before his premature death. In Germany and Austria the men who were in constant debate with Croce — Karl Vossler, Friedrich Meinecke, and Julius von Schlosser — have left no successor.[35] What one can take for granted is that scholars will have to use the facts collected by Croce even if they do not like his ideas. Croce the scholar will be indispensable for a long time to come even to those who care little for Croce the philosopher. In the matter of Neapolitan history, of Italian literature and history in general, and perhaps also of the history of aesthetic theories, Croce provides an immense amount of instruction. Oddly enough, nobody has yet attempted to place Croce's historical books within the history of modern historiography. It is easy to indicate Guizot's *Histoire de la civilisation en Europe* as the model for the *Storia d'Europa;* and the *Storia dell'età barocca* belongs to the tradition of German *Kulturgeschichte*. But the *Storia del regno di Napoli* and the *Storia d'Italia* are more difficult to classify and may well represent an original departure from the traditional type of national history. All these books were certainly new in Italy. They exercised an enormous influence which extended to mature historians like Gaetano De Sanctis and Luigi Salvatorelli, and gave Croce even in Fascist eyes the position of the greatest contemporary Italian historian. The notion that every history is contemporary history and therefore that books on the past serve to clarify problems of the present, the emphasis on the relations between politics and ethics, the sympathy with intellectual elites who find themselves in opposition to both the rulers and the masses were for a time typical of Italian history writing. Even now any debate on the history of Italy is bound to start with an examination of Croce's theses.[36]

But if we want to understand our own time, we shall certainly need to understand more clearly the meaning of Croce's philosophy as a whole. A great deal of good work has been done in Italy and abroad to analyze and criticize single aspects of Croce's thought—such as his ideas on art, his attitude to politics, his conception of history, and even his notions of religion and of nature. But only H. Stuart Hughes, to my knowledge, has attempted to relate the whole of Croce's philosophy to what he called the "reconstruction of European social thought 1890–1930." In Hughes's book (*Consciousness and Society,* 1958) Croce takes his place among those who, from Freud to Max Weber and Bergson, came to the conclusion that the former conceptions of a rational reality were insufficient. This is true enough. I wonder, however, whether there is not also a homelier aspect of Croce's attitude towards the world.

The philosophic system Croce built between 1900 and 1909 was in itself such as to put him automatically outside the mainstream of modern science. Nothing of the kind, to my knowledge, happened to Freud, Max Weber, and Bergson. By identifying language and poetry Croce lost contact with modern linguistic research—and never managed to reestablish it later.[37] By denying the character of true knowledge to natural sciences and mathematics, he offered strange support to those Italians who mistook Guglielmo Marconi—a good technician, but no scientist—for a new Galileo Galilei.

Croce's intellectual world was limited to literature (poetry) and history. We can now see what connected literature and history so closely in his mind. Both "represented" individual facts, "expressed" individual situations. Beyond individual situations Croce saw nothing but mystery. It cannot be emphasized enough that Croce never believed that the human mind can understand the whole of reality.[38] Mystery surrounds man. We cannot even talk of ourselves as personalities, as individuals—each with his own destiny. Each of us in each moment finds himself as a fraction of the whole in a position he cannot change. We can understand the circumstances of the present, if we have the intelligence to look at the past. But historical intelligence is not something we can be sure of acquiring. It comes as an act of grace. If Croce thinks that any error of judgment is to be attributed to a moral failure, he does not mean that by proper care and attention each of us can avoid mistakes. He means that if Providence does not put us in the right frame of mind, we shall never find the truth. Nothing is evil, simply because we have not the means to judge what is evil. If we had, we should have solved the riddle of the universe once and for all. Ludovico Antonio Muratori and the idiot he took as companion on his walks are, according to Croce, equally necessary to the harmony of the universe: we cannot assign different values to either of them.[39] Unconditional acceptance of what is given characterizes also Croce's distinction between politics and ethics. If human behavior has proved throughout the centuries to be different in political affairs from private affairs, there is nothing we can do about it. We can only recognize the existence of a double morality—Machiavellianism in politics, Kantian duty in private life.

Grace, Providence, humility are not words Croce uses rhetorically or analogically. They exactly define his attitude to life, which is one of acceptance of mystery and weakness.[40] One must read his *Filosofia della pratica* and even more his *Frammenti di etica,* which were the results of his meditations during the crucial years 1915–20. They are the essential texts for the understanding of Croce's view of the world. They explain why Croce, rather late, about 1906, found little difficulty in accepting Hegel's notion that what is real is rational, with the consequence that evil does not exist. In Croce's interpretation, "la positività del reale" meant that you and I have to take what is given, do the best we can, and never ask questions about ultimate meaning.

A personal god, in any interpretation of the word, was excluded from this world. The mystery was absolute mystery just because there was no personal god behind it. Those who put Croce's works on the *Index librorum prohibitorum* knew perfectly well what they were doing. But we may well ask whether such an interpretation of the position of man in the world does not represent, at least partially, a modernized, atheistic version of the Catholic education Croce had received. I am not speaking of Catholicism 1966—not even of the *ratio studiorum* Padre Gemelli, a medical doctor and an experimental psychologist, established in the Catholic University of Milan about 1922. In the *Contributo alla critica di me stesso* Croce described rapidly, but perceptively, the education in the boarding school to which he had been sent as a child: "collegio cattolico, non gesuitico in verità, anzi di onesta educazione morale e religiosa senza superstizione e senza fanatismi." He was grateful for that education. There was nothing new in Croce's article of 1942 "Perchè non possiamo non dirci cristiani."[41] It was silly to interpret it as a sign of conversion; but it was also unimaginative to take it as a political program for an alliance between Liberals and Christian Democrats against Communists. Croce uses in it the language he had repeatedly used in his *Frammenti di etica:* "Siate di buona fede e otterrete la fede buona." Perhaps this explains also why Croce preferred Vico to all other philosophers. It was not only *Lokalpatriotismus.* Vico put Providence in the center of his interpretation of history, but seldom mentioned Jesus Christ or the Incarnation.

The note of mystery and resignation in Croce's philosophy was reflected well in Croce's personal modesty, punctilious discipline, fear of moral weakness. "Non a torto la Chiesa considera l'errore quale suggestione della volontà cattiva."[42] On the other hand, the same attitude left him no illusion about the possibility of avoiding violence, punishment, economic inequality, and physical pain. The world to him was beyond human control.

I do not know whether Croce was personally satisfied with a theory which precluded any ultimate truth and any decisive modification of the human condition. His Goethean serenity was achieved at the price of a hard discipline—and he disliked too searching personal questions. But Croce was well aware that his contemporaries had not his Goethean temperament, and he treated them with that mixture of severity and sympathy, sheer amusement and curiosity, condescension and wholehearted solidarity, which was his fascination and his personal mystery.[43]

Notes

1. The three most useful bibliographical guides are E. Cione, *Bibliografia crociana*, Milan, 1956, which lists not only Croce's works, but also works on Croce (pp. 305-438); F. Nicolini, *L'editio ne varietur' delle opere di B.C.*, Naples, 1960, with unpublished documents; S. Borsari, *L'opera di Benedetto Croce*, Naples, 1964, which adds much new information. Croce himself published an introduction to his own work under the name of his secretary Giovanni Castellano (*B.C.: il filosofo—il critico —lo storico*) in 1924, 2d ed., Bari, 1936, which has a bibliography. *L'opera filosofica, storica e letteraria di B.C.*, Bari, 1942, is mainly a selection of papers on C.
The best guide to Italian philosophy in the period 1900-1943 is provided by E. Garin, *Cronache di filosofia italiana*, Bari, 1955, supplemented for the period 1945-50 by his essay in *La Cultura italiana tra '800 e '900*, Bari, 1962, pp. 211-351: this essay has been incorporated in the 3d edition of the *Cronache*, Bari, 1966. See also E. Garin, *Storia della filosofia italiana*, III, Turin, 1966, pp. 1261-1350. Garin is presupposed throughout my paper. See also C. Antoni and R. Mattioli, eds., *Cinquant'anni di vita intellettuale italiana (1896-1946)*, Naples, 1950. G. N. Orsini, *B.C.: Philosopher of Art and Literary Critic*, Southern Illinois University Press, 1961, is indispensable: he gives the necessary references to works by Croce or on Croce in English. I shall only add S. Hughes, "The Evaluation of Sociology in Croce's Theory of History," in W. J. Cahnman and A. Boskoff, eds., *Sociology and History*, New York, 1964, pp. 128-40. Among recent Italian works I mention: M. Abbate, *La filosofia di B.C. e la crisi della società italiana*, 2d ed., Turin, 1966; A. Bausola, *Filosofia e storia nel pensiero crociano*, Milan, 1965; A. Caracciolo, *L'estetica e la religione di B.C.*, Arona, 1958; R. Franchini, *Croce interprete di Hegel*, Naples, 1964; idem, *La teoria della storia di B. Croce*, Naples, 1966. The little book by A. Guzzo, *Croce e Gentile*, Lugano, 1953, includes personal impressions.
2. *Contributo alla critica di me stesso*, Naples, 1918 (it was written in 1915), later included in *Etica e politica*, Bari, 1931, pp. 363-411: R. G. Collingwood's translation with a preface by J. A. Smith, Oxford, 1927. It is important to see what C. writes about himself in *Storia d'Italia dal 1871 al 1915*, 1st ed., 1928, especially pp. 245-63. Parts of his diaries for the period September 1943-June 1944 are published in *Scritti e discorsi politici (1943-1947)*, I, Bari, 1963, pp. 171-344. The *Nuove pagine sparse*, I-II, Naples, 1949, are especially full of autobiographical recollections. (Earlier important drafts of the *Contributo* have now been published: B.C., *Memorie della mia vita*, Naples, 1966.)

3. Elena Croce, *Ricordi familiari,* 2d ed., Florence, 1962 (notice pp. 35–36 on the religious education of Croce's daughters); idem, *L'infanzia dorata,* Milan, 1966. *Cf.* also D. Marra, *Conversazioni con B.C. su alcuni libri della sua biblioteca,* Milan, 1952 (D. Marra was C.'s librarian from 1945).

4. *B. Croce,* Turin, 1962.

5. *Carteggio Croce–Vossler (1899–1949),* Bari, 1951. (*Cf.* now B.C., *Epistolario,* I–II, Naples, 1967–69 and the first volume of the letters by G. Gentile to C., Florence, 1973.)

6. The letters by G. Sorel were published partially in *La Critica,* 25, 1927, and following years.

7. *Cf.* the appendix to A. Labriola, *La concezione materialistica della storia,* Bari, 1938, pp. 267–312, to be found also in *Materialismo storico ed economia marxistica,* 6th ed., Bari, 1941, pp. 265–306.

8. E. Cecchi, *Ricordi crociani,* Milan and Naples, 1965, pp. 73–100. Among the interesting letters so far published notice those to R. Serra (in A. Grilli, *Tempo di Serra,* Florence, 1961) and to G. Amendola (in E. Amendola Kühn, *Vita con G. Amendola,* Florence, 1960).

9. This description by the historian F. Nitti is quoted by M. Corsi, *Le origini del pensiero di B.C.,* Florence, 1951, p. 182. Croce himself evaluated "La vita letteraria a Napoli dal 1860 al 1900" in *La Critica,* 8, 1910, pp. 241–62 = *La letteratura della Nuova Italia,* IV, pp. 293–319.

10. On all this it will be enough to refer to E. Agazzi, *Il giovane C. e il marxismo,* Turin, 1962, and to the introduction by E. Garin to A. Labriola, *La concezione materialistica della storia,* Bari, 1965: both give bibliography. E. Santerelli, *La revisione del marxismo in Italia,* Milan, 1964, pp. 29–80, is a partisan evaluation with few new facts.

11. The first version of the *Estetica,* 1900, is conveniently available (together with the first version of the *Logica*) in A. Attisani, *La prima forma della Estetica e della Logica,* Messina, 1924.

12. There is a very valuable anthology of these periodicals by D. Frigessi, *La cultura italiana del '900 attraverso le riviste, Leonardo, Hermes, Il Regno,* Turin, 1960, with an important introduction. *Cf.* also M. Puppo, *Croce e D'Annunzio e altri saggi,* Florence, 1964.

13. His *Opere* (the most important of which is *La persuasione e la rettorica*) were collected by G. Chiavacci, Florence, 1958: notice on p. 661 an opinion on Croce (written about 1908).

14. *Cf.* R. Serra, *Scritti,* II, Florence, 1938, pp. 265–71: "Il Croce di Prezzolini"; idem, *Le lettere,* Rome, 1914, pp. 39–47, 139–44; idem, *Esame di coscienza d'un letterato,* Milan, 1915 = *Scritti,* I, pp. 395–96, *cf.* pp. 444–45. E. Garin, "Serra e Croce," *Belfagor,* 21, 1966, pp. 1–14.

15. G. Papini–G. Prezzolini, *Storia di un'amicizia,* Florence, 1966, pp. 72, 136. See also Papini's review of Croce's first *Logica* in *Leonardo,* 1905, 3, 115 (D. Frigessi, *La cultura italiana,* p. 255). In general G. Prezzolini, *Il tempo della Voce,* Milan and Florence, 1960 (with several letters by Croce).

16. The identification of history (historiography) and philosophy was first formulated in the second *Logica,* 1909. For Croce's evolution on this point see for instance C. Antoni, in *Cinquant'anni di vita intellettuale italiana,* quoted I, pp. 68–77 (where bibliography).

17. Borgese's article, published in *La Stampa* (Turin), 10 April 1911, provoked C.'s reply in *La Critica*, 9, 1911, pp. 223–29 (*Pagine sparse*, I, 1943, pp. 329–38). Hence Borgese's attack, "Vico, Croce e i giovani," *Cultura Contemporanea,* 5 April 1912, pp. 110–73, reprinted in *La vita e il libro,* III, Turin, pp. 323–402.

18. See G. Prezzolini, *B.C.,* Naples, 1909.

19. *La Voce,* 6, no. 4, 28 February 1914, pp. 10–33 at p. 28, partly republished in the anthology of *La Voce,* ed. G. Ferrata, S. Giovanni Valdarno, 1961, pp. 447–59 (at p. 458).

20. *Le lettere,* 1914, p. 30.

21. *Cf. Storia d'Italia,* 1st ed., Bari, 1928, p. 345. In general *L'Italia dal 1914 al 1918: Pagine sulla guerra,* 3d ed., Bari, 1950.

22. *Cf. 2000 pagine di Gramsci,* I, Milan, 1964, p. 19; *Le riviste di Piero Gobetti,* a cura di L. Basso e L. Anderlini, 1961, p. 87 (from *Energie nuove,* 1918).

23. On this episode L. Salvatorelli, in F. Flora, ed., *B. Croce,* Milan, 1953, pp. 397–416.

24. *Cf. Cultura e vita morale,* 3d ed., 1955, pp. 253–59 (a defense of religious education in elementary schools written in 1923). A. Omodeo had written in 1914: "Il mito cristiano rinverdirà nell'atto in cui il padre si profonda nell'animo miticizzante del figlio" (*La Voce,* 6, no. 14, 28 July 1914). Prezzolini (ibid.) had answered: "Caro Omodeo, che l'idealismo difenda il valore preparatorio del grado religioso sta bene; ma che difenda per l'appunto il valore preparatorio del cattolicesimo di Papa Pio X non mi pare nè giusto nè opportuno." See also F. Nicolini, *Il Croce minore,* Milan and Naples, 1963, pp. 47–49, for interesting declarations by C.

25. The text in *Pagine sparse,* II, Naples, 1943, pp. 380–83. For Croce's point of view after Matteotti's murder in 1924, ibid., pp. 376–79. New evidence in G. Levi Della Vida, *Fantasmi ritrovati,* Venice, 1966, pp. 167–209. *Cf.* D. Mack Smith, *The Cambridge Journal,* 3, 1949, pp. 343–56; C. McArthur Destler, *Journ. Mod. History,* 24, 1952, pp. 382–90; G. Salvemini, *Il Ponte,* 10, November 1954, p. 1728.

26. Catholic philosophers, as is well known, varied in their reactions to Croce. E. Chiocchetti, *La filosofia di B.C.,* 1st ed., Florence, 1915; 3d ed., Milan, 1924, approves of the greater part of C.'s philosophy. F. Olgiati, *B.C. e lo storicismo,* Milan, 1953, is an invective. Further literature in G. Mastroianni quoted in note 35.

27. G. Pasquali, "Croce e le letterature classiche," *Leonardo,* 8, 1937, pp. 45–50. See Croce's reply, *Pagine sparse,* III, Naples, 1943, pp. 170–73.

28. On G. M. Hopkins, *Poesia antica e moderna,* 2d ed., Bari, 1943, pp. 421–46 (written in 1936).

29. Even in 1938 (*La storia come pensiero e come azione,* pp. 47–49) C.'s notion of liberty was ambiguous: liberty is both ubiquitous and aristocratic—independent of political regimes. See the interesting personal recollections by E. Chichiarelli, "Il limite della mia lezione crociana," *Riv. Studi Crociani,* I, 1964, pp. 482–98. Perhaps the most important analysis of Croce's liberalism is in N. Bobbio, *Politica e cultura,* Turin, 1955. See also N. Valeri, *Da Giolitti a Mussolini,* Florence, 1956, pp. 197–212 and E. Agazzi, "B.C. e l'avvento del fascismo," *Riv. Storica del Socialismo,* 9, 1966, pp. 76–103.

30. It would be worth examining in what sense and to what extent there was a group of "Crociani" in Italy between 1925 and 1940. The situation of course varied

not only according to years, but according to places: the Turin Crociani were different from those of Naples. The personality of two young Turin Crociani — L. Ginzburg and A. Mautino (the former died in jail as a victim of Nazi-Fascism) — emerges clearly from the posthumous publication of their writings: L. Ginzburg, *Scritti*, with an introduction by N. Bobbio, Turin, 1964; A. Mautino, *La formazione della filosofia politica di B.C.*, con uno studio sull'autore e la tradizione culturale torinese da Gobetti alla Resistenza di G. Solari, 3d ed., Bari, 1953. See more in general G. Luti, *Cronache letterarie tra le due guerre, 1920–1940*, Bari, 1966.

31. *Pagine sparse*, III, Naples, 1943, p. 138: "per questa via, la parola 'ario' finirà a prendere il significato d' 'imbecille.'" Croce's help to persecuted Jews, both Italian and foreign, was unlimited. *Cf.* E. Cione, *B.C. e il pensiero contemporaneo*, Milan, 1963, pp. 121 and 578 (the first edition of this book, under the title *Croce*, appeared in Milan, 1944: the author, a former pupil of Croce, became bitterly hostile to him).

32. A. Gramsci, *Il materialismo storico e la filosofia di B.C.*, Turin, 1948 (these notes must have been written about 1932), pp. 247, 250. *Cf.* also his notes on *Gli intellettuali e la organizzazione della cultura*, Turin, 1949, where there are typical judgments inspired by Croce, for instance p. 140: "la grandezza del Machiavelli consiste nell'aver distinto la politica dall'etica."

33. See C. Antoni, *Commento a Croce*, Venice, 1955, where the author puts together earlier papers: for Croce's approval see the preface.

34. *Cf. Filosofia e storiografia*, Bari, 1949, pp. 217–23 (1947) and the whole volume *Indagini su Hegel e schiarimenti filosofici*, Bari, 1952, and especially pp. 29–45 (1951). For existentialist criticism, *cf.* E. Paci, *Esistenzialismo e storicismo*, Milan, 1950. See also A. Bruno, *La crisi dell' idealismo nell' ultimo Croce*, Bari, 1964.

35. The Neapolitan group of "Crociani" now has its own journal, the *Rivista di Studi Crociani*, 1964 ff. *Cf.* G. Mastroianni, "La polemica sul C. negli studi contemporanei," *Società*, 14, 1958, pp. 711–37. I am not sure that J. W. Meiland, *Scepticism and Historical Knowledge*, New York, 1965, can be described as a book by a pupil of Croce. On C. and Meinecke, W. Hofer, *Geschichtschreibung und Weltanschauung*, Munich, 1950, pp. 389–403. On C. and Collingwood, Croce, *Nuove pagine sparse*, I, Naples, 1948, pp. 25–39 (1946). Collingwood's early essays on C. are now collected in *Essays on the Philosophy of History*, Austin, Texas, 1965.

36. The most important essay on Croce as a historian is by F. Chabod, *Rivista Storica Italiana*, 64, 1952, pp. 473–530. *Cf.* A.R. Caponigri, *History and Liberty: The Historical Writings of B. Croce*, London, 1955; F. Gaeta, *Riv. Studi Crociani*, 1, 1964, pp. 153–67; W. Mager, *Benedetto Croces literarisches und politisches Interesse an der Geschichte*, Graz, 1965. On the *Storia d'Italia*, V. de Caprariis in F. Flora, ed., *B.C.*, quoted pp. 291–301. On Chabod's interpretation of C., G. Sasso, *Interpretazioni crociane* (a collective volume), Bari, 1965, pp. 221–304 (interesting also for other points). See now also E. Ragionieri, *Belfagor*, 21, 1966, pp. 125–49 and K.-E. Lönne, *B.C. als Kritiker seiner Zeit*, Tübingen, 1967.

37. See C.'s paper of 1941 in *Discorsi di varia filosofia*, I, Bari, 1945, pp. 235–50, and also *Letture di poeti*, Bari, 1950, pp. 247–58. A useful collection of evidence in S. Cavaciuti, *La teoria linguistica di B.C.*, Milan, 1959; *cf.* T. De Mauro, *Giorn. Crit. Filos. Ital.* n.s., 8, 1954, pp. 376–91, and *Introduzione alla semantica*, 2d ed., Bari, 1966. But I should like to mention especially the little volume by E. Colorni (to whom the

present paper is dedicated), *L'estetica di B.C.*, Milan, 1932. Colorni died in 1944 as a victim of Fascism.

38. This was particularly well emphasized by F. Flora, *Croce*, Milan, 1927, p. 129. Croce's later work is no departure from this basic attitude. An important analysis of Croce's ideas on history in P. Rossi, *Storia e storicismo nella filosofia contemporanea*, Milan, 1960, pp. 287–330, with which I fundamentally agree. Perhaps less rewarding: D. Faucci, *Storicismo e metafisica nel pensiero crociano*, Florence, 1950; F. Albeggiani, *Lo storicismo di B.C.*, *Atti Accad. Palermo*, 4, 13, 2, 1953; R. Raggiunti, *La conoscenza storica: Analisi della logica crociana*, Florence, 1955. Among foreign critics it will be enough to mention two classics: M. Mandelbaum, *The Problem of Historical Knowledge*, New York, 1938; H.-I. Marrou, *De la connaissance historique*, Paris, 1954.

39. This example is given by Croce, *Frammenti di etica* in *Etica e politica*, Bari, 1931, p. 57.

40. See for instance his characteristic letter to K. Vossler on the war as "azione divina," *Carteggio Croce–Vossler*, pp. 206–7: "Come sai bene, le lotte degli Stati, le guerre, sono *azioni divine*. Noi, individui, dobbiamo accettarle e sottometterci. Ma sottomettere la nostra attività pratica e non quella teoretica" (1919).

41. It is reprinted in *Discorsi di varia filosofia*, I, Bari, 1945, pp. 11–23. *Cf. La religione di B.C.*, Bari, 1964; A. Bausola, *Etica e politica nel pensiero di B.C.*, Milan, 1966.

42. "L'indole immorale dell'errore e la critica scientifica e letteraria" (1906), *Cultura e vita morale*, 3d ed., Naples, 1955, pp. 88–94 at p. 89. Croce lived to regret his earlier (1909) eulogy of the Inquisition in *Filosofia della pratica*, 3d ed., Bari, 1923, p. 43.

43. (Among the innumerable publications inspired by the centenary, notice: *Terzo Programma*, 2, 1966, pp. 1–130 [various authors]; E. Paratore, *Il Croce e le lettere classiche*, Rome, 1967; G. Contini, "L'influenza culturale di B.C.," *L'Approdo Letterario*, 12, 1966, pp. 3–32; V. E. Alfieri, *Pedagogia crociana*, Naples, 1967; U. Benedetti, *B.C. e il Fascismo*, Rome, 1967; G. Sasso, *La Cultura*, 5, 1967, pp. 44–69, and above all the survey by V. Stella, *Giornale di metafisica*, 22, 1967, pp. 643–711.)

EIGHT

Julius Beloch

Karl Julius Beloch, more usually known as Julius Beloch, was German by birth, but became an Italian citizen in the last years of his life, having taught Ancient History at the University of Rome from 1879 to 1929. He was born at Petschkendorf, in the district of Lüben in Silesia, in the kingdom of Prussia, on 21 January 1854, the only son of Karl Julius, a well-to-do landowner (*Landwirt*), and Alwine Rösler, daughter of the landowner August Wilhelm Rösler of Hulm. The religion of his father's family had been Lutheran for at least three generations, and his mother was also Lutheran. The little that is known about Beloch's youth can be found in the "curriculum vitae" now in the archive of the University of Heidelberg (dated 1 July 1875) and in the autobiography published in 1926 in the series *Die Geschichtswissenschaft der Gegenwart in Selbstdarstellungen* (ed. Meiner, II, Leipzig) which in a general way contains reliable facts and observations, but leaves something to be desired in precision. His father died young. His mother—a secret writer of poetry—took a leading part in the upbringing of Beloch, who was educated privately. The boy showed a precocious interest in history, geography, and statistics, and learned the classical languages exceptionally well; already at that stage his favorite language was Greek. Then and throughout his life he was assisted by an extraordinary memory, which goes some way to explain the speed at which he worked. As an adult Beloch knew most of the *Iliad* and Thucydides by heart.

The fear that he might contract tuberculosis caused him to move to Italy around 1870, and he fell permanently in love with the sun-bathed lands of the Mediterranean. His first home was at Sorrento, which remained for him "the most beautiful spot on earth." Here he met Bartolomeo Capasso, who

"Giulio Beloch," *Dizionario Biografico degli Italiani* (1966), vol. VIII, pp. 32–45; *Terzo contributo* (1966), pp. 239–65. Translated by T. J. Cornell.

encouraged him to study the antiquities of Campania. His first work, on the topography of Sorrento (still unpublished?), formed the core of his book *Campanien,* which appeared in 1879 with a dedication to Capasso. From Sorrento he moved to Palermo where he obtained a teaching qualification and registered in the Faculty of Letters in 1872. Beloch asserts in his autobiography that he was the first student to be formally registered in the Faculty and to have followed with profit the course of A. Salinas. The destruction of the archives of the University of Palermo for those years makes it impossible to obtain further details. In the academic year 1873–74 and for part of the next he studied at the University of Rome, where among other things he followed courses in linguistics with G. Lignana, Roman antiquities with E. De Ruggiero, and ancient history with R. Bonghi, to whom, as teacher, he dedicated *Der italische Bund* (1880). Bonghi, who was Minister of Education from September 1874 to March 1876, broke off his teaching in 1874–75, but continued to give his encouragement to the young German who showed so much promise. The latter, who in Sicily had taken an interest in the history of the Greeks of Italy and in Homer, now at Rome devoted himself with equal fervor to epigraphy and to Roman and Italic antiquities. He was of course a frequent visitor to the Instituto di Corrispondenza Archeologica (later the German Archaeological Institute), and got to know W. Henzen and W. Helbig. The product of the year in Sicily was his first article in Italian, in the *Rivista di Filologia e Istruzione Classica* (2, 1873, pp. 49–62), on "Bronze and Iron in the Homeric Poems" (dated Breslau, July 1873), in which he made inferences about the composition of the *Iliad* from the mentions of iron; a revised version of this paper can be found in *Griechische Geschichte* (I, 2, 1913, p. 109). It was followed by other articles, also in the *Rivista di Filologia*: "On the Population of Ancient Sicily" (ibid., pp. 545–62) (dated Rome, April 1874); "An Addition to the Latin Anthology" (3, 1875, pp. 70–72) (on a stone inscription at Frascati: dated Frascati, June 1874); "On Restoring the Original Form of the Homeric Poems" (ibid., pp. 305–27) (dated Rome, October 1874); "On the Political Constitution of Elis," (4, 1875, pp. 225–38); "The Battle of Tanagra," (5, 1877, pp. 453–72).

In the spring of 1875 Beloch spent a few months at the University of Heidelberg, where he attended the seminars of H. Köchly, O. Ribbeck, and W. Stark, and the lectures of K. Fischer. On 7 August 1875 he passed the *examen rigorosum, summa cum laude,* taking classical philology as his main subject and archaeology and ancient history as secondary subjects. Two days later, on 9 August, he was awarded a doctorate for a dissertation *De Graecorum in Campania colonis* ("On the Greek Colonists in Campania"). This brief dissertation, of fifty-six handwritten pages, comprised three chapters: "Origines" ("Origins"), "Graecorum in Campania res gestae" ("The History of the Greeks in Campania"), and "Graeci Campaniae sub imperio barbarorum" ("The Greeks of Campania under Barbarian Rule"). The two referees,

Köchly and Stark, were far from satisfied with the dissertation, as can be seen from their comments, preserved in the archive of the University of Heidelberg and dated, respectively, 17 July and 7 June (almost certainly an error for July). While they praised the learning and acumen of the author, they recommended that the dissertation should be accepted only after revision. After Beloch's success at the "rigorosum" on 7 August, the Faculty accepted the dissertation subject to the proviso that it be partially revised and resubmitted. This does not seem ever to have been done. Not only was the dissertation never printed; there is no copy of it to be found in either the library or the archive of the University of Heidelberg. The material that it collected must have been used in the book *Campanien*.

Beloch immediately returned to Italy to continue working on the history of Campania. But even if we did not know it from his autobiography, we should have to deduce from the stream of articles that flowed from his pen that he made himself master of many areas of Greco-Roman antiquity. The forthrightness and rapidity of his conclusions disturbed his once amicable relations with the scholars who were then running the Instituto di Corrispondenza Archeologica. It was an argument over the site of the Battle of the Allia, which Beloch placed on the right bank of the Tiber, that caused the rupture with Henzen, who refused to include Beloch's study in the publications of the Institute (a résumé of Beloch's paper, and of Henzen's objections, is given in *Bull. Instituto Corrisp. Archeol.* [1877, pp. 55–56]; another quarrel, this time with F. von Duhn, is reported [ibid., 1878, p. 67] after which Beloch's name seems to disappear from the published proceedings of the Institute).

The quarrel with Henzen soon developed into a rift with the Institute in general; Beloch became a member only in 1925, almost on the eve of his death. When added to the equivocal outcome of his examinations at Heidelberg, the conflict with the powerful German group in Rome must have had a decisive influence on Beloch's decision to make his career in Italy. Given the pro-German tendencies of Italian politics and culture at that time, together with the patronage of Bonghi, it was not difficult. Precisely in 1876 a chair in Universal History at Palermo was awarded to another German, A. Holm, who however was soon to join the growing band of Beloch's enemies. In March 1877 Beloch took a university teaching degree (*libera docenza*) at the University of Rome, and on 21 January 1879, his twenty-fifth birthday, he was appointed in open competition to the post of junior professor (*professore straordinario*) in the chair of Ancient History in succession to Bonghi, who had had to vacate it as incompatible with his position as a member of Parliament (on which see F. D'Ovidio, *Nuova Antologia*, 144, 1895, p. 20). The appointing committee that awarded the chair to Beloch included P. Villari, M. Amadi, and D. Comparetti. Around this time he married the American Bella Bailey from Washington, D.C., whose family (according to Beloch's own account) were friends of Abraham Lincoln. They had two daughters, who have their own place in the history of Italian culture: Margherita (married name Piazzola), who was professor (*ordinaria*) of analytical geometry at the University of Ferrara, and Dorotea (d. 1952), a musician and pupil of P. Mascagni, who composed operas and operettas. Through his marriage Beloch gained a knowledge of English and of Anglo-American culture which was unusual at that time.

The young professor brought to Rome the methods of the German seminar and quickly attracted pupils there: among the earliest were Federico Halbherr, later an expert on Crete and a colleague of Beloch's at Rome, and Vincenzo Costanzi, later professor at Pisa. But his methods of teaching were not exactly those commonly used in Germany: relying on memory, Beloch came to the classroom without notes. By his own admission, he did not take his teaching too seriously in those years, and he preferred Frascati to Rome. He was made to wait for his promotion to full professor (*professore ordinario*), which in those days was not automatic; and for that reason in 1886 Beloch entered the competition for a full professorship in ancient history at Catania. He was successful, but nevertheless preferred to remain in Rome as junior professor (*straordinario*), and was finally appointed a full professor in 1891.

What Beloch was, and what he aimed at in the period 1879–90, is indicated by the extraordinary cycle of books: *Campanien* (Berlin, 1879); *Der italische Bund unter Roms Hegemonie* (Leipzig, 1880); *L'impero siciliano di Dionisio* (*Mem. R. Accad. Lincei*, 7, 1880; published in 1881); *Le fonti di Strabone nella descrizione della Campania* (ibid., 10, 1882); *Attische Politik seit Perikles* (Leipzig, 1884); *Die Bevölkerung der griechisch-römischen Welt* (Leipzig, 1886). To these must be added the revolutionary study of the Dorian invasion in *Rheinisches Museum* (45, 1890, pp. 555–98); the series of researches on Athenian finance in *Rheinisches Museum* (39, 1884, pp. 34–64, 239–59; 43, 1888, pp..104–22); *Hermes* (20, 1885, pp. 237–61; 22, 1887, pp. 371–77); research on Sicilian and Italiot history (ibid., 28, 1893, pp. 481–88; 630–34; 29, 1894, pp. 604–10; *Jahrb. f. class. Philol.*, 131, 1885, pp. 366–68); the analysis of the Roman censuses (*Rheinisches Museum*, 32, 1877, pp. 226–48); the study of the population of ancient Rome in *Bulletin de l'Institut international de statistique* (1, 1886, pp. 63–79; later reproduced in the volume on the *Bevölkerung*); and above all the start of the work on the population of medieval and modern Italy in the programmatic article in the *Nuova Antologia* (95, 1887, pp. 48–61) and in the paper on the 16th to 18th centuries (in *Bulletin* (cit.), 3, 1888, pp. 1–42; still not superseded in 1959, when it was reprinted in C. M. Cipolla, *Storia della economia italiana*, I, Turin, 1959, pp. 449–500), not to speak of so many other classic pieces of research on specialized topics, for instance on the organization of Timaeus's histories (in *Jahrb. f. class. Philol.*, 123, 1881, pp. 697–706; *cf.* ibid., 133, 1886, pp. 775–76) and on the native city of Theognis (ibid., 137, 1888, pp. 729–33).

These works perhaps contain what is most original and lasting in Beloch; we certainly find in them the most precise application of his method in all fields, including archaic Greek history, where its application was more open to question. Four qualities stand out in these early works of Beloch and were to remain characteristic of his later ones: the extraordinary capacity to keep constantly in mind all the evidence of the ancient sources, which he knew exceptionally well; the ability to make use of known facts to indicate preceding events that are not recorded in the surviving sources; competence in the evaluation of topographical and demographic matters; and finally, acuteness in textual criticism (exampes of this last characteristic in *Jahrb. f. class. Philol.*, 123, 1881, p. 391; *Hermes*, 28, 1893, p. 630; *Rivista Storica Antica*, 5, 1900, p. 603).

Something that mattered a great deal to Beloch was the careful reconstruction on the ground of the material conditions of ancient life. The understanding of the physical environment was the essential frame of reference for the calculation of population statistics, which Beloch throughout his life considered fundamental not only in the assessment of power relations between states, but also for the precise analysis of the internal events within any given state. In particular, Beloch soon realized that even an approximate idea of the population of the ancient world was impossible without a knowledge and assessment of the more abundant and secure data about the population of the medieval and modern world. For this reason he embarked on the demographic research in Italian archives that later had to be extended to various other European countries. On the twin bases of the measurement of territory and the calculation of population size he reconstructed institutions. He had little interest in the constitutional details of particular magistracies, but rather concerned himself with the administrative functions of urban centers, the structure of armies, and the nature and consistency of state finances. Within the state his interest was focused on the commercial and industrial classes, which he interpreted, with unabashed modernism, in capitalist terms; he gave little attention to agriculture except to determine basic relationships between cereal production and population. Nevertheless, Beloch retained a taste for political history as such: his books are filled with conflicts between individuals and parties, also modernized in terms of nationalist ideologies and rivalry between conservatives (aristocrats) and reformers (democrats). But it is easy to see that this interest in politics was not in perfect harmony with his other interests in economic and social history and in human geography. In *Attische Politik* it is clear that the reconstruction of Athenian finances and of the list of generals is not of much use in the analysis of politics. For that reason *Attische Politik* is in fact less original than *Der italische Bund* or *Die Bevölkerung der griechisch-römischen Welt.* It operates within the limits of the discussion of fourth-century Athenian politics that had been set by A. Schaefer and G. Grote, with the difference that Beloch admires the creators of strong states and therefore prefers Philip of Macedon to Demosthenes. The same admiration for strong states inspired the essay in Italian on Dionysius of Syracuse, but here for the first time an attempt was made to study the constitutional structure and the territorial extent of the empire of the Syracusan tyrant. This was acknowledged, in spite of the criticism of its (undeniably shaky) central thesis on the lifelong powers of Dionysius, in the hostile review by A. Holm in *Bursians Jahresbericht* (28, 3, 1881, pp. 48–55).

Der italische Bund, however, was something completely new. Moving on from his lengthy antiquarian and constitutional researches on Campania — which in other respects, particularly in the additions to the second edition (Morgenstern, Breslau, 1890), raised important questions about the chronology of the Greek colonies, the nature of Etruscan rule, and the oscanization of Campania — Beloch felt the need to understand the Roman conquest of Italy through a precise analysis of geographical extent of territory, administrative divisions, and demography. Everyone who has since worked on this subject (in Italy especially P. Fraccaro and his school) has started from Beloch.

Equally novel was the volume on the population of the ancient world. Criticism of traditional data went back to Hume (for further details see A. Momigliano in *Enciclopedia Italiana,* XXVII, s.v. "Popolazione [nel mondo antico]," p. 915), and there had been good work on some aspects of the subject, for example by J.-A. Letronne and H.-A. Wallon (*Histoire de l'esclavage,* I, 1847). In 1840 A. Zumpt had also tried, on the basis of traditional figures, to give a general idea of demographic change in the Greco-Roman world ("Ueber den Stand der Bevölkerung und Volksvermehrung im Altertum," *Abh. Berlin. Akad.,* 1840, pp. 1–92). But Beloch was the first to proceed critically to a systematic revision of all the ancient evidence based on the constant interrelations of population figures, size of territory, and means of subsistence. He was also the first to apply in a consistent manner the principle that figures for the size of armies or numbers of people taking part in political assemblies, although open to doubt, are more likely to be reliable than those for whole populations or numbers of slaves. For Beloch himself the criticism of earlier results worked better than the formulation of new figures; on this it is sufficient to refer to the observations of E. Ciccotti in the introduction to the Italian translation of *Die Bevölkerung* in V. Pareto's *Biblioteca di storia economica* (IV, 1909), as well as in *Valore e utilizzazione di dati statistici nel mondo antico* (1931), but Beloch himself had stressed the hypothetical status of his figures and had indicated the margins of error (*cf.* also the work of J. C. Russell cited below).

In all these studies (and also, as we shall see presently, in his skepticism about traditional data in archaic history and his attempts to replace them with inferences from later facts) there was nothing that cannot be called characteristically German. A specifically German trait was his preoccupation with economics and statistics, in which he reacted against K. Bücher's theories about the "household" character of the ancient economy (*cf.* his later polemic in *Zeitschr. für Socialwissenschaft*, 5, 1902, pp. 95–103, 169–79; and *Griech. Gesch.*, 2d ed., III, 2, p. 419). Equally German was the enthusiasm for Philip of Macedon, with its implicit identification of the Macedonians as Greeks, which he took from J. G. Droysen. More generally, the learned apparatus (source criticism) and the ideological equipment with which he operated—these too were German. It is not an accident, for example, that J. Jastrow, *Die Volkzahl deutscher Städte zu Ende des Mittelalters* appeared in 1886, the same year as *Die Bevölkerung*. But if Beloch was in harmony with certain currents of German culture around 1880, it cannot be said that he was in tune with the culture and interests prevalent among German ancient historians. He did not share the interest in administrative history and the constitutional orderliness of Th. Mommsen; he disliked the classicism of E. Curtius; he completely ignored the Dionysiac revolt of F. Nietzsche and E. Rohde; he never bothered with H. Usener's efforts to recover from later customs something of the popular morality and religion of ancient Greece and Italy; and finally he set himself against the revival of K. O. Müller's ideas about Greek mythology that was being championed by the young U. Wilamowitz. However great his debt to the imperialistic nationalism of the later Droysen (something which, apart from anything else, always kept Beloch away from Karl Marx, to whom he ought to have been drawn by his implicit materialism), he never adhered to Droysen's notion of Hellenism and never sympathized with his excessively analytical style. He could certainly refer to the example of A. Boeckh, but only inasmuch as the recent reissue of *Die Staatshaushaltung der Athener* (edited by M. Fraenkel, 1886), originally published in 1817, was a sign that the younger generation was going back to problems of social and economic history. There were other signs, it is true: perhaps the most conspicuous was the emergence of R. Pöhlmann who, among other things, published a monograph in 1884 on overpopulation in the big cities of the ancient world (*Die Ueberbevölkerung der antiken Grossstädte, Preisschriften der Jablonowskischen Gesell.*, XXIV), and reviewed Beloch in *Deutsche Literaturzeitung* (1887, col. 495–98). But this was precisely a change of direction by some of the young, which never became general; Pöhlmann like Beloch remained an exception. It is noteworthy that the first German historian to acknowledge the importance of Beloch's demographic researches and to follow them up on his own account was a contemporary who came from oriental history: Eduard Meyer (*cf. Forsch. z. alten Geschichte*, II, 1899, pp. 149–95, and the article "Die Bevölkerung des Altertums" in *Handwörterbuch des Staatswissenschaft* (II, 1891, p. 445).

It is not surprising therefore that the local rift between Beloch and the heads of the German Archaeological Institute in Rome grew into a conflict with official ancient history in Germany. Mommsen was prompted by certain chapters of *Der italische Bund* to condemn Beloch (*Hermes*, 18, 1883, p. 208; 22, 1887, p. 101). His cruel judgment — "rarely has a monograph been written with so little regard for specialized research, or a scientific expedition into unknown territory undertaken with so little equipment" — affected the rest of Beloch's career (Mommsen's opinion is probably reflected also in the review of O. Seeck in *Deutsche Literaturz.*, 1881, col. 402). More is now revealed in a letter from Mommsen to Wilamowitz of 1881 (*Briefwechsel*, 1935, p. 106). To judge by what Beloch says in his autobiography, Mommsen's veto was the main reason why he was not appointed to a chair at Breslau in 1889 (already in 1885 he had been an unsuccessful candidate for an assistant professorship at Leipzig). Beloch's desire to return to his homeland — all the greater for the growing hostility to him in official academic circles — is confirmed by his strange decision to stand for the German parliament in the elections of 1893 called by G. L. von Caprivi. What exactly Beloch's political opinions were in 1893 is not easy to say. In his autobiography he calls himself an anti-Bismarckian and a lifelong republican. He stood for the electoral district of Rügen-Stralsund at the last moment in place of R. Virchow as candidate for the Progressive Party (*Freisinnige Volkspartei*). His opponents were the outgoing deputy, R. von Keudell of the Reichspartei (formerly ambassador to Italy), the Social Democrat Rathmann, and finally the *Antisemitische Volkspartei* candidate von Langen, who was eventually elected after a second ballot against von Keudell. Beloch says nothing in his autobiography about the victorious anti-Semitic candidate who went on to sit in the Reichstag as an Anti-Semitic Conservative (*Antisemiten-Spiegel*, 2d ed., Danzig, 1900, p. 40); and this silence, in the light of what will be said about Beloch's anti-Semitism, seems significant. Beloch was evidently a victim of the electoral disaster that overtook his party. Personally he won votes, and in the city of Stralsund he obtained a majority. He consoled himself with a trip to Norway, which attracted him because of its natural beauty, to which he was always sensitive, and returned to his teaching in Rome with renewed vigor. Later he could make the Polybian boast: "Anyone who has stood for eight nights at the hustings in an election learns more than in eight years at the desk" (*Einleitung in die Altertumsw.*, III, 2d ed., p. 156).

It is extraordinary that Beloch, who spent all of his adult life in Italy, managed to remain so impervious to Italian culture. It seems indeed that not a single one of his ideas came from Italian scholars, not even from his own pupils. And yet Beloch was profoundly influenced by his residence in Italy; equally profound, and positive, was the effect he had on Italian culture.

Living in Italy gave Beloch an exact knowledge of environmental conditions that no other German scholar, with the exception of Mommsen, ever managed to achieve. Beloch's criticism of H. Nissen's *Italische Landeskunde* — "Half Baedeker, half *Corpus Inscriptionum Latinarum*" (*Römische Geschichte*, 1926, p. 215) — reflects his sense of superiority in this respect. This confident expertise in environmental matters was subsequently extended from Magna Graecia and Sicily to Greece, which he visited many times, although he never achieved the same level of familiarity with Greece as he had with Magna Graecia (and the consequences can be seen in his works on Greek history). He seems never to have gone to Asia Minor or Africa. But residence in Italy gave Beloch another advantage that is less easy to define: it freed him from the heavy atmosphere of subservience that pervaded German universities, and in particular from the "tyranny of Mommsen" which left its mark on contemporaries beyond the Alps. Lastly, it is impossible not to connect his Italian residence with that simplification of the German language, and perhaps even more the simplification of ideas, which is so characteristic of Beloch. Beloch's German language and German culture were reduced by distance to their bare bones. In a lesser man they might have become rigid and sterile; in him they were sharpened and clarified precisely because of this process of simplification. Hence his (justifiable) claim never to have written a superfluous word. With their extreme clarity and decisiveness, Beloch's ideas and methods of research were diffused and favorably received in Italy. Besides, if Beloch did not concern himself with Italian culture, he was nevertheless willing to give his time to even the most trivial needs of Italian education: teacher-training examinations, inspections, appointing committees. And he was bound by ties of friendship to colleagues such as Antonio Labriola and Ettore Pais, who honored him with the dedication of the first volume of his *Storia di Roma* (1898).

When Bonghi's friend L. Bodio, who had now achieved European fame as secretary of the new International Institute of Statistics, invited Beloch to collaborate with the *Bulletin de l'Institut International de Statistique*, which started in Rome in 1886, he contributed a number of articles (for Bodio's classical interests see F. Coletti, *Studi sulla popolazione italiana*, Bari, 1923, pp. 218–30). Between 1890 and 1900 his school transformed the study of ancient history in Italy: its products were G. De Sanctis (who graduated in 1892), E. Breccia, G. Cardinali, R. Paribeni, L. Pernier, etc. These were the years recalled by De Sanctis in his obituary of his teacher: "tall and erect in bearing, dignified in his long dark coat, swift in his actions and movements, his eyes restless and animated, his face serene, expressive and shrewd . . . with a trace of an accent and the occasional foreign phrase . . . his words simple, precise and clear" (*Riv. Fil. Class.*, n.s., 7, 1929, p. 141). The best dissertations produced by his school appeared in his *Studi di Storia Antica*, of which six volumes were published between 1891 and 1907, including thirteen monographs, among which were U. Pedroli, *I tributi degli alleati di Atene* (1891); G. De Sanctis, *Contributi alla storia ateniese dalla guerra lamiaca alla cremonidea* (1893); E. Breccia, *Il diritto dinastico nelle monarchie dei successori di Alessandro Magno* (1903); G. Cardinali, *Il regno di Pergamo* (1906). Other dissertations, like that of P. Varese on the *Calendario romano all'età della prima guerra punica* (1902) and of B. Bruno, *La terza guerra sannitica* (1906), are in fact elaborations of Beloch's own theories and as such are valuable for his ideas.

   Meanwhile Beloch had decided to write a history of Greece. Why Greece rather than Rome is easily explained. Apart from the danger of having to compete with Mommsen, Beloch disliked the Romans, whom he considered semibarbaric. His distaste for Roman imperialism (which he passed on, together with the idea of Indo-European superiority, to his pupil De Sanctis) became ever more definite and received its classic formulation in his vigorous paper of 1900 "Der Verfall der antiken Kultur" ("The Decline of Ancient Civilization") (*Hist. Zeitschrift*, 84, 1900, pp. 1–38), in which the ruin of Greece and of ancient civilization in general was laid at the door of the Romans, while Florence was exalted as a new Athens. Perhaps it is correct to assume in the young Beloch the feeling that Ludwig Curtius recognized in the old Beloch: "He knew no higher world than the Pentecontaetia," that is, the period from 480 to 431 B.C. (*Röm. Mitteil.*, 44, 1929, pp. iv–v). He undoubtedly believed, like the majority of his contemporaries in Germany, in the common Indo-European origin of the Greek genius and the German genius. The two Greek histories which had just begun to be published, those of G. Busolt (1885 ff.) and of his colleague and enemy A. Holm (1886 ff.), were such as to convince him of the need for a new Greek history. In Busolt's history Beloch respected only the footnotes; in Holm, whom he regarded as completely uncritical, even the notes were worthless (*cf.* the later explicit comments in *Griech. Gesch.*, 2d ed., I, 2, p. 15; Anhang, p. 422). In another sense his new Greek history was to be the continuation of his battle against the classicism of E. Curtius and the radicalism of Grote which had begun already in *Attische Politik*. But at least in archaic history Beloch was faced with a series of problems and methods of research with which he had not until now been much concerned. The Mycenaean civilization had been discovered by H. Schliemann, but the discovery of the Minoan civilization, which provided a background and a context for the Mycenaean, still lay in the future. Uncertainties of dating and interpretation were inevitable—all the more so given his attitude of radical skepticism towards the legends of Greek origins, not unlike that of Mommsen towards those of Rome. For Beloch, as for Mommsen, the only secure means of discovering anything about the archaic period was to draw inferences from the institutions of later periods. With such a starting point the criticism of literary sources could not be easily reconciled with the analysis of archaeological evidence. The history of the archaic period was to be the part that Beloch revised most often and most drastically in the successive editions of the *Griechische Geschichte*, and it would always remain the least satisfactory part;

even his theory about the Dorians underwent far-reaching modifications. (See the criticism of the first volume of the second edition by M. P. Nilsson in *Götting. Gelehrte Anz.*, 1914, pp. 513–47.)

A first attempt in Italian (probably connected with his promotion to full professor [*ordinario*]) appeared in Rome in 1891, of 146 pages and entitled *Storia greca, Parte Prima: La Grecia antichissima* ("Greek History, Part 1: The Most Ancient Greece"). The publisher was the eccentric dilettante Dr. Fr. M. Pasanisi (on whom see most recently P. Treves, *Athenaeum*, 40, 1963, p. 377 n. 28). Pasanisi prefaced Beloch's work with a foreword ("programma") so inconsequential that Beloch felt obliged to insert a disclaimer: "The author dissociates himself from it completely, and he is not pleased that the reader might be led to assume his agreement with the opinions expressed therein." As one might have expected, two years later a modified version of what had already been published in Italian, together with the rest of the history down to 416 B.C., appeared in German (*Griechische Geschichte*, I, Trübner, Strassburg).

In the Italian version Beloch maintained that the flowering of the Mycenaean civilization was somewhat later than Homer and belonged to the ninth to eighth centuries B.C., while the *Iliad* was dated firmly to the ninth century. The shaft graves of Mycenae were placed in the tenth to ninth centuries B.C. In keeping with the article published shortly before in *Rheinisches Museum* (45, 1890, pp. 555–98) Beloch denied the reality of the Dorian invasion: the Dorians were only the Achaeans under a different name. Phoenician colonization in Sicily and elsewhere was stated to have been later than that of the Greeks (*cf.* the vigorous article "Die Phoeniker am aegaeischen Meer" in *Rheinisches Museum*, 49, 1894, pp. 111–32). The German text (at least as it seems to me) had a slightly different view of the Mycenaean civilization, which was placed between the eleventh and the eighth centuries, with Homer dated to somewhere around the ninth to eighth centuries. Of these bold theories (which were not entirely novel: *cf.* E. Meyer, *Gesch. d. Altertums*, 2, 1893, p. 130) that which denied the Dorian invasion was rejected virtually everywhere except in Italy (De Sanctis, L. Pareti), while that on the chronology of the Mycenaean was quickly overtaken by the results of excavations on Crete; but that on Phoenician colonization was widely accepted (notice the reviews of Holm in *Berl. Phil. Woch.*, 1894, pp. 371–75, 400–404, and B. Niese in *Götting. Gelehrte Anz.*, 1894, pp. 890–904).

This first volume, however, included much more. It offered an original reconstruction of the economic life of archaic and classical Greece, with a strong emphasis on its capitalistic features (*cf.* also "Die Handelsbewegung im Altertum" ["The Movement of Trade in the Ancient World"]), *Conrads Jahrbücher für Nationalökonomie*, 3d ser., 18, 1899, p. 626–31, and "Die Grossindustrie im Altertum" ["Large-scale Industry in the Ancient World"],

Zeitschr. für Socialwissenschaft, 2, 1899, pp. 18–26). The section on religion is characteristic, in that Beloch clung to a naturalistic interpretation of the Greek divinities and found solar cults everywhere, more or less at the level of the first volumes of W. Roscher's "Lexicon" of Greek and Roman mythology; he gave only a small part to the cult of the dead under the influence of E. Rohde. Taking a minimal interest in the poetry of the archaic age — except for chronological questions such as the dates of Alcaeus, Sappho, and Theognis (*Rheinisches Museum*, 45, 1890, pp. 465–73; 50, 1895, pp. 250–68) — he dealt sympathetically with the move toward "enlightenment" associated with Euripides, Thucydides, and the beginnings of scientific research. His preference for the quantitative rather than the qualitative, though never taken to extremes, caused him to play down great personalities; another factor in this was his delight in appearing to be an iconoclast: "Anyone who regards individual personalities, or great men, as the driving force of historical development — rather than the masses, whose efforts are embodied in great men — would do well to leave ancient history alone" (I, p. 33). He denies any creative thinking to Pericles (I, p. 466), and he makes no secret of his antipathy to Socrates.

It should be noted, however, that Beloch's reputation for bold and ill-founded conjecture is based at least in part on theories that were advanced after the appearance of the first edition of the *Griechische Geschichte*. The denial of the historicity of Draco was reserved for the second edition (I, 1, p. 350); in the first edition Draco is historical (I, p. 307). So too the episode of Cylon was still placed before Draco (I, p. 352), not after Solon in 552 (I, 1, p. 370); and only in the second edition, and rather hesitantly, did he credit Pisistratus with the system of so-called Cleisthenic tribes.

The first volume of the *Griechische Geschichte* came out a few months before the second volume of Meyer's *Geschichte des Altertums*. Meyer was still in time to recognize in his preface the importance of the work of "my friend Beloch" and to welcome it as akin to his own in its aims and methods, despite his open avowal of a more conservative approach to the tradition. He then reviewed it in *Liter. Centralblatt* (1894, col. 109–14) in pages remarkable for their precision in noting points of agreement and disagreement, especially concerning oriental influences and social developments.

In point of fact we may now, after seventy years, be permitted to say that Meyer was far superior to Beloch in his treatment of archaic Greece (a comparison by I. Bruns can be found in *Beilage zur Allgemeinen Zeitung*, 21–22 June 1894, partially reprinted in *Vorträge und Aufsätze*, 1905, pp. 31–47). Less radical in his conjectures (he placed the peak of Mycenaean civilization in the fifteenth century B.C. and admitted the reality of the Dorian invasion), Meyer was above all much more subtle in the interpretation of culture and religion; it is sufficient to compare their respective treatments of Orphism. De Sanctis freely admitted in conversation that of the two works Meyer's had immediately struck him as the more profound, and had revealed to him the nature of the Greek "Middle Ages" (cf. A. Momigliano, *Secondo contributo,* Rome, 1960, p. 308 [above, p. 60]). It nevertheless remains true that Meyer and Beloch between them created a new situation in the study of archaic Greece, and it is arguable that this new situation had some influence on the contemporary works of Pais.

The second volume of the *Griechische Geschichte* appeared in 1897. Dedicated to Ettore Pais (a dedication later deleted for good reasons in the second edition), it covered the period from the Sicilian Expedition to the conquest of Asia by Alexander the Great.

The nineteenth-century approach to the interpretation of Athenian politics that had earlier been offered in *Attische Politik* was now extended to Greek history in general. Theramenes is esteemed as a moderate; Philip of Macedon is the Hohenzollern who unifies Greece. But his son Alexander was too international, too romantic, and — perhaps — too cruel for Beloch's bourgeois taste: Parmenion, the ancient von Moltke, was the true conqueror of Asia (II, p. 625). The most original part was once again the description of social and economic life. The first two volumes were translated into Russian by M. Herrschensohn (Geršenzon) in Moscow in 1897–99. The translator, a Jew, managed to eliminate some anti-Semitic statements (on which see below) and also incorporated some corrections made by Beloch himself.

While working on the third volume, which was to cover the Hellenistic world in the third century B.C., Beloch returned to his studies of population in the medieval world, largely based on first-hand archival research in Italy, France, Belgium, Germany, and Holland; there are also signs that he made use of manuscripts in the British Museum.

In 1899 he published a study of the population of the Venetian republic (*Conrads Jahrbücher für Nationalökonomie,* 3d ser., 18, 1899, pp. 1–49; cf. *Nuovo Archivio Veneto,* 1, 1903, pp. 5–49) and in 1900 a general sketch of the demographic history of Europe during the Middle Ages and Renaissance (*Zeitschr. für Socialwissenschaft,* 3, 1900, pp. 405–23; 765–86; later translated into Italian in the *Biblioteca dell'Economista,* 5th ser., 19, 1908). Notice also his studies on "Antike und moderne Grossstädte" ["Ancient and Modern Big Cities"], in *Zeitschr. für Socialwissenschaft* (1, 1898, pp. 413–23; 500–508); and "Das Verhältnis der Geschlechter in Italien seit dem 16. Jhdt." ("Family Relations in Italy since the Sixteenth Century") in *Conrads Jahrbücher für Nationalökonomie* (3d ser., 16, 1898, pp. 64–81). Around the same time he engaged in a dispute with O. Seeck, who in *Conrads Jahrbücher für Nationalökonomie* (3d ser., 13, 1897, pp. 161–76) had attacked Beloch's conjectures and set himself up as a champion of the tradition. Beloch replied (ibid., pp. 321–43) with a reasoned defense of his method and undoubtedly showed himself altogether more competent than his adversary in handling demographic problems. To specific problems concerning population in the ancient world he went back again and again: for example on the size of the Greek army at Plataea (*Fleckeisens Jahrbücher für class. Philol.,* 137, 1888, pp. 324–28); on the population of Sicily (*Archivio Storico Siciliano*, 14, 1889, pp. 1–83; 20, 1895, pp. 63–70); on the population of the Italian cities (*Atene e Roma*, 1, 1898, pp. 257–78); on the population of Gaul (*Rheinisches Museum*, 54, 1899, pp. 414–45); on the Roman censuses (*Klio*, 3, 1903, pp. 471–90). Beloch's calculations concerning Sicily aroused particular hostility (for which see Holm, *Geschichte Siciliens*, 3, 1898, p. 387). The importance Beloch attributed to numbers in determining the fate of civilizations, and incidentally in explaining the German victory over France in 1870, can be illustrated by the following remark: "[In the Renaissance] the Latins ("Romanen") had a significant numerical superiority over the Germans; the ratio was three to two. And this numerical superiority is the principal explanation of the essentially Romance character of European culture in the Middle Ages and the Renaissance" (*Zeitschr. für Socialwissenschaft*, 3, 1900, p. 785).

In 1904 the third volume of the *Griechische Geschichte* appeared, in two parts, one of text, the other appendices containing specialized research. The work, dedicated to Meyer, renewed in chronology, genealogy, and in his favorite field of historical geography the results of Droysen and Niese (the second of whom was held in low esteem by Beloch: *cf. Hist. Zeitschrift*, 85, 1900, p. 474).

The Hellenistic economy was described for the first time by someone completely familiar with the new science of papyrology. Beloch's tendency to modernize and his sympathy for bourgeois-capitalist society were given full rein. It is easy to see that J. Burckhardt's *Griechische Kulturgeschichte* could not have pleased him (see his review of it in *Zeitschr. für Socialwissenschaft*, 2, 1899, p. 928; 4, 1901, p. 479). On the other hand Beloch was certainly not the man to appreciate the elegance of Hellenistic art and the ambiguities of Hellenistic religion, nor the supranational atmosphere of Hellenistic culture. But he sensed the drama in the clash between Greek civilization and Roman power. The implicit parallel between Hellenistic civilization and that of nineteenth-century Germany was recognized and made explicit by W. F. Otto in a long and admiring discussion in *Zeitschr. für Socialwissenschaft* (8, 1905, pp. 700–712; 781–94). The young Otto recognized Beloch's exceptional capacity to "give shape." Even Wilamowitz, who was not well disposed to Beloch (the hostility was reciprocated), had to recognize the importance of the new work: a typical judgment in *Staat und Gesellschaft der Griechen* (2d ed., 1923, p. 213).

In his autobiography Beloch could justly say, "And this time it was a complete success." Without ever becoming a conspicuous force in German culture, Beloch had nevertheless found a public, especially in periodicals and handbooks of sociology and politics. Notice for example his article "Zinsfuss im klass. Altertum" ["Interest Rates in Antiquity"] in *Handwör-*

terbuch der Staatswissenschaft (Suppl. II, 1897) and his review of R. Pöhlmann entitled "Socialismus und Kommunismus im Altertum" (*Zeitschr. für Socialwissenschaft*, 4, 1901, pp. 359-64). Young ancient historians studied his work. If the new fashion of Hellenistic studies was largely connected with papyrology and led by U. Wilcken, the opinions of Beloch were widely discussed in Germany and elsewhere. That people in Germany were turning to look at Beloch is confirmed by the fact that he was invited to contribute a résumé of Greek history to the *Ullsteins Weltgeschichte* edited by J. v. Pflugk-Harthung. Published in 1909 (I, pp. 139-395), it gave Beloch an opportunity to rewrite the archaic period, to include the Minoan civilization, to connect it with the Mycenaean culture, and to separate Mycenae (16th–13th centuries B.C.) from Homer. The Mycenaean civilization was held to be non-Greek, even if its "bearers" were of Greek descent. This summary of Greek history—later translated into Swedish and Italian (Milan, 1912)—was subsequently reissued in revised and updated (and sometimes abbreviated) form in the *Propyläen Weltgeschichte* edited by W. Goetz (II, 1931, pp. 3–240), and in this new form represents Beloch's last thoughts on Greek history. It is not uninteresting to compare the texts of 1909 and 1931; there is for example a subtle change in the pages on Socrates (*Ullstein*, pp. 288–89; *Propyläen*, pp. 173–74). Meanwhile E. Norden invited Beloch to write for his *Einleitung in die Altertumswissenschaft* the history of the Hellenistic world and that of the Roman Republic (1st ed., 1914); the little volume, which was translated into Italian by G. Capone (Bari, 1933), is important because of the section on Rome, which brings together Beloch's views, published and unpublished, and has vigorous pages on method, particularly on the Etruscan question.

Amid all this flurry of research, which included a journey to Crete with the Italian mission in 1908 to study the Minoan civilization at first hand (*cf. Ausonia*, 4, 1909, pp. 219–37, where among other things the Cretan conquest of Greece is denied), Beloch remained a dedicated teacher. From 1900 to 1910 he took responsibility also for the teaching of ancient geography and founded a *Biblioteca di geografia storica*, which published three works by his pupils (G. Colasanti, *Fregellae*, 1906; idem, *Pinna*, 1907; E. Grossi, *Aquinum*, 1907; to which must be added *Fermo in Piceno* by G. Napoletani, which appeared in *Studi di Storia Antica*). At that time Beloch thought of composing a modern version of Ph. Cluverius's *Italia antiqua*, and he took advantage of his travels as government inspector to visit every corner of Italy again and again. The works of his pupils were evidently destined to prepare for this work (*cf.* his polemic with H. Nissen in *Woch. Klass. Philol.*, 25, 1908, nos. 6 and 12). From 1909 to 1912 he gave as part of his duties a course of lectures on ancient history in the department of education that was attached to the Faculty of Letters at Rome. He himself explains in his autobiography how he often had to stand in for Halbherr, who was active in Crete, in teaching

Greek epigraphy (records at the University of Rome show that he replaced Halbherr during his absences through all the academic years for 1897–98 to 1904–5 and again from 1910–11 to 1911–12). Beloch continued to command attention and influence as a teacher, even if the rise of the separate schools of Pais and De Sanctis and the new cultural interests provoked by the Idealistic movement and by modernism (the latter particularly prominent at the University of Rome) tended to reduce the attraction of his teaching.

In 1910 his thirty years as a teacher were celebrated by a volume in his honor of *Saggi di storia antica e di archeologia* ("Essays in Ancient History and Archaeology"). His principal pupil in the period 1900–1910 was Giovanni Costa, in whose support—more as the author of doubtful research on the Fasti than as an intelligent student of the late Empire—he risked quarreling even with his faithful pupils and friends De Sanctis and Cardinali. His courses were followed by G. Pasquali, G. Levi Della Vida, L. Salvatorelli, and other future masters of related disciplines. His demographic studies had now become models for many younger scholars. He himself continued to publish articles—for example on the population of Sicily under Spanish rule and on Modena (*Riv. Ital. Sociologia,* 8, 1904, pp. 28–45; 12, 1908, pp. 1–48) which were later combined in the *Bevölkerungsgeschichte Italiens.*

But above all his school was sustained by pupils of De Sanctis. With a loyalty which contrasting religious ideas, differences of historical temperament (rather than of method), and vigor of personal reactions never weakened for a moment, De Sanctis always considered Beloch's teaching as a necessary complement to his own. It became the normal practice for the best students of the Turin school to spend at least a year completing their studies at Rome. Thus Beloch came to have a direct influence on Luigi Pareti, who dedicated his *Studi siciliani e italioti* (1914) jointly to De Sanctis and Beloch as teachers, and who was perhaps, in his rationalist and skeptical attitude to tradition, closer to Beloch than to De Sanctis. Another who attached himself to Beloch was A. Ferrabino, who was later to become the most penetrating interpreter of Beloch's thought (*Riv. Fil. Class.,* n.s., 3, 1925, pp. 247–61; reprinted in *Scritti di filosofia della storia,* Florence, 1962, pp. 61–74) and who was especially stimulated by him, both in the study of Greek economics and military organization and in the formulation of the problems of national unity in ancient Greece.

In the years before 1914 P. Fraccaro was teaching in a secondary school in Rome. Fraccaro showed Beloch friendship and profound understanding, born of intellectual and moral sympathy. It is therefore all the more noteworthy that Fraccaro gave an impartial assessment of Beloch in *Riv. Fil. Class.* (n.s., 6, 1928, pp. 551–69; 7, 1929, pp. 267–76; *cf.* A. Momigliano, in *Mem. R. Accad. Lincei,* 8th s., 15, 1960, p. 363 [reprinted in *Terzo contributo,* p. 829]). But none of his pupils and friends continued Beloch's most characteristic work on the demography and economy of the classical world. Those Italians who did concern themselves with such matters — E. Ciccotti, G. Ferrero, C. Barbagallo — had no contact with him; he despised them as dilettanti, while they distrusted him as a representative of the pedantic and antidemocratic German tradition.

Meanwhile, prepared and accompanied by a long series of articles (several of which were published in the journal *Klio*), the new edition of the *Griechische Geschichte* began to appear in 1912 (I–II, Trübner, Strassburg, 1912–14; III–IV, De Gruyter, Berlin, 1922–27). The three volumes had thus become four, and each volume now included two parts, one of text and one of discussions (often previously published in periodicals, but always revised); in other words, the structure of the third volume of the first edition was now extended to the whole work.

The value of the new edition in relation to the first lay precisely in this great mass of detailed research, which was equivalent to a revision of all the evidence of the sources for the military history, genealogies, chronology, and political geography of the Greek world.

Because of its clarity of method, its systematic character, its brevity, and its acuteness, the work in this revised format became an indispensable aid to research and teaching which even today remains unsurpassed. It is naturally unthinkable that Beloch could have changed his collectivist-nationalist conception of Greek history; indeed he outlined it even more sharply, especially in the new introduction on "personality in Greek history," which was also translated into Italian in *Rivista Italiana di Sociologia* (16, 1912, pp. 1–15). It was not in Beloch's nature to give in to new fashions and to introduce local color or psychological refinements into his account (on the absence of these features see the review of H. Berve, in *Gnomon*, 4, 1928, pp. 469–79; for other criticisms R. Herzog, in *Hist. Zeitschrift*, 134, 1926, pp. 554–61). Also the criteria for archaic history were little changed, even if as early as 1897 (*Hist. Zeitschrift*, 79, 1897, pp. 193–223) Beloch had gone so far as to concede, under the influence of P. Kretschmer's linguistic researches, that other Greeks had preceded the Dorians in the Peloponnese. It was equally unthinkable that Beloch should have recognized the implicit conflicts between his liberalism and his nationalism, between his dislike of Rome and his love of Macedon, between his racism and his cult of numbers. The new introduction to the history of Greece must be considered together with the article, published around the same time, on "Die Volkszahl als Faktor und Gradmesser der historischen Entwickelung" ("Population Size as a Factor and Index of Historical Development"), in *Hist. Zeitschrift* (111, 1913, pp. 321–37), which was his opening lecture at Leipzig in 1912.

Beloch himself wrote in his autobiography: "Finally, when I was almost into my sixties, they remembered at Leipzig that I too existed." He was offered the possibility of a chair in succession to U. Wilcken, but the post, for which C. Cichorius also applied, was not uncontested. Having requested leave of absence from the University of Rome for family reasons, Beloch spent the academic year 1912–13 at Leipzig, where he had F. Oertel as an assistant. It was during this period, if not before, that he met U. Kahrstedt, who always admired him and was perhaps his only German disciple, even in the matter of the Dorian invasion (*cf. Neue Jahrbücher,* 1919, pp. 70–75; *Deutsche Literaturz.,* 1924, col. 802–13; 1926, col. 16–24). But at the end of the academic session Beloch decided to return to Italy and to resume his chair at the University of Rome. Apart from family reasons, including the fact that his American wife did not want to live in Germany, his decision to give up the chair at Leipzig immediately after accepting it—like the decision to accept it in the first place—was the product of a complicated cultural situation the main features of which need to be briefly outlined.

The idea, put forward around 1911, of appointing Guglielmo Ferrero, as an exceptional honor, to a chair of Roman history at the University of Rome unleashed a controversy which, largely thanks to Pais, eventually came to involve Beloch. Pais and Beloch were basically in agreement in not wanting Ferrero to have the chair, and in this they were supported by the authoritative opinion of D. Comparetti (*cf.* his *Poesia e pensiero del mondo antico,* 1944, pp. 555–56).

In an article in *Rivista d'Italia* (1911, 2, pp. 868–73) Beloch had pointed to Ferrero as an example of uncritical traditionalism; indeed he already hinted there at an idea that was later to become dominant in his *Römische Geschichte* of 1926, namely that history should not be narrated; the analytical part is the only one capable of rigorous treatment (*cf.* also "Storiografia e scienza storica" in *Riv. Ital. Sociologia,* 16, 1912, pp. 427–32, in reply to C. Barbagallo). But Pais used Ferrero's candidacy as an opportunity to stake his own claim to a chair of Roman history at Rome, and to make an underhand attack on Beloch, whom he called "a well-meaning visitor, a learned representative of Teutonic science," who had never taken Italian citizenship and did not even write his books in Italian (*Rivista d'Italia,* 15, 1912, pp. 43–61; 693–754; *cf. Studi storici per l'antichità classica,* 4, 1911, pp. 415–54; ibid., 5, 1912, pp. 194–221). Pais was suggesting that the new nationalism, which had been unleashed by the Libyan War, was sufficient reason to give an Italian the chair of the history of Rome at the University of Rome. Beloch's replies (ibid., pp. 535–37, 881–82) are firm and dignified; among other things he reminded Pais that he had been a pupil of Mommsen, "who was never a friend to me," and concluded, "I believed that I had become something more than a 'visitor' in my long years of residence in Italy, which I regard as my second fatherland." The decision to accept a chair in Germany was evidently not unconnected with the situation that had found expression in these polemics. Nationalism, of which Pais, breaking his old friendship, made himself the spokesman, disturbed and personally offended the historian who was now growing old and was aware of his own worth. It is possible moreover that he was feeling a sense of isolation even in relation to his own pupils.

But in Germany Beloch must have found other difficulties. He had the reputation in Germany of being of Jewish origin. Whether or not this notion had any basis in reality is of little importance. Notwithstanding the fact that it had been publicly denied on Beloch's behalf by his electoral committee in the elections of 1893, it was an opinion shared by everyone, even by those, like Wilamowitz, who were certainly not inclined to indulge in that sort of discrimination. His Jewish origin is referred to as an established fact by F. Oertel in *Gnomon* (5, 1929, pp. 461–64). It was given some credence by Beloch's appearance and his noble Semitic profile. To this suspicion of being Jewish Beloch responded by referring with every breath to "our Indo-European ancestors" and making a parade of anti-Semitism. Already in the first edition of the *Griechische Geschichte* he asserted, "A negro who speaks English is not for that reason an Englishman, and equally a Jew who spoke Greek did not pass in antiquity for a Greek any more than today a Jew who speaks German passes for a German" (I, 1893, p. 34 n. 1; the part concerning the Jews was omitted from the Russian translation, I, p. 27, but retained in the second German edition, I, 1, p. 67). Such anti-Semitic sentiments explain the particular animosity with which he later condemned the work of F. Münzer in the *Römische Geschichte* of 1926 and taint the whole of his autobiography; in his historical works he had little opportunity to express them, and they are bound up with his anti-Christian views.

Now these attitudes certainly did not go unobserved in Italy, and it was well known how much he tended to disparage universally respected men such as the Egyptologist G. Lumbroso, his colleague in the Faculty of Letters Emanuel Loewy, and his former pupil who was later to become director of the National Library of Florence, S. Morpurgo. But in Italy, where there was no Jewish problem, Beloch's anti-Semitism appeared to be one of his outlandish eccentricities, like his excessive fondness for the wine of the Castelli Romani, and could be shrugged off with a smile. Besides, the Jews were not the only ones to suffer from his sharp tongue (he had replied to De Sanctis, who had cited B. Croce, "You know, that man is an ass!"). Only after the racial campaign demanded by the Nazis was there any explicit comment in Italy on this aspect of Beloch's personality (E. Breccia, *Uomini e Libri*, Pisa, 1959, pp. 231–43, with letters of Beloch).

In Germany naturally things were different. Those who disapproved of anti-Semitism opposed Beloch as an anti-Semite. The anti-Semites however looked down on Beloch because they suspected that he was trying by this means to hide his alleged Jewish origin. And Beloch was responsible for

circulating at Leipzig one of those anti-Semitic epigrams that he found amus-
ing, the one against O. Hirschfeld as editor of Mommsen:

> "Jude, was treibst Du?
> Je nun: ich handle
> Mit Mommsens abgelegten Kleidern."
> ("Jew, what's that you're doing?
> Ah, now: I'm doing a nice deal
> In Mommsen's cast-off clothing.")

A local "Geheimer Regierungsrat" ("privy councillor") responded with the
verses:

> "Und Jude, was treibst Du?
> Je nun: ich veralbere Leipzig."
> ("And Jew, what's that you're doing?
> Ah, now: I'm poking fun at Leipzig.")

(Further details in O. Th. Schulz, *Bursians Jahresbericht*, 254, 1936, pp. 62–
65). It is not surprising that Beloch quickly took the road back to Italy. In
Germany he ended as a victim of the very anti-Semitism that he had
nourished throughout his life.

On his return to Italy Beloch was made Commendatore della Corona
d'Italia on 30 November 1913 (he had already been awarded a knighthood
of the Order of SS. Maurizio e Lazzaro in February 1911), to mark official
satisfaction that he had resumed his chair at Rome. It only remains to add
that, during his absence, not only the idea of creating a new chair of Roman
history, but also the next idea, which B. Croce among others opposed, that
a chair in the philosophy of history should be created at Rome for Ferrero,
had evaporated.

In 1914–15 Beloch made his voice heard, as he was entitled to, in support
of Italian neutrality. In the *Giornale d'Italia* of 9 February 1915 he published
an article on "Lo spettro germanico" ("The German Spectre"), a polemic
against the interventionism of Arturo Labriola, and he had no difficulty in
showing that Labriola was ill-informed about pan-Germanism. A curious
debate ensued, in which Labriola's response (ibid., 11 February) was again
answered by Beloch on 12 February, and during the following two weeks B.
Croce, N. Colaianni, P. Papa, and P. Bonfante all had their say, with great
fairness. In the end the affair petered out into a politically irrelevant anecdote. When war broke out—and at this stage it was not yet against Germany
—Beloch kept his chair, but by a resolution of the Academic Council of the
University of Rome his courses were suspended "for reasons of public
order." In a noble letter of 11 January 1916 (preserved in the University
archives) Beloch asked the rector if he might at least be permitted to put
on a course of reading classes on the work of an ancient author: "After

belonging to this Faculty for nearly forty years I would find it very hard to
have no dealings with those young people whom I have directed for so long,
whom I love, and from whom I have received so many proofs of affection.
An old teacher, if he is to stay alive, needs to teach." In a letter of 18 February
the rector refused this request. For the rest the vigilance of friends and the
good sense of F. Ruffini, Minister of Education in the Boselli cabinet,
ensured that he was not seriously molested. According to De Sanctis and
Breccia, it was made clear to Beloch in 1915 that if he wanted Italian citizenship it would be conferred upon him without formalities; but it was also on
the advice of De Sanctis that Beloch decided not to ask for it. After war was
declared on Germany in August 1916 there were further attacks on him,
one of them in Parliament by the Hon. De Felice-Giuffrida on 9 March 1917;
to judge from the parliamentary record it does not seem to have been taken
too seriously. The situation became critical only after Caporetto, and it
appears that some rash statements by Beloch played into the hands of his
enemies. He was officially pensioned off on 11 January 1918 and interned at
Siena, while his house and his books in Rome were impounded. His chair at
Rome was taken by Pais, who was now openly an enemy.

This was the beginning of a period of hardship for Beloch, all the more
so because his wife, who had stayed in Rome, died on 2 April 1918 (Beloch
had been allowed to return to Rome to be with her, and, on his own testimony in the autobiography, he received considerate treatment all the time
he was in Siena). In 1919 he was allowed to transfer to Florence, but he was
still considered an enemy alien (something which oddly he blamed on S.
Morpurgo). Later he recovered his house and his books in Rome, where he
went back to live. First Croce and then A. Anile as Ministers of Education
concerned themselves with getting his chair restored. The difficulty, apart
from psychological and bureaucratic obstructions, was the fact that in the
meantime it had become obligatory for university professors to have Italian
citizenship. Finally, by royal decree on 20 December 1923, Italian citizenship was conferred upon him. At the same time a new chair of Greek history was instituted at the University of Rome. To gain time, the job was
entrusted to Beloch for the academic year 1923–24, and then on 30 November 1924 he was restored to his post as permanent professor with all his
seniority since 1879 unimpaired.

Although old and infirm, Beloch returned to teaching with his usual
commitment. His students were now few, but among them at least one,
A. Gitti, became a disciple and later brought to a chair his master's theories
on archaic Greek history. In those years there began to form in the minds
of the younger generation an image of the grand old historian who every
evening, after hours of concentrated work, and having replaced all the
books on the shelf, would leave his house at Via Pompeo Magno 5, hunched
and unkempt, to go up to the Pincio to contemplate the sunset; then, if

company were available, he would proceed in his cups "to build a wall between the science of the evening and that of the morning." He was still teaching a class on 2 February 1929; on the night of 6 February he died while seated at his desk, after working throughout the day.

In the eleven difficult and eventful years since 1917 he had done nothing but work with ever-increasing tenacity, and with that love of truth and clarity which was in his nature and from which every trace of boorishness was burned and purified. His work gave him solace against increasing loneliness and the pain caused by the defeat of his distant and ungrateful country, to which he dedicated impassioned words in the conclusion of his autobiography. (On his political opinions during his last years, founded negatively on hatred of "Frenchmen, Jews, and socialists," see U. Kahrstedt, in *Nachr. Gesell. Wiss. Göttingen*, Geschäftl. Mitt., 1928–29, p. 81, and *cf.* also the characteristic passage of *Griech. Geschichte*, IV, 2, 1927, p. 291.) While under house-arrest in Siena (according to information provided by De Sanctis) he had composed the greater part of a *Wirtschaftsgeschichte Athens* ("Economic History of Athens"), recalling from memory the literary and epigraphic texts that he was unable to consult. The work (along with much else) remains unpublished. He completed, as has been noted, the *Griechische Geschichte* in 1927, adding an appendix to the second edition of volume I so as to bring it up to date from 1912. He wrote several articles on Greek history (for example on the authenticity of the Olympic lists, *Hermes*, 64, 1929, pp. 192–98; on Themistocles, ibid., 55, 1920, pp. 311–18; and on Epicurean texts in *Riv. Fil. Class.*, n.s., 4, 1926, pp. 331–36), various discussions of Hellenistic and Roman chronology (the last of which is in *Klio*, 22, 1929, pp. 464–66) returning again in 1927 to his beloved Homer (*Hermes*, 62, 1927, pp. 447–52). A couple of studies of the Second Punic War and its sources published in 1915 (*Hist. Zeitschrift*, 114, 1915, pp. 1–16; *Hermes*, 50, 1915, pp. 357–72) were not taken any further, perhaps because of the appearance soon afterwards of De Sanctis's history of the Punic Wars. But Beloch began during the war years, and published at Berlin in 1926, a substantial volume on archaic Roman history dedicated to past and present colleagues at the University of Rome (*Römische Geschichte*). The book consisted of analytical studies, not of narrative. In these investigations Beloch, who had always been anti-Mommsenian, referred only to Mommsen, ostentatiously and deliberately passing over everything that had been written in Italy, not only by Pais, but also by his own pupil De Sanctis. It is true that on some matters Beloch reproduced conclusions that he had originally arrived at many years earlier: for example he had already written about the dedication by the Latin League to Diana at Aricia, in *Fleckeisens Jahrbücher* (129, 1883, pp. 169–75) and on the supposed duplications in accounts of the Samnite Wars, in E. Pais's *Studi storici* (1, 1908, pp. 1–13). The first part presents a systematic revision of the tradition, and advances theories on the dictatorship (presented as the regular chief magistracy at Rome after the end of the monarchy), on the consular tribunes, on the date of the *Foedus Cassianum*; etc., which have been the point of departure for innumerable discussions and have subsequently been developed further by K. Hanell and the Swedish school. The second part completes and revises *Der italische Bund*. Problems of economic development and cultural life are not discussed. The book, which in Italy was subjected to the criticism of Fraccaro, in Germany to that of F. Münzer (*Gnomon*, 3, 1927, pp. 595–99), and in France to that of A. Piganiol (*Journ. des Savants*, 1928, pp. 104–13), would be enough on its own to make the reputation of a historian; the aged Beloch had lost none of his clarity, brevity, independence, and penetration.

Meanwhile he was continuing and developing his lifelong research on the population of medieval and modern Europe. To this end he began to travel once more in Italy and abroad each summer. At his death the history of the population of Italy was nearing completion and was gradually published, first by De Sanctis (*Bevölkerungsgeschichte Italiens*, I–II, De Gruyter, Berlin, 1937 and 1939), and then by L. Pareti (vol. III, 1961, and second edition of vol. II, 1961). Thus the youthful dream of giving Italy a history of its demographic fluctuations over the centuries was fulfilled. Beloch himself, perhaps without exaggeration, attributed the same level of importance to this work as to the *Griechische Geschichte*. The history of the population of all Europe was never completed, although unpublished material from this project survives. On the outstanding merits of Beloch's work on demography, which must of course be judged in relation to the methods used in such research during his lifetime, see R. Mols, *Introduction à la démographie historique des villes d'Europe* (I, 1954, p. 144); J. C. Russell, *Late Ancient and Medieval Population* in *Trans. Amer. Philosoph. Society* (n.s., 48, 1958); and P. J. Jones, *Engl. Hist. Rev.* (77, 1962, pp. 723–27). Beloch's demographic research, which appeared so late, has so far exercised only slight influence on works of Italian social history. But in a certain sense all of Beloch's work still has an unpredictable future. As a pioneer of the social history and the "quantitative" economic history of ancient Greece, he soon found himself isolated. When he published the second edition of the *Griechische Geschichte*, most people's interests were directed towards those aspects of civilization — such as religion, political theory, and "life-styles"— in which he was obviously too weak. On the other hand, those in Germany who sought to supersede him (which was never De Sanctis's aim) only carried his racism to extreme lengths, at a time when racism was no longer a way of thinking, but a way of killing, and they only succeeded in highlighting the elegance and subtlety of Beloch. The histories of Greece, or of "the Greek Man," by H. Berve, F. Schachermeyr, and M. Pohlenz certainly do not have the value of Beloch's. The true rival account remains, for the pre-Hellenistic age, that of E. Meyer. Outside Germany, the works of De Sanctis and of G. Glotz represent at least partial alternatives. Only now, more than thirty years after his death, are Beloch's works beginning to be studied by a generation whose principal interest is in social history.

Bibliographical Note

There is as yet no biography or bibliography of Beloch, and his essays have never been collected. It should be noted that he reviewed books in a variety of periodicals, such as *Litter. Centralblatt, Historische Zeitschrift, Deutsche Literaturzeitung, La Cultura, Rivista di Filologia, Zeitschrift für Socialwissenschaft*. A bibliography would naturally have to include a concordance between Beloch's numerous articles and his books. Given the impossibility of such a bibliography, I have attempted to indicate, in the course of the foregoing text, at least the more important articles, particularly those whose content is not refashioned in the larger works; for this purpose I have made use of the collection of Beloch's offprints belonging to his daughter, Professor M. Piazolla Beloch. Important for the reconstruction of Beloch's cultural milieu and his scholarly connections is the large "Miscellanea Beloch" (a collection of opuscula sent to Beloch) in the possession of the Institute of Archaeology and History of Art in Rome.

For the events concerning the elections of 1893 I have consulted the local newspapers of Stralsund.

The most important obituaries of Beloch seem to be the following: G. De Sanctis, in *Riv. Fil. Class.*, 57, 1929, pp. 141–51, reprinted with useful comments by P. Treves, *Lo studio dell'antichità classica nell'ottocento*, Milan-Naples, 1962, pp. 1231–46; E. Breccia, in *Bull. Soc. Archéol. Alexandrie*, 7, 1929, pp. 79–81; U. Kahrstedt, in *Nachr. Gesell. Wiss. Göttingen*, Geschäftl. Mitteil., 1928–29, pp. 78–82; C. F. Lehmann-Haupt, *Klio*, 23, 1930, pp. 100–106; E. Täubler, in *Zeitschr. Savigny-Stift.*, Rom. Abt., 49, 1929, p. 700. *Cf. Deutsches Biogr. Jahrbuch*, 11, 1929, p. 344. Among the characteristic judgments of Beloch notice for example B. Croce, *Storia della storiografia italiana nel secolo decimonono*, 3d ed., II, Bari, 1947, p. 247, already in *La Critica*, 27, 1929, p. 253, on which G. De Sanctis, *Riv. Fil. Class.*, 7, 1929, p. 567; U. Wilamowitz, in Mommsen-Wilamowitz, *Briefwechsel*, 1935, p. 487 (from the year 1894); R. Pöhlmann, *Grundriss der Griech. Geschichte*, 3d ed., 1906, p. 8 (with other references); H. Bengtson, *Il veltro*, 2, 1962, pp. 288–90; R. Bianchi Bandinelli, *Belfagor*, 20, 1965, p. 481.

NINE

Jacob Bernays

I

In 1839, at the age of twenty-four, Jacob Bachofen came to England to study medieval law. Fifteen years later the time he had spent in England still seemed to him the best of his life. The only unpleasant experience was a visit to Oxford: "Oxford entsprach meinen Erwartungen nicht."[1] But he escaped from Oxford to Cambridge, and there he found what he wanted. There he indulged in his favorite hunt for medieval "Prozessualisten." The good Cambridge dons did not quite understand what he was after, but apparently Magdalene College offered him a fellowship. Before the end of 1840 Bachofen was back in his native Basel where he settled down for the rest of his life.

His different reactions to Oxford and Cambridge are not surprising. Oxford was then in the middle of the Anglo-Catholic revival led by Newman. Mark Pattison, who was born two years before Bachofen in 1813, was busy transcribing medieval lives of saints, not medieval "Prozessualisten." At Cambridge, the Apostles were studying Niebuhr and Savigny, and even G. B. Vico. Connop Thirlwall, soon to become the Bishop of St. David's (1840), had translated Niebuhr and was writing a *History of Greece* according to Niebuhr's method.[2] Bachofen, a pupil of Savigny, was sure of a good reception in that group. Nobody could guess that within a few years Bachofen

"Jacob Bernays," *Mededelingen der Koninklijke Nederlandse Akademie van Wetenschappen,* Afd. Letterkunde, Nieuwe Reeks, Deel 32, no. 5 (1969), pp. 151–78; *Quinto contributo* (1975), pp. 127–58; French translation, *Problèmes d'historiographie ancienne et moderne* (1983), pp. 441–74; Italian translation, *Pagine ebraiche* (1987), pp. 157–80.

would have developed into the most fiery opponent of Niebuhr and would have disagreed with Savigny—affection notwithstanding.

Oxford went German when the Oxford Movement was defeated. In 1845 Newman left Oxford; in 1850 the Royal Commission was set up. The first to change, though gradually, was Mark Pattison himself, who emerged from the Oxford Movement as a free thinker in holy orders with a strong bias towards German *Wissenschaft*. His revulsion from Newman is best expressed by a passage in his *Memoirs:* "A. P. Stanley once said to me 'How different the fortunes of the Church of England might have been if Newman had been able to read German.' That puts the matter in a nut-shell."[3] The failure to become the Rector of Lincoln in 1851 gave Pattison ten years of sadness and of leisure which he exploited not only for solitary fishing in Yorkshire and Scotland, but also for visits to Germany. In 1859 he was there in his official capacity as an inspector appointed by the Education Committee of the Privy Council to report on elementary education in Prussia and other German states. More frequently he went to German universities to learn. When at last in 1861 he became the very influential head of his own college he made it his business to encourage Oxford dons to go to Germany to complete their studies.

John Sparrow, who knows more than anybody else about Mark Pattison, has recently devoted an absorbing little book to the difficulties in which Pattison involved himself by advocating in Oxford the Humboldtian idea of a university.[4] Pattison had started with the assumption that, in Oxford, colleges had to be developed as independent units and that college tutors, not the university professors, were the potential scholars in a German sense. He recognized at the end that the Royal Commission had transformed Oxford into a "cramming-shop." Examinations—not *Kultur*—had become the main preoccupation of tutors and undergraduates. Thus in 1868 Pattison wrote his suggestions for academic organization to reverse this trend. He now championed professors against tutors. He proposed the abolition of the colleges and of the fellowships and the transfer of their endowments to the university. Those colleges which did not become headquarters of Faculties might be used as non-compulsory halls of residence. In Pattison's dream students would flock to Oxford for the mere love of learning. If any of this was really meant as a practical suggestion, he lived long enough, until 1884, to be disabused.

The Warden of All Souls is not the man to miss the relevance of Pattison's experience to our 1965 or 1968 university problems. Old Pattison had to admit what young Pattison had not needed to know: that a vocational training and a liberal education are not interchangeable. But the Warden's account of Pattison is deliberately unilateral. He does not examine Pattison's scholarly work, nor does he examine the nature of his relations with

German scholars. Something is therefore inevitably lacking in his interpretation of Pattison's idea of a university.

II

The type of research which Pattison made his own and for which he remained famous was common neither in England nor in Germany.[5] This was the history of classical scholarship. Pattison also did other things after giving up the study of saints which Pusey and Newman had encouraged. His editions of Milton's sonnets and some of Pope's poems are described as first-rate by John Sparrow, who should know, but they did not take much of his time and appear to have been mostly "Parerga" of his old age.[6] He started his work on Casaubon in 1853 and published his biography of him in 1875. His biography of Scaliger dragged on from about 1855 to his death and was never completed.

In writing the lives of great scholars Pattison naturally wanted to advance the cause of pure, disinterested research, but he also tried to express some of his religious and social beliefs. In his view Casaubon had been sidetracked and then killed off by theology. All those years spent in refuting Baronius and helping King James to compile his theological tracts! Pattison is even impatient with Casaubon for filling pages of his *Ephemerides* with mere religious emotions. In one of his earliest biographical studies, on Bishop Huet, which he published in the *Quarterly Review* (1855), Pattison dramatized the conflict between Huet the scholar and Huet the philosopher.[7] The latter belonged to "that class of philosophers who have taken up philosophy not as an end, but as a means — not for its own sake, but for the support of religion." To such philosophers Pattison attributed "the desperate design of first ruining the territory they were preparing to evacuate."

There was only one scholar in Pattison's time who had a similar interest in the history of classical scholarship: Jacob Bernays. This name is not to be found in John Sparrow's book on Pattison and is not often mentioned in Pattison's own *Memoirs*, but one mention in the *Memoirs* is of great importance. When Bernays's book on Scaliger appeared in 1855, Pattison undertook to translate it into English. A letter from Max Müller to Bernays dated 5 February 1856 makes it certain that by that time Pattison was firmly committed to the translation of Bernays's *Scaliger*. Max Müller remarked about Pattison: "Seine Kenntniss der deutschen Sprache ist vielleicht nicht ganz gut, er kennt aber die Sache, die damalige Zeit, und ist eine ehrliche, obwohl etwas trockene Seele."[8] Pattison indeed summarized Bernays's book in two lengthy papers in the *Quarterly Review* (1860).[9] What the *Memoirs* reveal is that Pattison was persuaded by Christian Karl Josias von Bunsen, a former Prussian envoy to the Court of St. James's, to improve upon Bernays and to write another book about Scaliger: "I soon came to view in Scaliger something more than the first scholar of the modern age. The hint was given me in a conversation I had with Chevalier Bunsen at Charlottenburg in 1856. Speaking of Bernays' masterly monograph on Scaliger, just published, he pointed out that Bernays's creed had interfered with his seeing in Scaliger 'the Protestant hero.'"[10]

By linking Pattison with Bernays and Bunsen this passage provides a key to the understanding of the three persons involved. To see the Protestant hero in Scaliger proved to be more difficult than Bunsen had anticipated. Pattison never translated Bernays and never wrote his own book. One of his difficulties was that he himself was more anti-Catholic than Protestant. On the other hand, Bunsen was perhaps less certain of his Lutheranism than he cared to admit. In the twenty years 1818–38 in which he was a diplomat and a scholar in Rome, he was suspected of Catholic sympathies. His later work on the early Church and on oriental religions is, at least to one reader, not conspicuous for clarity of theological notions.[11] Both Pattison and Bunsen admired Scaliger for qualities which were beyond their reach. They also knew that Bernays was intellectually and morally closer to Scaliger than they were ever likely to be. It is a sign of their nobility that this awareness was the foundation of their long friendship for J. Bernays. Bernays returned their friendship with his characteristic warmth and devotion, but he had decided to remain alone. A Jew of unshakable faith, he sacrificed his scholarly career and much else in obedience to the law of his Fathers.[12]

III

Jacob Bernays was born in Hamburg in 1824 as the eldest son of Isaak Bernays. The father was an almost unique combination of orthodox Talmudic scholar and follower of Schelling. Something more must be said about him, because it is essential for the understanding of his son. Isaak ben Ja'akov Bernays was born in 1792 and died in 1849. In Würzburg he had been a pupil of Rabbi Abraham Bing and a close friend of Rabbi Jacob Ettlinger, but he had also been able to study at the University of Würzburg, thanks to the short-lived Napoleonic liberalization. In 1821 he published anonymously two instalments of *Der Bibel'sche Orient* which created a sensation. It was inspired by Schelling. Isaak Bernays never explicitly admitted that he was the author. In the same year, 1821, he came to Hamburg as Chief Rabbi with the task of creating a bridge between the Orthodox and the Reformed Jews of the city. The latter had set up their Tempel-Verein in 1817. The Jewish Community of Hamburg was then mainly made up of moderately affluent shopkeepers, who fought for their civic rights and wanted a modernization of their educational institutions.[13] The destitute and the very rich were on the fringe of the congregation, and among the very rich the dominant figure was the banker Solomon Heine. His nephew and protégé Heinrich had abandoned Hamburg two years before, in 1819, after failing both in business and in love, but the shadow of Heinrich Heine—the poet and the apostate—lingered on in Hamburg and especially in the Bernays family, which was somehow related to him.

Isaak Bernays wanted to be known not as a rabbi, but as a Chacham in the Sephardic tradition. He did not succeed in reuniting the Temple of the Reformed with the Synagogue of the Orthodox, but at least in the first twenty years of his office he managed to keep them together for political, legal, and charitable purposes and was obviously respected by both sides. He reformed the Jewish school system—the Talmud Torah—by including a great deal of ordinary German education. He lived long enough to see the de facto emancipation of the Hamburg Jews in 1848, but full legal equality was granted only in 1860. In June 1863 the Warburgs, just emerging to prominence, changed the name of their business from "Geldwechsler" to "Bankiers."

Isaak gave Jacob all the Jewish education he needed. Jacob became a master of the Hebrew language, was thoroughly acquainted with the Talmud, and was later able to teach Hebrew medieval philosophy. Isaak seems also to have been Jacob's first teacher in Latin and Greek. Jacob perfected his classical education in the local Johanneum. One special feature of the Hamburg situation was that the great classical school had been opened to Jews in 1802. Both Jacob and his younger brother Michael, later an eminent student of German literature, went to the Johanneum. Niebuhr's approach to classical scholarship permeated the school. Niebuhr's influence was also felt in Bernays's home because of the friendship between Chacham Isaak and Meyer Isler, a Jew who was a librarian in the municipal library and made his reputation by editing Niebuhr's lectures at Bonn. After a spell in the local Academy—das Akademische Gymnasium—Jacob Bernays went to Niebuhr's university, Bonn, in 1844.

IV

In Bonn Bernays studied with F. G. Welcker, Christian Brandis, and F. Ritschl. It is difficult to say what he owed to Welcker, though his interests in religion and religious poetry—such as tragedy—were related to Welcker's thought. Christian Brandis, the friend and biographer of Niebuhr, taught Bernays how to study the pre-Socratics and Aristotle, including the fragments of the lost dialogues, and opened to him the world of the scholiasts. But the beloved master—to Bernays, as to many others—was F. Ritschl. Though he did not succeed in interesting Bernays in what he himself was interested in at

the time—Dionysius of Halicarnassus—Ritschl understood and helped
Bernays in every way.[14] It soon became evident that Bernays, even as an
undergraduate, had developed critical methods of his own in the study of
Greek philosophy as well as of textual criticism.

In 1846 Bernays won the prize for a study on the manuscript tradition of
Lucretius. His paper, which was published by Ritschl in *Rheinisches Museum*
(1847), solved in all its essential elements the question of the relations
between the four branches of the tradition of Lucretius—the *Quadratus,* the
Oblongus, the *Schedae,* and the *Italici.* Lachmann's edition of Lucretius,
which appeared in 1850, inevitably obscured the merits of Bernays's essay.
Bernays himself, in his own edition of Lucretius published by Teubner in
1852, had nothing but admiration for Lachmann and minimized his own
contribution. Though Lucretian scholars such as Usener and Monro were
aware of the importance of Bernays's paper, the true state of affairs was first
reestablished by S. Timpanaro in his little volume *La genesi del metodo del
Lachmann* (1963). "Il metodo del Lachmann" was really to a great extent "il
metodo del Bernays."

Meanwhile, Bernays had obtained his doctorate in 1848 with a dissertation, *Heraclitea pars I,* which indicated a new way towards the study of the
pre-Socratics.[15] Following up a suggestion he had characteristically found
in a paper by Johann Matthias Gesner (1752), Bernays discovered the influence of Heraclitus on Pseudo-Hippocrates' *De diaeta.* In the second part of
his research on Heraclitus published in *Rheinisches Museum* (1850) he used
the same method to find Heraclitean material in Plutarch. Two years later
the discovery of the so-called *Philosophoumena,* first attributed to Origen,
then to Hippolytus of Rome, confirmed the validity of his method and gave
him new scope for the recovery of the lost Heraclitus. Th. Gomperz tells us
that Otto Jahn called his attention to Bernays's *Heraclitea,* "eine kleine
Schrift, die meinen Altertumsstudien eine neue Wendung gab."[16]

In the warm political atmosphere of 1848 all seemed easy. Immediately
after his doctorate, Bernays became a *Privatdozent* in Bonn. His *Habilita-
tionsvorlesung, De Philologiae Historia,* confirmed the interest in the history
of classical scholarship which he had inherited from his father. Under the
auspices of Ritschl he published two brief, but original, florilegia of
humanistic texts in the Bonn yearly program for the birthday of the king of
Prussia in 1849 and 1850. He also became an assistant editor of the *Rheinisches Museum* and contributed a chapter on Spinoza's *Hebrew Grammar* to a
book *Descartes und Spinoza* by his friend C. Schaarschmidt (1850), which
showed his command of Spinoza's philosophy.

Though very poor, Bernays found himself in a circle of friends which
included poets, aristocrats, and even near-royalties. One of his close
friends was Georg Bunsen, the son of the Prussian envoy to London. The
friendship with Paul Heyse was to last until the end of his life. It was his

only emotional friendship and was born out of their common interest in modern literatures. Paul Heyse in his *Jugenderinnerungen und Bekenntnisse* admitted that meeting Bernays had introduced a new element of serious-ness into his own intellectual life.[17] To Bernays he later dedicated his translation of Leopardi (1878). Bernays's letters to Heyse have only been partially published. Even so they touch upon a variety of subjects and of emotional experiences on which he was usually silent. The fact that Heyse had a Jewish mother, but was ignorant of Judaism and Christianity, allowed Bernays to speak to him about Jewish matters with irony and tenderness: "Wie traurig, dass Goethe nicht so gut hebräisch gewusst hat, wie ich...." (1856); "Gehörte ich nicht zum Volk des Spinoza, dem eine Portion hilaritas zum Erbtheil gegeben ist...." (1858).

Through Georg Bunsen Bernays became a frequent visitor to the house of the Fürst zu Wied, whose wife, Marie Prinzessin von Nassau, hung on his lips. Their daughter Carmen Sylva—or Elizabeth, queen of Rumania—devoted a whole chapter of her memoirs to Bernays, who had puzzled her so much in her childhood—because he refused to take food in her house and knew the New Testament much better than her parents.[18]

With the political reaction of the early 1850s it was soon clear that there was little hope for a Jew of getting a chair in a Prussian university. Christian Josias von Bunsen must have assessed the predicament of his son's friend realistically when he invited him to London in 1851 with the intention of introducing him to English scholars. Bunsen had had some part in trans-planting Max Müller, but Max Müller was not a Jew, and the East India Company was interested in his services. Bernays ate nothing and drank only tea at the Prussian embassy where he was a guest for about three months. He helped Bunsen in his work on Hippolytus, and as a parting gift he sent him that *Epistola critica ad Bunsenium* in which he showed how one could use Book X of the *Philosophoumena* to emend Books V–IX. During a visit to Oxford Bernays apparently signed a contract for a Latin commentary on Lucretius and established his friendship with Max Müller and Mark Pattison. If more was expected from Oxford, the times were unpropitious. Less than two months after Bernays's visit Pattison was defeated in the Lincoln election and retreated from Oxford affairs. Max Müller himself had to wait until 1868 for the chair of Comparative Philology.

Documents on the early relations between Bernays and Pattison, if they existed, do not seem to have survived. The unpublished letters between them which are preserved in Bodley belong to the period after 1859. Later on Pattison regularly sent the most promising Oxford dons to Bernays. In 1865 he introduced Henry Nettleship, a fellow of Merton; in 1868 he introduced Ingram Bywater as "a serious student of ancient philosophy": Bywater, as we know, became Bernays's English pupil and under his guid-ance put together the edition of Heraclitus (1877). In 1870 Pattison introduced D. B. Monro as a man "who takes a leading place in directing philological studies in this University." The correspondence, as we have it, contains some important letters from Bernays. There is a letter of 1865 in which Bernays gives his opinion on the authenticity of Plato's Seventh Letter and also an interesting judgment on F. A. Wolf (see appendix A).

We should like to known more about the relation between Bernays and Pattison in the 1850s when Bernays needed an academic position and Pattison was far from being firmly established in his own. What we know is enough to show that Pattison's *Memoirs* are no safe guide to the importance of Bernays for his early development. I do not believe that Pattison's interest in the history of classical scholarship was originally suggested by Bernays, though chronology would not be against this hypothesis; but if Pattison started independently, he soon had to take into account the standards of criticism and research set up by Bernays in his *Scaliger* of 1855.

What is more curious is that through Pattison and Bywater Bernays came to exercise a very deep influence on the reform of classical studies in Oxford. Even Oxford's special interest in Aristotelian research, as we shall soon see, cannot be separated from Bernays's example. But this poses two questions to which I shall not try to give an answer: (1) whether anyone in Oxford, Pattison or Bywater or Nettleship or W. L. Newman, had any suspicion that what they learned from Bernays was by no means typical of German scholarship; (2) whether any of them had at least a notion of what Bernays meant by his research.

V

The journey to England ended in failure. A few years later Bernays obtained the consent of the Clarendon Press to discontinue his work on the commentary on Lucretius which had reached 1.689 of the first book. In a letter of 7 November 1852, Christian von Bunsen made it clear to Bernays that England was the only alternative to conversion. This letter, to which a second part was added on 14 November, was far from being a cool analysis of the situation. Bunsen was a mystic and expected much from his friend's conversion. He quoted the Gospel of St. John. Evidently he himself felt that his invitation did not stand much of a chance. He was ready to welcome Bernays to his house again, "als Jude wie als Christ." Bernays's answer has rightly become a classic in Jewish-German literature.[19] The matter, as far as he was personally concerned, could not even be discussed.

The question of conversion was essential to German Jews from the beginning of the nineteenth century to the end of the First World War. Bunsen was a believer in Christianity. He was entitled to hope for the conversion of the Jews. But even liberals and atheists among the Germans asked the Jews to become converts as a demonstration of their loyalty to German institutions. Mommsen himself, the champion of the Jews against Treitschke, invited the Jews to conversion—apparently to make things easier for their defenders.[20] As men are better than their doctrines, Mommsen remained surrounded by unrepentant Jews to the end of his life: we shall find Bernays among them. "Taufjuden"—Jews who had chosen conversion not because they believed in Christianity, but as a concession to social pressure— became a demoralizing factor in German life, both on its Jewish and on its Christian side. As Bernays said in his reply to Bunsen: "Er selbst, Jesus von Nazareth selbst, jetzt als Jude geboren, würde es nicht können"—namely, to accept conversion under those conditions.

Bernays was soon to have a "Taufjude" in his own family. His brother Michael became a convert in 1856. He lived through another twenty difficult years before his outstanding contributions to the study of Goethe were recognized by the creation for him of a chair of German literature in the University of Munich. It is said that Jacob mourned his brother as dead. This would have been in keeping with the tradition of the Fathers who had preferred death to apostasy. But after Jacob's death the main part of his library passed to Michael. Jacob certainly made a will, because he bequeathed his manuscripts to the Bonn Library and his Hebrew books to the Jewish Theological Seminary of Breslau. What his testament said about his brother I do not know, but we must assume, until the contrary is proved, that Jacob did nothing to prevent the rest of his library from going to Michael. He certainly was intensely grieved by his brother's conversion. Fifty years later Carmen Sylva still remembered that sorrow and commented: "Ich muss sagen: er hatte Recht."

By the time of his brother's conversion Bernays had found an intellectual home as a teacher of classics and of Jewish philosophy in the newly created Jüdisch-Theologisches Seminar of Breslau. It is not possible to evaluate here the importance of the Breslau Seminary from the moment in which it was opened by Zacharias Frankel in 1854 to its destruction in 1938. The seminary's object was to train rabbis and teachers of the Jewish religion in up-to-date scientific methods. It also hoped to reinterpret the Jewish orthodox heritage through scholarly research. Heinrich Hirsch Graetz, the great historian, was, together with Zacharias Frankel, the dominant inspiration of the seminary from its inception. The *Monatsschrift für Geschichte und Wissenschaft des Judenthums* reflected their ideas. The thirteen years during which Bernays taught at the seminary between 1854 and 1866 were the most creative of his life. The friendship with Heyse was, no doubt, a primary factor in his profound concern for Aristotle's theory of tragedy. In one of the very few letters to Bernays which are preserved, Heyse expresses his full appreciation of the contribution which Bernays had made to his own ideas on art. Bernays acquired a new lifelong friend in Theodor Mommsen who was professor in Breslau from 1854 to 1858. At Breslau the newly married

Mommsen completed his *Römische Geschichte* and began to organize the *Corpus Inscriptionum Latinarum*. Bernays shared in the domestic happiness and in the intellectual vigor of his older friend Mommsen. He translated the Book of Job for Mommsen; he and Mommsen revised Heyse's translations from the Italian. They both contributed emendations to the *editio princeps* of Granius Licinianus by K. Pertz (1857). Bernays was able to follow Mommsen's intellectual development when the latter passed from Breslau to Berlin and from Roman political history to the Roman constitution. The essay which Bernays wrote in 1874 on Mommsen's *Römisches Staatsrecht* was a revelation to Mommsen himself. It determined his place in the history of classical scholarship. With all his contempt for reviewers Mommsen had to make an exception: "Gott helfe mir, oder Jahwe, wenn Sie das lieber hören, ich weiss keinen, der Ausnahme macht als Sie oder wenigstens wie Sie." The friendship between Bernays and Mommsen, as we can see from a detailed study by L. Wickert,[21] was more generous and delicate on Bernays's side than on Mommsen's. Bernays helped Mommsen ungrudgingly. He contributed an important paper on the *metuens* (*Gottesfürchtige*) in Juvenal for the *Commentationes in honorem Theodori Mommseni* in 1877. It is a famous academic anecdote that in the next year Mommsen asked Bernays's opinion on the meaning of *metuens*. Bernays answered in a tone which few would have permitted themselves with Mommsen: "Ich kann mich nicht enthalten gleich nach Empfang Ihres Breifes . . . zu danken für den eben so schlagenden wie schmeichelhaften Beweis, dass Sie meine Abhandlung des Gottesfürchtigen bei Juvenal, enthalten in dem grossen Band commentationes in honorem Theodori Mommseni, nicht gelesen haben." Mommsen admitted defeat for once: "Ja, lieber Bernays, auslachen können Sie mich immer, aber übel nehmen dürfen Sie das nicht. Es ist Ihnen ja auch nichts Neues von mir."[22]

But even in the Breslau days Bernays remained aloof. He had an excellent pupil for Hellenistic literature, Jacob Freudenthal, but he antagonized other students such as Hermann Cohen.[23] He continued to advise Bunsen and to contribute scholarly appendices (for instance on Sanchuniathon) to Bunsen's not very serious big works, until Bunsen died in 1860. He never quite identified himself with the religious opinions of the leaders of the Jewish Theological Seminary. As far as I know he took no part in the polemics provoked by the appearance of the *Darke ha-Mishnah* by Frankel in 1859. An increasing detachment from the surrounding world, a feeling of limited possibilities within the contemporary situation, were to characterize Bernays's activity.

In 1866 he consented to go back to Bonn. A full chair was still out of the question, though by that time he was recognized as one of the greatest classical scholars of Germany (chairs in Breslau and Heidelberg had been denied to him by the relevant ministries). As is well known, in 1865 the violent quarrel between F. Ritschl and O. Jahn shook German academic life. Ritschl left Bonn for Leipzig and took away with him his pupils E. Rohde and F. Nietzsche. O. Jahn died in 1869 after years of physical illness and mental anguish. Bonn's classical school had to be reconstructed from its foundations. Bernays was offered the direction of the university library and a chair as *extraordinarius*—which he accepted. He was fortunate in the two successors of Ritschl and Jahn. H. Usener, who came with him to Bonn in 1866, understood Bernays's mind as probably nobody else could. After Bernays's death in 1881 he made himself the editor of his *Nachlass* and his biographer. Bernays's *Gesammelte Abhandlungen,* published by Usener, are a monument both to the author and to the editor, as Wilamowitz realized. F. Bücheler, who returned to Bonn in 1870, in his more extrovert way loved the man who (as he wrote immediately after Bernays's death), "der Einsamkeit ergeben, las und bedachte unendlich viel, sinnend und ratend über Politik und Judentum, Philosophie und gelehrte Welt, den Geist spannend ohne Nachlass, bis das Hirn tödlich geschlagen ward."[24]

Bernays was also fortunate in his pupils of the Bonn years—Ingram Bywater and U. Wilamowitz-Moellendorff. Two of the best pages of the not very inspired *Erinnerungen* by the eighty-year-old Wilamowitz are an affectionate tribute to the master of his youth. This says much for a man who, already a professor, had had to apologize to Usener for his arrogant behavior as a student: "Er war nicht nur strenger Jude . . . sondern trug den Stolz auf sein Judentum zur Schau. . . . Es war eine sonderbare Sorte von Adelsstolz, der die meisten abstiess; mir hat er imponiert, denn da war alles echt, hatte alles Stil."[25]

After 1870 Bernays became very interested in politics. He disliked the new world of mass movements. He had no faith in democracy, but even less faith in Bismarck. A letter by him to Max Müller, dated 16 December 1870, is eloquent enough. His translation with commentary of the first three books of Aristotle's *Politics,* though—needless to say—a work of exquisite craftsmanship, was suggested by the political situation and appeared relevant to it when it was published in 1872. Bernays never moved from Bonn after his return there in 1866. One of the few glimpses into his private life of that period is provided by Berthold Auerbach, who tells of his Passover night, the Seder, with Bernays in 1867. Bernays was no good at singing and enjoyed the performance of Auerbach who, before becoming the favorite writer of the German upper bourgeoisie, had been trained as a rabbi.[26]

In 1880 Treitschke initiated his anti-Semitic campaign. Graetz and Mommsen were involved, and naturally Graetz resented Mommsen's defense almost as much as Treitschke's attack on the Jews. In a remarkable letter (15 December 1880) Graetz invited Bernays to answer Mommsen: "Dieser Bewunderer der Staatsstreiche scheint kein Gefühl für die Immoralität zu haben, die darin liegt, die Lüge eines Glaubensbekenntnisses, das

man vielleicht gar verabscheut, öffentlich auszusprechen."[27] We do not
know what Bernays replied to Graetz. He was probably aware that Graetz
had made some unwise remarks in his courageous public answer to
Treitschke. Nor would he easily have taken up his pen against his friend
Mommsen. But there is little room for speculation. In that very winter
1880–81 he began to feel ill. In May 1881 he suffered a stroke, and on 26
May he rejoined his Fathers. The anti-Semitic crisis, one suspects, had
killed him (see appendix B).

VI

From 1854 to 1881 the lines of Bernays's intellectual activity are firmly
drawn. He stated his credo in his monograph on Scaliger, which appeared
in 1855 and was dedicated to F. Ritschl. Scaliger was no Protestant hero to
Bernays, for the simple reason that Scaliger was not a Protestant hero in any
case. He was a man who had applied the same type of philological research
to the classical and to the Oriental worlds and had consequently unified the
two fields of research. Bernays emphasized this unity of method and vision.
He progressively acquired a formidable knowledge in the history of classical scholarship from the sixteenth century onwards, as the appendices of
his own works show and the admirable "Quellennachweise zu Politianus
und Georgius Valla" in *Hermes* (1876) confirm. He also studied the political
and historical thought of the eighteenth century in general, gave lectures
on Gibbon which Wilamowitz admired,[28] and hoped to publish a monograph on him. The notes he left on Gibbon have not lost their value after
a hundred years, but his book on Scaliger was not merely a contribution to
the history of classical scholarship: it was a declaration of method, and to
it we shall have to return in our concluding remarks.

Aristotle was another constant interest. His first important contribution
was an article in *Rheinisches Museum* (1853) in which he reconstructed
Aristotle's lost theory of comedy from the Anonymous Coislinianus. In
1857 he published the *Grundzüge der verlorenen Abhandlung des Aristoteles
über Wirkung der Tragödie* which created a sensation and provoked innumerable replies and discussions.[29] Bernays started from the simple observation
that *Katharsis* is a medical term and indicates the removal of impurity, the
purge of excess: it does not denote moral purification, as Lessing believed.
The remark was not entirely new, though neither Bernays nor his immediate critics were aware of the fact that Heinrich Weil—a German Jew like
Bernays, and like him unable to get a position in a German university
—had propounded the same medical interpretation of *Katharsis* in a paper
published in the *Verhandlungen der zehnten Versammlung deutscher Philologen*
(Basel, 1848, pp. 131 ff.). What was really new in Bernays was the development of the implications of the medical interpretation for the understand-

ing of Greek tragedy. Bernays connected the cathartic process with the ecstatic practices of the Dionysiac rites. The way was open for Nietzsche.

In 1872, after the publication of *Die Geburt der Tragödie*, Nietzsche wrote to Rohde: "Das Neueste ist, dass Jacob Bernays erklärt hat, es seien *seine* Anschauungen, nur stark übertrieben." Nietzsche went on to comment: "Die Juden sind überall und auch hier voran, während der gute teutsche Usener ... dahinten, im Nebel bleibt." Rohde answered in a suitable tone: "Vergleiche den Juden Bernays, der alles schon lange selbst sich so gedacht hat."[30]

What exactly Bernays thought and said about Nietzsche's book is another matter, but he was certainly entitled to see in this book an extreme development of his interpretation of *Katharsis*. The link between Bernays and Nietzsche — both, as we know, pupils of Ritschl — is obvious, but to us Bernays's analysis of *Katharsis* suggests the name of Freud even more than the name of Nietzsche. It is interesting that in 1931, after having said that "Das Wesentliche [on *Katharsis*] hat Jakob Bernays gesehen," Max Pohlenz added that through his theory of *Katharsis* "Aristoteles erwidert 'psychoanalytisch'" to Plato's criticism.[31] The discoverer of the Oedipus complex, who throughout his life had an insatiable curiosity for the classical world, became a nephew of Jacob Bernays by marrying Martha Bernays, a daughter of Berman Bernays, one of Jacob's brothers.

There is no doubt about what Chacham Isaak Bernays meant to Freud when he became engaged to Martha. In a letter he tells his fiancée how he entered into conversation with a little Jewish shopkeeper who turned out to have been a pupil of Isaak and to have known the whole Bernays family in his Hamburg days. The figure of the wise rabbi suddenly became archetypal for Freud, and he concludes his letter by a *sui generis* profession of faith: "Wenn die Form, in der die alten Juden sich wohl fühlten, auch für uns kein Obdach mehr bietet, etwas vom Kern, das Wesen des sinnvollen und lebensfrohen Judentums, wird unser Haus nicht verlassen."[32]

I have no evidence that Freud studied Jacob Bernays's works. Freud's biographer, Ernest Jones, is unhelpful on such matters,[33] and Ernst Kris, who went professionally into the question of Aristotelian *Katharsis*, is no better.[34] But I am not acquainted with the historical research on the development of Freud's thought. Michael Fraenkel must, however, have had some good reasons for dedicating his selection of Jacob Bernays's letters to Sigmund Freud. I should be surprised if Bernays's famous memoir on Aristotle's *Katharsis* was unknown to Freud in his formative years.

To go back to Bernays's Aristotelian studies, in 1863 he published and dedicated to Mark Pattison his book on the lost dialogues of Aristotle. Not much comment is needed here. We all know that Bernays was the man who effectively resurrected the exoteric Aristotle, that is, the only Aristotle who was known outside his school in the Hellenistic age. He was the first to show

how much one could learn about the lost Aristotle from neo-Platonic writings. His pupil Bywater followed him in discovering slices of Aristotle's *Protrepticus* in Iamblichus.[35] W. Jaeger and E. Bignone built on Bernays's foundations, and not everyone is certain that their building has the solidity of its foundations. The main disagreement between Bernays and Jaeger—on the existence of a "Platonic" stage in Aristotle's development—is still a controversial subject.

The third direction of Bernays's research was the study of texts bearing on the position of Judaism in the Greco-Roman world. He was not particularly fond of Jewish-Hellenistic literature as such, and explained why in the study he dedicated to Theodor Mommsen in 1856, *Ueber das Phokylideische Gedicht*.[36] Bernays recognized a Jew, or rather a Jewish proselyte, writing about the beginning of the Christian era, in the author of a poem transmitted to us under the name of Phocylides. The author, who wanted to appeal to the pagans, expressed himself ambiguously. He avoided a clear statement of Jewish beliefs. Bernays's comment is that the ambiguity explains why Jewish-Hellenistic literature was doomed to oblivion. Any attempt "das Concrete durch Compromiss oder Abstraction zu verflachen" is bound to be contemptible.

What Bernays liked best was to discover in pagan literature new pieces of evidence either for Jewish history or for the slow conversion of pagan minds to Jewish and Christian beliefs. In 1861 he published what may well be his masterpiece in historical interpretation, *Ueber die Chronik des Sulpicius Severus*. Bernays was exceptionally well acquainted with the political and religious situation at the end of the fourth century A.D. and subtly presented Sulpicius Severus's view of his own time. But the most sensational conjecture was that Sulpicius Severus's account of the destruction of Jerusalem summarized the now lost section of Tacitus's *Histories*. There is no doubt that Sulpicius Severus agrees with Valerius Flaccus (I, 13) against Flavius Josephus (VI, 4, 3) in stating that the destruction of the Temple was decided by Titus. As Bernays saw, the version of Josephus must be treated as an attempt to whitewash Titus in the eyes of the surviving Jews. Sulpicius Severus used Tacitus elsewhere, and this particular passage shows traces of Tacitean style under the early fifth-century veneer. It is therefore reasonable to conclude with Bernays that Sulpicius Severus depended on Tacitus. His conjecture has indeed been generally accepted. A recent attempt by Canon Hugh Montefiore to refute it is not convincing. Montefiore simply replaces the name of Tacitus as the source of Sulpicius by the name of the man who was probably the source of Tacitus, Antonius Iulianus: no gain and greater obscurity.[37]

I should like to include the book *Theophrastos' Schrift über Frömmigkeit* (1866) in the series of Jewish studies rather than in the Aristotelian series, though the method is that of the Aristotelian essays. Bernays proves beyond doubt that Porphyry's *De abstinentia* is largely based on Theophrastus's περὶ εὐσεβείας. The analysis is subtle and cautious. What interests Bernays most is that, approached in this way, Theophrastus becomes the first of the Greek writers directly available to us to have dealt with the Jewish religion. Furthermore, Bernays shows that Theophrastus developed a criticism of traditional Greek practices about sacrifices which implied a rapprochement to Judaism. Bernays's demonstration has since been refined and perhaps corrected in detail. Jaeger, for instance, has indicated in Hecataeus of Abdera a possible (but to my mind not probable) source of Theophrastus about the Jews.[38]

The little book on the letters attributed to Heraclitus appeared in 1869. As a lifelong student of this philosopher, Bernays had originally been interested in them as a source for Heraclitus's thought. He rightly suspected that the forger used Heraclitus's writings to lend plausibility to his products. During the progress of his research it became obvious that the letters were by several hands. Bernays tried to prove that some of the authors were either Jews or Christians in disguise. His demonstration was accepted for a long time. It now appears more probable that the letters in question (IV, VII, IX) are by a Cynic. But his analysis of the letters remains of basic importance. What Bernays gets out of these texts is truly astonishing. He was the first, as far as I know, to pose the problems of the relations between Cynicism and Jewish-Hellenistic literature.[39]

The study of Philo's *De aeternitate mundi* accompanied Bernays for many years. In 1863 he published his discovery that the text had been transmitted with chapters in the wrong order. This was a capital contribution to the understanding of the difficult text. In 1876 Bernays published an edition with translation in the *Abhandlungen* of the Berlin Academy, of which he had become a member in 1865. In 1882 Usener edited from the *Nachlass* the introduction to the text and an unfinished commentary — "Bernaysium nusquam magis Bernaysium videris," as he wrote to Wilamowitz.[40] According to Bernays, who knew he had predecessors as illustrious as G. Budé, the text cannot be by Philo. It maintains that the world is eternal and uncreated: which is not Philo's opinion in other works. It is hardly necessary to say that Bernays, as a constant student of Maimonides and Spinoza, lived in full awareness of the problem about the eternity of the world in Jewish thought. The solution adopted by Bernays was one of three possibilities, all of which he had considered. The second possibility was that Philo had changed his mind. The third was that he intended to refute the thesis of the eternity of the world in a lost section of the treatise.

F. Cumont defended the second solution in his edition (1891); other scholars (H. Leisegang among them) have opted for the third, which is indeed preferable. Nobody has ever denied that all the problems were first formulated by Bernays and that Bernays contributed enormously to the emendation and understanding of the controversial text.

We come now to the two works of Bernays's last years, in which a mysterious element of deep detachment from the world and even of revolt against it underlies the philological research. The book *Lucian und die Kyniker* appeared in 1879, two years before his death. Lucian's *Peregrinus* had traditionally been interpreted as an anti-Christian pamphlet. With the help of a hitherto unnoticed passage from Galen, Bernays clarified the background and showed that Lucian attacked Peregrinus not as a Christian (which he had been for a short time), but as a Cynic. Two elements emerge from Bernays's demonstration, which is followed, as usual, by a careful translation and annotation of the text. Lucian was no Voltaire. His irony and satire lacked the support of the serious and noble convictions which characterize Voltaire. Lucian hated the Cynics because the Cynics, in their contempt for ordinary social conventions, joined Jews and Christians in the protest against the world as it was. Even those who do not accept this interpretation admit, in Jacques Schwartz's words, that Bernays "a écrit la première étude sérieuse sur Peregrinos."[41] It was more than that.

Protest against political life — withdrawal from the city — was what characterized Greek philosophers in general, according to Bernays's last work, *Phokion und seine neueren Beurtheiler* (1881). Greek philosophers were normally émigrés or political rebels. With Alexander, and after him, they supported Macedon because they hated the ways of the polis. Phocion, who had been educated in the Platonic school, shared their dislike and was ultimately the victim of the democracy he disliked. Bernays's starting point was the difference of opinion on Phocion which began to emerge in the second part of the eighteenth century. Previously, admiration for Phocion had been almost as general as the admiration for his biographer Plutarch. Bernays saw that hostility to Phocion reflected the new democratic trend: it was to prevail in the nineteenth century. Bernays, who did not like democracy, reacted by returning to unconditional admiration for Phocion. He presented an analysis of the situation of the philosophers under Macedonian rule which for the first time focused attention on the political commitments of the philosophers and is still the starting point of any research on the subject. Wilamowitz, who had listened to Bernays's lectures on this topic in Bonn, declared his debt to Bernays even before the book on Phocion was published.[42] The whole volume on *Antigonos von Karystos* is hardly separable from Bernays's teaching, but the section on "Die Philosophenschulen und die Politik," the most important of the book, is literally unthinkable without Bernays. When in 1959 I tried to give a picture of the cultural situation in Athens at the time of the historian Timaeus, I had to return to Bernays. It was a shock to discover how little I had understood of his book when I first read it almost thirty years earlier during my study of Demosthenes and Philip of Macedon. Bernays's hostility to Grote, his sympathy with reactionary currents were not what in 1930 we expected from a great master who had lived in the happy year 1880. In 1959 it was at least clear that Bernays was not one of the many who idealized Macedon in order to justify Prussia. He had Treitschke in mind when he spoke of the inevitable opposition "zwischen dem selbständigen Hochsinn philosophischer Charaktere und der bald platten, bald wilden Politik demokratischer Stadtgemeinden."[43] We know that in his last years Bernays was working on a commentary on the prophet Jeremiah—the first work on a Biblical text he had ever undertaken. This perhaps indicates better than anything else where his thoughts were going.

VII

One has not the immediate sense of a premature death in the case of Jacob Bernays because every piece he wrote was a self-contained masterpiece. His control of philological techniques had been exceptional since his youth. Few have ever had a similar command of the language of Greek philosophy. He was good at emending texts, but above all an interpreter of rare thoroughness and acumen. He expressed himself in a lucid and minutely polished style and created a new type of philological treatise: short, closely argued, confined to the essentials, never deriving his assumptions from the work of another. He never worked on a subject which he did not consider intrinsically important. To his treatises he appended notes or excursuses, each of which was a little dissertation in its own right about points of the history of classical scholarship, of lexicography, of philosophy. His articles in learned journals were relatively few and in certain cases supplemented someone else's contributions, but even these articles were, as a rule, self-contained pieces of the highest distinction. I mention as an example his paper "Philon's Hypothetika und die Verwünschungen des Buzyges in Athen" (1876), which begins by clarifying the title of a lost work by Philo and ends by throwing much light on an Athenian rite. But if I had to choose a few pages for an anthology I would probably choose the little note published in *Rheinisches Museum* (1862) with the title "Ein nabatäischer Schriftsteller." Bernays emends an unintelligible sentence of Ammonius, the commentator of Aristotle, by identifying in it the name of a Nabataean god which he had read in Hesychius. By successive steps he conjures up a whole group of Greek writers in the Arabian city of Petra—a new paragraph in the history of Hellenism.[44]

Many of his emendations are no longer to our taste. None of us would eliminate an inconvenient θεοί in Pseudo-Phocylides by emending it into νέοι (l. 104). But I know of only one serious error made by Bernays. It is to be found in his last work on Phocion which shows signs of strain. Here Bernays undoubtedly misunderstood the political standing of Xenocrates, the leader of the Academy. He seems to have overlooked the evidence provided

by the *Index Academicorum Philosophorum Herculanensis,* though the text of it
had been revised by F. Bücheler in 1869. Theodor Gomperz, who admired
Bernays, but admired George Grote and Athenian democrats even more,
made this mistake an occasion for an unjustified attack against the whole
book on Phocion in *Wiener Studien* (4, 1882, pp. 102–20).[45]

Bernays had certainly intended to do more work on the history of classical scholarship, which he knew so well, but he did not share the interest in
the continuity of classical forms or in the transmission of classical texts
which was to become typical of Jewish scholars of the next generation, such
as Eduard Norden, Ludwig Traube, Ernst Kantorowicz, and of course Aby
Warburg. To him Scaliger was not a link in the chain, but an absolute. Like
any other Jewish boy Bernays carried in his mind—and almost in his
blood—the rule of Rabban Gamliel: "Make thee a master." Even more than
Ritschl, Scaliger was the master he gave himself. Scaliger was his master
because he had kept out of theological controversies and had worked out
a philological method which applied equally to Hebrew and classical writers and was beyond sectarian doubts. What Bernays wanted was an uncon-
troversial philological interpretation of what Greeks and Romans, Jews
and Christians had thought and done. Having received a faith, he did not
have to look to history for one, as many of his contemporaries did, including perhaps his friend von Bunsen.

When he formulated his program in 1855 in his *Scaliger,* he was in fact
propounding a *via media* between the wild Orientalizing speculations of
Creuzer and the sound classical distrust of Lobeck. When he died in 1881
there was perhaps general agreement that he had been right. But the
general agreement concealed a basic misunderstanding, a misunderstanding far more serious than the quasi-theological disagreements of thirty or
forty years before.

In the 1880s Wilamowitz and Wellhausen dedicated books to each other
and proclaimed that the method of dealing with the *Iliad* was the same as
the method of dealing with Genesis. Even more significantly, Eduard
Meyer, a product of the Hamburg Johanneum, was just embarking on his
History of Antiquity, where Amos and Hesiod, the Book of Samuel and
Herodotus were taken to be fragments of the same archaic world. Yet the
Jews whom Wilamowitz, Wellhausen, and Meyer were prepared to admit
into their own picture of civilization had all been dead before Cyrus, king
of Persia, allowed their descendants to go back to Jerusalem. It was the age
of the Prophets which belonged to the West—not what we call normative
Judaism, which was Bernays's Judaism. Hans Liebeschütz in his admirable
recent book *Das Judentum im deutschen Geschichtsbild* (1967) has shown to
what lengths German historians and theologians went in trying to eliminate Judaism from civilization.

Mohammedans and, to a lesser extent, Catholics received analogous treatment. This explains why Jewish and Catholic scholars were particularly committed to establishing standards of objective interpretation of unpopular beliefs, doctrines, historical periods. Bishop Karl Josef Hefele, Père Delehaye, Cardinal Ehrle are obvious names in this connection: so is the name of Ignaz (Isaak Iehuda) Goldziher, the secretary of the Jewish Community of Budapest, who introduced new understanding into the study of Mohammedan law and theology. Bernays is not quite in the same category. He neither needed nor wanted polemical attitudes: he never argued about his faith in public, and perhaps not even in private.[46] But he worked in the same direction. It is not by chance that he met with sympathy especially from Usener, who among the freethinkers was most aware of the problems of freethinking. In his mild way Usener had told Wilamowitz of their radical difference: "Sie suchen die Schöpfungen des Willens in der Geschichte, ich das unwillkürliche, unbewusste Werden."[47]

Appendix A: *Letter to Mark Pattison*[48]

Breslau (Wallstrasse I)
23. Juni 1865.

Verehrter Freund,

Zuvörderst sage ich den langgeschuldeten Dank für die schöne Scaliger-review, welche ich seiner Zeit ohne jegliche Porto-Belastung richtig erhalten habe. Ich ersuche Sie freundschaftlichst, dass Sie mir auch Ihre Arbeit über Stephanus nicht vorenthalten wollen. Wie Ihnen Mr. Nettleship schon berichtet hat, erbaute ich ex ungue leonem; die Auszüge im Examiner waren jedoch von sehr geringem Umfang, und ich möchte sehr gern mich an dem Ganzen erfreuen. Sehr gespannt bin ich auf Ihr Leben Wolf's, das Sie mir ankündigen;[49] ich denke, Sie haben bei näherem Studium gewiss auch erkannt, dass er mehr ein Mensch von grosser Wirksamkeit als ein grosser Mensch gewesen ist. Die charakteristischen Erzählungen über ihn in dem Goethe-Zelter'schen Briefwechsel (Band 2 u. 3) sind Ihnen hoffentlich nicht entgangen. Er ist dort unter dem nickname "Isegrim"— der in den deutschen Fabeln gebräuchliche Name für lupus—bezeichnet. Besonders ergötzlich sind die dort 2 p. 250 angeführten Gründe, weshalb er seinen Leichnam nicht secirt wissen wollte.

Arnold's Essays habe ich mit Interesse gelesen. Für die Engländer ist wohl der Aufsatz über Heine das Anziehendste (dass Heine nicht in Hamburg, wie p. 156 zu lesen steht, sondern in Düsseldorf geboren ist, hat der Vf. jetzt gewiss schon von Anderen erfahren). Mir war die Abhandlung on the litterary influence of Academies das Bedeutsamste; sie legt den Finger auf viele wunde Stellen der jetzigen englischen Litteratur und erklärt das, wie man sich nicht verhehlen kann, sehr beträchtliche Sinken ihres Einflusses auf den Continent. Zu Arnold's eigener geistiger Physiognomie frappirte mich besonders ein Zug, den ich nicht passender als mit dem griechischen Compositum ἀρρενόθηλυ zu bezeichnen weiss.

Nun zu den Scaligerana. Ich werde Ihnen für die Mittheilung des französischen Briefes sehr dankbar sein. Publiciren kann ich ihn in derselben Weise wie den früheren de igne purgatorio jetzt um so bequemer, da mich die Akademie jüngst, wie Sie vielleicht gehört haben, zugleich mit Max Müller zu ihrem korrespondirenden Mitglied ernannt hat. Das Liegnitzer Programm besitze ich auch;[50] der Scaliger'sche Brief an Bagarrius ist jedoch nicht ein ineditum, wie der Herausgeber meinte, sondern war bereits von Casaubonus in Scaliger's opuscula p. 574 veröffentlicht. — Das Kieler Programm besitze ich ebenfalls; Salmasius hat, wie ja auch der Herausgeber bemerkt, fast alles dort Notirte später gelegentlich in seinen Druckschriften angebracht. — Ueber mysterium der päbstlichen tiara ist mir nichts bewusst; ich solte aber meinen, dass wenn dergleichen auf mündliche oder schriftliche Äusserungen Scaligers zurückgeht, Näheres in seines Freundes Du Plessis Mornay: Mysterium Iniquitatis zu finden sein müsste. — Der Struve'schen Notiz werde ich gelegentlich nachspüren lassen; ich hege jedoch keine grosse Erwartungen, da die Leipziger Bibliothek oft von Kennern durchsucht worden.

Den 1. Juli soll der Druck einer grösseren Arbeit beginnen, die ich diesen Winter fertig gemacht habe; sie wird einen etwas grösseren Umfang gewinnen als das Büchlein über die aristotelischen Dialoge.[51] Gleich zu Anfang des nächsten Jahres denke ich Sie damit zu überraschen. — Das Aristotelicum,[52] von dem Ihnen Fleckeisen die Correkturbogen zeigte, kann ich Ihnen leider nicht schicken, da der Verleger sehr knickerig mit Freiexemplaren war, und einzelne Artikel der Sammlung nicht zu haben sind.

Mit dem 7. platonischen Brief scheint es mir wie mit den vier ciceronischen Reden pro domo etc zu stehen, welche Markland und Wolf für unecht erklären. Ich pflege bei den kritischen Problemen solcher Art Cassianum illud, Cui bono in Anwendung zu bringen. Da innere Beschaffenheit und äussere Zeugnisse keinen Zweifel daran aufkommen lassen dass die Schriften, wenn nicht von denen, unter deren Namen sie gehen, so doch von ihren allernächsten und sehr eingeweihten Zeitgenossen herrühren, so ist es ja für die gelehrte Anwendung nach den meisten Seiten, z.B. nach der stilistischen und historischen Seite, fast gleichgiltig ob man sie als platonisch und ciceronisch oder als pseudo-platonisch und pseudo-ciceronisch behandelt. Für die feinere Charakteristik Platons, gebe ich zu, macht es einen Unterschied ob man den Brief ihm selbst oder einem seiner nächsten Schüler beilegt. Aber eine solche Charakteristik hat auch innerhalb der unzweifelhaft echten Schriften genug Disparitäten zu überwinden, so dass eine Disparität mehr oder weniger die Hauptzüge des Bildes nicht wesentlich verändert. Man lasse also die Frage vorläufig ruhen, so lange nicht ein neues, Uebereinstimmung erzwin-

gendes Moment der Entscheidung zum Vorschein kommt. Nach der Dürf-
tigkeit unserer jetzigen Mittel zu urtheilen, darf man nicht hoffen dass der
Ertrag der Controverse ihre Mühen belohnen werde.

Ich schliesse aus einer Andeutung Ihres Briefes, dass Sie die nächsten
Ferien in Frankreich zubringen werden. Sollten Sie jedoch auch nach
Deutschland kommen, so bitte ich um rechtzeitige Mittheilung Ihrer
Reiseroute. Vielleicht kann ich es einrichten, dass wir irgendwo zusam-
mentreffen.

Mr. Nettleship hat mir sehr zugesagt. Ich wünsche seinem frischen Stre-
ben den besten Erfolg. Als ich ihm rieth, auch in Bonn einige Zeit zu ver-
weilen, waren die Zwistigkeiten, die zu Ritschl's Abgang geführt haben,
noch nicht ausgebrochen. Wie die Sachen jetzt liegen, ist es für Mr. N.
gewiss das Rathsamste, alle seine verfügbare Zeit in Berlin zu verbrin-
gen.—Behalten Sie in gutem Andenken

Ihren freundschaftlich ergebenen
Bernays.

This letter (Bodleian Library, Oxford, Ms. Byw. 61) is a good specimen
of Bernays's correspondence with Mark Pattison and Ingram Bywater,
which would deserve complete publication. His interest in Matthew Arnold
was reciprocated by Arnold, who in 1858 made extracts from Bernays's theory on *Katharsis* (*The Note-Books of Matthew Arnold*, Oxford, 1952, pp. 5–8)
and summarized it (p. 459: "Katharsis—a treatment of the obstructed person, which seeks, not to repress, but to stir up and drive forth the element
which obstructs him, and in this manner to give him relief"). Bernays also
spoke about Arnold in a letter to Pattison on 17 February 1880, from which
I quote an extract here because it is typical of the pessimism of his last
years:

Matthew Arnold hat mir seinen Wordsworth geschickt. Sie sehen ihn
wohl öfter und sind so gütig, ihm meinen Dank zu übermitteln, da ich
seine Adresse nicht habe. Die Meisterschaft des Stils habe ich in seiner
Einleitung sehr bewundert. Sein Versuch jedoch, W. dem continentalen
Leser näher zu bringen, hat wohl mit grossen Schwierigkeiten zu kämp-
fen. Diese idyllische und contemplative Poesie setzt, um genossen zu werden, feste Zustände und ein Gefühl der Sicherheit voraus, wie man es
jetzt nur in England haben kann, "that has settled on her lees." Der Continent hingegen vibrirt immer, und wird in Zukunft noch mehr als bisher
vibriren. Da bedarf man einer rauschenderen Muse, die wenigstens auf
Augenblicke die innere Unruhe, die Erdbeben-Stimmung, übertönt.

Arnold's hope of being able to interest Continental readers in Wordsworth, to which Bernays alludes, is also expressed in his letter to Miss
Arnold of 14 April 1879 (*Letters of M. Arnold*, London, 1901, II, p. 182).

Appendix B: *Jacob Bernays' last letter?*[53]

In the correspondence with Ingram Bywater (Ms. Byw. 56) Jewish themes were not infrequent. For instance, in a letter dated 12 February 1877 Bernays expressed interest in George Eliot's *Daniel Deronda* and admiration for her knowledge of Jewish ritual: "Hat sie sich auf eigene Hand dieses Wissen erworben, oder hat sie einen jüdischen directeur de conscience?" In a letter dated 14 July 1878 he wrote: "Jetzt wo die englische Flagge auf Cypern weht und also wohl auch bald Syrien und Palaestina anglisirt werden, könnte leicht in mir, wenn ich älter werde, wieder die Reiselust erwachen. Vielleicht besteigen wir dann noch einmal zusammen den 'mount Olivet,' und Pattison, den ich bestens grüsse, steigt vielleicht mit." On 2 January 1881 he alluded to the Berlin anti-Semitic episodes: "Wenn Sie von den deutschen, speciell den Berliner Verhältnissen etwa aus der Times Kenntnisse bekommen, so werden Sie sich vielleicht mancher meiner Gespräche und Vorhersagungen erinnern und ermessen können, dass mich diese traurigen Ausbrüche nicht überraschen. Was sagt denn Pattison dazu, der ja das Berlin von vor 1866 aus eigener längerer Anschauung kennt?" The same subject was in his mind in a letter of 11 May 1881, a fortnight before his death:

> Hier, lieber Freund, unter Kreuzband mein neues, kürzlich angekündigtes Buch. Vielleicht finden Sie Zeit, es zu lesen, bevor Sie den in Aussicht gestellten Abstecher nach Bonn machen, auf den ich mich herzlich freue. An Stoff zu Gesprächen, heiteren wie trüben, würde es freilich auch abgesehen von "Phokion" nicht fehlen. Ich werde Ihnen über Vieles, das jetzt bei uns vorgeht, so reinen Wein einschenken, wie man ihn nur mündlich aber nicht brieflich kredenzen kann.
>
> Zu der Paraphrase der Poetik wünsche ich so viel Muth und Glück, wie ein solches Unternehmen erfordert, und das ist freilich nicht wenig. Kennt man den Verfasser von "Rabbi Jeshua. An eastern story. London 1881"?
>
> Das zweite Exemplar des "Phokion" bitte ich Pattison zugleich mit beiliegendem Billet zu geben.
>
> Auf fröhliches Wiedersehen
Ihr Bernays.
>
> Bonn
> 11. Mai 1881.

Notes

ADDITIONAL NOTE: A biography of J. Bernays by H. Bach, Tübingen, 1974, has now appeared.

1. J. Bachofen, *Selbstbiographie und Antrittsrede*, ed. A. Baeumler, Halle, 1927, 18 ff.

2. K. Dockhorn, *Der deutsche Historismus in England*, Göttingen, 1950; D. Forbes, *The Liberal Anglican Idea of History*, Cambridge, 1952.

3. M. Pattison, *Memoirs*, London, 1885, 210.

4. J. Sparrow, *Mark Pattison and the Idea of a University*, Cambridge, 1967. *Cf.* V. H. H. Green, *Oxford Common Room*, London, 1957; W. R. Ward, *Victorian Oxford*, London, 1965.

5. *Isaac Casaubon*, London, 1875 (2d ed., 1892); *Essays*, ed. H. Nettleship, 2 vols., Oxford, 1889. One must compare the curious volume of *Sermons*, London, 1885.

6. A bibliography of M. Pattison was compiled by J. M. Hoare in an unpublished thesis of University College London, School of Librarianship, 1953.

7. *Essays*, I, p. 244.

8. M. Fraenkel, *Jacob Bernays: Ein Lebensbild in Briefen*, Breslau, 1932, p. 91. Further quotations from letters in the text are taken from this book.

9. *Essays*, I. p. 132.

10. *Memoirs*, p. 321.

11. *Aegyptens Stelle in der Weltgeschichte*, 1845–1857; *Christianity and Mankind*, 1854; *Die Zeichen der Zeit*, 1855; *Gott in der Geschichte*, 1857–58, etc. Bibl. in Bussmann, *Neue Deutsche Biographie*, III, 1957, pp. 17–19.

12. On J. B. in general: C. Schaarschmidt, *Bursians Biographisches Jarhbuch*, 4, 1881, pp. 65–83; Th. Gomperz, *Essays und Erinnerungen*, Stuttgart, 1905, pp. 106–25 (originally published in 1881); H. Usener in *Allgem. Deutsche Biographie*, 46, 1902, pp. 393–404 and in the introduction to Bernays, *Gesammelte Abhandlungen*, Berlin, 1885, 2 vols.; S. Frankfurter, *B. B. Mitteilungen für Oesterreich*, 5, 1933, pp. 173–83; W. Schmid in *Bonner Gelehrte* (Philosophie und Altertumswissenschaften), Bonn, 1968, pp. 137–43. M. Fraenkel's selection of letters (quoted above, n. 8) was reviewed by R. Harder, *Gnomon*, 8, 1932, p. 668. Some information is also in works by and on Max Müller (for instance *The Life and Letters of Friedrich Max Müller*, I., London, 1902) and on Chr. J. von Bunsen (on whom see below, p. 138, n. 1).

13. H. Krohn, *Die Juden in Hamburg, 1800–1850*, Hamburg, 1967. On Isaak Bernays (apart from usual reference books) H. Graetz, *Geschichte der Juden*, XI, 2d ed., 1900, pp. 387 and 506; E. Duckesz, *Jahrb. d. Jüdisch-Literarischen Gesellschaft*, 5, 1907, pp. 297–322. G. Scholem, *Leo Baeck Institute Yearbook*, 7, 1962, p. 249 (on L.B. as the author of *Der Bibel'sche Orient*, München, 1821).

14. O. Ribbeck, *F. W. Ritschl*, II, Leipzig, 1881, pp. 95–98. Bernays helped Ritschl for some time in his ill-fated edition of Dionysius's *Roman Antiquities*. The details are given by Ribbeck.

15. Reprinted in *Gesammelte Abhandlungen*, I. pp. 1–36. Bernays was in the Akademisches Gymnasium of Hamburg for one year before going to Bonn in 1844. See C. H. W. Sillem, *Die Matrikel des Akademischen Gymnasiums in Hamburg*, 1891, p. 189.

16. *Essays und Erinnerungen*, Stuttgart, 1905, p. 38 (the text is not unambiguous in its reference to Bernays): *cf.* H. Gomperz, *T. Gomperz: Briefe und Aufzeichnungen*, Wien, 1936, p. 146; p. 160.

17. *Jugenderinnerungen und Bekenntnisse*, 3d ed., Berlin, 1900, pp. 104–7.

18. *Mein Penatenwinkel*, I, 2d ed., Frankfurt a.M., 1908, pp. 57–71. It was probably through his friendship with the Wied family that Bernays became a member of a

committee to improve the situation of Balkan Jews in 1878: N. M. Gelber, *Leo Baeck Inst. Yearbook*, 5, 1960, p. 235.

19. M. Fraenkel, *J. B.*, pp. 50–60; reprinted in F. Kobler, *Juden und Judentum in deutschen Briefen aus drei Jahrhunderten*, Wien, 1935, pp. 290–93. *Cf.* Frances Baroness Bunsen, *A Memoir of Baron Bunsen*, II, London, 1868, p. 270, on the London visit.

20. Mommsen, *Reden und Aufsätze*, 3d ed., Berlin, 1912, pp. 410–26, especially pp. 423–24. The main texts of the controversy are now collected in W. Boehlich, *Der Berliner Antisemitismusstreit*, Frankfurt a.M., 2d ed., 1965.

21. *Hist. Zeitschrift*, 205, 1967, pp. 265–94. *Cf.* also Th. Mommsen-O. Jahn, *Briefwechsel*, ed. L. Wickert, Frankfurt a.M., 1962, p. 201 and elsewhere (Index s.v. Bernays). Bernays's essay on Mommsen in *Gesamm. Abhandlungen*, II, pp. 255–75.

22. M. Fraenkel, *Jacob Bernays*, p. 163.

23. Some information in M. Brann, *Geschichte des jüdisch-theologischen Seminars in Breslau*, Breslau, 1904, pp. 54–60; 124–26 (important for Bernays's Jewish interests). H. Cohen as a student left the Seminary after disagreements with Bernays. Even later he disliked his memory. *Cf.* H. Cohen, *Jüdische Schriften*, II, Berlin, 1924, pp. 420–21 (1904): "Es war kein lebendiges, schaffendes, aufbauendes Denken, welches in dieser gewaltigen Maschine arbeitete . . . Daher empfand er den Trieb nicht in sich, die Ideen des Judentums, das fortwirkende Wesen desselben seinen christlichen Freunden bekannt und deutlich zu machen."

24. *Kleine Schriften*, 2, 1927, p. 424 (from *Rheinisches Museum*, 36, 1881, p. 480). On B. in Bonn *cf.* also P. E. Hübinger, *Hist. Jahrb.*, 83, 1964, p. 162. In 1869 I. Bywater spoke of "the critical tact and poetical insight into the mind of antiquity by virtue of which he [B.] stands so completely alone among living scholars" (*Journ. of Philology*, 2, p. 55).

25. *Erinnerungen*, 1928, pp. 87–88.

26. B. Auerbach, *Briefe an seinen Freund Jacob Auerbach*, Frankfurt, a.M., 1884, I, p. 328; *cf.* II, p. 459 where Bernays's dictum is quoted: "Man habe kein Recht die Tradition aufzulösen."

27. The letter is reprinted in the Tel-Aviv *Leo Baeck Institute Bulletin*, 4, 1961, p. 321 by M. Reuwen. It was originally published in *Der Morgen*, II, 1935–36, p. 365 by M. Fraenkel.

28. H. Usener-U. Wilamowitz, *Ein Briefwechsel*, Berlin, 1934, p. 36.

29. *Cf.* for instance S. H. Butcher, *Aristotle's Theory of Poetry and Fine Art*, 2d ed., London, 1898, p. 236; G. Finsler, *Platon und die Aristotelische Poetik*, Leipzig, 1900, p. 96; I. Bywater's Commentary on the *Poetics*, Oxford, 1909, *ad l.* (pp. 152–61); L. Golden, *Trans. Am. Phil. Ass.*, 93, 1962, pp. 51–60; D. W. Lucas, Commentary on the *Poetics*, Oxford, 1968, pp. 273–90. F. Ueberweg-K. Praechter, *Philosophie des Altertums*, 1926, pp. 120–21, gives a bibliography until 1925. See also L. Cooper and A. Gudeman, *A Bibliography of the Poetics of A.*, New Haven, 1928; M. T. Herrick, *Am. Journ. Phil.*, 52, 1931, p. 168. The fortunes of Bernays's interpretation of *Katharsis* deserve a special investigation. (See K. Gründer's introduction to the reprint of the *Grundzüge*, Hildesheim, 1970.)

30. *F. N's. Briefwechsel mit Erwin Rohde*, Leipzig, 1923, pp. 273–80.

31. *Griechische Tragödie*, Leipzig, 1930, I., pp. 529–33.

32. S. Freud, *Briefe 1873–1939,* Frankfurt a.M., 1960, pp. 19–24. *Cf.* D. W. Lucas, *Commentary on Aristotle's "Poetics,"* 1968, p. 289.

33. E. Jones, *Sigmund Freud: Life and Work,* I, London, 1953, p. 112.

34. E. Kris, *Psychoanalytic Explorations in Art,* London, 1953, pp. 62–63.

35. *Journ. of Philology,* 2, 1869, pp. 55–69. *Cf.* W. Jaeger, *Aristotle,* Engl. transl., 2d ed., Oxford, 1948, p. 60; A.-H. Chroust, *Symb. Osloenses,* 42, 1968, pp. 7–43.

36. Now in *Ges. Abhandlungen,* I, pp. 192–261. F. Dornseiff amusingly tried to save this poem for Phocylides in *Echtheitsfragen antik-griechischer Literatur,* Berlin, 1939, pp. 37–51. See also Bernays's note "Zur vergleichenden Mythologie" (*Rheinisches Museum,* 1860), now *Ges. Abhandlungen,* II, pp. 294–96, with its characteristic conclusion in the style of Heine.

37. J. Bernays, *Ges. Abhandlungen,* II, pp. 81–200 (dedicated to Max Müller); H. Montefiore, *Historia,* 11, 1962, pp. 156–70.

38. W. Jaeger, *Diokles von Karystos,* Berlin, 1938, pp. 134–53; *Scripta minora,* II, Roma, 1960, pp. 169–83. For later research the ed. by W. Pötscher, *Theophrastus, περὶ εὐσεβείας,* Leiden, 1964.

39. *Cf.* E. Norden, *Jahrb. f. class. Philol.,* Suppl. 19, 1893, p. 386 and the very different opinion in *Agnostos Theos,* reprint 1923, pp. 389–90; I. Heinemann, *Pauly-Wissowa,* Suppl. V, 1931, pp. 228–32. *Cf.* E. Schürer, *Geschichte des jüd. Volkes,* III, 4th ed., 1909, pp. 624–25, also for Diogenes *ep.* 28 studied by Bernays.

40. Usener-Wilamowitz, *Briefwechsel,* p. 26.

41. Lucien de Samosate, *Philopseudès et De Morte Peregrini,* Paris, 1951, p. 63.

42. *Antigonos von Karystos,* Berlin, 1881, pp. 182 n. 4, 339.

43. *Phokion,* p. 97.

44. *Ges. Abhandlungen,* II, pp. 291–93 with an important addition to the original text in *Rheinisches Museum.* Another admirable piece of research discovered interpolations in Pseudo-Apuleius, *Asclepius,* which were suggested by antipagan laws of the fourth century A.D.: see *Ges. Abhandl.,* I, p. 328 and A. D. Nock-A. J. Festugière, *Corpus Hermeticum,* II, 1945, p. 288 n. 2.

45. *Cf.* G. Maddoli, "Senocrate nel clima politico del suo tempo," *Dialoghi di Archeologia,* I, 1967, pp. 304–27.

46. H. Cohen, *Jüdische Schriften,* II, p. 421 spoke of the "Schellingscher Mystizismus" which J. Bernays inherited from his father. This is not apparent in his writings, though a letter to Heyse after Schelling's death in 1854 (M. Fraenkel, p. 75) implies admiration for, and perhaps personal acquaintance with, Schelling. Bernays's interest in Neoplatonic thought, even if it was originally inspired by Schelling and Creuzer, was later independent of their influence. Bernays's sympathy with Voltaire and Gibbon is not easily reconcilable with the alleged "Schellingian mysticism"; but as I have said, Bernays never made public his deepest beliefs.

47. Usener-Wilamowitz, *Briefwechsel,* p. 7.

[Additional note (April 1969). My colleague Professor G. J. Weiss had drawn my attention to a letter from Sigmund Freud to Arnold Zweig in their recently published *Briefwechsel* (Frankfurt a.M., 1968, p. 59) which shows that Freud took a direct part in the publication of M. Fraenkel's book *Jacob Bernays: Ein Lebensbild in Briefen,* 1932 (above, p. 143). Furthermore, I should like to refer to N. Rubinstein, "Il

Poliziano e la questione delle origini di Firenze," in *Il Poliziano e il suo tempo,* Florence, 1957, p. 108 for the importance of Bernays's discovery that Politianus read Johannes Lydus. Finally, I should like to mention Louis Robert's "De Delphes à l'Oxus: Inscriptions nouvelles de la Bactriane," *C.R. Acad. Inscr.,* 1968, p. 451 on the question of Clearchus's reference to the Jews which had interested Bernays in connection with Theophrastus (above, p. 147)].

48. In accordance with Jacob Bernays's will, letters from his correspondents were returned to them. Bernays's letters to Pattison are therefore together with Pattison's letters to Bernays in the Bodleian Library. But the letter from Pattison to which this letter is a reply has apparently not been preserved. I was therefore unable to identify the "Kieler Programm" to which Bernays alludes in answer to Pattison.

49. See Pattison, *Essays,* I, pp. 337–414.

50. Epistola Josephi Scaligeri ad Petrum Rogoseum Bagarrium, in F. Schultze, *Epistolae virorum doctorum ineditae,* Lignitii, 1827.

51. *Theophrastos' Schrift über Frömmigkeit.*

52. "Zu Aristoteles und Clemens," in *Symbola philologorum Bonnensium in honorem Frid. Ritschelii collecta,* Lipsiae, 1864, p. 301.

53. Letters by I. Bywater to Bernays in W. W. Jackson, *I. Bywater,* Oxford, 1917, pp. 102–6. The query about *Daniel Deronda* answered on p. 105. P. Vidal-Naquet called my attention to O. Rank, *Das Inzestmotiv in Dichtung und Sage,* Leipzig, 1912, p. 4 on B. and Freud.

TEN

J. G. Droysen
Between Greeks and Jews

If asked what we mean by Hellenism, we should probably answer that we mean the historical period which goes from the death of Alexander the Great (323 B.C.) to the death of Cleopatra in 30 B.C. Egypt was the last important survivor of the political system which had developed as a consequence both of the victories of Alexander and of his premature death. With the absorption of Egypt into the Roman Empire, that political system came to an end. Even today, however, there is considerable disagreement among historians as to what the word *Hellenism* is intended to signify. Hellenism suggests to us more the idea of a civilization than the idea of a mere political system. When used to indicate a civilization, the word *Hellenism* is seldom confined to the chronologies and spatial limits within which we use it to indicate a political system. We often speak of Hellenism in the Roman Empire to indicate the cultural tradition of the Greek-speaking part of the Roman Empire: we even incline to extend the Hellenistic tradition into the Byzantine empire. On the other hand, the word Hellenism is often associated with the cultures of Carthage and Rome—not to speak of southern Italy and Sicily—which were never part of the empire of Alexander.

As a rule terminological ambiguities should never detain a scholar for long. We all know what a waste of time the word *Renaissance* has represented. But at the root of this particular terminological ambiguity there are the ambiguities of the *Geschichte des Hellenismus* by Johann Gustav Droysen, one of the greatest historians of any time.[1] It was J. G. Droysen who

---

"J. G. Droysen between Greeks and Jews," *History and Theory,* 9 (1970), pp. 139–53; *Quinto contributo* (1975), pp. 109–26; *Essays in Ancient and Modern Historiography* (1977), pp. 307–23; French translation, *Problèmes d'historiographie ancienne et moderne* (1983), pp. 383–401; Italian translation, *Tra storia e storicismo* (1985), pp. 211–31; German translation, *Wege in die Alte Welt* (1991), pp. 177–91. (501)

introduced the word Hellenism to designate the civilization of the Greek-speaking world after Alexander. He himself was not very clear about the chronological limits he intended to give to this word. There are passages of his work in which it is applied to the whole period before the Arab invasion of Egypt and Syria, whereas more frequently he calls Hellenism the period between Alexander and Jesus, which roughly corresponds to our usage.[2] But what matters to us is that Droysen himself never reached clarity about the main characteristics of the period he set out to explore. I do not intend to return here to those aspects of Droysen's thought which are best known.[3] The problem with which I shall be dealing here is new, at least to the best of my knowledge.[4]

A tradition which goes back to antiquity makes the decline of Greece coincide with the death of Alexander the Great—or rather with the death of Demosthenes. This is a deserved tribute to the role of Athens in Greek civilization. In literary terms it means classicism. To quote Plutarch only, both Demosthenes and Cicero ended their lives as soon as their countrymen ceased to be free (*Demosthenes* 3). Such a tradition, however, does not account for the poor reputation of Egypt and Syria and Pergamum as political, social, and cultural organizations of the third and second centuries B.C. Here two factors played their part: one is ancient, the other modern. One factor was the contempt in which the Romans held their Greek-speaking enemies after they had reduced them to impotence in the first part of the second century B.C.—a contempt which was shared by influential Greek observers such as Polybius. The other factor is the paucity of the literary evidence about the third century B.C. The literary fragments of the third and second centuries B.C. seemed to confirm by their very nature the impression of decline and fall. After Theocritus, Callimachus, and Apollonius Rhodius, there seemed to be a desert in Greek literature of the third and second centuries B.C.—except for epigrams. No historian or philosopher of the third century B.C. has come down to us in a complete text. True enough, the loss of third- and second-century Greek literature happened in the Middle Ages and has nothing to do with the conditions of the period between the death of Alexander and Roman rule in the East. But it is difficult to resist the first impression that there is something wrong with an age which has left an insufficient account of itself. When Droysen wrote his doctoral dissertation *De Lagidarum regno Ptolemaeo VI Philometore rege* in 1831, it was still necessary for him to apologize for dealing with an age which "propter sterilitatem suam atque languorem negligi, a Romanarum rerum scriptoribus despici, a Christianarum deformari defamarique solet."[5]

As we all know, it was precisely J. G. Droysen who first decided to explore thoroughly the Greek-speaking world in the centuries after Alexander. Alexandrian literature had been put on the map by a famous essay by C. Gottlob Heyne, *De genio saeculi Ptolemaeorum,* in 1763.[6] Later on, the discovery of the Armenian Eusebius was to inspire a fundamental essay on the political and dynastic events of the third century B.C. by Niebuhr (1819). Inscriptions and papyri were attracting increasing attention. Champollion's decipherment of Egyptian hieroglyphics naturally added interest to those Greek inscriptions of Egypt from which his discovery had started. In France an epigraphist of genius, Jean Antoine Letronne, showed what one could do with these inscriptions in his *Recherches pour servir à l'histoire de l'Égypte sous la domination des Grecs et des Romains* (1823). Droysen learned all these things from his teacher Boeckh at the University of Berlin. From Boeckh he also learned to reflect on the differences between Classical civilization and Christian civilization. Boeckh returned regularly to the subject in his lectures on *Encyclopädie und Methodologie der philologischen Wissenschaften,* which he gave twenty-six times between 1809 and 1865. He did not, however, offer any precise suggestion about the process of transition from the pagan to the Christian world. The theologians and philosophers of Berlin University were much readier to produce ideas on this question of the transition. Droysen listened to several of them: the theologian August Neander, Eduard Gans, the pupil of Hegel, and Hegel himself. Hegel had offered one solution in his *Philosophie der Weltgeschichte.* This solution was to find in Roman civilization, and more precisely in the Roman state, the preparatory stage for the development of the Christian idea. Droysen meditated on Hegel and accepted his basic presupposition that history moves forward by thesis, antithesis, and synthesis. But Boeckh saved him from *a priori* speculations about the course of history and very probably also directed his attention towards the Greek-speaking states of the post-Alexandrian era.

Whatever the precise origins of his ideas may be, they matured very rapidly. In December 1833, two years after his rather crude dissertation, Droysen published his *Geschichte Alexanders des Grossen,* 584 pages thick, in which his idea of Hellenism is clearly formulated.

The word itself, *Hellenism,* already existed in scholarly terminology.[7] It was originally taken over from Acts of the Apostles 6:1, where Ἑλληνισταί are opposed to Ἑβραῖοι. Scaliger spread the notion of Ἑλληνισταί as Jewish speakers using Greek in the synagogue service: Ἑλληνισταί *Iudaei graecis Bibliis in Synagogis utentes* (*in Eusebium,* ed. Lugduni, Bat., 1606, 124 *b*). The existence of a special Greek dialect for these Jewish speakers in Greek was hotly debated in the seventeenth century. Salmasius denied it in a discussion with D. Heinsius and wrote one of his most famous polemical pamphlets, or rather books, on this subject: *Funus linguae hellenisticae* (1643).[8]

The notion of *lingua hellenistica* to indicate the Greek of the Old and New Testaments survived Salmasius. Later, in the eighteenth century, the word *Hellenismus* was extended to cover the way of thinking of those Jews who spoke Greek. Herder used *Hellenismus* repeatedly in that sense.[9] Closer to Droysen, J. Matter, a French scholar who was under the influence of German scholarship, wrote in 1820: "Les études auxquelles se livrèrent les Juifs en Égypte produisèrent cette manière de penser et d'écrire qu'on désigne sous le nom d'Hellénisme." (*Essai historique sur l'école d'Alexandrie*, I, p. 203). The originality of Droysen was to take Hellenism to mean, not specifically the way of thinking of Jews under the influence of Greek language and thought, but generally the language and way of thinking of all the populations which had been conquered by Alexander and subjected to Greek influence. In other words, he used the word Hellenism to indicate the intermediary and transitional period between classical Greece and Christianity. As we shall see later, the Jews interested Droysen much less than the Egyptians, the Babylonians, the Syrians. Hellenism was to Droysen essentially that stage in the evolution of paganism which led from classical Greece to Christianity—not via Judaism, but via other Oriental religions. It was a stage in the evolution of paganism which resulted from the contact between Orientals and Greeks in the empire created by Alexander and subdivided by his successors. So conceived, Hellenism had two aspects. It was a cultural movement which produced a new synthesis of Oriental and Greek ideas. It was also a political development which resulted in the constitution of a system of states in which Oriental natives were governed by a Greco-Macedonian aristocracy.

Droysen was perhaps never fully aware that the notion of Hellenism he propounded had two very different aspects—the political and the cultural—and that there was a problem in relating one aspect to the other. This was not a serious difficulty in the initial stage of his work, when he wrote the history of Alexander. In the original plan the volume on Alexander was meant to be only the necessary introduction to the history of Hellenism proper. The question of the relation between political history and cultural (and religious) history was bound to become serious, indeed decisive, when he entered the specific field of Hellenism.

In a sense he never gave an answer to the question. Droysen devoted the only two volumes of the *Geschichte des Hellenismus* which he was actually to write (one published in 1836, the other in 1843) to the political history of the period 323–221 B.C. The volumes he had intended to write on the period from 221 to Augustus and on the cultural history from Alexander to the Arabs were never written, and we do not know what Droysen meant to put into them. After 1843 he devoted more than forty years of his scholarly activity to the history of Prussia, on which he became the highest authority: *Vorlesungen über das Zeitalter der Freiheitskriege* (1st ed., Kiel, 1846); *Das Leben des Grafen Yorck von Wartenburg* (Leipzig, 1851); *Geschichte der preussischen Politik* (Leipzig, 1855–85). One might have thought that he had forgotten his former field of study. But in 1877–78 he surprised everyone by providing a revised, fully up-to-date edition of his work on Hellenism. One of the new features of the new edition was that the volume on Alexander was now explicitly the first part of the *Geschichte des Hellenismus* instead of being an introductory volume. Readers are advised to remember that *Geschichte des Hellenismus,* volume I of the first edition, has become *Geschichte des Hellenismus,* volume II in the second edition. It is this new edition, which was translated into French by A. Bouché-Leclercq, that started the great revival of studies in the political and institutional history of the Hellenistic period in the last decades of the nineteenth century and in the early twentieth century. Like the first edition, the renewed *Geschichte des Hellenismus* contained a program of cultural and religious history, but was in fact exclusively an examination of the political history of the period 323–221 B.C. We are therefore faced with the following paradox. Droysen set out to write a history of the transition from paganism to Christianity and never changed his mind on this. Though in the second edition of 1877–78 he modified the text of some of his programmatic declarations of the first edition, he never departed from his original interpretation of Hellenism as the period of three centuries in which Greeks and Orientals met and made Christianity possible. On the other hand, Droysen never wrote about these cultural developments. He never went beyond programmatic declarations on them. What he really achieved was a political history of one century—a political history which became a classic as soon as it was published. We may sharpen the paradox by a further remark. If there was an historian Droysen disliked, it was his contemporary Ranke.[10] Ranke represented for Droysen the very image of the detached historian, of the *Quellenforscher,* who does not take sides and prefers mild diplomacy to battles of ideas doubled by battles of swords. Yet what we have of the history of Hellenism closely resembles the masterpiece of Ranke's youth, *Geschichten der romanischen und germanischen Völker* (1824). Both works are histories of relations between states belonging to the same civilization.

Droysen's paradox used to be explained in a simple way. Droysen started as a Hegelian historian of ideas, but soon turned to political history. He discovered that what mattered in Hellenism was the power of the Macedonian army. Macedon being the Prussia of antiquity, he was consistent in proceeding from Macedon to Prussia. The history of Hellenism was a *praeparatio evangelica* to the history of Prussia. I am of course making this explanation simpler than it is. Ultimately it goes back to Droysen himself. In his *Antrittsrede* to the Berlin Academy in 1867 he said that he had interrupted his *History of Hellenism* because his appointment as a professor in Kiel (1840) had made him more acutely aware of the political problems of Germany. Kiel was "in the border zones, already imperiled, of German life" ("in den schon gefährdeten Grenzgebieten deutschen Lebens").[11] In its two most sophisticated versions, provided by historians such as F. Meinecke and F. Gilbert, this explanation takes into account Droysen's profound concern with the Christian faith.[12] Yet even in these subtlest versions such an interpretation leaves out something.

Droysen worked for twelve full years on the history of Hellenism before turning to modern history (and not just to the history of Prussia), and in these twelve years he never lost sight of his aim of making Christianity intelligible in historical terms. He was then, and remained afterward, an unorthodox Lutheran. Religion mattered to him. He always felt that Providence had been at work in sending Alexander and in making East and West meet in the kingdoms of his successors. The statements to this effect are many in the *History of Hellenism* and in the *Correspondence*. In the last chapter of the final volume of the *History of Hellenism* (1843) he says solemnly: "Truly history has now created the body for the Holy Spirit of the New Revelation and of the New Covenant. Around it congregates the community of the Believers, the Church of Christ."[13]

The most striking document of this religious attitude is the so-called *Theologie der Geschichte,* an open letter to his friend J. Olshausen. It was originally meant as an introduction to the 1843 volume of the *Geschichte des Hellenismus* (volume II). Droysen must, however, have felt that this was more a profession of faith than an historical essay, and he published it separately in a few copies for private circulation. The paper became generally accessible only after Droysen's death when it was included in the *Kleine Schriften zur Alten Geschichte* in 1893. The title of *Theologie der Geschichte* is to be found in the reprint by E. Rothacker (1925), not in the *Kleine Schriften.* Droysen here stated his belief of how Providence worked in the obscure and despised centuries he called Hellenism.

It is therefore remarkable that in the same decade 1833–43 Droysen showed far more interest in the classical than in the postclassical literature and religion of the Greeks. Though the importance of Droysen's work on Aeschylus and Aristophanes is acknowledged, the implications of it for his attitude towards Hellenism have not yet been sufficiently considered. In 1832 Droysen published his translation of Aeschylus, which contributed much to the interpretation of the poet in literary and historical terms. But epoch-making was the translation of Aristophanes in three volumes which appeared in 1835, 1837, and 1838 respectively. Nobody had previously understood Aristophanes so well in relation to Athenian social and political life. The care which Droysen put into this work is shown by his paper "Des Aristophanes Vögel und die Hermokopiden," which appeared in *Rheinisches Museum* (1835–36)[14] and has since remained the standard work on the scandal of the desecration of the Herms in 415 B.C. In later years Droysen returned to Aeschylean problems under the influence of F. G. Welcker, whose admirer and correspondent he was. He wrote papers on the questions of the Trilogy in 1841 and 1844, with further contributions to the political interpretation of Aeschylus' *Persae*.[15] In 1842 he published a revised edition of his translation of Aeschylus.

As is evident from many of his remarks on Aeschylus and Aristophanes, Droysen intended to contribute to contemporary artistic life. He considered it important to make Athenian classical poetry accessible to the German public. The first volume of his Aristophanes translation was dedicated to Felix Mendelssohn-Bartholdy, the composer, and to Albert Gustav Heydemann, a fellow student; the third volume was dedicated to Eduard Bendemann, the painter. His appreciation of Aristophanes was enhanced by his personal acquaintance with Heine. The performance of the *Antigone* in Berlin in 1842, with Mendelssohn's music, was an occasion for a literary manifesto by Droysen on the situation of the contemporary theatre.[16] It is unnecessary here to expatiate on the well-known friendship and collaboration between Droysen and Mendelssohn.[17] It was Droysen's ambition and pride to provide his friend with words for his music. The revival of Greek classical art was the aim of this collaboration, at least as Droysen saw it.

Droysen was aware of the roots of Athenian art in Athenian society. Just as he was abandoning the classical world for modern politics in 1847 he produced a paper on "Die attische Communalverfassung,"[18] which for almost thirty years remained his last substantial contribution to classical studies. It was a searching and original analysis of the political life of the Attic villages in the archaic and the classical age. In Droysen's interpretation, Solon and Clisthenes allowed freedom in religious, patrimonial, and administrative matters to the villages of Attica. They created a characteristic balance between the Athenian polis and its individual components which eliminated any rivalry "zwischen Staat und Commune" and contributed much to the liberty of the Athenian citizens. No doubt Droysen had in mind contemporary problems of the Prussian state in speaking of the balance "zwischen Staat und Commune," but he also felt that there was some connection between the varied and free life of Attica and the varied and free poetry of Athens. His perception of such a connection was never very clear, but it was certainly more definite than anything he ever thought about the relations between Hellenistic institutions and Hellenistic culture.

The surprising fact is that while he was working on Hellenistic political history Droysen did not concurrently study Hellenistic poetry, philosophy, and religion, as we should have expected. He was reading, translating, interpreting, popularizing Attic literature, and clearly considered it the center of his emotional life. While he was intellectually convinced that Providence had guided mankind along the path of Hellenism in order to produce Christianity, he found the pagan literature of pre-Hellenistic Athens far more satisfying. He claimed that Hellenism interested him as a Christian. But he recommended Aeschylus and Aristophanes to his contemporaries.

In other words, literary classicism kept him away from Hellenistic culture, though culture, including religion, was supposed to be the principal object of his study of Hellenism.

Nor was classicism the only obstacle in Droysen's attempt to explain Christianity historically. He had started his work on Hellenism on the assumption that the rise of Christianity could be explained by the situation of the pagan world in the Hellenistic age. He was no theologian and knew little of Judaism. What he knew had apparently convinced him that Christianity was nearer to Greek paganism than to Judaism. One of the theses he offered for discussion at the oral examination for his doctorate in 1831 was "a doctrina Christiana Graecorum quam Iudaeorum religio propius abest."[19] Of course, theses offered for discussion at an examination need not be stated on oath. Sophistry is part of the game. But Droysen's point of view, at least in the first two volumes of his Hellenistic work (1833 and 1836), is in agreement with this doctoral thesis. When he speaks of Christianity, the emphasis is invariably on the encounter of Greeks and non-Jewish Orientals: Jews are left out.

The appearance of the *Life of Jesus* by D. Strauss in 1835–36 shocked Droysen as it shocked many others. But there was nothing in the work of Strauss which caused him to change his mind about his interpretation of Hellenism. What Droysen felt after reading Strauss (and later Bruno Bauer) was an increased distrust of Hegel's methods, if they could lead to such blasphemous conclusions.[20] There was, however, other research in progress which Droysen was bound to examine with greater care in relation to his own studies. In the early 1830s a remarkable upsurge of interest in Philo and Alexandrian Judaism in general was noticeable in Germany. The purpose of this research was to ascertain whether Philo had influenced St. Paul and altogether contributed to the development of Christianity. It will be enough here to mention two books which are still worth consulting today: A. Gfrörer, *Philo und die alexandrinische Theosophie* (1831) and A. F. Dähne, *Geschichtliche Darstellung der jüdisch-alexandrinischen Religionsphilosophie* (1834). This new research added to the importance of a relatively older book by one of Droysen's teachers: the *Genetische Entwickelung der vornehmsten gnostischen Systeme* by A. Neander, which had appeared in 1818. Neander had propounded a distinction between Jewish and anti-Jewish Gnostics and had indicated the relevance of Jewish Gnostics (among whom he included Philo) to the origins of Christianity. The topical interest of Neander's book was recognized by F. C. Baur, who developed Neander's thesis in his book *Die christliche Gnosis* (1835) to the point of connecting Schleiermacher with anti-Jewish Gnosis and Hegel with Jewish or pro-Jewish Gnosis.[21]

The whole of Baur's research in those years underlined the significance of Jewish-Greek contacts for the origins of Christianity. Baur believed that the Essenes had been influenced by the Pythagoreans and that in their turn the Essenes had influenced early Christianity (*Apollonius von Tyana und Christus*, 1832). The interpretation of St. Paul, with which Baur's name is connected forever, implied that Pauline doctrines were an internal development of Judaism in the direction of the Greco-Roman world. The fact that Baur had turned from Schleiermacher to Hegel in his research on the Christian origins may not have been a point in his favor with a disillusioned Hegelian like Droysen. But Droysen was too good a scholar to remain indifferent to all the serious research which was going on around him on the relations between Judaism and Christianity. The notion of Gnosis, which Neander and Baur had forcibly made a contemporary issue, competed with his own notion of Hellenism. Gnosis indicated a combination of Jewish and Greek factors in the origins of Christianity, whereas Hellenism implied a purely pagan approach to Christianity.

There are signs that Droysen reconsidered his position in the years between 1837 and 1843, while he was writing his third volume on Hellenism. In 1838 he published a very important review of G. Bernhardy's *Grundriss der griechischen Litteratur,* volume I, in which he formulated a distinction between the learned and the popular literature of Hellenism.[22] He took the popular (*volksthümliche*) literature to include the expressions of non-Greek people writing in Greek—such as Philo and the Septuaginta translation of the Old Testament. He recognized that it was a mistake on the part of classical scholars to leave such a literature in the hands of theologians. It is therefore not surprising that in the last chapter of the *History of Hellenism,* volume II (1843) Judaism is mentioned for the first time as an important factor in the origins of Christianity. The mention is cursory, but Droysen is aware that he is saying something new.[23] A few months later, in a letter to F. G. Welcker of 12 September 1843, we find Droysen talking about the Sibylline oracles and the Hellenistic books of the Old Testament. He expresses his intention of extending his reading to the vast mass of Apocrypha.[24]

To sum up, at least from 1838 onward Droysen became more interested in Judaism. He included Jewish books in the popular literature of which he intended to make a special study. He was not indifferent to the mounting research on Alexandrian Judaism, on the Essenes, and on Paulinism. He seemed to be preparing himself for the next volume of the *History of Hellenism.* Yet nothing happened. He must have soon interrupted his readings. He never expressed any articulate opinion on what he had already read.

Once again we are faced with the question: why did he not pursue this obviously fruitful line? Once again, no easy answer will do. What Droysen envisaged in his study of Oriental texts was in many ways premature. A glance at R. Reitzenstein's *Poimandres,* which appeared in 1904 and can be said to have been written in Droysen's spirit, is enough to show how much of the evidence was still unknown in 1843. Inscriptions, papyri, Egyptian texts, even literary texts, such as Hippolytus' *Philosophoumena*, were later additions to knowledge. Yet what was available in 1843 was more than sufficient for spade work. Droysen did not suspend his work for lack of evidence.

The classicism of his literary tastes may have helped to delay his research on Jewish texts, but does not explain why he interrupted his work on them once he had started it. In 1838 Droysen had satisfied himself that new research on Jewish texts was necessary—and possible. The reasons for his unwillingness to pursue it, if it can be explained at all, must be sought elsewhere. Increasing involvement in the German national problem is certainly part of the story. But it is also true that Droysen had reached the point in his exploration of Hellenism at which he had to decide whether to include or exclude Judaism. The inclusion would have meant a radical revision of the original conception; it would have involved him in the difficult exegetic problems raised by the Tübingen theologians; and it would have touched intimate recesses of his personal life. The last aspect deserves special attention.

As a student and young teacher in Berlin, this son of a Lutheran pastor found his friends and his first wife in a circle of highly educated Jewish converts to Protestantism. He dedicated his book on Alexander to Gottlieb Friedlaender, who was the grandson of David Friedlaender, the champion of Jewish emancipation. He married Marie Mendheim, the sister of Gottlieb Friedlaender's wife. Marie Mendheim was the daughter of a Jewish bookseller who apparently changed his name Mendel to Mendheim when a convert. Her mother belonged to the Friedlaender family. Droysen's other two closest friends, F. Mendelssohn and E. Bendemann, were both of Jewish origin. Heine and Gans belonged to the same society. It is interesting to note that G. Bernhardy, whose history of Greek literature Droysen discussed from the point of view of religious history, was himself a convert from Judaism. Less near, but influential, was another convert, August Neander, born David Mendel—at that time perhaps the most eminent and respected Lutheran theologian. Some of these converts thought hard about Judaism before and after their conversion. Neander made a thorough study of Philo. Both Gans and Heine had belonged before conversion to the *Verein für Cultur und Wissenschaft der Juden*. Gans had presided over it. This was a society for the study and reform of Judaism, and it was deeply under the influence of Hegelian ideas. For a while Hegelianism and Judaism had seemed to be reciprocally compatible, an attitude which perhaps explains why Baur had classified Hegelian philosophy as Gnosticism of the Jewish variety.[25] Readers of Heine are in no need to be told that all his work, even after conversion, was a continuous *confessio iudaica*—as indeed it has been called. I am less clear about the religious ideas of Felix Mendelssohn and Gottlieb Friedlaender, but both are said to have combined deep Christian beliefs with devotion to the memories of their respective Jewish grandfathers. Conversion was taken seriously, but did not mean oblivion of the Jewish ancestry and tradition. Yet surrounding society asked these men and women to behave as if they had no Jewish past, and in general they complied with this requirement. Heine had greater freedom because he was in exile in Paris. Silence on Judaism was the official line. Droysen seems to have conformed absolutely to this convention in his relations with his friends of Jewish origin. His letters to Gottlieb Friedlaender, Mendelssohn, and Bendemann, as far as I remember, never touch upon Jewish subjects. Even the marriage to Marie Mendheim must have happened under this unwritten law. Gustav Droysen, himself a historian, who left a good unfinished biography of his father Johann Gustav, never mentions the circumstance that his mother was Jewish. The taboo was deeply ingrained, and I wonder whether it did not affect Droysen as an historian. He had started from the notion that Christianity can be explained with little reference to Judaism. He had perhaps come to realize the weakness of such an exclusive approach. The work of the Tübingen school had indeed shown that it was difficult to talk seriously about the origins of Christianity without a prolonged study of the Jewish background. Droysen did some work on Jewish texts, but he never brought himself to face the whole problem of the relation between Judaism and Christianity. It was the problem which at a personal level had deeply concerned his best friends, his wife, and his relatives — and it was going to affect his own children. He must have known that his friends were thinking about it in their silences. He remained silent, too. The *History of Hellenism* was never finished.

To write chapters of the history of historiography with references to social taboos about allegedly unpleasant subjects is a dangerous task — and I do not claim to be on safe ground. But certain consequences for the concept of Hellenism must now be considered.

As we have seen, Droysen claimed that Hellenism was an avenue (or rather *the* avenue) to Christianity, but he himself studied it as a political phenomenon. His two approaches — one programmatic and the other effective — conditioned the research of the next generations. Hellenism, as a religious phenomenon, attracted the minds of many great scholars at the end of the nineteenth century: Usener, Cumont, Reitzenstein are the most distinguished. They were mainly interested in the interplay of Oriental and Greek beliefs: syncretism was their guiding notion. Reitzenstein undoubtedly cherished the hope of explaining the origins of Christianity in Hellenistic terms. His hope seemed to come near fulfillment when the Mandaean texts attracted his attention. It was his thesis that these were documents of a pre-Christian faith connected with St. John the Baptist. As we all know, the Mandaean question proved to be more intractable than Reitzenstein had anticipated.[26] But other documents, such as the Egyptian Gnostic texts, too late for Reitzenstein to use, have raised analogous hopes in more recent researchers.

Meanwhile great progress was also being made in the study of Hellenism inside Judaism. E. Bickerman's recent work, *Four Strange Books of the Bible* (1968), is perhaps the most striking product of this trend of research, of which the volume by Martin Hengel, *Judentum und Hellenismus* (1969), provides an up-to-date summary in 692 pages.

Even the proto-monks of Qumran have not remained immune from the suspicion of Hellenistic influences: their *Manual of Discipline* has been compared with the rules of Hellenistic religious associations. However, to start from Hellenism in the interpretation of Christianity does not necessarily mean to end with Hellenism. A great specialist of Hellenistic religious movements, A. D. Nock, indicated the points in which Christianity appeared to him original: conversion was one. So much for the religious side of Droysen's approach to Hellenism.

On the other side Droysen inspired research on political history and political institutions. Such research was helped by the discovery of new epigraphical and papyrological material. The more one knew about Hellenistic institutions, especially of Egypt, the stronger the temptation became of presenting Hellenism as a bourgeois, capitalistic civilization. The bureaucratic apparatus, the growth of urban centers, the realism in art, the banks, the international traffic, the development of science and technology reminded the historians of conditions in France and Germany in the middle of the nineteenth century. U. Wilcken, K. J. Beloch, U. Wilamowitz, J. Kaerst, and later of course M. Rostovtzeff, described the modern features of the Hellenistic world. The new papyri of Menander and Herodas confirmed this impression of a bourgeois culture. Even the combination of superstition and of technological progress seemed to fit into the bourgeois pattern. The major departure from Droysen was in the new insistence on the purely Greek character of Hellenistic civilization, at least in its creative phase. In that vigorous survey of Hellenistic history which is the first volume of *Hellenistische Dichtung in der Zeit des Kallimachos* (1924), Wilamowitz presented Hellenistic culture as the imperialistic achievement of Greek conquerors. The continuity between Greek and Hellenistic civilizations was also the main theme of Kaerst's fine work. W. W. Tarn indeed saw his Greco-Macedonians as precocious Englishmen and Scotsmen settling on colonial land. He idealized the Greek kingdoms of Bactria and India as the predecessors of the British Raj. Even the very recent *Kulturgeschichte des Hellenismus* by the theologian Carl Schneider (1967–69) is imperialist and racist.[27] Nobody saw any basic contradiction between the image of Hellenistic man in need of religious salvation and the image of the Hellenistic state providing the comforts of life for a capitalist society. The two directions indicated by Droysen appeared after all to be not incompatible with each other, especially after some rectifications by his successors.

It is, however, doubtful whether this harmony is likely to last. Decolonization and Marxism have in recent years contributed to a shift in attention towards the poorer natives and the slaves, while a reassessment of the intellectual achievements of Hellenistic thinkers, scientists, and scholars is now in progress. The suspicion is growing that the benefits gained by science from state protection were short-lived and fraught with evil consequences.[28] At the same time pre-Christian Judaea, which produced the skepticism of Ecclesiastes, the revolution of the Maccabees, and the monasticism of Qumran within a period of perhaps seventy to eighty years, is once again forcing itself on the attention of scholars not exactly as a Hellenized country. But it is too early to be sure that the dual interpretation Droysen encouraged both by his word and by his silence is now on the wane.

Notes

1. On Droysen, in addition to the works quoted below in the text and in the notes, see especially O. Hintze, *Allgem. Deutsche Biographie*, 48, 1904, pp. 82–114, reprinted in *Gesammelte Abhandlungen*, II, 2d. ed., Göttingen, 1964, pp. 453–99 (*cf.* also the later [1930] paper reprinted there, pp. 500–518); and G. Droysen, *J. G. Droysen*, I, Leipzig and Berlin, 1910. Hintze and G. Droysen speak about Droysen's political activity (the latter only up to 1848); R. Hübner, "J. G. Droysens Vorlesungen über Politik," *Zeitschrift für Politik*, 10, 1917, pp. 325–76; H. Astholz, *Das Problem "Geschichte" untersucht bei J. G. Droysen*, Berlin, 1933; J. Wach, *Das Verstehen*, III, Tübingen, 1933; H. Diwald, *Das historische Erkennen*, Leiden, 1955, pp. 50–76; W. Hock, *Liberales Denken im Zeitalter der Paulskirche: Droysen und die Frankfurter Mitte*, Münster, 1957; P. Hünermann, *Der Durchbruch geschichtlichen Denkens im 19. Jahrhundert*, Freiburg, 1967, pp. 49–132. Among the general histories of historiography G. von Below, *Die deutsche Geschichtschreibung*, 2d. ed., Munich and Berlin, 1924, pp. 49–50, is still best on Droysen. A criticism of Droysen from the point of view of Holy Roman Empire ideology is made in H. von Srbik, *Geist und Geschichte vom deutschen Humanismus bis zur Gegenwart*, I, Salzburg, 1950, pp. 367–77. *Cf.* also G. G. Iggers, *The German Conception of History*, Middletown, Conn., 1968, pp. 104–19.

2. *Cf. Geschichte der Nachfolger Alexanders*, Hamburg, 1936, Vorrede, pp. xv–xvi, which seems to include, at least on the literary side, even Byzantine history in the notion of Hellenism.

3. My *Contributo alla storia degli studi classici*, Rome, 1955, pp. 165–93, 263–73, with bibliography, contains two papers which I wrote in 1933 and 1934 devoted to these aspects of Droysen.

4. I have been led to reconsider the notion of Hellenism in Droysen by the appearance of a remarkable book on him by Benedetto Bravo, an Italian who

teaches in Poland: *Philologie, histoire, philosophie de l'histoire: Étude sur J. G. Droysen, historien de l'antiquité*, Warsaw, 1968. Some observations which I formulated in a review of Bravo's book in *Riv. St. Ital.* in 1969 were the starting point for an article of mine in *Saeculum,* "Hellenismus und Gnosis," in the *Festschrift J. Vogt,* 1970.

5. Now in *Kleine Schriften zur Alten Geschichte,* II, Leipzig, 1894, p. 351.

6. *Opuscula,* I, Göttingen, 1785, pp. 76–134.

7. See the history of the term in the deservedly famous essay by R. Laqueur, *Hellenismus,* Giessen, 1925. St. John Chrysostom gave an interpretation of the term which must have inspired Scaliger, in Homily XIV on the Acts: *Opera,* IX, Paris, 1837, p. 129.

8. *Cf.* D. Heinsius, *Aristarchus Sacer* in *Sacrarum Exercitationum ad Novum Testamentum libri XX,* Lugduni Bat., 1639, pp. 653, 668, and elsewhere. The story of this dispute deserves further research.

9. R. Pfeiffer, *Philologische Wochenschrift,* 46, 1926, pp. 961–66; Momigliano, *Contributo,* p. 183 n. 58; R. Pfeiffer, *Ausgewählte Schriften,* Munich, 1960, p. 151. In 1926 Pfeiffer showed that Herder even included other Oriental nations in his notion of Hellenism.

10. *Cf.* J. G. Droysen, *Briefwechsel,* I, ed. R. Hübner, Berlin and Leipzig, 1929, p. 119 (letter to F. Perthes, 8 February 1837), where Droysen quotes the motto "Das wahre Faktum steht nicht in den Quellen." Note the significant episode in O. Hintze, *Allgem. Deutsche Biographie,* 48, p. 98, and in general G. Birtsch, *Die Nation als sittliche Idee: Der Nationalstaatsbegriff in Geschichtsschreibung und politischer Gedankenwelt J. G. Droysens,* Cologne, 1964.

11. *Historik,* ed. R. Hübner, Munich and Berlin, 1937, pp. 425–28. *Cf.* O. Hintze, *Allgem. Deutsche Biographie,* 48, p. 88; G. von Below, *Die deutsche Geschichtsschreibung,* p. 48; T. Schieder, *Neue Deutsche Biographie,* 4, 1959, p. 135.

12. F. Meinecke, *Historische Zeitschrift,* 141, 1930, pp. 249–87, reprinted in *Schaffender Spiegel,* Stuttgart, 1948, pp. 146–210, and *Zur Geschichte der Geschichtsschreibung,* 1968, pp. 125–67; F. Gilbert, *J. G. Droysen und die preussisch-deutsche Frage,* Munich and Berlin, 1931. *Cf.* also K. Jordan, *Archiv f. Kulturg.,* 49, 1967, pp. 262–96, and J. Rüsen, *Begriffene Geschichte: Genesis und Begründung der Geschichtstheorie J. G. Droysens,* Paderborn, 1969, pp. 28–49.

13. *Geschichte der Bildung des hellenistischen Staatensystemes,* 1843, p. 584.

14. *Kleine Schriften,* II, pp. 1–61.

15. *Kleine Schriften,* II, pp. 75–145.

16. *Kleine Schriften,* II, pp. 146–81.

17. C. Wehmer, *Ein tief gegründet Herz: Der Briefwechsel Felix Mendelssohn-Bartholdys mit Johann Gustav Droysen,* Heidelberg, 1959, adds nothing to the material in the *Briefwechsel,* ed. Hübner.

18. *Kleine Schriften,* I, pp. 328–85.

19. *Kleine Schriften,* II, p. 431.

20. *Briefwechsel,* I, pp. 103, 118.

21. This question deserves reexamination. *Cf.* H. Jonas, *Gnosis und spätantiker Geist,* I, 3d. ed., Göttingen, 1964; S. Wagner, *Die Essener in der wissenschaftlichen Diskussion,* Berlin, 1960; F. Parente, *La Parola del Passato,* 95, 1964, pp. 81–124; P. C. Hodgson, *The Formation of Historical Theology: A Study of F. C. Baur,* New York, 1966.

22. *Kleine Schriften,* II, p. 74.

23. *Geschichte der Bildung des hellenistischen Staatensystemes,* p. 581.

24. *Briefwechsel,* II, p. 253. Droysen's failure in his Hellenistic project may be taken either as a contribution to, or as a symptom of, the decline in the importance of ancient history which is evident in German universities after 1840: *cf.* J. Engel, *Historische Zeitschrift,* 189, 1959, p. 346.

25. Hans Liebeschütz, *Das Judentum im deutschen Geschichtsbild von Hegel bis Max Weber,* Tübingen, 1967, on Droysen pp. 86–90; M. A. Meyer, *The Origins of the Modern Jew: Jewish Identity and European Culture in Germany, 1749–1824,* Detroit, 1967. On the political side, H. Fischer, *Judentum, Staat und Heer in Preussen im frühen 19. Jahrhundert,* Tübingen, 1968. *Cf.* also the introduction by K. Wilhelm to the selected papers on *Wissenschaft des Judentums im deutschen Sprachbereich,* 2 vols., Tübingen, 1967.

26. *Cf.* K. Rudolph, *Die Mandäer,* Göttingen, 1960, for a summary of the question.

27. *Cf.* the important review by O. Murray, *Classical Review,* 19, 1969, pp. 69–72, with further bibliography on Hellenism.

28. Claire Préaux, "Réflexions sur l'entité hellénistique," *Chronique d'Égypte,* 40, 1965, pp. 129–39, and in general all the historical research by this author, beginning with *L'Économie royale des Lagides,* Brussels, 1939; S. K. Eddy, *The King is Dead,* Lincoln, Nebraska, 1961. *Cf.* for new points of view R. Pfeiffer, *Ausgewählte Schriften,* pp. 148–58; R. Lévêque, *Le Monde hellénistique,* Paris, 1969. The standard political history of the Hellenistic age is now E. Will, *Histoire politique du monde hellénistique,* 2 vols., Nancy, 1966–67. Louis Robert occupies a place apart through the invaluable contributions to our knowledge of all aspects of Hellenism provided by his work on inscriptions: see especially his series *Hellenica,* Paris, 1941 ff.

ELEVEN

The Ancient City
of Fustel de Coulanges

To E. J. Bickerman
'sodali fusteliali'

When one talks of the ancient city as a society within which institutions operate and ideas circulate, the first modern historian whose name comes to mind is Fustel de Coulanges. We think of him above all because in the very title *Cité antique* he defined his dependence upon and his distance from the greatest ancient interpreter of the city, Aristotle. Like Aristotle, and through the influence of Aristotle, Fustel places the city at the center of his interpretation; but it is the ancient city, not the city as such and not even specifically the Greek city.

Furthermore, with Fustel we can now see the characteristic beginnings of French historiography of the ancient world in the elements that distinguish it from the German historiography of the ancient world on which my generation in Italy was still reared. When we were young we were naturally aware that it was French and Belgian scholars such as H. Francotte and G. Glotz who were describing the Greek city. Indeed, in the first pages of his admirable *Cité grecque* of 1928 Glotz referred to Aristotle and Fustel as his two predecessors. But I am afraid that we did not make a clear distinction between these works and the so-called *Staatskunde* of the German scholars, as exemplified, after A. Boeckh, in the fundamental *Griechische Staatskunde* by G. Busolt and H. Swoboda (1920–26) or, on a lesser scale, in the successive contributions by B. Keil and V. Ehrenberg respectively to the second and third editions of the *Einleitung in die Altertumswissenschaft* of Gercke and Norden. We did not clearly understand the origins of the psychological

"La città antica di Fustel de Coulanges," *Rivista Storica Italiana*, 82 (1970), pp. 81–98; *Quinto contributo* (1975), pp. 159–78; English translation, *Essays in Ancient and Modern Historiography* (1977), pp. 325–43; French translation, *Problèmes d'historiographie ancienne et moderne* (1983), pp. 402–23; German translation, *Wege in die Alte Welt* (1991), pp. 192–208. Translated by Judith Landry; translation revised by T. J. Cornell.

and ethnological interests, the "perpetuelles contaminations d'idées et de coutumes" which were characteristic of Glotz's books. While the German treatises distinguished between public law and private law, Glotz conflated them: he saw in the *polis* a patriarchal society. Following Francotte (1856–1918) whose studies of the *polis* had been accompanied by works on the industry and finances of the Greek cities, Glotz arrived at the *Cité grecque* after his well-known thesis on the *Solidarité de la famille dans le droit criminel en Grèce* (1904) and a volume on *Le Travail dans la Grèce ancienne* (1920). L. Gernet, several years his junior, combined a whole series of basic papers and textual commentaries on purely juridical problems with a study on economic history, *L'Approvisionnement d'Athènes en blé au Vᵉ et au IVᵉ siecle* (in *Mélanges d'histoire ancienne*, ed. G. Bloch, 1909, pp. 269–391), with a thesis of an ethical-legal nature, *Recherches sur le développement de la pensée juridique et morale en Grèce* (1917), and lastly with a religious history of Greece, *Le Génie grec dans la religion* (1932), in collaboration with André Boulanger.

Today there is no doubt about the origins of this complex interest in Greek society, seen variously in its economic, intellectual, legal, and religious aspects. Born in 1862, Glotz was a student at the École Normale in the years in which it was dominated by Fustel. The Belgian Francotte passed from the study of the Encyclopedists (1880) to the study of Greek law and economy (c. 1890) under the influence of the problems formulated in France. Gernet began to work under Paul Girard, the author of a volume on *L'Éducation athénienne au Vᵉ et au IVᵉ siècle av. J.C.* (2d ed., 1891). Girard was a pupil of Fustel and a biographer of Fustel's biographer, Paul Guiraud (1908). In Guiraud, who wrote his biography of Fustel in 1896, the economic aspect of the school of Fustel is particularly marked: *La Propriété foncière en Grèce jusqu'à la conquête romaine* (1893) and *La Main-d'oeuvre industrielle dans l'ancienne Grèce* (1900).

The other main characteristic can equally clearly be traced back to Fustel: the comparative method. It is enough to open the introductory pages of Glotz's *Solidarité de la famille* to see that he is caught up in a discussion between jurists on the respective merits of the comparative method and the historical method. By Glotz's time this discussion was circulating throughout Europe. It entered Italy, for instance, with the translation of P. Bonfante and C. Longo (1906) of the *Grundriss der ethnologischen Jurisprudenz* by A. H. Post (1894–95). But it originated with H. S. Maine's *Ancient Law* (1861) in England, and the *Cité antique* by Fustel in France (1864); and it is well known that Fustel was writing without knowing Maine. In France the first application of the comparative method in the study of ancient law was by Fustel. The French jurists' awareness of the value of the comparative method was subsequently enriched by the particular theorization of this method on the part of a pupil of Fustel who followed a path of his own: Emile Durkheim.[1] Already in Glotz, and more noticeably in Gernet,[2]

Fustel's influence was inseparable from that of Durkheim, at least in the sense that Durkheim interpreted and generalized Fustel's system of observation of social facts. Anyone wanting to assess the more recent developments of this French school must devote at least as much attention to Durkheim's reelaboration and generalization as to the original inspiration of Fustel. In Gernet, who died in 1961, and was the general secretary of the *Année Sociologique* in the last years of his life, the direct legacy of Fustel, treasured in the École Normale and the Sorbonne, is possibly of less importance than the new spirit of research that he found in the company of his sociologist friends Robert Hertz, killed in the First World War, Marcel Mauss, and Marcel Granet (to whose *Études sociologiques sur la Chine* he wrote a preface in 1953).

I have especially the Italian situation in mind in emphasizing this complication of Durkheim's intervention in giving a new meaning—more rigorous and also broader—to Fustel. In Italy there has been an attempt to present *La Cité antique* as a work that should be assimilated into our culture. And it is typical of the intelligence of Giorgio Pasquali that it should have been he, apparently so remote from French culture, who noted Fustel's absence from our midst and who pointed out his importance.[3]

But Pasquali's introduction to the Italian translation of the *Cité antique* by G. Perrotta (1924) was inevitably affected by the bias of its author, who believed on the one hand that Fustel had never read either Niebuhr or Mommsen, and on the other hand that he had "found successors only in Germany in Rohde, and in the Scandinavian countries in Wide and Nilsson" (pp. v–vi).

We shall have more to say about the systematic neglect of modern historians that Fustel displayed in the *Cité antique*. The assertion that Fustel found his successors outside France, and that he should be seen so to speak as a part of a German-Scandinavian tradition of the history of religion, is certainly misleading. If the name of Glotz were not enough, that of Durkheim with all that it entails would be sufficient to refute this interpretation. Moreover, the extent of Fustel's influence on Rohde should not be exaggerated. Nothing could be further from the truth than the assertion in the *Enciclopedia Italiana* that he was "a fully conscious successor" of Fustel. In two notes to his *Psyche* (4th ed., 1907, I, p. 166 n. 2; p. 253 n. 2) Rohde accepted Fustel's postulate that the state is more recent than the family, and showed sympathy for the idea of the worship of ancestors preceding other cults, but refused to follow Fustel into the world of prehistory. *La Cité antique* was translated into German only in 1907, and as we see from the review by L. Wenger in the *Deutsche Literaturzeitung* (1907, col. 1733–37 and 1797–1801) and from an observation by B. Keil in *Einleitung in die Altertumswissenschaft* (III, 2d ed., 1923, p. 429), it was never very widely read and had even less authority. V. Ehrenberg repeatedly defined it as "sachlich wie methodisch phantastisch, aber bedeutende Konzeption mit zum Teil tiefer Erkenntnis der religiösen und sippengebundenen Kräfte des Staates" (most recently *Der Staat der Griechen,* 1965, p. 305), which is incidentally an intrinsically contradictory judgment. Not only does Fustel fit rightfully into the French sociological tradition—as is borne out by the dedication to him of Durkheim's Latin thesis on Montesquieu—but he contributed to this tradition by establishing the connection between economic structure and religious beliefs. More particularly, Fustel saw in the worship of the dead the first justification of private property.

The relatively short life of Numa-Denis Fustel de Coulanges (1830–89) is divided, as far as intellectual activity is concerned, between the two decades of the Second Empire and the other two of the still shaky Third Republic.[4] Educated at the École Normale, where he studied under V. Duruy, A. Cheruel, and J.-D. Guigniaut but found sustenance in Descartes, Guizot, and Tocqueville, Fustel took his doctorate in 1858 with a French thesis on *Polybe ou la Grèce conquise* and a Latin thesis on *Quid Vestae cultus in institutis veterum privati publicisque valuerit.* The first thesis already contained the substance of the conclusions of the *Cité antique,* while the second, within the limits we shall shortly indicate, foreshadowed its beginning. Only six years elapsed between the thesis and the publication of the *Cité antique,* written at Strasbourg when he was already a professor. Before his doctorate, as a pupil at the French School at Athens, Fustel had explored Chios between 1853 and 1855 and had written a *Mémoire sur l'île de Chios* which appeared in 1856 and was republished by Camille Jullian, pupil and editor of Fustel, in *Questions historiques* (1893): this was a history of the island of Chios from its origins to the nineteenth century.

A basically conservative and religious interpretation of political life, such as that contained in the *Cité antique,* naturally made Fustel *persona grata* at the court of Napoleon III. He was appointed, on Duruy's recommendation, to give history lectures at the École Normale in Paris in February 1870 and immediately invited to give a special course to the Empress Eugénie and her suite. Clearly it was remembered that Ranke had lectured for Maximilian II of Bavaria in 1854. The lectures were published only in 1930 by P. Fabre with the title *Leçons à l'Impératrice sur les origines de la civilisation française.*

When the Second Empire fell, Fustel became the upholder of the French character of Alsace against Theodor Mommsen and defended it with a remarkable clarity of ideas about the principle of nationality (*Questions historiques,* 1893, pp. 506–12). These and other pages by Fustel could still be reprinted during the First World War as being of real relevance.[5]

In 1872 he was writing the manifesto of the new French historiography, as he wanted it to be after the disaster of 1870. The German victory had been made possible partly by the difference in the attitude of historians in the two countries. German scholars were united in celebrating Germany, while the French had given themselves over to diatribes against France's past, particularly against the pre-1789 regime. "In France scholarship is liberal, in Germany it is patriotic." "True patriotism is not love of one's native soil, it is love of the past, respect for the generations who have gone before us." In other words, Fustel was asking for respect for prerevolutionary France, for the *ancien régime*, as a sign of French patriotic unity after the defeat. He did not want an imitation of patriotic German scholarship. He hankered after the scholarship "si calme, si simple, si haute de nos Bénédictins, de notre Académie des Inscriptions, des Beaufort, Fréret"—themselves products of the *ancien régime*. But if it was necessary for France, he was ready to encourage a militant historiography around "les frontières de notre conscience nationale et les abords de notre patriotisme" (*Questions historiques*, 1893, pp. 3–16).

This anti-German ideology was echoed by the general tendency of the work already outlined in the lectures at Strasbourg, but actually written in Paris, on the *Histoire des institutions politiques de l'ancienne France*, of which the first volume came out in 1875. Rewritten and largely posthumous, the definitive edition appeared in six volumes, edited and completed by C. Jullian, between 1891 and 1893. Fustel aimed at separating the history of France from its Germanic roots. As he wrote in 1877: "I have talked neither of the spirit of freedom of the Frankish warriors, nor of elective kingship, nor of national assemblies, nor of popular juries, nor of the confiscation of the lands of the conquered, nor of the allodia distributed to the conquerors. I have sought for all this in the documents and I have not found it. On the other hand some definite facts are to be found there: for instance the preservation of the right to landed property without any modification; the continuity of the administrative regime, at least in its outward forms, particularly the persistence of the same social distinctions, and the existence of an aristocracy to which many Germans certainly belonged, but which was not exclusively German" (*Histoire des institutions politiques de l'ancienne France*, volume II, *L'Invasion germanique*, 1891, pp. xi–xii). Fustel gave new significance to the eighteenth-century polemic of J. B. Dubos and H. de Boulainvilliers and came to the defense of Dubos's theory that the roots of modern France lay in the Roman world, not in the Germanic one. As he says in another passage: "It is indisputable that the link between Rome and Gaul was not broken at the will of the Gauls, but by the Germans. We shall see again in the course of our studies that the Gallic population preserved all it could of what was Roman and was intent on remaining Roman, as far as was possible" (*Histoire des institutions politiques de l'ancienne France*, volume I, *La Gaule romaine*, 1891, p. 96).

This thesis included a defense of the antiquity of private property among the Gauls, which resumed a basic idea of the *Cité antique* and was further reinforced in the essay of 1889 on *Le Problème des origines de la propriété foncière* (*Questions historiques*, pp. 19–117).

Although he was sometimes suspected of Bonapartism, Fustel continued to prosper after 1870. In 1875 he obtained a teaching post in Ancient History at the Sorbonne; in 1880 he became director of the École Normale and remained there for three years. He found the ideal position in the chair of Medieval History at the Sorbonne created specially for him in 1878. He also outlined a plan (c. 1872?) for the reform of the Constitution of the Republic and declined an invitation from Thiers to become the official historian of the defeat. One may well acknowledge that his political position was genuinely uncertain. His defense of the *ancien régime*, his hostility towards German intellectuals and his vague religious sense endeared him to the Right: later on he became the favorite of Maurras and Daudet.[6]

But the men of the Right never managed to convince their adversaries, even after Fustel's death, that he was entirely theirs. The harshest attack, from H. d'Arbois de Jubainville, in *Deux manières d'écrire l'histoire* (1896), was primarily the attack of a *chartiste* against a *normalien*—diplomatics and palaeography versus literary and legal sources; Mabillon versus Condorcet and Taine. There was a certain irony in setting Mabillon against Fustel, who about 1870 had looked upon Mabillon as one of the glories of French historiography. But the truth is that in France there was never an open revolt against Fustel. Not even the bias of Marc Bloch and Lucien Febvre for Michelet really signified opposition to Fustel. Bloch, whose father was one of Fustel's most eminent pupils, felt able to take part without any qualms in the celebrations for the centenary of his birth in 1930.[7] With the foundation of the *Annales* in 1929 and the appearance of *Les Caractères originaux de l'histoire rurale française* in 1931 the centenary in fact coincided with the start of a new phase of French historiography.

Let us now return to the two theses of 1858 and the *Cité antique* which grew out of them. Paul Guiraud tells us that Fustel defended his theories "with extraordinary asperity and that on several occasions he treated his examiners somewhat roughly." They nonetheless praised Fustel's theses unreservedly, particularly because, as they said, they really were theses (*Questions historiques*, p. vii n. 2). The short book on Polybius aimed at clarifying a single but important point. Polybius, for Fustel, offered the explanation of why Greece willingly yielded to Rome: "He is frankly on the side of the conquerors, one feels that he is happy to see Greece obey" (*Questions historiques*, p. 121). Why was this? Polybius's patriotism could not be doubted. But in Greece civil war was hampering civil life: a war of aristocracy against democracy, or rather of rich and poor. Revolutions there were not political, but social. The redistribution of wealth in a more legitimate way was not a part of the revolutionary program. The winners despoiled the losers, and city alliances reflected these opposing movements. For this reason the citizen became estranged from the city, became a mercenary, sold himself, allowed himself to be corrupted. Polybius "rose above the petty interests which divided his fellow-citizens" (p. 140). He was an exemplary man, like Philopoemen, and a moderate. Like all moderates he began as impartial and ended by desiring foreign domination. When he arrived in Rome he was won over by the Romans and especially by their aristocracy. He understood that if the Romans had conquered the empire, it was because they deserved it (p. 194). In reality, concludes Fustel, there was more to Roman domination than the renewal of the life of the city. There was the disappearance of the political regime in the precise sense of a regime of independent and sovereign cities. The virtues of the cities had been great: they had taught a taste for freedom and had contributed to the progress of literature and the arts. But now the cities were no longer enough for the needs of men's souls. "Those principles of exclusion and hatred against the foreigner and against the inhabitant of the neighbouring city, the blinkered patriotism which generated so many wars and covered the land with ruins, began to sicken men. Relations had become too general, minds understood one another too well, philosophy and the arts had made too much progress for society not to change shape" (p. 208). The internal struggles of the Greek cities, which provoked or facilitated foreign intervention, are therefore for Fustel a mysterious means by which it became possible for the peoples to come together. Note the exact phrase: "Les mêmes luttes . . . ont été le moyen mystérieux par lequel les peuples ont réussi à s'unir" (p. 209).

It seems that Fustel never believed in God: he had himself buried as a Catholic as a token of respect towards his ancestral faith, not out of personal conviction. When he was accused by a critic of the *Cité antique* of being a reactionary romantic, he protested and declared himself a rationalist. He made it quite clear in his reply to C. Morel in the *Revue Critique* of 1866 (pp. 373 ff.) that he was in agreement with his critic about the human origin of the religion of the ancients and about the absence of individual freedom in the ancient world. Even more precisely, in an important letter of 7 April 1868 to another of his critics, Louis Ménard, Fustel stated: "You are more pagan than I; I am not more Christian than you" (E. Champion, *Les Idées politiques et religieuses de F.d.C.,* 1903, pp. 18 ff.). Yet his reply is not entirely unequivocal. Atheistic Catholicism has a long history in France, which may have ended with the condemnation of the *Action française* in 1926.[8]

For Fustel it was providential that Rome should have intervened to save the Greeks from themselves. By saving Greece the Romans substituted a new principle for that of city government — and protected private property from the dangers of frequent alternating revolutions. Polybius "renounced independence at first out of fear of democracy, then out of admiration for Rome" (p. 207). He recognized in Rome the defense of private property and the end of the ancient city. The Roman cosmopolis was later to become the Christian cosmopolis. In 1858, the year of Orsini's assassination attempt and the eve of the Italian War, the Second Empire complacently presented itself as a revival of the imperial idea, of order, hegemony, and defense of property.[9]

Contrasted implicitly with Tacitus (and the antithesis has a long history), Polybius was interpreted by Fustel with discernment and a basic fidelity to the conditions of the second century b.c, but also with some rather obvious interpolations due to nineteenth-century ideologies.

Fustel had therefore isolated in Polybius, the truest historian of Rome, the final phase of the ancient city, and more exactly of the Greek city. Its beginning, as we have already said, was outlined in the other thesis. Vesta, the goddess of the hearth, represented the nucleus of the domestic and family religion which was, according to Fustel, the first phase of civilized development in all Aryan peoples. However, the notion that the principle of private property was derived from domestic religion—which is essential in the *Cité antique*—is absent from the thesis on Vesta.

"The religion of the sacred fire dates from the distant and dim .epoch when there were yet no Greeks, no Italians, no Hindus; when there were only Aryans" (*The Ancient City,* Doubleday Anchor Books, New York, p. 29). The *Cité antique* would have been inconceivable without the arrival of the Aryans on the scene of ancient history. The Celts and the Slavs entered Fustel's mental horizon later on. As far as I know, he concerned himself with them only after 1875—mainly in connection with the problems of property. In the *Cité antique* only the Indians figure alongside the Greeks and Romans. His information on the Indians is based on readings of the Vedas and the laws of Manu in translation, and probably on E.-L. Burnouf, *Essai sur le Vêda* (1863).

Fustel therefore believed that he had arrived at the origins of human society and that he was giving an explanation of the institution of property which on the one hand refuted the notion of a primitive communism and on the other precluded any superficial parallel between the Greco-Roman city and modern society. Fearful of the revolutionary intoxication which had identified the ancient heroes with the protagonists of the Terror, Fustel deepened the gulf which separates our conflicts from the ancient ones and made it virtually unbridgeable: "The ideas which the moderns have had of Greece and Rome have often been in their way. Having imperfectly observed the institutions of the ancient city, men have dreamed of reviving them among us. They have deceived themselves about the liberty of the ancients, and on this very account liberty among the moderns has been put in peril" (*The Ancient City,* p. 11). The contrast between ancient and modern freedom, already formulated by B. Constant, is here taken up not to be developed, but to lead back to the religious principles of ancient organization. It will be observed that the Bible and Jewish history are left *a priori* out of consideration. Whether or not this was simply a matter of prudence, Fustel is addressing himself, as an Aryan, to Aryans. Salomon Reinach, of course, realized this immediately (*Manuel de philologie classique,* 2d ed., 1883, p. 222 n. 1). What characterized Aryan society, according to Fustel, was the cult of the dead, who were considered divine. But the worship of the dead was closely connected with the worship of the hearth, with the cult of Agni, Vesta, and other hearth deities. Ancestors lived, like Lares, in the hearth. The hearth was therefore the symbol of the cult of the dead, who reposed near the hearth itself. Fire was lit there to honor the ancestors, and the fire itself in some way kept them alive or at least represented their still watchful souls (p. 27).

The worship of the dead had its effects. Religion was centered not in a temple, but in the house and in the tomb, which (Fustel adds rather inconsequently) was near the house, in an adjoining field. Every family had to possess both the hearth and the tomb with the field containing it in perpetuity, because without this permanent possession the worship of the dead was not possible. It was not the laws which protected private property, but religion. The limits of the inviolable domain were the Termini, themselves treated as gods. The worship of the dead, the family, and property had a single origin; they were three indissolubly interconnected concepts. For this reason property was in origin inalienable (p. 71). One cannot sell one's own ancestors. "Found property on the right of labour, and man may dispose of it. Found it on religion, and he can no longer do this; a tie stronger than the will of man binds the land to him" (p. 70). It also follows that dispossession would be impossible, and that property would not be individual, but of the family. The son inherits from the father because he is responsible for worship. The daughter does not inherit, because she is not qualified to worship. The son is *heres necessarius:* there is no need for a will. "The property is immovable, like the hearth, and the tomb to which it is attached" (p. 74). But in order that the unity of the family be maintained, it is necessary that the first-born son should be the sole heir and, so to speak, should watch over the indivisibility of the patrimony (p. 85). Fustel points to traces of this law of primogeniture in India and in Greece: in Rome he himself admits that he could not find them, but postulates them (p. 84).

According to Fustel, the true family, the original family, is what the Greeks call *genos,* and the Romans *gens,* i.e., all the descendants of a common ancestor through the male line. The family of Latin terminology (*pater familias,* etc.) is therefore the product of a later development with the separation of the various branches of the *gens.* But the later family tends to retain the essential characteristics of the organization of the *gens* in the authority of the *pater familias* and the laws of inheritance. In Rome the connection between *familia* and *gens* was kept up by personal nomenclature, as well as being at the basis of the right of *agnati* and *gentiles* to inherit.[10]

A characteristic of the original *gens,* and consequently of the family, was that it included not only the physical descendants of a common ancestor, but also the slaves. If a slave was later freed, he became part of the *gens* or family as a client. Furthermore the *gens,* according to Fustel, had nothing above it: it was a state run by the *pater,* in which the *liberi* were the aristocracy and the clients were the lower orders, to be distinguished from the *plebs.* Each *gens* had its worship, its territory, and its egoistic ethics, devoid of charity towards anyone who was outside it.

Through a religious development, the cause of which is apparently not discussed by Fustel, it became possible for several *gentes* to join together in a common worship; this gave rise in Greece to the *phratria,* in Rome to the *curia,* with a leader, *phylobasileus* in Greece, *curio* in Rome. The new worship could not be that of ancestors. Instead, it addressed itself to nature. Evidently Fustel considered it probable that certain nature gods had already been recognized within the *gens* before the setting up of the *curiae* and corresponding Greek institutions (p. 120). But the very recognition of a new type of divinity, no longer linked to the family and ancestors, encouraged the association of the various *gentes* into *curiae,* as it subsequently encouraged the association of the various *curiae* into tribes, and of the tribes into cities.

There is no point here in repeating in detail what can easily be read with enjoyment in the original. It should simply be emphasized that the city was constructed on the model of the *gens:* it was based on a common religion, it was limited by inviolate territory; it honored the founder as its head, almost an ancestor; it contained in particular an altar to Vesta; it periodically confirmed its unity with sacred banquets for the citizens; it assigned to the king absolute powers, on the religious basis of the *pater familias;* it excluded the foreigner, as the *gens* excluded anyone who did not belong to it. Since the city incorporated the *gens* and was modeled on it, it naturally recognized the right of family property.

But gradually the city favored the dissolution of the *gens* into families, facilitated the disappearance of the right of primogeniture, and undermined clientship. Those who did not have citizenship and in Rome were called plebeians gradually managed to get themselves admitted into the city and to obtain the right to convene for religious ceremonies.[11] In Rome at the time of Servius Tullius the plebeians were admitted into local tribes and, according to Fustel, became responsible for celebrating sacrifices and festivals (*compitalia, paganalia*), which became their religion: "le plébéien eut une religion."

Fustel gives a schematic account of this process of dissolution of the primitive city based on the *gens.* He speaks of a first revolution in which power was removed from the king, and of a second revolution in which the *gens* broke up into families, the right of primogeniture disappeared or was weakened, and the clients were freed. The third revolution was that of the plebeians' entry into citizenship. With the fourth revolution democracy was attained, as well as a humanization of the law, by now the product of assemblies. Fustel continues:

> When the series of revolutions had produced an equality among men, and there was no longer occasion to fight for principles and rights, men began to make war for interests. . . . As men departed from the ancient system, a poor class began to grow up. Before, when every man belonged to a *gens* and had his patron, extreme poverty was almost unknown. A man was supported by his chief. . . . Inequality of wealth is inevitable in every society which does not wish to remain in the patriarchal state or in that of the tribe. The democracy did not suppress poverty, but, on the contrary, rendered it more perceptible. Equality of political rights made the inequality of conditions appear still more plainly (pp. 336–37).

The right of property was no longer respected because the religious sanction was lacking: "the religion of property has disappeared . . . men no longer saw the superior principle that consecrates the right of property" (p. 338).

We are back at the situation described in the thesis on Polybius: Roman intervention. But what was merely implicit in the thesis on Polybius becomes explicit in the last pages of the *Cité antique*. Christianity arrives to combine the reform of the organization of the state with a new element. Fustel says: "Christianity is the first religion that did not claim to be the source of law. It occupied itself with the duties of men, not with their interests" (p. 395). According to Fustel, Christianity therefore made possible the transformation in the right of property, based no longer on religion, but on labor (p. 396).

From Fustel's point of view it is an ambiguous conclusion. It is not clear if this new basis of the right of property represents progress or retrogression for Fustel, if it affords the same guarantees of stability as the religious conception of property had ensured for the ancient city in its golden period. In his reply to C. Morel in the *Revue Critique* of 1866, Fustel defended his right not to take up a position on contemporary problems in a book devoted to ancient civilization.

The ambiguity of the conclusion accorded well with the situation of Fustel, who then and later found himself torn between attachment to a religion in which he did not believe and a nostalgic admiration for a primitive society which had worshiped its own ancestors and had made them the guarantee of private property.

Something about the composition of the *Cité antique* is revealed to us by two letters from Fustel published by L. Halkin in *Mélanges Bidez* (volume I, 1934, pp. 465–74). A German scholar who for a long time had been professor of Law at Liège and had now retired to Stuttgart, L. A. Warnkoenig, had said that he would be willing to review the *Cité antique* in a German periodical. He did in fact publish a long and admiring review in *Jahrbücher der deutschen Rechts-wissenschaft* (II, 1865, pp. 81–94). Fustel thought it expedient to explain to him the method he had used in writing the book. He stated without false modesty that "his type of mind was such that he could not be content with details." His method had been the comparative one. By comparing the Rig-Veda with Euripides, the laws of Manu with the Twelve Tables or Isaeus and Lysias, he had arrived at the conclusion of a remote community of beliefs and institutions among Indians, Greeks, and Italic peoples. He had not troubled to read what the moderns had written. Indeed he had imposed upon himself the principle of not reading them, and in particular of not reading the works of Mommsen, until he had almost finished his book. He insists on this independence from modern authors also in the reply to Morel, where the books of Becker and Marquardt are specified among those not read. It is nonetheless clear that these claims only go to demonstrate that Fustel was fully informed about contemporary historical research and made a distinction, for instance, between Marquardt and Mommsen. If the *Cité antique* is haughtily devoid of references to modern authors while revealing an enviable familiarity with classical texts, one must deduce from this not simple ignorance, but intentional disregard: the same disregard that led Hegel to ignore Niebuhr's critical method and that made Bachofen (with certain exceptions) indifferent to Mommsen's methods. The attitude they have in common is one which repudiates modern criticism of the sources in order to preserve the sources' data. In his inaugural lecture at Strasbourg in 1862 Fustel declared: "I then resolved to have no masters on Greece other than the Greeks themselves, nor on Rome than the Romans." Even more explicitly, in fragments published after his death: "I would rather be mistaken in the manner of Livy than that of Niebuhr; and in the manner of Gregory of Tours than that of Mr. Sohm." And he added more generally about his adversaries: "They put themselves up as critics because they have no critical spirit" (*Revue Synthèse Hist.*, 2, 1901, pp. 249–50, 257–58). Later, in writing, or rather in rewriting the *Histoire des institutions politiques de l'ancienne France*, Fustel confessed with regret that he had had to yield to the new fashion of presenting all the scholarly material (*Histoire*, I, *La Gaule romaine*, 1891, p. iv n.).

The history which he brought to the attention of his readers was therefore composed of four main elements:

1. the development of the organization of the state from *gens* to city through *curia* and tribe;

2. the parallelism of Indian, Greek, and Roman institutions;

3. the evolution of religion from the worship of ancestors to the gods of nature;

4. the prehistoric origin of private property safeguarded throughout the whole evolution of the ancient world by religion, and more precisely by ancestor worship. At the margins of the ancient city Christianity appeared and brought to an end the security of private property founded on religion. A new epoch began in which labor became the justification for private property.

Fustel's critics are naturally free to stress one or other of the four main principles of his *Cité antique* as the most important and significant. Hitherto critics, particularly in Germany, have seen Fustel as the theoretician of ancestor worship and of the *gens* as the predecessor of the state. To me there seems little doubt that anyone who surveys the development of the studies on ancient history over the last century will emphasize the link between the history of private property and the history of ancient religion. Not only does this question play a part in post-Marxist interest in the problem of the origin of property (in its relations with religion); it is also important for the specific reason that the new social history of the ancient world was born in France through the reconsideration of Fustel, converting his theories into sociological categories (Durkheim), extending his analysis to other civilizations (Egypt, China), and above all keeping religion at the center of socioeconomic life.[12]

Appendix I

FUSTEL AND DURKHEIM. I do not know of any detailed studies on the relationship between the thought of Fustel de Coulanges and Durkheim, but the literature on Durkheim is only partly known to me: I have followed the bibliographies in the books of T. Parsons, *The Structure of Social Action*, 1937; H. Alpert, 1939; K. H. Wolff, ed., 1960; R. A. Nisbet, 1965, on Durkheim; and, also by Nisbet, *The Sociological Tradition*, 1966; *cf.* R. Aron, *Les Étapes de la pensée sociologique*, 1967 (and S. Lukes, *Emile Durkheim: His Life and Works*, Allen Lane, 1973).

There is no doubt about Fustel's influence on Durkheim. The dedication *"Memoriae Fustel de Coulanges"* of Durkheim's thesis on Montesquieu (*Quid Secundatus politicae scientiae instituendae contulerit*, Burdigalae, 1892) is more than an act of formal homage. The link between Montesquieu and Fustel was in everyone's mind during those years (*cf.* A. Sorel, *Mém. Acad. Sciences Morales et Politiques*, 18, 1894, p. 229). To Fustel Durkheim owed above all his sociological interest (*cf. Année Sociol.*, I, 1896–97, pp. i–vii): Fustel had said, "History is the science of social facts, that is to say sociology itself." There was, however, a certain distance between Durkheim and Fustel. In his youth Durkheim showed himself to be sympathetic towards socialism (*cf.* for instance M. Mauss, *Oeuvres*, III, 1969, p. 505), concerned himself with the problem of the division of labor, which was alien to Fustel, and stressed the interdependence of division of labor and the evolution of property. In fact, it is in *De la division du travail social* (1893) that Durkheim's well-known criticism of Fustel occurs: "M. Fustel de Coulanges has discovered that the primitive organization of societies was based on the family and that, furthermore, the formation of the primitive family had religion as its base. However, he has taken the cause for the effect. After putting forward the religious idea, without deriving it from anything, he deduced from it the social arrangements that he observed, whereas on the contrary it is the latter which explain the power and nature of the religious idea" (I, VI, 1, 6th ed., 1932, p. 154). But Durkheim's socialist sympathies paled with the years, though his group of pupils largely retained socialist sympathies. The orientation of his researches altered accordingly. About 1911 Georges Davy could write in his *E. Durkheim*, p. 44: "He began to study religious phenomena only after having written the *Division* and the *Règles* and it was this new study which revealed to him the importance of the ideal factors."[13]

In the *Leçons de Sociologie*, published posthumously in 1950, which apparently date back to 1898–1900, Durkheim turns back to Fustel's idea that property has a religious basis, but criticizes the connection with the cult of the dead and replaces it with the new concept of collective religious representation. This position is substantially the same as that of M. Mauss in 1906 (*Oeuvres*, II, pp. 139–42).

In the *Formes élémentaires de la vie religieuse* (1912), religion creates the social system. Although the most elementary form of religio-social awareness, totemism, is certainly not identical with ancestor worship, which Fustel considers the elementary form, for Durkheim individual souls are originally the reincarnation of the souls of ancestors and in point of fact are "of the same substance as the totemic principle" (II, 8, 2, ed. 1912, p. 355).

The most interesting difference for our purposes between the Durkheim of the *Formes élémentaires* and his master in the *Cité antique* is the former's uncertainty about the relation of religion to economic life. While Fustel resolutely derived private property from religion, Durkheim has a note in his conclusion to *Formes* (p. 598 n. 2) in which he declares that some connection exists between ideas of economic value and ideas of religious value, but that it has not yet been studied. The very nature of Australian societies, with which Durkheim was primarily concerned in *Formes*, made the study of property in relation to religion difficult; but from the book as a whole it is evident that Durkheim had lost interest in the problems of the origin of property that were central to *De la division* (this point does not seem to me to emerge from G. Aimard, *Durkheim et la science économique*, 1962).

Another important difference between Fustel and Durkheim is in the implicit religious experience which underlies their conceptions. For Fustel, born a Catholic, the idea of individual immortality was essential: it was at the root of his ancestor worship. For Durkheim, of a rabbinical family and originally destined to become a rabbi, individual immortality counted for rather less than the collective sense of the community preserving itself and laying down laws throughout the centuries. It is interesting that Australian totemic society should have been Judaized by Durkheim and should have come to resemble one of those small communities, no longer agitated by waves of mysticism or Messianic fervor, that Durkheim, born in 1858, must have known in the Alsace-Lorraine of his precocious and earnest childhood.

Appendix 2

THE ARYAN IDEA IN FUSTEL. The notion of Aryan unity is already quite clear in the dissertation of 1858, *Quid Vestae cultus in institutis veterum privatis publicisque valuerit,* dedicated to J.-D. Guigniaut, the expounder and biographer of Creuzer. We read on p. 2: "*Nempe Persarum, Scytharum, Graecorum ac Romanorum ut idem fuit genus, ita communis religio. In ultima antiquitate et in ultimis Asiae regionibus ortus est apud homines cultus Vestae.*" An unpublished piece of evidence for this conviction of Fustel's is found in the *Cours d'histoire grecque* at the École Normale of 1876–77: the notes on this course taken by E. Groussard are in manuscript in the library of this school, and I owe the permission to read them to the librarian (P. Petitmengin). In stressing the importance of the Aryan origin of the Greeks, Fustel claimed: "Let us now compare the customs, the institutions, and the beliefs that we have just expounded with the customs, the institutions, and the beliefs of the Semitic peoples. The whole is completely different: we find no relationship from any point of view; it is an absolutely different world from our own." Even more significant is the fact that Fustel should make an exception: the law of property. He finds among the Semites, and in particular among the Jews, the "instinctive conception of family property" (*Nouvelles recherches,* p. 30). As A. Sorel observed (*Mém. Acad. Sciences Morales et Politiques,* 18, 1894, p. 215), the question of the origin of property "became a positive obsession with M. Fustel."[14]

Notes

1. See Appendix 1.

2. *Cf. Hommage à Louis Gernet,* Paris, 1966, with essays by G. Davy, J.-P. Vernant, and others. A selected bibliography of L. Gernet is also appended to *Anthropologie de la Grèce antique,* 1968. On Gernet and the school of Durkheim cf. S. C. Humphreys, *History and Theory,* 10, 1971, pp. 172–96.

3. The *Cité antique* was translated into Italian a second time in the same years by G. E. Calapaj (Laterza, Bari, 1925). The most interesting German review of the original publication of 1864 is possibly that by F. Liebrecht, *Gött. Gelehrte Anz.,* 1865, pp. 841–80.

4. An excellent bibliography on Fustel is given by Jane Herrick, *The Historical Thought of Fustel de Coulanges,* Catholic University of America, Washington, 1954 (a thesis supervised by F. Engel-Janosi). Apart from the biography by P. Guiraud, 1896, it is sufficient to mention: J. Simon and A. Sorel, *Mém. Acad. Sciences Morales et Politiques,* 18, 1894, pp. 33–72, 185–230; G. Monod, *Portraits et Souvenirs,* 1897, pp. 135–54; E. Jenks, "Fustel de Coulanges as a Historian," *Engl. Hist. Rev,* 12, 1897, pp. 209–24; C. Jullian, "Le Cinquantenaire de la Cité antique," *Revue de Paris,* 23, 1916, pp. 852–65; H. Leclercq and Cabrol, *Dict. d'archéol. chrét.,* V., 1923, pp. 2717–32; J. M. Tourneur-Aumont, *Fustel de Coulanges,* 1931; G. Dodu, *Rev. Ét. Hist.,* 100, 1933, pp. 41–66; H. de Gérin-Ricard, *L'Histoire des institutions politiques de Fustel de Coulanges,* 1936 (Gérin-Ricard is the co-author with L. Truc of a *Histoire de l'Action Française,* 1949). A *Catalogue des livres composant la bibliothèque de feu M. Fustel de Coulanges* was published in Paris in 1890. *Cf.,* also A. Grenier, *Camille Jullian,* 1944, pp. 117–49; *Lettres de C. Jullian à H. d'Arbois de Jubainville,* Nancy, 1951, pp. 12–13.

5. *Questions contemporaines,* Paris, 1916. For a similar rebirth of interest in Fustel in Italy after the Second World War *cf.* the preface by F. Martinazzoli to his translation of Fustel's *Polybe,* Laterza, Bari, 1947.

6. *Cf.* C. Maurras, *La Bagarre de Fustel,* Paris, 1928 ("Cahiers d'Occident," II, 1). The book by H. de Gérin-Ricard quoted above is, on a higher level, of the same tendency. So also is A. Bellesort, *Les Intellectuels et l'avènement de la Troisième République (1871–1875),* Paris, 1931, pp. 189–217 (and, now, S. Wilson, "Fustel de Coulanges and L'Action Française," *Journ. Hist. Ideas,* 34, 1973, pp. 123–34).

7. M. Bloch, *L'Alsace Française,* 19, 1930, pp. 206–9 (not seen by me). *Cf. Mélanges Historiques,* I, 1963, pp. 100–106.

8. H. Stuart Hughes, *The Obstructed Path,* New York, 1966, pp. 66–67, and bibliography mentioned.

9. *Cf.* my essay on Caesarism in *Secondo Contributo,* 1960, pp. 273–82, and more generally P. Stadler, *Geschichtschreibung und historisches Denken in Frankreich, 1789–1871,* Zürich, 1958, pp. 249 ff.

10. I have not yet managed to ascertain what influence Fustel's ideas on the *gens* have had on scholars of Roman law (e.g., Bonfante). The impression I have gained from running through the vast material collected and elaborated by L. Capogrossi Colognesi, *La struttura della proprietà e la formazione dei Iura Praediorum nell'età repubblicana,* I, Milan, 1969, is that H. S. Maine is better known than Fustel (*cf.* particularly pp. 79–80). One exception is V. Arangio-Ruiz, *Le genti e la città,* Messina, 1914, reprinted in *Scritti giuridici raccolti per il centenario della casa editrice Jovene,* Naples, 1954, pp. 109–58. Incidentally, in his thesis on Vesta of 1858 Fustel still accepts that the family preceded the *gens.*

11. *Cf.* also *Questions historiques,* 1893, pp. 411–52 (a piece which dates from the years of 1867–68, published posthumously by C. Jullian). For Athens the article "Attica Respublica" by Fustel in Daremberg-Saglio, *Dict. des Antiquités,* I, 1877, emphasizes the development from *genos* to the city and confirms the central importance attributed to the problem of private property. According to Fustel the nonnobles were admitted into the land-owning classes by Solon—an interpretation already rejected in the same *Dict. des Antiquités* by C. Lécrivain, s.v. "Eupatrides." For private property in Sparta, Fustel, *Nouvelles recherches,* 1891, pp. 54 ff. For property

among the Germans, *Recherches sur quelques problèmes d'histoire,* 1885, pp. 319–56. *Cf.* R. Schlatter, *Private Property: The History of an Idea,* London, 1951, pp. 266–67.

12. A study of Fustel's alterations to the successive editions of the *Cité antique* has not yet been undertaken, as far as I know. The corrections made to the 2d ed. of 1866 and the 6th ed. of 1875 should be particularly important. I have not been able to study the 1st ed. A comparison I made between the 2d ed. of 1866 (Hachette) and the 7th ed., 1878, seems to indicate only one substantial addition to the text after 1866: in part III there is a new chapter XVI, "Les confédérations, les colonies," with the result that the original chapter XVI becomes chapter XVII. But several other points in the text were altered (for instance the penultimate paragraph of I, 1) and there is much new source material in the notes. The change of title in II, 10, 4, and III, 7, 3, does not imply any alteration in the text. My French quotations are from the 18th ed., 1903. The exposition in the *Cité antique* should be complemented by the articles in *Dict. des Antiquités:* "Attica Respublica" already quoted; "Epula" (II, 1, pp. 736–38); "Lacedaemoniorum Respublica" (III, 2, pp. 886–900); "Regnum" (IV, 2, pp. 821–27); "Romanorum Respublica" (IV, 2, pp. 878–91).

13. *Cf.* also G. Davy, *Sociologues d'hier et d'aujourd'hui,* 2d. ed., Paris, 1950, pp. 79–122. Of course the discovery of the classificatory systems of kinship also stands between Fustel and Durkheim. *Cf.* for instance U. Bianchi, *Storia della etnologia,* Rome, 1965, pp. 79, 112.

14. *Cf.* T. C. Barker, *Aryan Civilization . . . based on the work of De Coulanges,* 1871. For the considerable coincidences in E.-L. Burnouf, *Essai sur le Vêda,* 1863, with Fustel, *cf.* p. 183: "In the eyes of the Vedic Aryans the role of the Ancestors is fused, at least in some measure, with that of the gods." On pp. 441–69 Burnouf stresses the opposition between Semites (Jews) and Aryans (Indians).

TWELVE

Introduction to a Discussion
of Karl Reinhardt

I

When we discussed Wilamowitz at the Scuola Normale Superiore di Pisa a few years ago,[1] I deliberately excluded the relationship between Wilamowitz and Karl Reinhardt, because Reinhardt seemed to me to be, among the pupils of Wilamowitz, not only the most significant in himself but, in terms of relations with his teacher, also the most difficult.[2]

If there is a well-known page of Karl Reinhardt it is the one that describes Wilamowitz on a bicycle: "His pedaling was supreme ... and Wilamowitz's trousers were without compare, even among contemporaries." Admiration for Wilamowitz, which came close to envy, accompanied, stimulated, and disturbed Reinhardt throughout his life. But the Olympian role which Reinhardt reserved for Wilamowitz on a bicycle is that of a black-figure Hermes, an archaizing and ambiguous role.

Reinhardt was born in 1886. His father was a classical philologist and, more importantly, a schoolmaster who, having been director of the Frankfurt Gymnasium and having worked at the Ministry of Education, was in old age the cofounder of the famous aristocratic school (for spiritual "Führer") in the castle of Salem of Prince Max of Baden. At home Reinhardt found the intellectual atmosphere that was to shape his life: here he got to know Hermann Usener, who was more stimulus, largely negative, than teacher to Wilamowitz, and Paul Deussen, the friend of Nietzsche and Schopenhauerian translator of the Upanishad. K. Reinhardt would attempt in the course of his life to combine loyalty to Wilamowitz with loyalty to the

"Premesse per una discussione su Karl Reinhardt," *Rivista Storica Italiana* 87 (1975), pp. 311–18; *Annali della Scuola Normale Superiore di Pisa*, 3d ser., V, fasc. 4 (1975), pp. 1309–17; *Sesto contributo* (1980), pp. 351–59. Translated by T. J. Cornell.

enemies of Wilamowitz, Nietzsche and Stefan George. When in 1947 Reinhardt wrote "Akademisches aus zwei Epochen," two chapters of an autobiography, George had faded into the background and become one name among many. The volume of 1927, *Platons Mythen*, dedicated to Kurt Singer, who in the same year produced *Platon der Gründer* in the spirit of S. George, is enough to present Reinhardt in a different perspective. In 1941 in "Die Klassische Philologie und das Klassische" Reinhardt took up a position in relation to Nietzsche, Wilamowitz, and Jaeger, not in relation to the George-Kreis; in any case we should take note of an incidental phrase: "Jaegers dritter Humanismus kam, im Gegensatz zu den Erneuerungstendenzen des George-Kreises, nicht aus einer Offenbarung." The Third Humanism then did not derive from a revelation, like the revivalist tendencies of the circle of George.

The life of Reinhardt was in general quietly academic, after travels and the experiments of gymnasium teaching. Professor at the age of thirty at Marburg, then in 1919 in the new and fertile University of Hamburg, in the shade of the Warburg Library (this was when he published his *Poseidonios*, 1921); from 1923 to 1941 in Frankfurt, the city of Goethe and of his own early childhood; from 1941 to 1945 at Leipzig, and return to Frankfurt after the war. He died in Frankfurt on 9 January 1958. The only dramatic moment was on 5 May 1933, when he decided to hand in his resignation as professor. The Ministry advised him to stay on, and he accepted its advice. One cannot demand from anyone that he should emigrate if there is no necessity, when so many others were emigrating because they had no choice. Reinhardt was immunized against Nazism, negatively by being apolitical, positively by his absolute integrity. That Reinhardt received a blow from which he was unable to recover is perhaps indicated by the simple fact that he never again wrote anything comparable to *Sophokles*, which appeared precisely in 1933. The essays, notable though they are, collected in the volume *Von Werken und Formen* of 1948, do not have the same conciseness and assurance. The *Aischylos als Regisseur und Theologe* of the following year is strange. One would like to define it—to accentuate its importance for understanding Reinhardt's personality—as partly an autobiographical game. In philology—our discussion will take us to this conclusion— Reinhardt vacillated between regisseur and theologian.

The only curious fact is that he arranged to transfer during the war to Leipzig, where the Nazi rector, the ancient historian Helmut Berve, protected some of his non-Nazi colleagues. Rooted in German thought and in the cultural and emotional life of a society that was brought up on Nietzsche, George, Hofmannsthal, and Strindberg—and through them on Goethe—Reinhardt cannot in truth be imagined outside Germany. But it would be a mistake to emphasize his experiences of literature, philosophy, music, and even painting—even if he was such an intense admirer of

Cézanne. These experiences were thoroughly enjoyed by his friends and colleagues and by his few disciples, including U. Hölscher. But the academic community is never without its delicate and semimystical spirits, especially in Germany. One hears more about Reinhardt the ironical man of culture, reticent in his beliefs, paradoxical and surprising in the lecture theater no less than in the drawing room, than of Reinhardt struggling, sometimes desperately, with problems of interpretation. Information about Reinhardt the philologist comes almost exclusively from his pupil Hölscher and from his colleague, the philosopher who deals with problems of hermeneutics, H.-G. Gadamer.

II

Almost everyone was a pupil of Wilamowitz in the first thirty years of the century in Germany, even if they did not all write their dissertations under him.

Eduard Fraenkel had him as teacher after F. Leo, P. Maas after E. Wölfflin and K. Krumbacher, K. Latte after L. Deubner, R. Pfeiffer after O. Crusius, E. Kapp after Ed. Schwartz, and so on. Reinhardt started at Bonn with Buecheler and ended at Berlin with Wilamowitz. And since all were pupils of Wilamowitz, Wilamowitz could not signify the same thing for all of them. Choices were made not between teachers, but in front of the teacher. The least typical pupil was precisely the one whom Wilamowitz wanted to succeed him at Berlin—which implied passing over the infinitely greater F. Jacoby. W. Jaeger fixed upon the political-humanist element of his teacher and developed it in an original manner, giving the greatest weight to Plato, Aristotle, Neoplatonism, and the interpenetration of Greek philosophy and Christianity. It gave birth to a philological-humanistic movement of thought which was dominant in Germany between 1925 and 1935, but which then collapsed for political and perhaps more for racial reasons. It was impossible for Jaeger to make this Third Humanism acceptable to the Third Reich. Among Jaeger's pupils W. Schadewaldt and R. Harder compromised with Nazism. The teacher and other pupils were forced to flee to America. No other pupil of Wilamowitz founded a school of this philological-political type.

It is not possible to make a distinction on this point between those who preferred to stay in Germany (among them, with consequences that were far from happy, a Jew, K. Latte) and those who emigrated. There is no doubt that what Jacoby, Maas, Eduard Fraenkel and Hermann Fränkel (another Göttingen scholar who would be incomprehensible without Wilamowitz), Pfeiffer and P. Friedländer constructed elsewhere was of necessity composed of materials taken from outside German thought and inserted into other cultural contexts, English or American, and inevitably bore the mark of an individual contribution to a different world. Eduard Fraenkel, a born teacher, had a truly great influence in the Anglo-Saxon world, greater, I should say, than that exercised by Jaeger at Harvard. But Fraenkel transmitted a technique and an ethos rather than problems of culture, still less of politics; he had more influence in Greek than in Latin, in which he had more original ideas. If K. Dover and H. Lloyd-Jones derived their technique from Fraenkel, their problems were taken from E. R. Dodds, J. D. Denniston, and even Gilbert Murray. What is significant for the purposes of our analysis is that even the pupils of Wilamowitz who remained in Germany — J. Geffcken, L. Malten, O. Regenbogen, as well as K. Latte when after 1945 he had a period of authority in his country — rarely transmitted their complex cultural interests to their pupils.

The problem of why post-Wilamowitzian philology was not communicated except in matters of technique holds true of all — with the exception of Jaeger, who paradoxically was a failure. It is therefore worth investigating the most extreme case of one who remained in Germany, admired by all, followed by very few. The case is exemplary because Reinhardt deliberately refrained from transmitting the research technique he possessed, and consequently condemned himself to isolation. His style of interpretation forced him into this position.

Wilamowitz had represented the triumph of interpretation. The master had managed to combine a rigorous interpretation of texts with a more than personal satisfaction in the act of interpreting them. Not only did interpretation come naturally to him and without hesitation, although he had the highest awareness of the difficulties and responsibilities of interpretation; but he found sufficient opportunities for integrating his interpretations within the aristocratic and bureaucratic world and within the intellectual bourgeoisie (often Jewish) of contemporary Prussia. His public lectures at Berlin attracted crowds, and his translations of Greek tragedies were performed. Not everything went smoothly. His son Tycho rebelled; the Plato composed in the middle of the First World War left a sense of emptiness. But it was not empty for Wilamowitz himself. With Reinhardt interpretation remained central, as it had been for his teacher, but the pacific satisfaction with the results was no longer guaranteed, as it had been for Wilamowitz.

Having excluded any conscious modernizing on the one hand, Reinhardt equally excluded any historicizing on the other. His distaste for the Third Humanism was balanced by loathing of nineteenth-century historicism.

The historical dimension upheld by Wilamowitz, which became a program of research into the history of historiography for Jacoby and which was otherwise accepted by almost all the disciples (more specifically by Fraenkel and in a Christian sense by Pfeiffer), was nonetheless, at least programmatically, suppressed by Reinhardt. It was suppressed not only in the interests of Reinhardt but even in the interests of the authors he studied. Posidonius the historian counts for little in Reinhardt's general framework of research on Posidonius (the chapter on the "historian" concerns ethnography). Herodotus is studied in connection with oriental narrative forms, Thucydides is taken out of his world for a timeless comparison with Machiavelli. What remains is the bare necessity of making the text speak, of asking it to make a response about itself. Reinhardt's techniques of interpretation are twofold. The first is to restore unity to fragments of thinkers who have, so to speak, vanished—to recover that internal structure that will recreate the personalities of Parmenides (1916) and Posidonius (1921; 1926; 1928; 1954). The second direction is the relocation of the myths of Plato (1927), Sophocles (1933), Aeschylus (1949), and finally Homer (posthumous, 1961) in objective situations. As for the fragments, dissatisfaction with his own results is at least obvious in the case of Posidonius: there are three stages of interpretation (*Poseidonios*, 1921; *Kosmos und Sympathie*, 1926; and the article "Poseidonios" in Pauly-Wissowa (1954), as well as an essential supplement (*Poseidonios über Ursprung und Entartung*, 1928). In terms of time, Posidonius must have cost Reinhardt at least fifteen years of his life. In the interpretation of complete texts, which is not limited to ancient ones, it is the very nature of the text—almost always a myth—that challenges the interpreter. The doubt arose as soon as the volume on the myths of Plato was published (1927), which had ended with an arrogant assertion of certainty: "Aber Platon ist selbst wieder Abbild eines Urbilds-Schöpfungsmythos."

Significantly in each case the struggle with the mythical material is complicated by the struggle with Wilamowitz. On the one occasion where a peaceful harmony is achieved, in *Sophokles*, Reinhardt feels himself supported by Wilamowitz junior against Wilamowitz senior. In the latest books, on Aeschylus and Homer, the effort to free himself from Wilamowitz is explicitly acknowledged and, with a delicate smile, declared impossible. In the Homer, which was left unfinished after years of revision, the aged pupil, precisely because of his age, can no longer manage to put up that first line of defense, habitual in earlier books, of giving the research a form of his own. The method is the analytical method of Wilamowitz, and later on the omnipresent influence of W. Schadewaldt makes itself felt. Reinhardt's friendship with Schadewaldt was, one suspects, only partly genuine.

The "Reinhardt case" is therefore extreme in the school of Wilamowitz and at the opposite pole to the "Jaeger case." In Jaeger the political program, the project of *making* new history; in Reinhardt the renunciation of history. In the matter of interpretation he did not admit the historicist preoccupation that was characteristic of Wilamowitz and of the majority of his school. The reason for this renunciation of history does not need to be sought out because it is clearly stated by Reinhardt himself. Wilamowitz idolized his own scholarship, not Plato, not Sophocles, not Homer. "This attitude is the end of all humanism . . . or rather it would be, if Wilamowitz were not held by the spell of contradiction between the thought and the man." Reinhardt was right at least in this sense: he had noted that his fellow-pupils were incapable of communicating anything more than technique, except in what he considered the deplorable case of Jaeger; he was also prepared to face up to isolation and with a shrug to withdraw into silence in mid-sentence. As R. Pfeiffer wrote, "Even in other circumstances he knew so well how to keep a thoughtful silence." Or rather, "so *schön* nachdenklich schweigen." Between a philology which, although historical, or indeed because it was historical, was no longer able to make itself heard, and the characteristic art of solitary interpretation, Reinhardt decided in favor of the latter.

It was not then a choice that could remain undisturbed. Reinhardt had no doubt about the possibility of interpretation. But he was not certain what kind of realities it would reveal. Naturally he had nothing to do with Christian hermeneutics. Hierophancy, revelation, and spontaneity are his characteristic words, just as they were for the George-Kreis. In the books on Plato and Sophocles and, perhaps less decisively, in those on Aeschylus and Homer, he appears sometimes to admit the *reality* of the Greek myths, which speak and impose their form. He prefers the Greek gods of his friend W. F. Otto to the Greek faith of his teacher Wilamowitz. Walter F. Otto believed in the reality of the gods. Still in 1951 Reinhardt can say of Hölderlin: "The plays of Sophocles are for him rediscovered sacred texts," and he appears to approve. *Appears,* because the decisive identification of interpretation and revelation, of hermeneutics and illumination, albeit discontinuous, is never, as far as I know, to be found in Reinhardt. Indeed, in "Nietzsches Klage der Ariadne" (1936), one of his most important essays, the myth of Ariadne is, or rather could be, the symbol of the mask "which sees itself as mask" and of the text "which interprets itself as interpretation." The objectivity of revelation is, at the last moment, discarded; just as, at the last moment, Reinhardt avoided going into the George-Kreis in order to preserve (as he himself declared) his liberty.[3]

Reinhardt therefore stands alone, against the Third Humanism, against the majority of his historicist fellow-pupils in the school of Wilamowitz, and finally against those who, for good or ill, accepted a revelation. Admittedly his interpretation inclines toward the latter group. If one wants to classify Reinhardt as an existentialist, at least in the period when he was preparing *Sophokles,* I do not see anything wrong in that: Heidegger certainly played a part in his life. More vaguely the contrast between existence and appearance preoccupied and fascinated Reinhardt from the time when he was working on Parmenides. But there is little to be gained from these labels, or from obvious parallels that come to mind in the shape of W. Benjamin and H. Schaeder, the orientalist. That Reinhardt should repudiate Jaeger seems to us perfectly natural. The detachment from Wilamowitz, insofar as it implies criticism of the majority of the school, is more disturbing. My impression, at least, is that it indicates an element of weakness in the school itself. Reinhardt's hermeneutic solution would in theory be a solipsism not reinforced by revelation. In practice, however, one may doubt if Reinhardt really intended to listen to a voice of unknown provenance. Meanwhile, where fragments are concerned, we see an extraordinary capacity to follow the traces of a tradition by procedures which from H. Diels onwards may be considered conventional.

Then the method of internal form, which is called upon to integrate the results of conventional source criticism, is justifiable — or open to criticism — without recourse to questions of transcendence. We are dealing with style, with *forma mentis*. On the other hand it seems legitimate to assert that the analyses of Sophocles, Aeschylus, and Homer accomplished by Reinhardt present themselves as attempts to understand the situation of each poet in the face of specific traditions. The tradition creates a factual datum accepted by the poet.

The analyses themselves have varying degrees of persuasiveness: probably in descending order from Sophocles to Homer to Aeschylus. They are analyses which in each case need to be reconsidered with a more secure knowledge than Reinhardt ever had of the society and the mental world in which the poet operated. But anyone who has read these books, even the Aeschylus, has a better understanding of the poets in question. Isolated within the school, Reinhardt communicates to his readers his interpretations of certain creative situations. He communicates it even to those who do not indulge in mystical experiences in philology. Neither the Posidonius nor the Sophocles of Reinhardt can be overlooked, and much remains persuasive in the Parmenides, the Aeschylus, the Homer, and in the lesser essays, even in the Plato.

It follows that we must take account of the twofold — or rather the threefold — division in the school of Wilamowitz. If the Third Humanism is not, at least for the present, a serious problem, the antithesis between the historicist inclinations of the majority and the Nietzschean-existentialist hermeneutics of Reinhardt should be registered without surprise. Above all the antithesis goes back to the youthful clash between Nietzsche and Rohde on the one side and Wilamowitz on the other. In the second place it exists within Wilamowitz himself. The spell, the "charme" that Reinhardt felt in Wilamowitz was due to his daemonic aspect, to his intuition.[4] Behind the historicism of Wilamowitz stands a violent appropriation of the divine order of Hellas, difficult to justify in terms of normal historical procedure.

Finally, two other pupils of Wilamowitz found themselves in serious difficulties with the historical premises of the master — Paul Friedländer and Hermann Fränkel. Each would require separate treatment on his own, the first in his connections with the George-Kreis, the second in his specifically hermeneutic preoccupations that grew out of his twofold experience as an Indianist and a Hellenist. It will suffice now to cite them in confirmation of the opportunity to restore the "Reinhardt case" to the hermeneutic dissonances in classical philology, specifically those which are visible within the school of Wilamowitz.

Notes

1. "Premesse per una discussione su Wilamowitz," *Riv. St. Ital.*, 84, 1972, pp. 746–55; reprinted in *Annali della Scuola Normale Superiore di Pisa*, 3d ser., III, 1, 1973, pp. 103–17.

2. Among the papers on Reinhardt (to some of which I obtained access thanks to L. E. Rossi, who also took part in the discussion on Reinhardt at the Scuola Normale Superiore di Pisa in April 1975) the following may be noted: H.-G. Gadamer and K. Hildebrandt, *Neue Rundschau*, 69, 1958; M. Gelzer and U. Hölscher, *Gedenkreden auf K. R.*, Klostermann, Frankfurt, 1958; H. Rahn, *Paideuma*, 6, 1958, pp. 464–72 (which refers to connections not otherwise known to me between Reinhardt and L. Frobenius); W. Schadewaldt, *Schweizer Monatshefte*, 38, 1958, pp. 737–44 = *Hellas und Hesperien*, 1960, pp. 1030–37 (*cf.* pp. 296–300); R. Pfeiffer, *Jahrb. Bayer. Akad. Wissenschaften*, 1959, pp. 147–52; B. Snell, *Deutsche Akad. f. Sprache u. Dichtung* (Darmstadt), 1959, pp. 134–35; W. Jens, *Zueignungen*, Munich, 1962, pp. 74–78; W. Jaeger, "Ordre pour le mérite," *Reden*, III, Heidelberg, 1958, pp. 23–30; U. Hölscher, *Die Chance des Unbehagens*, Göttingen, 1965, pp. 31–52 (which includes earlier pieces, among them *Die Gegenwart*, 13, 1958, pp. 110–13); H.-G Gadamer, *Neue Zürcher Zeitung*, 30 April 1966, p. 20. The minor writings of K.R. are collected in the two volumes *Vermächtnis der Antike*, (Göttingen, 1959), *Tradition und Geist* (Göttingen, 1960), with excellent introductions by Carl Becker, who has also arranged for a good selection, *Die Krise des Helden*, Munich, 1962.

3. For relations with Stefan George it is necessary to start from the article of K. Hildebrandt in *Neue Rundschau*, 1958, and from his memories of George, even if they are challenged by U. Hölscher, *Die Chance des Unbehagens*, p. 88 n. 6. As is well known, K. Hildebrandt is the author of the most violent attack by the Georgians on Wilamowitz ("Hellas und Wilamowitz") in the *Jahrbuch für die geistige Bewegung*, 1, 1910, pp. 64–117, republished in abbreviated form (also published previously) in G. P. Landmann, *Der George-Kreis*, Cologne-Berlin, 1965, pp. 141–49. It is worth comparing F. J. Brecht, *Plato und der George-Kreis*, Leipzig, 1929, reviewed by K. von Fritz, *Gnomon*, 7, 1931, pp. 356–63.

4. *Cf.* my analysis in the article cited above, "Premesse per una discussione su Wilamowitz" [see now V. Poeschl, *Annali delle Scuola Normale Superiore di Pisa*, 3d ser., V, 1975, pp. 969–83].

THIRTEEN

Introduction to a Discussion
of Eduard Schwartz

I

Eduard Schwartz was born in 1858. His father was a doctor, later professor of Gynecology at Göttingen for about thirty years, from 1862 to 1890. His mother was the sister of the archaeologist and archaeological historian Adolf Michaelis. He was a relative of one of the greatest and most original German philologists, Otto Jahn, the friend of Mommsen, and he was connected by family ties with the historian J. G. Droysen and the archaeologist Eugen Petersen. The family belonged therefore to the upper academic bourgeoisie, devoted to Prussia but never wholly identified with it. Ed. Schwartz began his studies at his father's university, Göttingen, in 1875; he moved to Bonn — a philological university *par excellence*, and Prussian too — in 1876, where he was drawn especially to Hermann Usener, an attachment which he later described in an essay on his teacher.[1] He spent some time at Berlin in 1878, where thanks to family connections he established a friendship with Mommsen, which is once again described with typical modesty in his writings about him.[2] Later Mommsen, by then an old man, decided to help Schwartz with the edition of Eusebius's *Ecclesiastical History,* preparing the edition of the Latin supplement including the two books added by Rufinus to his translation of the text of Eusebius. This link with Mommsen cannot be separated from the fact that in 1879 Schwartz transferred to Greifswald, a small university, to work with Mommsen's son-in-law Wilamowitz, the rising star. Wilamowitz had also studied at Bonn, but unlike Schwartz had been a recalcitrant and arrogant student of Usener.

"Premesse per una discussione su Eduard Schwartz" (introduction to a seminar at the Scuola Normale Superiore in Pisa, February, 1978), *Rivista Storica Italiana*, 90 (1978), pp. 617–26; *Annali della Scuola Normale Superiore di Pisa*, 3d ser., IX, fasc. 4 (1979), pp. 999–1011; *Settimo contributo* (1984), pp. 233–44. Translated by T. J. Cornell. (600)

The reconciliation of Wilamowitz and Usener, who had taken as an insult a disrespectful poem by his pupil, occurred in 1877; it is hardly an accident that this happened shortly before Schwartz moved to Berlin and then to Greifswald. Schwartz, who was about ten years younger than Wilamowitz, remained his friend for life. Everything Schwartz wrote about Wilamowitz — a very great deal — expresses devoted friendship, recognition, and deep appreciation of his unique qualities.[3] But a certain strain between them is undeniable (subtly expressed in a letter from Schwartz to a would-be biographer of Wilamowitz, published in *Quaderni di Storia*, 7, 1978, p. 211). For this reason Schwartz felt that he had to make his own way and to find a field of study far removed from that of Wilamowitz; while Wilamowitz for his part was frankly critical of certain works of Schwartz, such as the first volume of the edition of the scholia to Euripides (1886)[4] and, more harshly, the book on the *Odyssey* of 1924, to which Wilamowitz reacted with a book of his own in 1927. At all events, Schwartz returned to Bonn in 1880 to take his doctorate; his ambitious thesis on a Hellenistic mythographer, *De Dionysio Scytobrachione*, was soon disproved, as he himself smilingly acknowledged.[5]

All his life Schwartz had a liking for biographical sketches, of both ancients (the two volumes of *Charakterköpfe* of 1903 and 1909) and contemporaries. As a result his work contains a wealth of autobiographical material, both direct and indirect. At some points he even seems to identify philology with the understanding of individuals. To this one should add a remarkably candid sketch of his own intellectual life sent to the Academy of Vienna in 1932 and published in *Gesammelte Schriften*, II. Among the obituaries published after his death in 1940, the essay of A. Rehm is especially notable: "Eduard Schwartz' wissenschaftliches Lebenswerk" (in *Sitz. Bayer. Akad.*, 1942, p. 4).[6]

II

For the sake of clarity it is worth reminding ourselves at the start that the research of Eduard Schwartz, exceptional for its quality and quantity, can be divided into eight distinct categories, which often, but not too often, overlap:

1. His activity as an editor of texts is surprisingly varied, and only in the case of major texts coincides with his historical interests. The edition of the scholia to Euripides (1886–91), an extension of his interest in mythography, was followed by the edition of Tatian, *Oratio ad Graecos* (1888), and the *Apologia* of Athenagoras (1891). The great edition of Eusebius's *Ecclesiastical History*, a model of unprejudiced recension of a tradition (and at the same time an example of research into the successive redactions of a single work) was finished in 1909.[7] Immediately afterwards he began preparing the edition

of the Acts of the Councils, which, although not finished, include the acts of the Council of Constantinople of 553, the Council of Ephesus of 431, and the Council of Chalcedon of 451. The Syriac texts are translated into Greek. Among the results of this preliminary work was the identification of the so-called Egyptian Apostolic Canons as the work of Hippolytus of Rome (1910). The luxury editions of the *Iliad* (1923) and the *Odyssey* (1924) are important for their use of the Alexandrian critics. Even on his deathbed Schwartz was publishing—for the first time in critical form—the lives of the Palestinian monks by the sixth-century Cyril of Scythopolis.[8]

2. Studies in the history of Greek historiography include all or almost all the Greek historians in Pauly-Wissowa from *A* to *E*—that is, Apollodorus, Appian, Arrian, *Chronicon Paschale*, Diodorus, Cassius Dio, Diogenes Laertius, Dionysius of Halicarnassus, Ephorus, and Eusebius, as well as the Latin historian Curtius Rufus.[9] In addition to these articles, all of which are fundamental and are really monographs, he published papers in journals on Xenophon (1889), Callisthenes (1900), Ephorus (1909), Timaeus (1899), etc. The 1919 volume on Thucydides was followed by two general essays on Greek historiography in 1920 and 1928, and was preceded by a programmatic survey of ecclesiastical historiography in 1908. We may add the extremely important study of the tradition about the Catilinarian conspiracy (1897) and the late work on the sources of Pausanias for the Messenian wars (1937). Schwartz also left his mark on the study of the Roman annalistic tradition (1903).

3. The analytical studies of Greek poetry include essays on Homer, Hesiod, Tyrtaeus (1899; later repudiated in 1937), and Theocritus, and culminate in the volume on the *Odyssey* of 1924. He also found time for an influential paper on Demosthenes (1893) and an edition of the pseudo-Virgilian *Aetna*, notable for its bold emendations (1933).

4. The studies of ancient geography and chronology began with investigations of the king-lists of Eratosthenes and Castor in 1894, and continued throughout his life, perhaps culminating in the works on the calculation of the date of Easter (1905), which are technically difficult and are replete with important insights into relations between Judaism and Christianity.

5. A fundamental volume on the Greek novel in relation to Greek historiography (1896).

6. Historical and biographical studies (*Charakterköpfe*), of which the best known is the monograph on Constantine and the Christian Church, published in 1913 and later revised. His historical research was essentially concentrated on ecclesiastical politics of the fourth century, with particular reference to Athanasius (nine monographs), and of the sixth century (Justinian). Here the importance of Schwartz as a pioneer is beyond dispute.[10]

7. New Testament studies, particularly on the fourth Gospel; although Schwartz himself was later uncertain about their value, he nevertheless held

on to his view that the study of the Bible was a matter for philologists, not theologians.

8. Studies of Greek ethics, first formulated in the "Problems of Ancient Ethics" of 1906 and leading to the posthumous publication in 1951 of the *Ethik der Griechen*, the product of classes given in the years 1933–35.

With such a mass of work one might suppose that the life of Ed. Schwartz was entirely academic and straightforward. That is true only up to a point. His scholarly qualities were quickly recognized; he received grants to travel abroad, which took him now and again to Italy and made him familiar with Italian, in which he became proficient enough to write a brief paper of archaeological-mythological character for the German Institute in Rome. On the other hand, although a formidable Hellenist, he never went to Greece. In 1884 he was a lecturer at Bonn; in 1887 at the age of 29 he was professor at Rostock, and in 1893 at Giessen; in 1897 he was invited to take up an appointment at Strassburg, where he was a colleague of Richard Reitzenstein. This was a period in which Strassburg, a German university in Alsace which had been torn from France, had political aspirations to prestige and to Germanization—matters on which Schwartz was to reflect in his later years with a clear mind. In 1902 he moved to Göttingen, as successor, in fact though not in title, to his teacher Wilamowitz. It seemed to be a decisive step. And it was decisive in the sense that his meeting with Julius Wellhausen, the historian of the Jewish and Arab world who at precisely that period had passed on to New Testament studies, had even greater significance than the meeting of Wellhausen and Wilamowitz at Greifswald. Wellhausen pointed out or at least confirmed to Schwartz the new way— the nontheological study of Christianity—that he had been searching for when defining himself in relation to Wilamowitz. On Wellhausen's death in 1918 Schwartz wrote his most penetrating and intimate biographical essay. What he had admired in Wellhausen was to a large extent the clearly recognized legacy of the school of Wilamowitz: "The way to a spiritual content goes through linguistic form" (*Ges. Schriften*, I, p. 354). But it was with nostalgia and a sense of his own inadequacy that Schwartz viewed Wellhausen's historical constructions. A Lutheran pastor's son, full of the simple joys of living, Wellhausen had become an unbeliever, but had managed to salvage something from the parsonage which he had left and had understood with rigorous philological criticism the preurban culture of the Jews and Arabs. Following Wellhausen's advice Schwartz, whose linguistic abilities were exceptional, added Arabic to the Syriac and Armenian that he had learned in order to study ecclesiastical history (although Armenian, he declared, was "almost the death of me"). But other aspects of Göttingen failed to satisfy him, and he left in 1909 for Freiburg before returning in 1913 to Strassburg, where he spent the war years. Two of his sons died in the war (one of them, Gerhard, had been a most promising philologist), and a third came back permanently disabled. In October or November 1918 he had to flee from Strassburg, and for a time he lost his house, his books, and his papers. He took refuge in Freiburg and only in 1919 regained a chair, this time at Munich. He recovered his books and papers through the intercession of foreign friends, the Dane Heiberg and the Belgian Cumont. He remained at Munich for the rest of his career, having refused, so it is said, the chair at Berlin in succession to Wilamowitz. He retired in 1929, before the Nazis gained power, although he twice gave classes during the Nazi regime on classical and Hellenistic ethics—but certainly not with a Nazi slant or in order to please the Nazis. He died in 1940, without ever having said anything, as far as I know, that could be taken as approval of the Nazi regime. Two of his pupils, one I think of Jewish origin, the other a non-Jew, Ernst Kapp and Kurt von Fritz, left Germany; they were among the few who in nobility of character and intellectual stature could be considered his true disciples.

His influence was more evident in the form of respect and admiration than of true approval or collaboration. Of Wilamowitz we have already spoken. With Felix Jacoby, the other scholar who together with Schwartz had inherited from their common teacher Wilamowitz an interest in Greek historiography, the wide areas of agreement were less significant than the points on which they differed. The theologians watched reluctantly as Schwartz invaded their territory of ecclesiastical history. Harnack never concealed his dislike of Schwartz, and was repaid in the same coin. In 1908 Harnack sought to demonstrate to the Berlin Academy that Schwartz, in publishing a Syriac document of a synod of Antioch in 325, had been taken in by a forgery. Schwartz openly fought his opponent on his own ground in the reply he gave that same year at the Göttingen Academy, of which the editors of the *Gesammelte Schriften* have had the bad judgment to reprint only a small part.[11]

Abroad, Schwartz's name is invariably remembered in connection with specific problems, and it cannot be said that anyone has given much thought to his work as a whole. Three of his non-German friends have been well known to me: Georgio Pasquali, Plinio Fraccaro, and Norman Baynes. Pasquali studied under him at Göttingen, and his interests in patristic studies must undoubtedly have been encouraged by that; later he admired and commented on the book on Thucydides; and he always regarded the edition of Eusebius as a model. But what he had to say about Wilamowitz was matched by a corresponding silence about Schwartz. About the youthful friendship between Fraccaro and Schwartz (after 1919 Schwartz never went back to Italy) I was informed by Emilio Gabba and not, as far as I can remember, by Fraccaro himself. Baynes went to Germany to talk to Schwartz about Constantine and ecclesiastical politics, but it is not my impression that he considered him a kindred spirit.[12]

All the major German classical philologists of the period 1870–1930 were devoted subjects of the Prussian state, which had become the German empire. The reaction against Bismarck's policies, which Mommsen displayed after 1870, was not shared by the younger generation of classical scholars and ancient historians. Eduard Schwartz was certainly no exception. At Strassburg he saw himself as a representative of German culture at the frontier. During the First World War he shared the current patriotism and paid the price both personally and through his family. After the war he deprecated what he considered the demagogy of the Weimar Republic. What separated him from others was the clarity of his judgment. Schwartz was not deluded into thinking that Alsace considered itself German and was happy to have been made part of Germany. He knew that its language was German but that its feelings were French. In a confidential paper in 1916, and later in a public speech in 1929, he stated this unequivocally. The text of the 1929 speech was published at the time and later reprinted in *Gesammelte Schriften*, I. The text of the 1916 paper is referred to in the autobiographical memoir of 1932, but up to now it has been available only in the Italian translation that L. Canfora deserves credit for having published in *Quaderni di Storia*, VI. Schwartz regards the Prussian policy of assimilating Alsace as a manifest failure. His suggested remedy is to annex Alsace to Prussia: that is, to replace persuasion by force.

In Schwartz there is a disparity between the subtlety of his insights and the one-sidedness of his feelings. For him the supreme entity is the state, in which free men defend their liberty against outsiders. That there are objective conflicts of classes and interests within the state, that there is a culture which transcends ethnic divisions, and indeed that there is a religion which is not conterminous with political units: these notions do not seem to have formed part of his political awareness, although he was naturally conscious of them. His aristocratic ethos, which echoes the ethical values of archaic and classical Greece (down to Pericles), is effectively free from all religious assumptions. To him individualism and cosmopolitanism were ruinous. That is not to say that he did not recognize their importance at particular periods, and did not appreciate the value, in an age of decadence, of the Epicurean ideal of friendship or the Stoic ideal of public service in the Roman period. His sympathy for the Hellenistic monarchies (at least in his essay of 1906) was due to their Macedonian origin, which for him, brought up as he was on Droysen, unambiguously recalled Prussia.

If there is anything which defines Schwartz's place within the school of Wilamowitz, it is his direct and decisive intervention in the history of Christianity. This is not a matter, as it is with other pupils of Wilamowitz such as J. Geffcken, of a generalized interest in the decline of ancient culture. Nor can it be seen as a leftover from the teaching of Usener, whose historical-religious interests Schwartz did not share. Here Schwartz felt himself to be an innovator in his own right, and at least at certain moments (almost all during the Göttingen period) chastised himself with the sense of being a revolutionary. In Schwartz's view the history of the Church was divided into two stages: the first, that of the Gospels, was for him the formation of the myth of Christ; the second was the interplay of factions within the Church which degenerated into power rivalries and led to the heresies and schisms which the Councils sought to resolve.

It is difficult to say whether Schwartz subjectively attributed more importance to the first period or to the second. In the years of open conflict with the "theologians" (Harnack), the criticism of the Gospels was probably most significant for him. He was conscious of depending on Wellhausen—of agreeing with him about the need to connect the study of the New Testament with that of the Old Testament—and of being able to use his own exceptional analytical abilities in dissecting (which meant undermining) the most important "theological" document: the fourth Gospel. His ambition in these years was to understand the formation of the original Christian tradition without any religious presuppositions and purely with the instruments of philological analysis. Later, things must have appeared to Schwartz in a different form. He implicitly acknowledged the failure of his criticism of the fourth Gospel, and in general he never again undertook a task of such ambitious scope in biblical criticism. The revolution, it must be admitted, never materialized, and the theologians remained in control.

The second phase, concerning the political struggle within the Church from the fourth to the sixth century, interested and occupied Schwartz from 1910 onwards. The actual volume of material to be published and interpreted was enormous. If the Councils were key points in political struggles, Athanasius and Justinian were, at opposite poles, the prototypes of ecclesiastical politics. As always, it would be to undervalue Schwartz to reduce him to his own formulae. In his last years he studied the Palestinian monks of the age of Justinian with great subtlety. But it was always the moment of political-ecclesiastical conflict, not the moment of faith, that prevailed in his research. If Schwartz did not concern himself with economic conflicts, he compensated by interpreting religious conflicts as political ones. And it must be said: in the criticism of the fourth Gospel (and of the Acts of the Apostles) Schwartz inevitably entered the "holy of holies" of theology. However, in his history of ecclesiastical struggles he chose that type of document which coincided most closely with his (non) theological tastes, and virtually left untouched the doctrinal formulations of Tertullian, Origen, the Cappadocian Fathers, Augustine, etc. That is to say, he recognized, albeit unwillingly, the distinction between Church history and the history of the Church's teachings. The distinction does not diminish the importance of the work done by Schwartz in Church history, but it attenuates its revolutionary character. Added to the admission that there was something wrong with the attempt to reduce the problem of the Gospels to a philological problem, this abandonment of the properly theological zone in the fourth to sixth centuries explains why few have noticed that Schwartz remains, in spite of everything, alongside Usener as a figure who stands for the renewal of philology.

What then lessens Schwartz's revolutionary attitude? It is necessary to return to the function that philology served for him. For him, the task of philology was naturally to reconstruct people's conscious thoughts. The objectivity of the heuristic process guarantees that one does not attribute to a writer or speaker ideas that are not his. Here we find the fundamental honesty of a philologist who interprets according to explicit rules and is prepared to recognize that he is wrong if someone proves to him that the rules of the game have not been observed. I would also say that it is implicit in the attitude of this philology (which for convenience we shall call the school of Wilamowitz, although Usener also fits into it) that it is prepared to recognize that its own rules could be erroneous, even if I could not at present point to a clear example of this recognition of error in the given rules. But after the function of establishing the conscious thought of writers who are being analyzed, Schwartz gives philology another task—that of revealing through contradictions, obscurities, and lacunae the existence of a process of development. This process of development can be simply due to the additions of the author himself who has changed his ideas, but can also be the result of extraneous interventions, such as interpolations, modifications, and corrections. Schwartz was obviously not the only one to have sought to reconstruct the formation of a text by means of analysis. Homer and the Bible were in his day, and perhaps still are, the object of daily exercise for analytical philologists. What was exceptional in Schwartz was his belief that it was possible to reconstruct vanished personalities, otherwise undocumented aspects of known personalities, and indeed historical situations, by no other means than the analysis of texts, since analysis reveals inconsistencies and contradictions. All of Schwartz's Homeric criticism was aimed at uncovering lost poets hidden beneath the surviving text, the least interesting being the poet (or "redactor") who put together the *Odyssey* we now possess. The book on Thucydides—of extraordinary richness, and even today in Italy the model for L. Canfora's researches on Thucydides—is a typical example of this second aspect of Schwartzian philology. Schwartz maintains that Thucydides radically changed his view of the Peloponnesian War after the defeat of Athens. After the defeat, Thucydides was much better able to appreciate the value of Pericles' policy and composed the funeral speech which is both a description and a celebration of it. On the other hand Thucydides died leaving the work unfinished, and therefore containing many elements which would otherwise have been eliminated; these include the documents which Schwartz, here following Wilamowitz, believed incompatible with the rules of Greek historical style. What is more

Schwartz found elements in Thucydides that had been added by the posthumous editor who published the work. The book must be read for its freshness and pathos to be fully appreciated; a book written for consolation during the First World War, and with certain elements that one would be tempted to call autobiographical if Schwartz had not informed us that it was completed in 1917 before the defeat of Germany.

It is evident that in this second task, which was not unique to Schwartz, but was strongly emphasized by him—the analysis of the process of development through the investigation of internal contradictions—the rules of the game became more relaxed and almost uncontrollable. One cannot overlook the fact that Schwartz was after all a contemporary of Freud, for whom the rules of the game were and are far more arbitrary and subjective than Freud himself ever suspected.[13] Late nineteenth-century philology has been one of the many ways of reaching the unconscious—or the undocumented. Philology is therefore the hallmark of the vision of Ed. Schwartz, but philology is divided into two: the high road is the interpretation of coherent thought, and the low road is the perception of what makes thought incoherent. This in part explains why the disagreement was so sharp between Wilamowitz and Schwartz over the *Odyssey*, where Wilamowitz refused to recognize those poetic personalities whom Schwartz detected lurking behind what for him was the work of a rather unintelligent compiler. In my opinion this is also the difference between Schwartz and Jacoby. Jacoby's chief interest was in the Greeks' methods of historical research; this meant recognizing a much greater variety of historical genres and having less need to resort to real or supposed contradictions as the criterion of interpretation. One might add that Jacoby, while agreeing with Schwartz in giving central importance to the political element in Greek historiography, attributed equal importance to rationalism, which Schwartz tended to undervalue.[14] To us the similarities between Schwartz and Jacoby as interpreters of the Greek historians may seem more significant than the differences; neither was much concerned with the relationship between the historian and his public—in other words with the problematic position of the historian in Greek society.[15] There is no doubt that the subjectivism of Schwartz the philologist did not suit Jacoby. However, as far as I know, Schwartz's disagreements with Wilamowitz and Jacoby were never pursued in a systematic way by either party. Even those (like R. Pfeiffer[16]) who have resumed the debate, at least in relation to Homer, have not touched the heart of the matter. The question was, and is: What is the value of coherence as a criterion of interpretation?

It is this second aspect of philological criticism—the intuitive—that permitted Schwartz to introduce his political and religious (or antireligious) leanings into the fabric of philological interpretation. Not that his principal enemies, the theologians, behaved any differently. By giving this second aspect of Schwartz's philological method the importance it deserves, one can begin to understand why the philological revolution, which he promised at certain moments, and to which he was certainly more inclined than Wilamowitz or Jacoby, never took place.[17]

Notes

Introduction to a seminar on Eduard Schwartz held at the Scuola Normale Superiore, Pisa, in February 1978. Particular aspects were illustrated by G. Arrighetti (Homer); M. Isnardi Parente (Greek ethics); F. Parente (studies on Christianity); E. Gabba (Greek historiography). The best bibliography of Ed. Schwartz is in *Ges. Schriften*, IV, 1960, pp. 329–44.

The *Ges. Schriften* are an unreliable selection; in my paper I have presupposed the full texts of the original papers.

1. Ed. Schwartz, *Ges. Schriften*, I, 1938, pp. 301–15.

2. *Ges. Schriften*, I, pp. 281–300.

3. *Ges. Schriften*, I, pp. 362–82; "Wilamowitz-Moellendorffs Ilias und Homer," *Ges. Schriften*, II, 1956, pp. 25–41; review of the *Platon, Hist. Zeitschrift*, 122, 1921, pp. 290–300, and elsewhere. *Cf.* the preface to *Mommsen und Wilamowitz: Briefwechsel*, 1935.

4. Wilamowitz, *Deutsche Literaturz.*, 8, 1887, pp. 1111–13.

5. *Cf.* E. Bethe, *Quaestiones Diodoreae Mythographiae*, diss., Göttingen, 1887, and the article by Schwartz himself in Pauly-Wissowa, V, 1903.

6. Note also the important obituary by Walter Otto, *Hist. Zeitschrift*, 162, 1940, pp. 442–46. Less significant is that by J. Stroux, *Forschungen und Fortschritte*, 16, 1940, pp. 166–68.

7. See the assessment of it by G. Pasquali, *Storia della tradizione e critica del testo*, new ed., 1952, pp. 135 ff.; 408 ff. It should not be forgotten that the book is dedicated to the "fatherly friends," Ed. Schwartz and G. Vitelli.

8. *Kyrillos von Skythopolis*, 1939; note also "Drei dogmatische Schriften Justinians," *Abh. Bayer. Akad.*, 18, 1939, and the earlier essay of 1912 "Johannes Rufus, ein monophysitischer Schriftsteller" (*Sitz. Heidelb. Akad.*), and the seminal piece of 1922 on the "capitula" of Nestorius (*Sitz. Bayer. Akad.*).

9. The principal articles were collected in a volume, *Griechische Geschichtschreiber*, Leipzig, 1959.

10. The programmatic aspects are emphasized in *Ges. Schriften*, I, pp. 110–30 and 135; *Hist. Zeitschrift*, 104, 1910, pp. 609–14 (review of R. Sohm), and elsewhere.

11. "Zur Geschichte des Athanasius VII," *Nachr. Gesell. Wiss. Göttingen*, 1908, pp. 305–74; notice the programmatic page 373.

12. *Cf.* N. H. Baynes, "Constantine the Great and the Christian Church," *Proceed. British Acad.*, 15, 1929.

13. Here it is relevant to cite S. Timpanaro, *Il lapsus freudiano*, Florence, 1974, because it is a critique by a philologist. My own position is stated in *La composizione delle storie di Tucidide* of 1930.

14. Notice the succession of articles by F. Jacoby and Ed. Schwartz in *Die Antike*, 2, 1926, and 4, 1928, on Greek historiography.

15. On this see my paper in *Annali della Scuola Normale Superiore di Pisa*, 3d ser., VIII, fasc. 1, 1978.

16. R. Pfeiffer, *Ausgewählte Schriften*, 1960, pp. 8–25 (written in 1928); but *cf.* also his fine portrait of Schwartz, from 1952, in *Von der Liebe zur Antike*, 1969, pp. 87–93.

[17. *Cf.* now L. Canfora, *Intelletuali in Germania*, Bari, 1979.]

FOURTEEN

Liberal Historian and Supporter of the Holy Roman Empire: E. A. Freeman

I

Born in 1823, orphaned in early infancy, brought up first by a grandmother with high religious ideals and then in the house of a High Church clergyman, the five-year-old Edward Augustus Freeman put the following question to a theologian friend of the family: "Do you believe that St. Paul wrote the Epistle to the Hebrews? If he is called the Apostle to the Gentiles, why would he have written to the Hebrews?" At the age of eleven he knew not only Latin and Greek, but also a little Hebrew. A few years later he wrote, among numerous lyric and tragic verses, a tragedy on St. Thomas of Canterbury, in sympathy with the Oxford Movement which was later to carry Newman to the bosom of the Roman Church. He continued to be a poet (in public) even after his university years down to about 1850. As far as one can tell, he preferred as a matter of personal choice to avoid the traditional rigors of public school and to continue to be educated privately in the vicarage of his tutor until his admission to Trinity College, Oxford, as an undergraduate in 1841. He arrived in Oxford betrothed to the daughter of his tutor, Eleanor Gutch, whom he was to marry in 1847. Trinity College was precisely Newman's original college and one of the centers of the Oxford Movement; the choice of college will not have been fortuitous. Freeman certainly took part in some aspects of the movement, sharing its taste for asceticism, the liturgy, and Gothic cathedrals. Already at that time he showed

"Uno storico liberale fautore del Sacro Romano Impero: E. A. Freeman" (introduction to a seminar at the Scuola Normale Superiore in Pisa, February 1981), *Rivista Storica Italiana,* 92 (1980), pp. 152–63; with slight variations, *Annali della Scuola Normale Superiore di Pisa,* 3d ser., XI, fasc. 2 (1981), pp. 309–22; *Settimo contributo* (1984), pp. 187–200 [the later version translated here]. Translated by T. J. Cornell.

skill in drawing buildings and talent as an architectural historian. But he decided not to go into the Church (as a married man he lost the fellowship of Trinity College that had been given to him for scholarly achievement), and he soon ceased to concern himself with theological aspects of the movement. He does not seem ever to have been tempted to follow Newman on the road to Rome (1845).

As his parents had left him enough of a fortune to live as a country gentleman, he was not faced with a serious problem of choosing a profession. The absence of a public-school education in keeping with the conventions of his class probably contributed to the relative isolation of his adult life and certainly prevents us from considering him a typical Victorian. But in other respects Freeman conforms well enough to the stereotype of the age: conspicuous individualism; a certain lack of prejudice underlying the conventions; love of the life of a country gentleman (which he began around 1848 in Gloucestershire and never abandoned, although he moved twice: near Cardiff in Wales in 1855 and then near Wells in Somerset in 1860). He was a tenacious and methodical reader and writer, a high-class correspondent and conversationalist, with a passion for riding despite a far-from-athletic physique, a traveler with wide horizons, and above all a political animal. A beard which grew ever longer with the years must have contributed to his personal defensiveness.

To the end of his life Freeman considered himself a Christian. To one of his ecclesiastical friends who doubted this he wrote in 1888, four years before his death: "You ask if I am still a believer. Certainly. That is to say, I believe that the Christian religion comes from God, and not only in the sense that all things come from God." However, his Christianity diminished rapidly, while another semireligious influence on him was making itself felt, the myth of German civilization, which was communicated to him, according to his own testimony, by Thomas Arnold.[1]

II

Thomas Arnold, headmaster of Rugby School, became Regius Professor of Modern History at Oxford, and delivered his famous inaugural lecture there precisely in 1842, shortly after Freeman's arrival. There was indeed something in this lecture to excite the fantasy of an intelligent and fundamentally solitary young man. Arnold began with few preambles: "We are living in the latest period of the world's history. No other races remain behind to perform what we have neglected or to restore what we have ruined. [It follows that] the interest of modern history does become intense, and the importance of not wasting the time still left to us may well be called incalculable.... Our existing nations are the last reserve of the world; its

fate may be said to be in their hands—God's work on earth will be left un-
done if they do not do it."[2]

The apocalyptic tone must be taken together with what Arnold had
affirmed a few minutes earlier: "I say nothing of the prospects and influence
of the German race in Africa and in India: it is enough to say that half of
Europe, and all America and Australia, are German more or less completely, in race, in language, or in institutions, or in all." Arnold, it seems,
had been converted to the belief in the superiority of the Germanic race by
Chr. Karl Bunsen, the founder of the Instituto di Corrispondenza
Archeologica in Rome and later Prussian Minister in England. The myth of
the superiority of the youthful Germanic nations, of which England was
one, which formed in the minds of educated Christian classicists like Bunsen and Arnold, must naturally not be identified with the ignorant brutali-
ties of German and Italian racists of the 1930s; but some elements of this
later development are already present, and in more than embryonic form,
for example, the justification of colonialism.

Forty-two years later Freeman, who after many difficulties and somewhat
unexpectedly was in a position to call himself Arnold's indirect successor in
the Regius Chair of Modern History at Oxford, solemnly declared: "It was
from Arnold that I first learned the truth which ought to be the center and
life of all our historic studies, the truth of the unity of history." And what
this unity of history recognized by Arnold amounted to he specified in
his own inaugural lecture: "It was ruled by the Teutoburg wood that there
should be a free Germany to plant a free England, and a free England to
plant a free America."[3] The festive occasion of an inaugural address might
have caused Freeman to exaggerate his debt to Arnold, but there can be no
question about the essential accuracy of his statement, and for a reason of
which Freeman himself was perhaps not entirely conscious.

To hear at Oxford in 1842 a declaration of the centrality of German history, and consequently of Germanic destiny—into which British history
could be made to fit—could not but represent an alternative to Newman's
message, which entailed a return to Rome. There was an old and well-
established connection between Arminius and Luther, between the Teutoburg Forest and the League of Schmalkalden. Classicist, Christian, and
Germanophile, Arnold showed the young Freeman a way out of the Oxford
Movement that would not cause him discomfort.

We can follow this withdrawal in a field in which the Oxford Movement
was heavily involved, namely the evaluation of medieval church architecture. Freeman, as we know, was skilled and interested in architecture; in his
youth he even toyed with the idea of becoming an architect. But, once he
had decided on a career as an independent scholar, he produced as his first
important work a general history of architecture (1849). Freeman had not
at that time been out of England.

The value of this history of architecture in relation to contemporary studies I am not competent to judge, but its lines are clear and vigorously drawn. According to Freeman, whatever the merits of the ecclesiologists, who concerned themselves with medieval churches and gave the Gothic style the recognition it deserved, ecclesiology is not a satisfactory alternative to antiquarianism (antiquarianism was one of the terms of abuse which Arnold used frequently and with relish). Second to none in his admiration for the Gothic style, particularly in its severe phase, Freeman nevertheless wants to understand the whole history of architecture from its origins to modern times. He wants "a philosophic history of the science of architecture, whose task it would be to indicate its artistic principles and its symbolism—the symbolism, that is, of styles and of entire buildings, not that of mere details."[4] Shortly afterwards (1851) Freeman dedicated another, more technical, work to the windows of medieval English buildings. By way of architecture Freeman freed himself from the religion of his youth and became a historian of politics and civilization.

He nevertheless continued throughout his life to go around drawing buildings and observing architectural structures. After 1860 his curiosity for places and buildings had every chance of fulfillment in the increasingly long and frequent journeys to France, Italy, Switzerland, and western Germany—and to a lesser extent in travels in Dalmatia and Greece in the years around 1878. The requests—and for years the commissions—to write for newspapers and magazines provided scope for this activity of description and draughtsmanship. The educated English public were eager to read in weekly and monthly periodicals about places they had already visited or were able to visit. Notwithstanding his basic financial independence, Freeman loved to supplement his family fortune with work that he found easy, gave him the opportunity to travel, and apparently ended up providing him with five hundred pounds a year. A long and continuous commitment of particular importance was his association with the *Saturday Review* between 1855 and 1877. His reputation as a journalist went some way to compensate him for the lack of success which, for reasons that are not entirely clear to me, dogged him in politics and academic life. Political ambitions could be considered natural in a man who lived the life of a country gentleman. In Wells, which as we have said was near his home from 1860 on, he seems to have been much appreciated in local circles; he became a magistrate, and in 1870 published a well-received history of Wells cathedral. But his persistent efforts to enter Parliament on a liberal platform close to Gladstone were unsuccessful. The same has to be said of his repeated attempts to obtain one of the chairs of History at Oxford; in 1858 he was passed over for the chair of Modern History which was a royal appointment and therefore the object of political patronage; in 1861 he failed to gain the chair of Ancient History (the *Camden Chair*); and in 1862 he was unsuccessful with the *Chichele Chair* of Modern History. Contacts with Oxford as an examiner in Modern History, and participation in discussions about university reforms (even minor ones), would have been slender consolation.

What needs to be emphasized, however, is that even when his academic prospects were bleak, Freeman always considered journalism a secondary activity, and worked solidly on works of history any one of which would have been enough to make the reputation of a historian.

III

Freeman's interest from 1850 onwards extended to all of classical antiquity, the European, Byzantine, and Arab Middle Ages, Modern Europe, and Anglo-Saxon America. It was expressed not only in books but also in essays, often of great originality. His concern with architecture and town planning and his interest in political and cultural problems were linked by his competence in historical geography, to which he devoted a volume (1881), revised after his death by J. B. Bury (1903).

The belief in the superiority of the German race was connected by Freeman with a series of constitutional and political problems, of which he stressed both the classical antecedents and the modern consequences. The first theme he tackled in political history was the history of federal government, of which he published only the first volume in 1863, dedicated to Greek federalism. It was his intention to continue the theme and to investigate how federal government, after the attempts described by Polybius, had been taken up by the Romans and brought to life again by the Germans in the Middle Ages and in Switzerland in the modern period. An immediate coincidence—the American Civil War of 1861–65—was perhaps the most powerful stimulus for embarking on this work, but there were other questions of contemporary politics to which Freeman hoped to contribute with his original plan for this history: whether the situation of modern Greece and the Balkans in general might not point to the utility of a federal government in that area; whether a federal system might not suit Italy; whether there were reasons for some kind of federal reorganization of British dominions in Ireland, Canada, and Australia; and finally whether the monarchies of modern Germany might not be brought together in a federation. Already in 1854, in a letter to George Finlay, the historian of medieval and modern Greece, who remained a lifelong friend, Freeman put forward the federal solution as the most suitable for Greece; it was one of the first signs of his growing interest in the Balkan world and in the destiny of the Islamic empire, past and present. In another letter to Finlay in 1860, Freeman extended his preference for a federalist solution to the Italian question, save that he nevertheless accepted the conquests of Savoy as inevitable. Concerning Britain, then and later, Freeman eschewed federalist solutions, which would have compromised the power of the British parliament, but on the other hand he made himself an advocate of Home Rule for Ireland. With the publication of the first volume Freeman set himself to the business of working on the second volume with a trip to Switzerland, which recalls the earlier visit of G. Grote: like Grote, Freeman considered himself at that time (1863) vaguely republican. Two unfinished chapters of this second volume were added to the first in the second edition which was published posthumously by J. B. Bury in 1893. But the rest of the second volume was never written, and the material that had been assembled served in part for other works, among which was a concise study of the development of the English constitution (*The Growth of the English Constitution*, 1872).

In the years around 1870 Freeman was less interested in the federal idea in itself than in the contribution of the Germans to the constitutional structures of Europe, particularly of England. Whereas federalism had Greek origins, he considered parliamentary government (in accordance with a precise tradition of juridical thought) to be of German origin. In this version of the history of medieval institutions the Normans acquired a central position, first in northern France and England, then also in Sicily. To the Normans in England Freeman devoted the work of his maturity, the most substantial and elaborate he ever wrote. *The History of the Norman Conquest* appeared in six volumes between 1867 and 1879. The bulk of it was already written by 1872. The intensity of his commitment to the Normans is confirmed by the massive two-volume monograph on William Rufus (1882) and the smaller one on William the Conqueror (1888). Norman Sicily was his intended destination, after a journey through ancient, Byzantine, and Arab Sicily, in the work which he undertook in the last years of his life and which he left unfinished in four volumes down to the fourth century B.C. in 1892. The general idea behind this history of Sicily is made clear by a little volume of 1892 entitled *Sicily: Phoenician, Greek and Roman*. For Freeman the Normans, who came to England as Frenchified conquerors, resumed their Germanic character through the resistance and influence of the Anglo-Saxons. Together with the Anglo-Saxons, and on Anglo-Saxon foundations, they created the typical institutions of medieval feudalism, including the bicameral parliamentary system which, in contrast to the organization of (three) Estates General in France, was the cornerstone of modern English liberty. The providential vitality of the Germanic element among both the Anglo-Saxons and the Normans triumphed over bad French instincts. "The Norman was a Dane who, during his sojourn in Gaul, had taken on a light French colouring and was coming to England to rid himself of it." In Sicily then, the Normans not only introduced parliamentary life, but for the second time saved the island from becoming Semitic (the first occasion occurred in the fifth and fourth centuries B.C. when the Greeks had defeated the Phoenicians); thus the Normans helped in their own way to keep Europe Aryan.

The years in which Freeman worked on the Normans in England were those in which his Germanic enthusiasm reached its peak. Factors that contributed to it (or followed from it) were his antipathy to Benjamin Disraeli, the prime minister of Jewish origin, and his loathing (there is no other word for it) of Napoleon III. The Prussian victory was hailed by him as a success for England, against the prevalent view of English public opinion, which was concerned about German expansion. It is not surprising that by now Freeman found it difficult to distinguish between Germans and Indo-Germans (or Aryans). Much of this was derived from the German who championed the idea of the unity of Aryan culture, Max Müller, now active at Oxford.[5] Freeman developed linguistic interests and obsessions. He not only liked to understand the structure of the Indo-Germanic languages and to etymologize accordingly, but he dedicated himself as systematically as possible to the task of excluding from his vocabulary all words of Latin origin, giving preference to Germanic roots. He even reproved Mommsen for using too many Latin words. These interests and obsessions are widely documented in his correspondence with his daughters, his more intimate friends, and certain other scholars who shared his convictions.

Among his correspondents (apart from J. R. Green, the historian, his frequent traveling companion from 1871 onwards) one in particular merits attention: Viscount Strangford (Percy Ellen Frederick Smythe, eighth Viscount Strangford). A true linguistic genius, Strangford, while still a student at Oxford in 1845, had been sent to Constantinople as an attaché at the British Embassy; later he played a part of some importance in the Crimean War; between 1857 and 1861 he lived, it seems, among dervishes in Constantinople. Later he traveled in the Balkans and died prematurely in 1869. He had succeeded in acquiring what was said to be a perfect command of Turkish, modern Greek, and Persian, and a good knowledge besides of Indian, Slavic, and Celtic languages. As evidence of his ability to analyze languages and dialects there survive a few published writings and numerous letters assembled by his widow, herself an oriental traveler of notably enterprising spirit: *Selected Writings* in two volumes (1869); *Original Letters and Papers* (1878). In the volume of letters one can trace the influence of Strangford on Freeman as guide and corrective on linguistic matters. It was from Strangford that Freeman learned about the spread of Gaelic in Scotland, about Maltese as a dialect of Arabic, about the relationship between Albanian and Greek, and about other things. But it was Strangford above all who gave Freeman some idea of discipline in linguistics.[6] While he was writing the history of the Norman Conquest Freeman was contemplating—and rapidly drafted in 1872—one of his most important works, *Comparative Politics,* which sought to give an idea of Indo-European institutions with particular reference to the Germans. In 1872 Freeman wrote to E. B. Tylor, author of *Primitive Culture* (1871): "I have chosen a topic which makes a good sequel to your works and those of Max Müller, and I am calling it, for want of a better title,

Comparative Politics." Without knowing, except vaguely (as far as can be deduced from the preface), of Fustel de Coulanges, but certainly well aware of Maine, Freeman applied the method of comparative philology to Indo-European (or, as he would have preferred to say, Aryan) institutions. The elements of this method are already present to some extent in the history of federalism, but there it had been a question of tracing the evolution of a well-defined type of institution. But now in *Comparative Politics* Freeman proceeded to compose a mosaic of Indo-European institutions out of pieces drawn from later ages: in their turn the later institutions were elucidated in the light of their original Aryan unity. The method was, as we know, successful. It was used not many years ago by one of the greatest philologists of our time, E. Benveniste. This is not the place to discuss its strengths and weaknesses, which are in fact rather obvious.

IV

Freeman's concerns in the years around 1870 were concentrated on these linguistic and institutional themes, because it seemed to him that the combination of linguistics and the study of institutions could help to resolve contemporary political problems. Too English and too much of a gentleman to throw himself headlong into ethnological speculations on the future of humanity, he placed his hopes in some sort of renaissance of the Holy Roman Empire. One of the unpublished chapters (later included in Bury's edition) of the *History of Federal Government* had already prophesied something of the kind. It would presumably have been a question of a Holy empire under joint Prussian and English control, into which the Italians, having freed themselves from the Pope and from other superstitions, would have been fraternally welcomed, while the French would have had to expiate the sin of having endured Napoleon III. The Holy Roman Empire (to which J. Bryce had dedicated his famous book a year after the appearance of the *History of Federal Government*) would make it possible to preserve the values of the ancient Roman Empire, and therefore of classicism, within the framework of German supremacy.[7] Ancient Rome, after all, had been the model for the Germans. The coexistence of the cities of the Roman Empire could be interpreted in accordance with a federalist model. In 1872 Freeman could say to his Cambridge audience: "The history of Rome is the history of the European world. The true meaning of Roman history as a branch of universal history, or rather the absolute identity of Roman history with universal history, can only be fully understood by giving special attention to those ages of the history of Europe which are commonly most neglected."[8]

In this Anglo-Teutonic perspective there was no place for the Hapsburgs, whom Freeman despised almost as much as Napoleon III. The same applied even more to the Turkish empire, which for Freeman was the ultimate manifestation of oriental despotism in contrast to European civilization. Already in a course of popular lectures in 1855 on the *History and Conquests of the Saracens* (reissued with a new preface in 1876) the opposition between Orient and Occident (which then was the equivalent of the opposition between Semites and Aryans) was vigorously asserted. Freeman returned to the theme in 1877 with *The Ottoman Power in Europe,* on the eve of the Congress of Berlin, and again in 1881 he assembled his impressions of travels in Venetian lands under the significant title *Subject and Neighbour Lands of Venice:* Venice had suffered from the nearness of both empires, the Austrian and the Turkish.

Not that Freeman felt so secure in his ideological positions at this time. During the Congress of Berlin he began as champion of Turkey but by the end had become a partisan of Russia, which nevertheless he distrusted, however Christian and Indo-Germanic its population might be. He can elsewhere be seen to have been hesitant about the position England ought to take towards Prussia. For all his admiration for Teutonic institutions and for the Holy Roman Empire, Freeman was not so blind as not to recognize that English institutions were different from Prussian ones and that the community of interest between the Germans and the English was precariously based on a shared distrust of France and Russia. Nor would he ever have consented to a reduction in the power of England if that had been the price to pay for entry into a federal organism. If anything, especially after 1880, he would have been ready for the English to make sacrifices in order to strengthen and formalize links with the United States.

Freeman's hesitations are most clearly documented in articles and semi-theoretical studies which went to fill four volumes of *Historical Essays* between 1871 and his death in 1892. Notice for example the essay of 1877 on race and language, which was followed, significantly, by a brief article on the Jews in Europe of the same year. Freeman on the one hand admits the distinction between race (a complex of psychic qualities) and language, but then adds that "the natural instinct of mankind connects race and language." The consequence (if there is any logic) is a distinction between natural nations, based on community of race and language, and artificial nations, such as Switzerland. On the other hand, with one eye on Britain, Freeman is not then disposed to give equal weight to all nationalist aspirations: "Scots (Highlanders), Welsh, Bretons, French Basques (if not Spanish Basques) undoubtedly have memories of a national past, but no political aspirations or hopes"—an affirmation which, even if true in 1877, was later to prove false. The Jews appeared to Freeman to be precisely an example of a racial unity, which would have had theological and practical consequences, on which he declared explicitly (and therefore all the more significantly, given that anti-Semitism was already raging again in Germany and

Romania) that he had no intention of dwelling.[9] His vacillation on this point amounted to a deliberate ambiguity. There is confirmation in the famous lecture on the *Unity of History* delivered at the University of Cambridge in 1872. On the one hand Freeman stated that the most important revolution in historical method was the introduction of the comparative method in linguistics and mythology, which had made it possible to eliminate the distinction between the classical world and the barbarian world, between the ancient world and the modern world. Once the predominance of classicism is broken, the unity of history is restored: "As man is the same in all ages, the history of man is one in all ages." But notice that at that point what seemed to be a vindication of the unity of mankind becomes a celebration of the Aryan tribe or race: "The history of the Aryan nations of Europe, their persons of rank, their languages, their institutions, their dealings with one another, all form one long series of cause and effect, no part of which can be rightly understood if it be dealt with as something wholly cut off from, and alien to, any other past." The jump has no theoretical justification; indeed it occurs surreptitiously: "Looking then at the history of man, at all events at the history of Aryan man in Europe, as one unbroken whole, no part of which can be safely looked at without reference to other parts...." All that is needed is a turn of phrase, a mere "at all events," to move from the history of man to the history of Aryan man.

V

His appointment as Regius Professor of Modern History at Oxford in succession to his younger friend Stubbs, who had become a bishop, came in 1884, too late to be much more than an acknowledgment of an eminence that was by now recognized internationally and in truth indisputable. It would not be uninteresting, however, to investigate how Freeman concerned himself with teaching and published a methodological introduction to historical studies which is even today of some use to Oxford students. The other event of the last ten years of Freeman's life was a lecture tour of America in 1881, which gave him the chance to gain a direct acquaintance with the great Anglo-Saxon federation across the Atlantic and persuaded him to give up the exclusive interest in European affairs he had had for the previous decade.[10] Yet the task to which Freeman intended to devote the years of his old age was a twofold return to the classicistic interests that had never been extinguished and to the problem of the effect of the Normans on the history of Europe—in other words, it was the aforementioned history of Sicily. The marriage of his favorite daughter Margaret to the archaeologist Arthur Evans—the future discoverer of the Minoan civilization on Crete—could have had some weight in the formulation of the new project. When Freeman died unexpectedly from smallpox in Spain in 1892, the responsibility fell to Evans of editing the unfinished work, which he did with an expert hand. No one can say how this work of detailed narrative would have finished. Among other things, Freeman was well aware of the worth of Amari as a historian of Arab Sicily and was in contact with Ugo Balzani, the specialist in medieval Italian chronicles who was linked to Oxford society. Like the history of the Norman Conquest, the history of Sicily followed the narrative tradition made canonical by Macaulay and followed, for example, by T. Hodgkin, the historian of the barbarian invasions of Italy. When he was about seventy the end came for a historian who, for breadth of vision, for capacity to raise problems, and for talent as a narrator, had few rivals in nineteenth-century English historiography. The themes of federalism, of the comparative study of political institutions, and of the Normans in Europe remain connected with his name. Something that remains characteristic is the link he forged between federalism and Teutonic culture by way of the Holy Roman Empire.

The question of his sources for the idea of federalism is another matter, and yet another is the question of the legacy of Freeman. In the Bodleian Library in Oxford in January 1979 I cut the pages of the copy of the history of architecture published in 1849.

Notes

In our annual seminar on an ancient historian, E. A. Freeman represents a particularly difficult case because after all Freeman remains the historian of the Normans. Freeman's very personality must be viewed against a British nineteenth-century tradition that is not easy for an outsider to define. For that reason, even more than in earlier years, our partial contributions must be considered exploratory and are presented with some diffidence.

1. The principal source of information is the two-volume work of W. R. W. Stephens, Dean of Winchester, *E. A. Freeman: The Life and Letters,* London, 1895. *Cf.* the article in the *Dictionary of National Biography,* XXII. The letters I have cited in the text are taken from Stephens. But an essential supplement for an understanding of the intellectual environment is in the letters to Freeman from the historian J. R. Green, which form the larger part of the volume *Letters of J. R. Green,* ed. Leslie Stephen, 1901. These letters, apart from being an unforgettable record of the friendship that began in 1862 and ended only with the premature death of Green (1837–83), also contain the most penetrating criticism known to me of Freeman as a historian. Green used to reprove his friend for indifference to social and moral forces (pp. 332; 363), and once observed: "You have never left Oxford" (p. 168). Green, who like Freeman gradually abandoned Anglicanism, although he remained a clergyman, inclined in the direction of a humanitarian Christianity, considered himself "southern rather than Teutonic" (pp. 214–15), and in opposition to the imperialistic federalism of his friend showed a strong interest in communal life (p. 309), which gave him a predilection for medieval and modern Italy. For a

precise comparison of Freeman and Green see G. P. Gooch, *History and Historians in the Nineteenth Century*, 2d ed., London, 1952, pp. 323–34, with further bibliography [*cf.* now J. W. Burrow, *A Liberal Descent*, Cambridge, 1981, pp. 155–228].

2. *Introductory Lectures on Modern History*, Oxford, 1842, p. 39; *cf.* p. 35.

3. E. A. Freeman, *The Office of the Historical Professor*, London, 1884, p. 9; reprinted in *The Methods of Historical Study*, London, 1886, pp. 5–6 and 33.

4. *A History of Architecture*, London, 1849, p. 11.

5. *Cf.* in general G. L. Hersey, "Aryanism in Victorian England," *Yale Review*, 66, 1976, pp. 104–13. Also D. J. De Laura, *Hebrew and Hellene in Victorian England*, Austin, 1969. For the German reaction notice the book, which strangely ignores Freeman, of C. E. McClelland, *The German Historians and England*, Cambridge, 1971.

6. Viscount Strangford, *Original Letters and Papers*, London, 1878; the correspondence with Freeman, of the first importance, is particularly dense for the years 1865–67.

7. J. Bryce, who became a friend of Freeman, wrote a fine profile of him, which is reprinted in *Studies in Contemporary Biography*, London, 1903, pp. 262–92. Here it is noted that Plato, Carlyle, and Ruskin are the three writers most detested by Freeman. This is not the place to speak at length on the quarrel with Froude.

8. *The Unity of History*, The Rede Lecture, London, 1872. The lecture is reprinted in *Comparative Politics*, London, 1873, pp. 296–339 (the quotation is from p. 327).

9. "Race and Language," "The Jews in Europe," respectively, in *Historical Essays*, London, 1879, III, pp. 173–226 and 226–230.

10. *Lectures to American Audiences*, Philadelphia, 1882.

FIFTEEN

Introduction to a Discussion of Eduard Meyer

I

In a few laconic pages in 1923, Eduard Meyer, who was born in Hamburg on 25 January 1855 and died on 31 August 1930, sketched an outline of his life: the years of apprenticeship, the rapid career which took him, before the age of forty, to the chair at Berlin, the composition of the *History of Antiquity*, the passion with which he changed from scholar to propagandist and defender of Germany in the early years of the war, the rectorship at Berlin immediately after the war, retirement in 1923, the mistrust of the new Weimar Germany.[1] There is little about his family: only that he was married (he does not say to whom) in 1884, that he had seven children, of whom one died in the war in 1915, and that in 1919 he lost his esteemed brother Kuno, the great specialist in Celtic languages and literature. He does not even give the name of his mother. Since she belonged to the Dessau family, she was almost certainly of distant Jewish origin.[2] One might ask if the oriental interests and the fierce nationalism of her son were not an ambivalent reaction to this suppressed inheritance. He is explicit, however, about his paternal descent. His father was a gymnasium teacher, a student of ancient and modern history, and a commentator on Goethe. He was, it seems, his son's first Greek teacher. Eduard soon became a star pupil at that most excellent school, the Hamburg Johanneum. Its head at that time was Johannes Classen, the commentator on Thucydides, who as a young man had lived in Niebuhr's house in Bonn as tutor to his son Marcus. From Classen Meyer received, explicitly, the mantle of Niebuhr, not as historian

"Premesse per una discussione su Eduard Meyer" (introduction to a seminar at the Scuola Normale Superiore in Pisa, 12–13 February 1981), *Rivista Storica Italiana*, 93 (1981), pp. 384–98; *Settimo contributo* (1984), pp. 215–31. Translated by T. J. Cornell.

of Rome, but as historian of antiquity. Meyer dedicated the first volume of the *History of Antiquity* to Classen in 1884 and again acknowledged his debt to him twenty years later in the speech he gave when entering the Prussian Academy.[3] From Classen Eduard Meyer naturally learned also to understand and admire Thucydides, and it must be noted that another eminent specialist on Thucydides, L. Herbst, was one of his teachers at the Johanneum. Meyer always identified his historiographical method with that of Thucydides: a remarkable thing for a universal historian who declared that religion was his special interest.

The subjects studied at the Johanneum included biblical Hebrew as well as the classical languages, while Meyer learned Arabic outside the curriculum from another Hamburg teacher. Pupils were also encouraged to do personal research. The paper with which Meyer received his university teaching degree in 1879, the *Geschichte des Königreichs Pontos*, had already been drafted by him ten years earlier while still a pupil at the Johanneum. From there, after an unsatisfactory start at the University of Bonn, where he stayed for one semester, Meyer went to Leipzig, at that time the center of German oriental scholarship, where he obtained a deep knowledge of Arabic and hieroglyphic Egyptian and acquired the rudiments of Sanskrit, Persian, and Turkish, to which he later added Assyrian; Aramaic is not mentioned, perhaps because it was too obvious. His dissertation, which was in Egyptology under G. Ebers and dealt with a topic of religious history, Set-Typhon, was produced in 1875 when he was only twenty. Ebers, a strange combination of technical expert and visionary, who wrote historical novels and maintained a personal contact with the ancestral Jewish tradition from which his parents had separated themselves by becoming converts, was important also in the later intellectual life of his pupil, as is demonstrated by the essay Meyer dedicated to him in the form of an obituary.[4] There followed a year and a half in Constantinople as tutor to the son of the English consul general Sir Philip Francis; he must therefore already have had good English. After the consul's death, Meyer stayed for a further six months with the family in England, and there, in contact with the British Museum, he wrote his history of the Troad which appeared in 1877. Hamburg was noted for its special relationship with England and for its Anglophilia. In those years, and for a long time afterwards, Ed. Meyer remained sympathetic to Anglo-Saxon culture. We may note now that he was to go to Chicago as professor in 1904 and to Harvard in 1909 as part of a system of exchanges between German and American professors which it was hoped would become regular. From Great Britain he received three honorary degrees (Oxford, Liverpool, St. Andrews). In 1879, after his return to Germany and after a period of military service, he became a university teacher at Leipzig.

That he would become not just an Orientalist, but a comprehensive expert on both the Orient and the Classical world, was already implicit in his training at the Johanneum. In five years of prodigious activity Meyer was ready in 1884 to publish the first volume of his *History of Antiquity*, which went down to the foundation of the Persian empire and contained a preliminary elucidation of method in the introductory chapter. It may be observed that between 1881 and 1882 Meyer had presented a sample of his penetrating scholarship in three different fields: in the study of the sources for Antiochus III the Great, in an investigation of the biblical account of the conquest of Canaan, and in a paper on the Roman sources of Diodorus (in which his criticism went directly against Mommsen and even today remains fundamental). Recognition, as has been noted, came quickly: full professor at Breslau in 1885, then an invitation to Halle in 1889. In twelve years at Halle — in the company of men like C. Robert, W. Dittenberger, and G. Wissowa — Eduard Meyer managed to publish four more large volumes of the *History of Antiquity*. Already in 1887 he had rewritten and continued the history of ancient Egypt in a volume which, as far as I am aware, is the only one of his works to have been translated into Italian. Nor was this all. The two substantial volumes of *Forschungen zur alten Geschichte*, published respectively in 1892 and 1899, contain the best and most lasting studies from the whole of the nineteenth century on the history and historiography of Greece from its origins to the end of the fifth century B.C. They can be linked in importance — and probably should be linked genetically — to the *Römische Forschungen* of Mommsen: the significance of this link is obvious when it is set against the clear disjunction between Meyer and the systematic Mommsen of the *Staatsrecht*. 1896 saw the revolutionary volume, which is still very much alive today, on *Die Entstehung des Judentums*, which for the first time placed the formation of postexilic Palestinian Judaism in close relation to the political directives and even the terminology of Persian imperial administration. Then in 1898 there appeared the essay on slavery in antiquity, which was sufficiently important to be still in 1980 the point of departure for Moses Finley's attack on the methods of his predecessors.[5] Collaboration on the *Handwörterbuch der Staatswissenschaften* placed Meyer beside Beloch, who became a personal friend, as a pioneer in the study of the ancient economy: hence the articles on the population of the ancient world, on Greek finances, on oriental and Greek monetary systems, etc. And as if that were not enough, there appeared in 1894 the researches on the Gracchi and in 1895 those on the origin of the tribunate of the plebs, as well as dozens of encyclopedia articles in Ersch and Gruber, Pauly-Wissowa, Roscher, and later in the *Encyclopaedia Britannica*. Although later Meyer rarely wrote reviews, in that period he was also active in this field.

    I do not know when Ed. Meyer came into direct contact with Max Weber; perhaps it was when they were both collaborating on the *Handwörterbuch der Staatswissenschaften*. In any event it is not an accident that the bond became closer when Ed. Meyer almost paradigmatically concluded this first phase of his activity in 1902 (while the fifth volume of the *History of Antiquity* was being published) with the essay "Zur Theorie und Methodik der Geschichte" —to which Weber responded.[6]

In 1902 Meyer went to Berlin, and in 1904 he was elected an ordinary member of the Prussian Academy. For decades he was a leading member of the Deutsche Orientgesellschaft and other archaeological institutions. Something evidently changed as a result of this transition. The *History of Antiquity* was no longer continued, and only in part and at infrequent intervals rewritten in sections that had already been completed. Before considering what this change meant, let us first attempt a general assessment of the preceding phase, before the move to Berlin in 1902.

II

The tradition of universal history was still flourishing in Germany: precisely in the years around 1880 it was engaging the aged Ranke. As part of universal history the history of antiquity was traditionally divided into four parts: the great monarchies of the ancient Near East, the history of the Jews down to Jesus, and naturally the histories of Greece and Rome. That is how, more or less (but with the inclusion of India), it had been set out by Max Duncker, who was Meyer's immediate predecessor and was recognized as such.[7] But Ed. Meyer did not simply continue this tradition. Rather, with his competence and vigor as a researcher, he transformed the detailed results of previous research and spoke in his own name: none of his predecessors had had his command of languages and his strong critical sense. In the second place, around 1880, anyone who concerned himself with the history of antiquity in general had to take a stand against powerful currents of thought that were unfavorable to such an enterprise. Many argued that the only valid history was national history. More precisely, it was maintained that the very fact of putting Greeks and Orientals together belittled the Greeks. Finally, in biblical history there existed two mutually contrasting tendencies, both of which, however, were opposed to the universal history pursued by Meyer. On the one hand the theologians proclaimed biblical history as the history of revelation; on the opposite side there now existed a group of ex-theologians who were prepared to leave revelation in the shade and to seek in the Semitic world, and especially among the Arabs, the terms of comparison for Jewish society; but even these ex-theologians had never been in favor of immersing the Jews in a general history of the classical and oriental world. When speaking of national history in antiquity one thinks immediately of Mommsen; and the Mommsen of 1880 had by now linked his name to reductive tendencies within national history, because he preferred institutional to political history. It was not by chance that Meyer, without naming Mommsen, would declare in his essay on method of 1902 that a historian should presuppose, but should not construct, a system of public law. Among those in favor of isolating the Greeks stood the young Wilamowitz—six years older than Meyer. There is no sign that in their youth the two liked each other; a different picture emerges from their mutual relations during the many years when they were colleagues at Berlin. Finally, as would soon appear from the dispute between Wellhausen and Ed. Meyer over the *Entstehung des Judentums,* there was no chance of reaching an understanding even with the ex-theologians among students of the Bible. The internal evolution of Judaism mattered to Wellhausen, just as the internal evolution of Greek civilization mattered to Wilamowitz; for that reason Wellhausen and Wilamowitz understood each other, and Wilamowitz took Wellhausen's biblical criticism as a model for his own Homeric criticism. Meyer, who was ready in those years to follow Wellhausen on many points of biblical criticism, saw Ezra and Nehemiah essentially as working officials of the Persian empire.

In the situation that existed around 1880 Meyer's notion of the history of antiquity was therefore in one respect the continuation of an old idea of universal history now in decline, but was in another respect an affirmation of concrete political and cultural relations extending from Mesopotamia to the Iberian peninsula, which were not generally recognized by contemporaries. It is impossible even now, a hundred years later, to read this first volume of Ed. Meyer's *History of Antiquity* without being dumbfounded by the intensity and accuracy of the research. He gave ancient history its first rigorous framework after the decipherment of hieroglyphic and cuneiform and, it must be said, after the new wave of biblical criticism which culminated in Wellhausen. The twenty-five-page statement of method with which the volume opens aroused interest above all because it affirms the priority of the state: "A man without a state is unthinkable." Gaetano De Sanctis was among those who in the succeeding decades accepted this affirmation. But in these twenty-five pages Meyer also found a way of clarifying his position on the question of linguistic groupings, in which he vigorously supported the notion of Johannes Schmidt that a linguistic unit consists of dialects which reciprocally influence one another. Religion was presented by Meyer as a projection of social conditions. There followed a preliminary definition of the relation between anthropology (or ethnology) and history with which Meyer was later to feel dissatisfied: anthropology looks for general facts of human development, whereas history presupposes these trends and concerns itself with sectional and untypical developments. Races, including the Indo-Europeans, would therefore be the subject of anthropology, not of history. This explains the subjectivity of history, which is always viewed by every historian in relation to his own specific interests, rather than to

general laws: "There can be no history without assumptions." The exclusion
of India and China from ancient history was for Meyer justified by the fact
that India and China had only rare contacts with the ancient Near East.
And ancient history ends with the victories of the Germans in the West and
the Arabs in the East.

The second volume, which followed in 1893, already contained new
thoughts and corrections to the first volume. The Indo-Europeans were
permitted to enter history as of right, whereas previously they had seemed
to belong to anthropology, and with that Meyer was able to indulge in arguments about their superiority of feeling (that is, about his own), which I
have been unable to detect in the first volume. But the great effort of this
volume, which aroused enormous attention when it appeared, and in Italy
had a decisive influence on the recently graduated Gaetano De Sanctis, was
in the understanding of the rise of the Greeks and above all in the definition of the place of the recently discovered Mycenaean civilization (the
Minoan had yet to be brought to light). The intermediate period was connected by Meyer with the Dorian invasion; he defined it as the Greek Middle Ages: a relatively innocent notion in this context, but, as we shall see,
anything but inoffensive in another context. In the same volume Meyer
outlined the age of the aristocracy of the seventh and sixth centuries B.C.
and included an epoch-making evaluation of aristocratic religion and
aristocratic values. Within this Greek framework it was not easy to insert
Etruscans, Romans, and Carthaginians. However, the brief sketch of the
archaic Roman state and the spread of Etruscan domination in Italy, as well
as the expansion of the Carthaginians in Africa, represented a novelty (and
an advance on Mommsen). It introduced the Greco-Persian conflict that
was to dominate volumes III–V and to condition the history of postbiblical
Judaism. Meyer felt himself to be particularly qualified to investigate the
values put into play by three political-religious structures as different as the
Persian, the Greek, and the Jewish. The paradox was that in this way the admirer of Thucydides aligned himself with Herodotus and perhaps even
with the biblical historians. We are now perhaps in a position to appreciate
more precisely what determined the abandonment of the *History of Antiquity,* so to speak in midair, in the fourth century (circa 350 B.C.) — while
Meyer's creative energies were intact.

That the first volume of the *History* could no longer stand up after twenty
years of new discoveries goes without saying. And Meyer was deeply involved in the new discoveries. Among other things it was a matter of
finding a place for the Sumerians, the Minoans, the Hittites, and the unexpected Jewish military colony in Egypt at Elephantine. The whole chronology of the ancient Near East had to be revised. For Greece, precisely for the
first half of the fourth century, there was now the new text of the *Hellenica
Oxyrhynchia.* While Meyer set himself to understand all these new facts, he

also recognized that the theoretical foundations of the *History of Antiquity* needed further justification in view of all the end-of-the-century disputes about the methodology of history in relation to sociology and psychology; K. Lamprecht was at the center of one of these controversies. Then there was Max Weber; and however little Ed. Meyer might have wanted to reckon with Marx and Engels, he did not ignore them.

III

In 1904 an entire volume appeared on Egyptian chronology. In the great academic memoir of 1906 Meyer was the first to reconstruct the relations between Sumerians and Semites in Mesopotamia on the basis of the archaeological evidence. In 1909 he published a volume on the *Hellenica Oxyrhynchia* important not for its historiographical analysis, which led him to an improbable identification of the author with Theopompus, but for the attendant historical studies. In 1912, after preparatory work, he published the volume on the Jewish colony at Elephantine; among the documents bearing on this Meyer had the satisfaction of finding confirmation of his thesis on the authenticity and the interpretation of biblical documents in Aramaic that originated in the Persian chancellery. In 1914 he gave a preliminary sketch of the history of the Hittites, before the decipherment of their texts. Four books, then, on new discoveries. To 1906 also belongs the memorable study of the most ancient history of the tribes of Israel, another contribution to the revision of the first volume of the *History of Antiquity*. A new edition of a part of this volume in fact appeared in two sections: the first in 1907, in which the twenty-five pages of the first edition dealing with anthropology now became two hundred fifty; the second in 1909, in which the history of the earliest civilizations down to the sixteenth century B.C. was covered in around nine hundred pages. In a third edition of this second section which appeared four years later in 1913 the number of pages had grown to around a thousand. We may add that in 1903 and 1905 Meyer published extremely significant essays on Augustus and universal monarchy, and that in 1910 he published an original inquiry into the ages of Hesiod which soon became a classic. Then in 1912 he issued an unexpected, and in truth extraordinary, product of his travels in America, the history of the Mormons in three hundred pages: *Ursprung und Geschichte der Mormonen*. Meyer seems to have been the first to notice that the appearance of a revealed religion, so dependent on sacred texts, in the middle of the nineteenth century, could illuminate not only the civilization of America but the study of the revealed religions of antiquity: Meyer refers specifically only to Islam, but it is clear from an excursus that he was also thinking of Judaism and Christianity.

At the risk of passing over much else of importance, I should like to confine myself here to observations on three points: Meyer's conception of historical method in this decisive phase; his notion of Judaism and Christianity, for which I shall also have to take account of developments in his research after 1919; and finally the outcome of his work on the ancient economy.

In the 1907 volume on anthropology Meyer was evidently seeking to make use of new research on particular points, for example on the position of women in the Semitic world, or on the male groups illuminated by H. Schurtz in *Altersklassen und Männerbünde* (1902), or more generally on the results of studies of religion in prehistory. But it is much more difficult to identify, at this distance, the opponents whom Meyer had in mind in restating his own methodology: M. Weber apart, it is not clear to me how much Meyer had become a point of reference for the sociologists.[8] As was already evident in the essay of 1902, Meyer seems to have envisaged history as the analysis of a process by which various lines of action (that is, causes) intersect, insofar as this process leads in any given case to unique results. History is therefore individualizing in the sense that it fixes upon those processes which appear important to the spectator — or future player — who views them from his own particular vantage point. As such, it remains for Meyer selective and subjective. But in another sense history is universal, because any given moment sees the interaction of infinite numbers of events arising from the whole range of human activity. The individual is the more culturally developed the more he can make judgments and take action as an individual; but his individuality can be affirmed the more strongly the more capable he is of dominating and controlling his relations with the world around him. It could be said that for Meyer the awareness of living in universal history is the condition for thought — with this essential reservation: that Meyer's natural sympathies go to those political and religious organisms in which a strong national sense is the accompaniment to universal thought. He likes the Egyptians, the Persians, and above all the Greeks and the Germans (between whom he does not always distinguish). The Jews are too tribal, the Romans too internationalized. In the fundamental identification of himself with the Greeks we can recognize in Meyer a distinct preference for the Greeks of the time of Alexander, who present themselves in a balanced equilibrium between nation and universalism. In a long essay of 1905 on Alexander the Great and absolute monarchy, there are striking affinities between the Macedonian monarchy, with its elements of ruler cult (introduced by Philip II), and the divinely anointed Prussian monarchy.

Now all this — whether Meyer realized it or not — implied new objects of research, among them the continuity of the notion of absolute monarchy in later periods, which entailed an understanding of the relative position of Caesar and Augustus, already outlined in another essay of 1903 on Augustus. In theory such projects could have been developed in further volumes of the *History of Antiquity* dedicated to Rome. But in Meyer's new specialized concentration on the religious foundation of political authority, or conversely on the function of religion as support for state authority, the old framework of universal history that had been followed up to that point was too broad. In fact—whatever may have been the ultimate reasons— Eduard Meyer decided to present these problems between 1918 and 1923 in monographs: that is, first in the volume that became a best-seller, on Caesar's monarchy and the principate of Pompey, and then in the three volumes on the origins and rise of Christianity.

Reference should be made here to the volume of 1906 on *Die Israeliten und ihre Nachbarstämme,* in which Ed. Meyer for the first time clearly set out his idea of a dualism within Jewish history which he never retracted, right down to his last paper on the subject in the year of his death. On this view Moses, no longer a historical figure but a mythical one, is the representative of the religion of the Levites, a sacerdotal group centered on the oasis of Qadesh and devoted to the cult of a volcanic god, Yahweh. It was this Levitic group that always retained a nomadic ideal, of a rough and warlike morality bound to a rigorous monotheism. The later representatives of this Levitic ideal were the prophets, particularly in the kingdom of Judah. The fact that they operated in the context of urban states resulted in the utopian character of their preaching. And for that reason, in spite of the high moral standing of these prophets and particularly of Amos, whom Meyer was not the only one to compare to Hesiod, they failed. If Judaism, beginning with the Deuteronomic code of the eighth century B.C., retained something of the Levitic ideal, that was due to favorable political circumstances, of which the most important was the postexilic restoration organized by Persia. At times Meyer let his sympathy show for the Israelites of the north, who were more open to international contacts and less fanatical; from there came the historians, comparable to Herodotus, who gave such a vivid account of the reigns of David and Solomon.

For postexilic Judaism, particularly that of the Greco-Roman period, Meyer had no sympathy; he found it bigoted and anti-Greek, the predecessor of medieval and modern Judaism, for which his antipathy was evident, even if he usually (though not always) kept it within the bounds of civility.

But is it certain that he thought any differently about Christianity? I am not sure, and I confess that his interpretation of Christianity is more clear to me in matters of detail than in its general outline.

According to Meyer, postexilic Judaism had already been influenced by Persian, Zoroastrian, dualistic elements, which had taken the form of new ideas about evil, about universal judgment, and about the resurrection of the dead, and had encouraged a kind of reversion to the universalist tendencies of the better prophets. Jesus, who presented himself as a Messiah, not as a god, had appropriated this "Weltanschauung der iranischen

Propheten" (*Ursprung*, II, p. 441). Jesus therefore combined in himself the Semitic prophet and the Iranian prophet. We know that Meyer had sympathy for the Persian world, but not to the point of preferring it to the Greeks. Since St. Paul, whom Meyer considered the true founder of Christianity, could not be viewed as the Hellenizer of the new faith—and since Meyer, as far as I know, never expressed any definite opinions on the Alexandrian Christianity of Clement and Origen—it is difficult to say what he thought about the progressive Hellenization of Christianity. It is equally difficult to know precisely how to evaluate expressions which tend to identify Jesus with the Kantian categorical imperative (just as H. Cohen had similarly identified it with the message of the Israelite prophets). But it is not without significance that in the paper of 1925 on "Blüte und Niedergang des Hellenismus" he saw a sign of the victory of the Orient over Greece in the replacement of political struggle by religious struggle. Further comments on the negative influence of Calvinism on the Anglo-Saxon mentality could also be found in Meyer. If then he had no doubts about the importance of Christianity for the political conscience not only of medieval but also of modern Europe, we could equally well ask—though we should not get any clear answer—if his evaluation of this intervention of Christianity was positive or negative. We have now arrived at the point where it is perhaps legitimate to attempt a general outline both of what has hitherto seemed more elusive in Ed. Meyer's historical vision and of his intervention, passionate and well-defined as it was, in German politics during the First World War.

IV

The history which Ed. Meyer knew supremely well, with critical understanding, was of course ancient history. He also had an unusually good knowledge of modern history, but less good and more ingenuous than he himself believed. Convinced as he was that his Germany—that is, the empire founded at Versailles after the defeat of France—was the ideal *Kulturstaat,* he accordingly maintained that everything had to be measured against that ideal, and that for religion, civilized values, and social organization one could be satisfied with the mixture of religious hypocrisy and pietism, of the state of law and racial and social oppression in administration, of extreme nationalism and elite cultural cosmopolitanism which characterized the world of professors and civil servants in which he lived. The very idea, that the ferment of civilizations that existed in the ancient East, in Greece, and in Rome should have culminated in the Prussia of the late nineteenth century, was difficult to believe: but Ed. Meyer was one of those who truly did believe it.

One consequence was evident in his very conception of ancient history. When it came to the point, the real worth of the civilization of the Greek poleis, the significance of the reaction of Jews and Christians to Greece and Rome, and the character of the Roman attempt to create a supranational empire and ultimately to identify it with Christianity, remained only half-assimilated experiences for Ed. Meyer, however well he knew the facts.

Something else that was not absorbed into a revised version of the *History of Antiquity* was the multiple series of researches on social and economic history that Meyer had produced in such a promising way in the last decade of the nineteenth century. I am alluding, apart from the essays already cited on slavery in 1898 and on the Gracchi in 1894, to the famous paper (a hundred pages long) of 1895 on the economic development of antiquity. This paper begins as a refutation of the theories of Rodbertus and Bücher on the ancient economy as an economy based on the self-sufficient household unit. Meyer indeed had no difficulty in disproving these theories. But at a certain point, when he arrived at the Roman Empire, which is no small part of the economic development of antiquity, one has the impression that Meyer lost his way. In fact he was pursuing another path: that of the intellectual decline of antiquity and the consequent growth of superstition. How all this relates to the economic development of the empire is not clear, at least not to me. Cultural history interferes with economic history without clarifying it. One suspects that Meyer is more interested in the spread of Christianity than the spread of latifundia. In a not dissimilar manner ancient slavery disappears at the moment when Meyer seems close to characterizing it. He makes precise observations about ancient slavery that explain the authority his paper has had in subsequent research, as the work of his direct pupil W. L. Westermann is sufficient to indicate. Meyer distinguishes slavery of the helot type from classical slavery (that which he calls *Kaufsklaverei*), places the latter in connection with the development of the polis, and indicates the element of competition between free men and slaves which accompanied this development. But at this point an extraeconomic element once again steals the limelight. Meyer was convinced, as we know, of the substantial affinity between Greek and Hellenistic civilization on the one hand and modern European civilization of the Prussian stamp on the other. In his view both civilizations emerge from a medieval phase. For that reason the ancient slave appears to him to be the equivalent of the modern industrial worker (or agricultural laborer), who can achieve independence and even wealth. Meyer is not blind to the objection: why has modern capitalist society not resorted to slavery except in relatively marginal areas? His reply is once again based on extraeconomic considerations: the unity of civilization created by Christianity made it impossible in Europe for slave raiding to take place between neighboring states. The dominant preoccupation for Meyer was to maintain the equivalence between Greece and modern Europe (or, more precisely, between Greece and modern Prussia) even at the cost of obliterating the characteristics and functions of slavery in the Greco-Roman world.

Now in the years 1914–18 Ed. Meyer found himself involved in a war in which, rightly or wrongly, the right of the Prussian state to remain what it was was called in question. Prussia had been promptly attacked by England and later by America, with which Meyer had personal relations of sympathy and collaboration. It would be untrue to say that Meyer lost his head, because fundamentally he continued to reason as before, and as before to persuade himself that he understood modern history. And so in 1915 he dashed off a slim volume on the development of England and then, after the Armistice, another on America. He wrote numerous articles and pamphlets, which like the two booklets were neither ignorant nor stupid, but still unworthy of a great historian: rather it was journalism of the type exemplified in Italy by G. A. Borgese but avoided by serious men like Croce and De Sanctis. One of the least known of these pieces—but for obvious reasons one of the best informed—concerns ancient Italy, with only a brief postscript on modern Italy. It appeared in the *Süddeutsche Monatshefte* of June 1915 and certainly shines by comparison with the juvenile piece that accompanied it, on rhetoric in Italy, by Eduard Fraenkel. A more balanced comparison, however, is offered by another essay in the same issue, by Robert Davidsohn on anti-German feeling in medieval Italy, which seems to me to be full of facts.

In addition Ed. Meyer engaged in political activities to put immediate pressure on the government, for example in favor of vast annexations and of submarine warfare, in collaboration with his friend Dietrich Schaefer—efforts which do not seem to have produced results. The emotional involvement is confirmed by a series of letters written at that time to Victor Ehrenberg, which are now published in part.[9] The nationalist tension was to continue even after the end of the war and was to find a more limited but practical outlet in his activity as rector of the University of Berlin in 1919–20. Eduard Fraenkel liked to recall having worked with him in assisting students of the university, and how the rector used to arrive at the university late in the morning with a thermos of hot soup after staying up until the small hours—because only the nights were left for him to work on his history of the origins of Christianity. His address on 15 October 1919, with which he took over the rectorship, "Preussen und Athen," has to be read with the greatest respect even now as an unusual statement of loyalty to the old Prussia; Meyer felt himself to be the Thucydides of the new Athens after its defeat. It is probable that the Kapp Putsch of March 1920 had his sympathies, but I am not aware of any documented collusion between him and the right-wing students: all in all Wilamowitz seems to have been closer than Meyer to Kapp.[10] A characteristic sign of Ed. Meyer's state of mind is the fact that he, the great universal historian, believed that the universal history that he dreamed of had at least partly been realized by a dilettante like Spengler — as is demonstrated by the well-known and basically approving essay of 1925. Another major paper of the same year on "Blüte und Niedergang des Hellenismus in Asien" is written under this Spenglerian influence.

However Meyer did not conclude with Spengler. There was detailed research in the three volumes on the origins of Christianity, accompanied as usual by academic memoirs, important among which is the one on the Zadokite text of Damascus, which we now know as part of the Dead Sea Scrolls but for which Meyer's exegesis of 1919 should still not be ignored — and seems to be in the ascendant. In 1917, among all the preoccupations of the war, he had found time to write the revolutionary paper on Apollonius of Tyana and his alleged source Damis, which would be sufficient to glorify the reputation of a lesser scholar.[11] And in 1923 he published those researches on the Roman army which remain, even in the opinion of Fraccaro, the point of departure for any study of the subject. After a visit to Egypt in the winter of 1925–26 Meyer prepared two volumes of the revised edition of the *History of Antiquity* between the sixteenth and the eighth centuries B.C.; the first was published in 1928, the second, by then posthumous, in 1931. The two volumes were splendid in the way they interwove the cultural and political history of the centuries and the civilizations he knew best. In 1930, on the eve of his death, he turned once more to one of his favorite topics with a memoir for the Berlin Academy on the cultural, literary, and religious development of the Israelite people in the earliest monarchic period — probably his last work.

Loyalty to the old Prussia and loyalty to his chosen task as a historian of antiquity were never simply superimposed in Meyer; if we consider the root of the matter they were perhaps even potentially contradictory. But Meyer possessed both together, with a simplicity and frankness all his own. Evidence for these traits that should not be overlooked can be found in the review he published in December 1928 of Wilamowitz's memoirs. His youthful hostility to Wilamowitz is unequivocally admitted, and what is more he expresses the reservation of a systematic historian about the continuing brilliant improvisations of his colleague (whose works of the last fifteen years are given preference). All the more convincing is the awareness of having shared with Wilamowitz the same culture, the same upbringing, the same epoch that was now at an end.[12]

With this evaluation of his great rival we may take our leave of the old maestro, but not without a personal recollection. In the late summer of 1930 I happened to mention to Croce, in his house at Meana in the Val di Susa, the death of Eduard Meyer. Croce had not yet heard about it, and after a moment of silence he observed: "Such a great historian can pass away, and one doesn't even get to know about it."

Notes

BIBLIOGRAPHICAL NOTE: There is an excellent bibliography of Ed. Meyer which includes reviews of his work (also a biographical essay by U. Wilcken) edited by H. Marohl, Stuttgart, 1941. The best introduction is the chapter in K. Christ, *Von Gibbon zu Rostovtzeff*, Darmstadt, 1972, pp. 286–333, which is presupposed here. Among older literature it is worth consulting the obituaries of W. Otto, *Zeitschr. Deutsch. Morgenl. Gesell.*, 85, 1931, pp. 1–24; V. Ehrenberg, *Hist. Zeitschrift*, 43, 1931, pp. 501–11; E. Täubler, *Zeitschr. Savigny-Stiftung*, Rom. Abt., 51, 1931, pp. 604–6. Of the later bibliography, limited to just one aspect, but of great importance, is H. Liebeschütz, *Das Judentum im deutschen Geschichtsbild von Hegel bis Max Weber*, Tübingen, 1967, pp. 269–301.

1. Reproduced in H. Marohl, *E.M. Bibliographie*, 1941, pp. 9–12.

2. H. Liebeschütz, *Das Judentum im deutschen Geschichtsbild*, p. 291.

3. *Sitz. Berl. Akad.*, 1904, pp. 1012–15. On Niebuhr as a universal historian *cf.* K. Christ, "Römische Geschichte und Universalgeschichte bei B.G. Niebuhr," *Saeculum*, 19, 1968, pp. 172–96.

4. *Biog. Jahrb. und deutscher Nekrolog.*, 3, 1897, pp. 86–89; reprinted in *Kl. Schriften*, 1910, pp. 504–24.

5. M. I. Finley, *Ancient Slavery and Modern Ideology*, London, 1980, pp. 44–49.

6. M. Weber, *Gesammelte Aufsätze zur Wissenschaftslehre*, Tübingen, 1922, pp. 215–90 (from 1905). On Max Weber and E.M. *cf.* my *Sesto contributo*, 1980, I, pp. 285–93. It should be noted that if Max Weber demonstrated the fragility of the notions of efficacy, chance, and biography, as defined by Meyer, he presupposed the legitimacy of the type of history that Meyer was writing. As a historian Meyer was never called in question by Weber.

7. On Duncker, apart from the biography of R. Haym (1891), the article of H. v. Petersdorff in *Allgem. Deutsche Biographie*, 48, pp. 171–99. The *History of Antiquity* does not go beyond the middle of the fifth century B.C.

8. For the orientation of a contemporary historian close to Meyer, G. von Below, *Die Entstehung der Soziologie*, Jena, 1928, is instructive.

9. By H. Liebeschütz in the chapter of *Das Judentum* cited above (n. 1). V. Ehrenberg gave me a copy of the complete text of these letters many years ago, which I have kept.

10. L. Canfora, *Intellettuali in Germania*, Bari, 1979, p. 149. *Cf.* also by the same author, *Cultura classica e crisi tedesca*, Bari, 1977.

11. Also partly belonging to the war period are the studies of the Second Punic War collected in *Kl. Schriften*, II, 1924. Here too is the fundamental paper on the Battle of Pydna of 1909.

12. *Deutsche Literaturz.*, 49, 1928, pp. 2489–94. It is worth comparing what Meyer wrote on Mommsen in 1903, now in *Kl. Schriften*, I, 1910, pp. 539–49.

SIXTEEN

New Paths of Classicism in the Nineteenth Century

Introduction

In our time there is a great danger that those who talk most readily about historians and scholars may not know too much about history and scholarship. Housman's homosexuality or Wilamowitz's erratic behavior with his father-in-law Mommsen are easier to describe than Housman's achievements as an editor of Manilius or Wilamowitz's understanding of Aeschylus. Equally it is easier to criticize Eduard Meyer's political pamphlets during the First World War than his analysis of the papyri of Elephantine or of Egyptian chronology. Though it would be a pity to forget those imponderable elements of a scholar's personality which are his hidden strength or weakness, we have to shift discussion toward specific scholarly achievements if we want to avoid the danger of superficial and partisan evaluations. The fact that Georges Dumézil was, we are told, a supporter of the Action française is not an argument against his theories on Indo-European society. In an age of ideologies, we must be increasingly careful to submit scholarly results to the sole legitimate criterion of evaluation, which is the reliability of the evidence.

The only justification for the history of scholarship is the promotion of scholarship itself. This means that we must go into the past of the discipline we profess in order to learn something new or to be reminded of something which we had forgotten, which is almost the same. Generally speaking, the history of classical scholarship should point to new desirable directions of classical scholarship. Thus a history of classical scholarship should not only

New Paths of Classicism in the Nineteenth Century, History and Theory, Beiheft 21 (1982), 64 pp.; Italian translation, *Tra storia e storicismo* (1985), pp. 99–192; German translation, *Wege in die Alte Welt* (1991), pp. 108–76.

be organized according to problems, but some distinction should be established between viable themes and dead issues. It is ultimately the discovery
that certain scholars of the past still have something to teach that makes the
study of past scholarship acceptable.

If, therefore, one has to write history of historiography or of scholarship
by choosing one's own problems, pursuing them backward, and trying to
involve past scholars in one's own investigation, I shall be justified or at least
excused in my subjective choice of classical themes in the present occasion.
I happen to be working on the two themes which I am discussing here.
Whoever studies early Rome has to face the problems raised by the nature
of land-tenure in Roman law and practice; these problems are strictly connected with the interpretation of the basic elements of early Roman society,
such as the clan or *gens,* the curia, the family. If Niebuhr initiated the modern study of early Roman agrarian problems, it is with Maine and Fustel de
Coulanges that the whole problem of the interrelation between landownership and social structure becomes central. On the other hand, whoever
faces the problems of the interrelations between paganism, Judaism, and
Christianity in the Roman Empire notices a new atmosphere, a new attitude toward the understanding of ancient religions about 1870–80. Here no
single name is as obvious as the name of Niebuhr is for the understanding
of early Rome. The choice is far more personal. In my choice of Hermann
Usener as the starting point, I may have been influenced by a remark I
heard from Arthur Darby Nock perhaps thirty years ago that Usener was
the most attractive student of ancient religions of the nineteenth century.
But I am certainly still with the impression of a seminar on Usener I conducted in Pisa in February 1982. Usener after all never meant much to Italian classical scholars, and even in Germany he is no longer a living force.
One cannot escape the conclusion that his pupil and rival Wilamowitz
rather effectively displaced him. Yet in the Scuola Normale of Pisa, Usener
suddenly returned to life for all of us—and we were a good sixty or seventy
in the lecture room—and we argued about him for four days. We felt that
Usener's peculiar use of philology to clarify problems of religion and custom—and especially problems of transition from paganism to Christianity
—was saying something to us. The old professor of Bonn, who had died in
1905, had suddenly become a real teacher in the Scuola Normale of Pisa,
which is traditionally a stronghold of Wilamowitz's method.

In any case I am interested in experimenting with an approach to the
history of classical scholarship which aims at defining more exactly the territories that classical scholars have explored in succession. Though it may
be a platitude to remark that scholars differ between themselves not so
much in the tools they use as in the subjects they are interested in, the implications of this remark are not equally obvious and are not often taken into
account by those who write history of classical scholarship.

I: Niebuhr and the Agrarian Problems of Rome

1

Barthold Georg Niebuhr himself always declared that his very early investigation of Roman agrarian history, which he conducted when still employed by the Danish government in Copenhagen about 1804, was the foundation of all his future work on Roman history. Niebuhr never published this early dissertation (which seems to have had the provisional title *Zur Geschichte der römischen Ländereien*). Perhaps he considered it replaced by his pages on the same subject in his *Roman History,* the first edition of which appeared in 1811–12. The manuscript, or rather the various drafts of the unfinished juvenile work, is now preserved in the Berlin Academy after having been in private hands. Projects for publication were shattered by various difficulties, the most serious being the unfinished character of the manuscripts themselves. But in 1981 Professor Alfred Heuss published in the *Abhandlungen* of the Göttingen Academy a treatise of more than five hundred pages in octavo on "Barthold Georg Niebuhrs wissenschaftliche Anfänge" which gives a paraphrase and extracts from the difficult texts and illustrates them in a masterly way exactly from the point of view of the history of agrarian problems. He has therefore provided a new departure both by the material he offers and by the investigations through which he illustrates them. By a curious coincidence, I had called attention in 1980 to an aspect of Niebuhr's agrarian interests which had remained unnoticed by previous students, though explicitly declared by Niebuhr himself: the decisive importance of his knowledge of Indian agrarian problems in helping him to clarify ancient Roman agrarian problems.[1] This Indian side of Niebuhr's interests is not specifically noticed by Heuss either. But a text he publishes now serves as documentary confirmation of what I had thought I could deduce from what Niebuhr himself had written in his *Roman History.* The last part of this chapter will be a discussion of the new text.

We may now start our examination of the modern research on the agrarian problems of Rome by reminding ourselves of what the Romans thought they knew about landownership in the earliest stages of their own city. The Romans were not in any doubt that there had been a formal act of foundation of Rome. From at least the beginnings of the third century B.C., this foundation was unanimously attributed to Romulus after he had killed Remus. Any act of a foundation of a city would imply a division of the land among the citizens. As the Romans had in their turn been founders of colonies for a long time, there was some actual experience behind the speculations or conjectures about the modalities of Romulus's foundation. It is, however, puzzling that Livy, of all people, should maintain silence on the original form of the distribution of land in Rome. Whatever explanation we choose to give of his silence, we have to turn to other sources. In the available sources for this aspect of the foundation of Rome, we can notice two contrasting tendencies. Some sources state explicitly that the city since its foundation had been divided into rich and poor, or more precisely into patricians and plebeians. Cicero in *De republica* 2, 16 was of this opinion, and this must also be the opinion of at least some of the sources behind Dionysius of Halicarnassus, *Roman Antiquities;* for he states in II, 8 that the city was divided by Romulus into wealthy patricians and poor plebeians. In the previous chapter (II, 7) Dionysius seems, however, to contradict himself, because he asserts that Romulus divided the land into thirty equal portions and assigned one of them to each curia. He concluded that such a division of the land "involved the greatest equality for all alike." One can of course try to reconcile the two passages by arguing that though each of the thirty curiae received the same amount of land, the families inside each curia received unequal portions; but this solution of the difficulty is made improbable by the statement that the Romulean distribution involved the greatest equality for all alike. It is more probable that Dionysius put together two sources which did not agree with each other. While Plutarch, *Life of Romulus* 13, seems to share the notion that Rome knew inequality since its foundation, other authors attributed to Romulus the distribution of two *iugera* of land for each citizen. The main text is Varro, *De re rustica* 1, 10, 2; but the same notion returns in Pliny, *Natural History* 18, 7 and elsewhere. Mommsen observed that those who explicitly attribute to Romulus the division of the land into parcels of two *iugera* are not historians, but antiquarians. Two *iugera* (about half a hectare or one acre) were in fact the minimum measure of land given to individual colonists in the foundation of Roman colonies, such as that of Terracina in 329 B.C. (Liv. 8, 21, 11). A third current of thought is perhaps perceptible in the information we find in the *Life of Poplicola,* chap. 21, by Plutarch, that, when Attus Clausus migrated to Rome with his clients about 505 B.C. he received twenty-five *iugera* of land for himself and two *iugera* for each of his clients. Here the distinction between rich patricians and poor plebeians or clients is respected, but the clients of the patricians get the traditional two *iugera.*

In any case nobody in antiquity doubted that Rome had known private property since her beginnings. But the Roman state as such was a land-owner, too: the owner of the land called *ager publicus,* which would be extended by conquest, unless the government decided after each successful war that it would hand over the conquered land to individual citizens as private property. As a matter of fact, tradition liked to emphasize that the early kings had distributed new land to the citizens or to the poorest of them (*cf.* Dion. Hal. II, 15, 4; III, 1, 4–5; Cicero, *De republica* 2, 33). The problematic side of the story, in the opinion of Roman historians and antiquarians, was not the existence of private property, but the inclination of the patricians, or at least of the rich, to grab for themselves some or all of the land the state owned as *ager publicus*. Tradition therefore emphasized the various attempts made by the government (or suggested by the plebeians) to limit the amount of *ager publicus* which could legitimately be in the hands of one holder. The so-called agrarian laws of Rome, which culminated in the laws of the Gracchi, were all attempts to define the amount of public land which any one individual might hold.

It is an essential part of our story that the texts which tell us of these laws are not models of clarity. We may quote here the two capital passages on an agrarian law—the Licinian Law—earlier than the Gracchan ones which limited the occupation of the public land by each individual Roman citizen to five hundred *iugera*. According to Plutarch, *Life of Tiberius Gracchus*, chap. 8:

> Of the territory which the Romans won in war from their neighbours, a part they sold and a part they made common land, and assigned it for the poor and indigent among the citizens, on payment of a small rent into the public treasury. And when the rich began to offer larger rents and drove out the poor, a law was enacted forbidding the holding by one person of more than five hundred *iugera* of land. For a short time this enactment gave a check to the rapacity of the rich.... But later on the neighbouring rich men, by means of fictitious personages, transferred these rentals to themselves and finally held most of the land openly in their own names.[2]

Plutarch emphasizes the accumulation of public land in the hands of the rich, notwithstanding the legal prohibition to occupy more than five hundred *iugera*. Appian, who wrote less than half a century after Plutarch, has a different account in his book 1 of the *Civil Wars* (chap. 7). He first explains that the Romans, after a victorious war, would either assign to colonists the previously cultivated part of the land they had conquered or would sell it or would lease it. But they would allow the free occupation of yet uncultivated land on condition that the occupier (presumably a Roman citizen) paid a tithe on the crops. As the rich took advantage of this clause to exploit as much land as they could through their slaves, the government imposed a limit of five hundred *iugera* on the exploitation by individuals. This limit was not respected, and Tiberius Gracchus had to reimpose the limit of five hundred *iugera* in his agrarian law. Appian introduces the qualification, unknown to Plutarch, that the land anyone may occupy is previously uncultivated land.

Even now there are still many question marks about the original regime of landed property in early Rome and about the origins and developments of the occupation of public land by individual citizens.[3] The notion that a Roman could originally own only two *iugera* is puzzling both in itself and in comparison with five hundred *iugera* of public land he was apparently entitled to occupy. Two *iugera*, it is generally admitted, can in conditions of primitive agriculture just keep an unmarried man alive through the year. They cannot give enough food to a growing family. As the distribution of two *iugera* to each colonist happened at the foundation of colonies, there must have been means of supplementing the food production through the exploitation of public land. But are we to follow Appian and believe that the purpose of the Licinian Law was to limit to five hundred *iugera* the apportionment of unexploited land? Plutarch, as we have mentioned, does not make any difference between previously exploited or unexploited land. The possibility of diametrically opposed interpretations of the regime of property in early Rome is shown by the fact that Mommsen came to the conclusion that Rome had known a stage of collective landowner-ship. According to Mommsen, the tradition of the two *iugera* distribution would have represented the earliest stage of the formation of private prop-erty in Rome, when private property would still have been limited to the house and the surrounding orchard, whereas the fields would have been exploited collectively by the whole clan or *gens* (*Staatsrecht*, III, pp. 22–27). Mommsen, one can see, complicated his reconstruction by inserting between the collective property of the community and the private owner-ship of the individual family the collective property of the clan or *gens*. More recent scholars have generally been persuaded by Robert von Pöhlmann[4] to repudiate Mommsen's theory of a primitive communism in Rome; but a glance at the volume by L. Capogrossi Colognesi, *La terra in Roma antica* (Rome, 1981), shows there is no unanimity about what to do with the two *iugera* tradition. Is it just an element of colonial policy unduly transferred to the beginnings of the metropolis, Rome?

Mommsen's introduction of the *gens* into the problem will retain our attention in a later context (part II, below). His name was brought in at this point because it offers a guarantee that notions of primitive communism in Rome, with all their implications about the later agrarian laws, were not necessarily fancies of revolutionary minds unacquainted with the ancient evidence. The evidence is difficult to interpret in any case. But at the end of the eighteenth century, there was even less experience than now in dealing with difficult texts of this kind: comparative study of land-tenure was still in its infancy. Furthermore, at the end of the eighteenth century a revolution was shaking Europe, and there were wild and obscure speculations about the possibility of the introduction of some agrarian law in France and in other countries. The regime of landownership in Rome suddenly became a hot topic, even in academic circles. It is not surprising that young B. G. Niebuhr, who preferred public service to an academic career but had grown up in an atmosphere saturated with historical experience, while very sensitive to contemporary issues, should recognize the study of the communal land of the Romans as an urgent task.

2

Barthold Georg Niebuhr, as we know, was born in the year in which Gibbon published the first volume of his *Decline and Fall* and the American colonies proclaimed their independence. He was a German subject of the King of Denmark. His father, Carsten, had been the most famous traveler of the eighteenth century. He had penetrated into Arabia, reached Persepolis, and ended with India in an expedition organized by the University of Göttingen and patronized by the King of Denmark in order to explore the conditions of life of the Semites in their original countries and therefore to throw light on the Bible. The man who had conceived the idea was, apparently, the Göttingen professor J. D. Michaelis, the author of a work on *Mosaisches Recht*. Carsten Niebuhr was a sturdy and shrewd peasant who liked to satisfy through his son the ambitions in matters of scholarship and public influence in which he himself felt frustrated after a short season of glory as an explorer. The King of Denmark had ultimately given Carsten a modest position as a land-surveyor at Meldorf in his native Holstein, and there young Niebuhr grew up to precocious maturity, instructed by his father in the disciplines, including Arabic, in which the latter had a more or less self-taught knowledge. He studied law at Kiel, and at the age of twenty-two he received a Danish *stipendium* to get to know Great Britain, its language, and its problems. Interestingly enough, Niebuhr spent far more time in Edinburgh, where there was a university, than in London, where there was none, and went back to Denmark in 1799 with a remarkable knowledge of contemporary finance and politics, including the agrarian questions of Ireland and of India. His mixture of conservative and liberal attitudes, quite unusual on the Continent, was to remain for life a consequence of his British experience. His previous democratic sympathies had been challenged by the Terror. In his Roman years as an ambassador, he declared to his protégé Franz Lieber, later a great man in the United States, that most of his English friends were Whigs, and the Whigs had saved England in 1688.[5] As a Danish civil servant, Niebuhr reached the position of manager of the Danish State Bank in 1804. This is more or less the time in which he decided to tackle the Roman agrarian questions systematically, while reflecting, and preparing to act, on the contemporary Danish and German situations: the liberation of the serfs was at stake in both countries. While writing and rewriting his essay, he was persuaded by the Prussian minister Freiherr vom Stein to change country and employment. In 1806 he moved to Berlin as an expert on governmental banking, but was soon advising on other subjects. The monograph on the communal lands of Rome was never finished. In 1810 he was compelled by Hardenberg's policies to leave office. Appointed a member of the Prussian Academy and a nominal "Hofhistoriograph" of Prussia, he acquired the right to give lectures at the new University of Berlin without becoming a professor. There in 1810–11, in an extraordinary concentration of thought, he virtually created the modern study of Roman history. Though he lived until 2 January 1831 and was never intellectually idle, most of his original ideas crystallized in those two years. He returned to ancient history in earnest after his period as an ambassador in Rome from 1816 to 1823. He rewrote his first two volumes and added a third to reach the Punic Wars. He also gave lectures on other subjects, ancient and modern, at Bonn, where he settled down, not without difficulties, near the new university. But he will continue to be remembered for what he wrote in 1810–11. In its turn what he wrote then is based on an understanding of the role of the Roman *plebs* suggested to him by the study of the agrarian situation of early Rome.

Paradoxically he was moved to this study much more by the intentions attributed to the French than by the actual events. Niebuhr himself was a supporter of the liberation of the serfs, which had been enacted in Denmark in 1788 and was extended by the Danish government to Schleswig-Holstein in 1804 after the prolonged opposition of the local German aristocracy had been overcome. After 1806 Niebuhr was also vitally concerned with the liberation of the peasants in Prussia and wrote memoranda which contributed to the royal edict of 9 October 1807 to that effect. As Niebuhr's memoranda show, he was aware of the danger, inherent in any liberation of the peasants, of leaving them unprotected against the consequences of a free market in land. But this was not the theme of his historical studies. His effort as a student of Roman agrarian history was to prove that the Romans had never used agrarian laws to undermine the private ownership of the land. If French revolutionaries had tried to justify their ideas of a redistribution of the land and had proposed a *loi agraire* toward that end, they should not be allowed to claim to be imitating the Romans.

True enough, about 1792 there had been a great deal of talk about a *loi agraire* for the purpose of the redistribution of land in France. "Loi agraire égalité réelle" was one of Babeuf's mottoes. Departmental meetings debated the subject. No doubt many people, not only in France, but throughout Europe, must have feared that it might become a reality. We can imagine the French aristocratic émigrés, who were concentrated at Koblenz, spreading this fear. But Robespierre repudiated the law. He defined it as "a phantasm created by scoundrels to terrorize imbeciles." The Declaration of 1793 recognized the right of private property. The mystery is how Niebuhr could still be so emotional about that fear in 1804—by which time, one would say, Napoleon had represented the end of it for several years. Yet the opening pages of Niebuhr make it clear that he was moved to write in order to refute "the mad and detestable sense given to the agrarian law by a criminal gang." In the French Revolution, he added, the "very word of agrarian law had sunk into the most odious of all demagogic assaults."

Perhaps this only confirms the old theory that real fear starts when the danger is over.

What the French Revolution had certainly taught scholars like Niebuhr (and we shall soon see that he had at least one predecessor) was not to leave difficult passages of classical writers half-interpreted. The Babeuf group would not have been able to use the agrarian law of the Romans as its favorite weapon if the passages of Appian and Plutarch had not been misinterpreted to purport that the agrarian law imposed a maximum limit to private property and therefore authorized confiscation of property above that maximum. There were excuses for that misinterpretation. To understand Plutarch and Appian correctly was not a simple question of Greek. It was necessary to know what made the difference in Roman law between private property and hereditary exploitation of public land. As we shall soon see, it was the merit of Niebuhr to formulate this difference in proper legal terms, but he could do it only because a Roman lawyer of the caliber of Savigny had come to his help.

Machiavelli, who is explicitly quoted by Niebuhr, took it for granted that the Roman agrarian law limited private property altogether within five hundred *iugera.* Harrington in his *Oceana* must have interpreted the law in the same sense, because he suggested to Cromwell a ceiling to private landownership, though he formulated it in money terms. Harrington's admirer Walter Moyle was indeed explicit on this interpretation of the five hundred *iugera.* In 1671 Wilhelm Goes, a Dutch lawyer, wrote an influential book, *Antiquitatum agrariarum liber singularis,* which stated that the Licinian Law took private land away from the rich to give it to the poor. Goes was well known to Niebuhr, who appreciated him. The notion that five hundred *iugera* was the maximum allowed for private property became a commonplace in the handbooks of ancient history which began to get into the market at the end of the seventeenth century and multiplied in the early eighteenth century: for instance those by the Englishman Laurence Echard, the two Jesuits Catrou and Rouillé, and Charles Rollin. Even the more sophisticated student of the Roman revolutions, the Abbé de Vertot, and the critical interpreter of the traditions of early Rome, Louis de Beaufort, agreed on this.

The first to decide that the supporters of the agrarian laws were not only dangerous people, but also bad scholars, was, not surprisingly, Christian Heyne, the great classical master of Göttingen. He did that at the right moment, in an academic speech, naturally in Latin, delivered in March 1793, with the self-explanatory title, "Leges agrariae pestiferae et execrabiles." Göttingen was a center of English influence at that time, especially in political philosophy. Heyne, who sympathized with it, had a domestic problem of his own because his estranged son-in-law Georg Forster—the pioneer anthropologist dear to young Friedrich Schlegel—had just embraced the cause of revolution. Thus Heyne—when he was deprecating those "homines inter Francos fanaticos et furoribus civilibus lymphatos," those French fanatics made furious by political strife, who were thinking of grabbing land not belonging to them—was in fact addressing a member of his family.[6] Heyne was not exactly aiming at an antithesis between the Romans and their self-styled modern imitators (which was to be Niebuhr's strategy). He was altogether suspicious of the Romans because of the proscriptions in which they had indulged at the end of the Republic. But he could at least absolve the Romans from having made the agrarian law an instrument of social subversion. Heyne was the first to point out unequivocally that the agrarian law did not affect private land, but only the distribution of public land. This was, however, stated rather than demonstrated because even Heyne did not command the lawyer's ability to prove the point.

When Niebuhr turned to the same problem more than ten years later, he was of course acquainted with Heyne's piece. If he felt the need to consolidate Heyne's demonstration, notwithstanding his declared conviction that Heyne was basically right, more than one consideration must have prompted him. No doubt, as I said before, he was persuaded that the danger of having a modern agrarian law was not yet over. It was necessary, therefore, to deprive any new proposal for an agrarian law of the support it might receive from a misunderstood Roman agrarian law. As a supporter of the liberation of serfs in Denmark and Prussia, he wanted to keep that good cause uncontaminated by any propaganda for the redistribution of private property. His attitude, in general terms, was the one he had learned from Julius Möser and saw confirmed by all his experience: a free peasantry enjoying moderate prosperity on its land was necessary to the prosperity of the state and represented the best safeguard against foreign attacks. Though he did not want to interfere with private property as such, he was, however, prepared to encourage the English government to give the Irish peasants hereditary tenure of the land they tilled. He wanted to prevent the extinction of the Irish peasantry, which, in his opinion, would lead to the inevitable decline of England. Thoughts on the Irish question are coordinated in a manuscript memorandum which was found after Niebuhr's death and published in his *Nachgelassene Schriften nichtphilologischen Inhalts* (1842). It seems to belong to the years around 1805.

There was, however, a more specific inducement for Niebuhr to take up the Roman agrarian question after Heyne. In the article of 1980, I drew attention to a very interesting indication provided by Niebuhr in the second edition of his *Römische Geschichte*. There Niebuhr said that he would never have been able to understand the real nature of the *ager publicus* in Rome if he had not been acquainted with the Indian agrarian situation. He went on to explain that in India the state is the owner of the whole land: the peasants of the villages hold their land in hereditary concession by paying

a fixed sum which is collected by a state officer, the *zamindar*. In this statement Niebuhr clearly took sides in a controversy of primary importance for
English rule in India. Especially in Bengal the English had found themselves the heirs of an agrarian situation which was by no means clear. *De
facto* the *zamindar* was considered the owner of the land of the village (the
Persian word means "landholder"). But what were his precise legal rights?
What was his precise legal function between the sovereign and the peasants? The question could also be put in a different way: was it the right policy for the English to support and therefore consolidate the position of the
zamindar and his exploitation of the peasantry now that the rule of native
princes had been replaced for all practical purposes by an English administration? The legal position of the *zamindar*, the expediency of being able to
count on his cooperation, and the moral justification of English rule were
three, not necessarily coinciding, points of view. More subtly, a fourth consideration interfered: the opportunity of giving the Indians a system of
landownership which would be recognizably similar to the European one
and therefore easily administrable by Europeans.

From the text of the *Römische Geschichte* itself, it was possible to guess that,
by denying the *zamindar* the rights of a landowner and reducing him to a servant of the Crown, Niebuhr was following the legal line supported by James
Grant, who had been general superintendent for taxation (or *serrisfahder*) in
Bengal from 1786 to 1789 on behalf of the East India Company. In 1790 James
Grant published his *Inquiry into the Nature of the Zemindary Tenures in the Landed
Property of Bengal*. This *Inquiry*, with its main thesis that the *zamindar* had no
hereditary property rights, but was simply there to collect taxes for the Crown,
was vastly controversial and came up immediately against the opposition of
Charles William Boughton-Rouse, who in the next year published a by
no means improvised *Dissertation concerning the Landed Property of Bengal*.
Boughton-Rouse, himself a former employee of the East India Company and
a trained Orientalist, defended both the hereditary rights of the *zamindar* and
the convenience for the English authorities of confirming them permanently.
In his turn Grant answered back in the Prefatory Remarks to the second edition of his *Inquiry*, which appeared in the same year, 1791.

Now we knew from Niebuhr's letters that during his stay in Scotland in
1798–99 Niebuhr had got to know personally a man he called "Mr. Grant of
Redcastle," a place near Inverness. He had visited his home and had discussed with him Indian agrarian problems.[7] Even from these letters it
would have been easy to infer that the Mr. Grant mentioned by Niebuhr was
the famous author of the *Inquiry*. But this identification escaped me in 1980
and, as far as I know, has never been suggested. It is now made inevitable by
a passage of Niebuhr's dissertation of 1804, which Heuss has published
for the first time without, perhaps, appreciating its importance. Here is the
translation of the remarkable passage:

It would be a worthwhile undertaking . . . to follow up the process of the variations in the landownership through the history of the Roman emperors (on the foundation of Arabic colonies I hope to speak another time), to investigate the rise of those princely estates, which in times of decline of the empire gave enormous incomes to the aristocratic families, and finally the origin of the serfdom in that milder form which developed in Italy and France during the Middle Ages out of the relations between the landowner and the overseer of the Roman epoch. But these researches belong to an extensive work, to a comprehensive "Spirit of the Laws of Landownership," which I have been encouraged to undertake by my learned friend Mr. Grant of Redcastle. His own researches have clarified beyond doubt the characteristics of the right of landownership in Asia.[8]

The allusion to James Grant's *Inquiry* is obvious in the last sentence, and therefore the identification of Mr. Grant of Redcastle with James Grant is, I would maintain, certain. I may add that James Grant was in fact living at Redcastle in 1799. What is revealed here is that Niebuhr had originally envisaged his research on the agrarian laws of the Romans as a section of, or a preliminary contribution to, a larger investigation in the style of Montesquieu about agrarian history. This larger work had been suggested to Niebuhr by Grant. The study of Roman agrarian laws was first conceived in this wider frame. For his part Niebuhr had used the model proposed by Grant for the *zamindar* to explain the situation of the Roman *ager publicus*. Like the *zamindar*, the Roman patrician had taken advantage of his position to transform into hereditary and permanent ownership his control of public land. In Rome the agrarian laws, far from redistributing privately owned land, tried to reduce the abusive control of public land by patricians. Obviously James Grant and Barthold Georg Niebuhr were expecting the English government to reduce the abuses of the *zamindar* in India as the Gracchi had tried to reduce the abuses of the *nobiles* (if no longer of the patricians) in Rome. The equation of the *zamindar* with his Roman counterpart could not of course be complete, because there was no question in Rome of whole communities or villages being controlled by patricians or other aristocrats and because in the Roman state there was large and small private property surrounding the stretches of the *ager publicus*. Besides, the patricians were not exactly acting as intermediaries between the state and the peasants. All the same, Niebuhr thought he had been able to understand the legal situation of the *ager publicus* better because he had compared it with the agrarian situation of India as interpreted by Mr. Grant of Redcastle.

By one stroke Niebuhr, the great admirer of the English constitution, had managed both to subtract the Roman agrarian law from the perspective of the French Revolution and to insert it into the perspective of the British Empire, with all the implications it provided of moderate reforms and sensible evaluation of circumstances. Heyne was vindicated in his contention that the Roman agrarian law was concerned with public land, but at the same time the new English setting was an implicit refutation of Heyne's distrust of a Rome capable of proscriptions. So much at least becomes obvious that the months in Scotland in 1799 were of decisive importance for the formation of Niebuhr's historical interest in land-tenure.

There was still something Niebuhr was not really able to grasp while writing in 1804–5. It was the precise difference existing in Roman law between ownership of private land and permanent and hereditary occupation of public land. This was probably clarified in Berlin in the contact which Niebuhr established with Savigny when he had the opportunity of developing his views on archaic Rome before an audience of the University of Berlin in 1810. The audience included Savigny, who had just been made a professor in Berlin and later considered those lectures by Niebuhr the beginning of a new era in the understanding of Rome. Savigny himself had been in some doubt about questions of Roman ownership. In 1803 he had elaborated the distinction between property and possession in *Das Recht des Besitzes,* the book to which he owed his sudden rise to fame. There he had made clear the distinction between the full *dominium ex iure Quiritium* and the *possessio* basically protected by interdict. He himself had admitted that he could not entirely explain the origins of the *possessio.* Now an integration was possible between his theories and those of Niebuhr. He was able to offer Niebuhr the notion of *possessio* as being the most suitable to explain the hereditary control of the *ager publicus,* but in return accepted from Niebuhr the suggestion that this hereditary control of the *ager publicus* was in fact the earliest instance, and probably the model, of *possessio.* With typical generosity the two men acknowledged their debt to each other. The later editions of Savigny's *Das Recht des Besitzes* include a paragraph (12a) which makes the addition suggested by Niebuhr evident. It was then the good luck of Niebuhr to discover in the palimpsest of Gaius in Verona what I believe to be the earliest extant example of the term *dominium ex iure Quiritium* (I, 54; II, 40). The sharp distinction between right of private ownership and right of occupation as formulated by Savigny and Niebuhr has ever since been the center of discussion, interpretation, and doubt in any comparison between Roman property law and other legal systems.

Niebuhr always considered the interpretation of Roman agrarian conditions his principal achievement. He presented it in these terms to Goethe. It was certainly the precondition of his understanding of ancient Rome. Having established that the plebeians had been the victims of the patricians, he went into the study of the patrician society which had originally controlled Rome. His sympathies were for the plebeians. The plebeians had been the free peasants of the neighborhood of early Rome: they preserved their simplicity and honesty. They were different from the clients who depended on the patricians. Niebuhr attributed the best of Roman virtues to the plebeians. They were the authors of those historical ballads to the glory of their ancestors in which Niebuhr sought the source of the tradition about early Rome as we find it in Livy and Dionysius of Halicarnassus. No page of Niebuhr's history is so naively prejudiced as that in which he opposes the forgeries of the pontifical chronicle operated by the patricians to the pure and fresh popular poetry of the ballads about the kings which had been composed by the plebeians.

Niebuhr followed up the conflicts between patricians and plebeians to their final reconciliation in the same spirit with which he worked in Denmark and in Prussia for the recognition of the peasantry by the aristocracy. He was a conservative at heart, and he did not want the dissolution of the aristocracy. With an eye to the English noblemen (and perhaps to the Prussian aristocrats who had accepted him), he wanted to save the aristocracy from itself. He remained, however, an outsider in his aristocratic society, conscious that his father had been of peasant stock and had never received the recognition he deserved for what he had done. He had even derived from the professional knowledge of his father—a land-surveyor turned explorer but later returned to land-surveying in his native country—his first knowledge of land-tenure in East and West.

II: From Mommsen to Max Weber

1

When we discussed Niebuhr we did not hear much about the two *iugera* allegedly granted by Romulus to his companions in the foundation of Rome. In the climate of the French Revolution, or rather in the ensuing period of fear, many thought that they had not heard the last of Babeuf's dreaded *loi agraire*. Niebuhr's main concern had been to separate what he considered the just claims of agrarian reform from the unjust attacks against private property. He had made the Gracchi respectable again by showing that they were totally unlike the French revolutionaries.

In the next fifty years the scene changed. Marx and Engels published their *Manifesto*. Primitive communism became a subject of learned research. The books by Georg Ludwig von Maurer which appeared in 1854 and 1856 told historians and lawyers who were ready to listen about the primitive German "Markenverfassung," the German variety of village collectivist society. Another German aristocrat, August von Haxthausen, in studies published in German, English, and French between 1847 and 1853, illustrated the primitive communistic features of the Russian village, the *mir*. Village collectivism appeared to be a sign of primitive life uncontaminated by Roman individualism: as such it appealed to German lawyers and aristocrats, even if they found it in the rather unclean hands of Slavs and, later, Turks. The whole question of the historical development of private property had obviously taken a new turn in these researches about survivals of collectivist institutions in modern villages of Europe. We can now say that it was one of the most momentous changes in our understanding of ancient civilizations.

Exactly in 1856 Theodor Mommsen showed that the early Romans had not lagged behind the early Germans in their collective attitudes. Mommsen, who was a victim of post-1848 reaction in German universities, was, however, no revolutionary. In the second edition of his *Römische Geschichte* of 1856, he revised and enlarged a less definite text of 1854 into the account which remained substantially unchanged in later editions. He presented a description of early Rome in which the land was collectively owned by the *gens* or clan (not by the nuclear family). He explained the tradition of the two *iugera* for each household by the assumption that they represented the orchard attached to the household at a time in which the real agricultural land was still undivided within the clan. To speak with gross approximation, the two *iugera* (half a hectare) were the garden belonging to the nuclear family, while the fields belonged to the *gens* and were distributed in rotation to the householders according to communal rules and under communal supervision. For Mommsen the reform by King Servius Tullius in the middle of the sixth century B.C. was indicative of the end of this situation. The military and political organization of Servius Tullius presupposed rich householders with plenty of land of their own: it signified that the clans had lost control of the fields which must have been divided up among the householders.

Whether Henry Sumner Maine had read his Mommsen when he published his *Ancient Law* in 1861, I do not know. He certainly knew his Niebuhr, as any Cambridge man born in 1822 would have done. What matters more, he was well acquainted with von Maurer and von Haxthausen and had already directed his attention to the Indian village. On this he had been preceded by Niebuhr, but as an Englishman soon to be involved in governing India, he did not need Niebuhr's example. He quoted Mountstuart Elphinstone's *History of India* to illustrate the similarities between the Indian village community and the Roman *gens*. Here are the foundations of his theory that the original landownership of the Indo-Europeans was based on the communal property of a clan or *gens*. It must, however, be said that the pleasure of finding out what the Aryan fathers were like was never dominant in Maine's mind. When pressed by opponents who accused him of ignoring matriarchy and similar novelties, he had to fall back on the Indo-European limitations of his interests. But what he had really set out to prove in the *Ancient Law* was that English lawyers had trusted Blackstone for too long. The unchallenged occupancy of the *res nullius* by the individual was not the beginning of private property. Maine, as we all remember, argued that "Ancient Law ... knows next to nothing of Individuals. It is concerned not with Individuals, but with Families, not with single human beings, but groups."[9] He went on arguing that "the mode of transition from ancient to modern ownerships, obscure at best, would have been infinitely obscurer if several distinguishable forms of village communities had not been discovered and examined."[10] He had of course in mind his German, Slavonic, and Indian examples. He went on to explain: "Private property, in the shape in which we know it, was chiefly formed by the gradual disentanglement of the separate rights of individuals from the blended rights of a community."[11] He suggested, on lines which were to be developed by Pietro Bonfante, that the *res mancipi* of early Roman Law including land, slaves, and beasts of burden, were the "commodity of first consequence to a primitive people." The *mancipium* was consequently the oldest form of alienation of previously nonalienable commodities. Maine was not prepared to say much on the *gens,* the original owner of the land: "The *gens* were also a group on the model of the family; it was the family extended by a variety of fictions of which the exact nature was lost in antiquity."[12] He argued, however, that Roman law, which does not know primogeniture, must have been preceded by rules (of which he also found traces in India) defining a society run by the eldest male of the oldest line. In other words, primogeniture served to choose the chieftain of a *gens* who was also the administrator of a common patrimony or estate.[13] The revival of primogeniture in feudal Europe was for Maine a return to a collective form of succession which had existed before the development of private property as Roman law knew it: "Civil society no longer cohering, men universally flung themselves back on a social organization older than the beginnings of civil communities."[14]

Maine developed his ideas on the village community in the volume *Village Communities of the East and West* in 1871: it was enriched in the third edition of 1876 by the addition of his Rede Cambridge Lecture of 1875, "The Effects of the Observation of India on Modern European Thought." He had by then resided in India for seven years as a legal member of the Indian Council and had been chiefly responsible for the codification of Indian law. When he undertook to compare the results of von Maurer's studies on the Mark with what he himself knew of the Indian village, he was in the unique position of a man who had access to all available Indian data. Speculations on the Indo-European past might well yield precedence to a description of the contemporary situation. But the comparative interest was still very strong in Maine and became even stronger when in 1874 he extended his researches to early Irish law in his *Lectures on the Early History of Institutions.* He was helped on Irish law by his friend Whitley Stokes. In this volume (the last of his basic contributions to early law) we find the very

illuminating sentence: "It has often occurred to me that Indian function-
aries, in their vehement controversies about the respective rights of the various classes which make up the village community, are unconsciously
striving to adjust by a beneficent arbitration the claims and counter-claims
of the Eupatrids and the Demos, of the Populus and the Plebs."[15]

Village Communities of the East and West, as far as I know, was not promptly
translated into French, while the *Lectures on the Early History of Institutions*
were. The latter (together with *Ancient Law*) were therefore more discussed
on the Continent than the former. Fustel de Coulanges took notice of them
in his work after 1870, whereas he had not yet known *Ancient Law* when he
published *La Cité antique* in 1864. After 1875 it can be said that in Continental juridical thought Maine came to personify the acceptance of village
communism as the most primitive form of landownership, whereas Fustel
appeared, and liked to appear, as the defender of the existence of private
property since the origins of documented history.

2

If he did not know Maine, Fustel de Coulanges must have known Mommsen's chapters in the *Römische Geschichte* well when he published *La Cité
antique* in 1864. But, at least in that period of his life, he was not the man
to quote a contemporary if he could help it. Born in 1830 and educated at
the École Normale of Paris, he was then a young professor at the University
of Strasbourg. He was unusually sensitive to his position of a watch on the
Rhine. In his inaugural lecture at Strasbourg in 1862, he declared: "I had
then resolved to have no masters on Greece other than the Greeks themselves, nor on Rome than the Romans." More explicitly, in an undated fragment which was published after his death, he declared roundly: "I would
rather be mistaken in the manner of Livy than that of Niebuhr." If Niebuhr
could be left out in 1864, it was even easier to forget Mommsen. And Fustel
was not only reluctant to confront his contemporaries on the other side of
the Rhine. He was also capable of baffling, oracular answers about himself.
When in 1868 a critic defined him as a Christian, he replied: "You are more
pagan than I, I am not more Christian than you." Later he could be taken
both as a Bonapartiste and as a partisan of the Third Republic, as a man of
the Right and as a man of the Left. Charles Maurras tried to make him an
unqualified predecessor of the Action française, and of course he failed.
But what exactly Durkheim—a pupil with socialist sympathies—meant by
the dedication of his Latin thesis (1892) on Montesquieu to his dead
teacher Fustel is not obvious either.

What remains remarkable is the rapid succession of basic works on an-
cient societies in that decade 1861–71: Maine's *Ancient Law,* 1861; Bachofen's
Mutterrecht, 1861; Fustel's *La Cité antique,* as I said, 1864; J. F. McLennan's
Primitive Marriage, 1865; E. B. Tylor's *Primitive Culture,* 1871.

The recent arrival of the Indo-Europeans on the scene was no doubt one of the stimulating factors. But Fustel, even less than Maine, was not really committed to the reconstruction of an Indo-European society. At the time of writing the *Cité antique* he knew far less than Maine about Germans and Slavs. He had read something of the Vedas and of the laws of Manu in translation and was of course familiar with the work of some French Indianists, such as E.-L. Burnouf. But almost all his specific statements are still founded on Greek and Roman materials. His quest for the primitive society still took its start from the classical lands. It is on pure Greek and Latin evidence that he tries to demonstrate the central proposition of his book: "The time when men believed only in the domestic gods was the time when there existed only families." True enough, he adds: "In such a State the whole Aryan race appears to have lived for a long time. The hymns of the Vedas confirm this for the branch from which the Hindus are descended." But the Vedas are not frequently quoted by Fustel. It is from Roman and Greek texts that he tries to conjure up the picture of a preurban society in which people claiming to have the same ancestors live together on privately owned ground. This ground is sanctified by the tombs of the ancestors themselves and by the hearth in which the spirits of the ancestors are supposed to live perennially as gods.

Here we begin to appreciate what in a sense is the most extraordinary feature of Fustel's style of arguing. He has plenty of texts to support his discourse. But the texts very seldom support exactly the point he wants to make. His main arguments are in fact gratuitous assumptions. It is a gratuitous assumption (as I shall have to emphasize more than once) that the ancestors are normally buried in the precincts of the family residence. It is also an unwarranted assumption that the fire must be kept alive in order to keep the ancestors alive: the relation between fire and ancestors is never so crude in the Greco-Roman world. It is an altogether gratuitous assumption that the dead are the root both of religion and of ownership. Having made these large assumptions, Fustel goes on to deduce consequences. The daughters are excluded from inheritance because they do not take part in the cult of the ancestors, and they do not take part in the cult of the ancestors because they marry outside the family and join the ancestors' cult of the husband. As ownership is conceived in terms of absolute sovereignty by the head of an extended family, the first son must inherit the priestly and political rights of the father: therefore rights of primogeniture must be postulated even for early Rome, which is more than Henry Maine was prepared to ask for. Finally, Fustel has to explain how the primitive community of the family dissolved and the association of families which we call city came into being. He has to admit that the picture he had so far kept before our eyes was in fact incomplete. He now tells us that not all the members of the family were the descendants of the ancestors they worshiped. Outsiders had been admitted to the family as clients. In exchange for the help they received from this admission, the clients agreed to worship the ancestors of their patrons; but of course they were never entirely happy in their subordinate position, which involved the renunciation of their own natural ancestors. Furthermore, we are told that there even existed families which were unable either to worship their own ancestors or to accept the cult of somebody else's ancestors. These unfortunate families remained for a long time outside what we might perhaps call the original civilization of the Aryan *gentes:* they were in a near-beastly condition. But somehow a new religion developed which was not concerned with the families and the ancestors, but was directed toward the natural elements (such as the sky, the sun, the moon, and the stars). This new religion suited dissatisfied clients and barbarous outsiders. It gave the former, of course, the opportunity to do something more satisfactory than worshiping somebody else's ancestors, and it provided the latter with a genuine religious emotion. So the cities came into being, because dissatisfied clients and impervious outsiders (let us call them plebeians) joined forces in worshiping new gods and building new societies. The old families, the patricians, could not stay out and had to compromise; they joined the cities and the new cults. In the long run the city resulted in the victory of naturalistic polytheism over the ancestor cult. But the ancestor-worshiping aristocracies initially had enough resources to allow them to join the cities on their own conditions. They imposed on the city some of the features of the original domestic cult. This explains why the city had a common hearth and a common fire—personified in Rome, even more precisely than in Greece, by the goddess Vesta. Rather loosely, but vividly, Fustel finds in Aeneas the symbol of that stage of political life in which an aristocratic hero transfers his own penates to the city which he is about to found. If the aristocrats had enough faithful clients, the new city would be particularly advantageous to aristocratic pretensions: in Rome the outsiders, the plebeians, were kept down for a long time. The description of early Rome given by Fustel deserves to be quoted because it indicates how he conceived the relation between the patricians who were the ancestor worshipers and the primitive plebeians:

> At Rome the difference between the two classes was striking. The city of the patricians and their clients was the one that Romulus founded, according to the rites, on the Palatine. The dwellings of the plebs were in the asylum, a species of enclosure situated on the slope of the Capitoline Hill, where Romulus admitted people without hearth or home, whom he could not admit into his city.... One word characterizes these plebeians—they were without a hearth, they did not possess, in the beginning at least, any domestic altars.... They had no father—*pater.*[16]

The entry of the *plebs* into the city was due to the alliance which developed between the plebeians and the kings against the patricians.

In all these developments, which are largely a brilliant construction *a priori,* two elements require special attention. The first is the assumption which we have already noticed that the family tomb created a decisive title to landownership. The second is the assumption we have not yet made evident that, for the purpose of the argument, the *gens* in Rome and the *genos* in Greece are taken to be identical with the family in its primitive organization, rights of ownership, and cult of ancestors. Let us examine these two points more closely.

The custom of burying the dead on the family estate was by no means universal either in Rome or in Greece. As Sally Humphreys has remarked: "Tombs in antiquity were usually placed beside roads, and although land used for burial became private property and might in various ways be safeguarded from abuse or alienation, there is no evidence that it was regarded as particularly desirable to be buried in land that formed part of a larger family holding."[17]

In Rome, no doubt, some *gentes* are known to have had a specific burial reserved for each of them, but I know of no evidence that the burial ground was placed in what could be called the gentile estate. Suetonius tells us in the *Life of Tiberius* that the Claudian *gens* had its burial ground on the slope of the Capitoline Hill. The Capitoline Hill was very distant from the territory of the tribe Claudia, where the Claudii had presumably their oldest estates. The Capitoline Hill was not the original site of the Claudii. It looks as if the Claudii bought a piece of land beneath the Capitol for their burial place when they were well established and respected in Roman society. It is better to regard the burial places for a family or a *gens* as a consequence of the availability of land for those who could pay for it rather than as a cause of the constitution of private property in Rome.

But far more disturbing is Fustel's second assumption, that the *gens* was both the most aristocratic and the oldest form of the family. The fact that *gens* and *genos* are two words, one Latin and the other Greek, with comparable meanings and an identical root, does not authorize us to identify the Roman social unit called *gens* with the Greek social unit called *genos*. Here it is enough to emphasize one difference. The Roman *gentes* can be either patrician or plebeian — that is, they are not ipso facto aristocratic. In Greece we are not so certain, but at least in Athens the notion of *genos* seems to apply only to aristocratic groups which can boast of remote common ancestors. In Greece, or at least in Athens, the *gene* seem to be connected with aristocratic privileges, such as access to priesthoods and magistracies. It is therefore difficult to agree with Fustel in his three assumptions that the *gens* and the *genos* are the same thing, that this thing is essentially precivic, and that it represents the full organization of the family as it was before the family was absorbed into the city. We shall add to this point later. We now return to Fustel's concern with tombs.

It has become well known from Philippe Ariès's pioneering book *L'Homme devant la mort* that the regulation of cemeteries was a matter of special anxiety after the French Revolution, and was proposed as a subject for an essay competition by the Institut de France in 1801. At least one of the essays submitted on that occasion correlates respect for the tombs with respect for private property—the notion which became central to Fustel's thought when he was writing *La Cité antique*. At that time he was perhaps more interested in the interdependence between the religion of ancestors and the formation of private property than in the defense of private property as such. To judge this stage of Fustel de Coulanges, one must keep in mind the chapter of the *Cité antique* in which he tries to explain what he calls the entering of the plebeians into the city. He thought, not unjustifiably, that the struggle between patricians and plebeians was the consequence of the disappearance of the kings who had in one way or another attracted the plebeians to Rome and protected them. But, says Fustel, "let us not unreasonably accuse the patricians or suppose that they coldly conceived the design of oppressing and crushing the plebs. The patrician who was descended from a sacred family . . . understood no other social system than that whose rule had been traced by the ancient religion."[18]

The patricians could not conceive of absorbing the plebs other than by transforming them into clients, but that was exactly what the plebeians objected to. They did not want to become clients of the patricians. Hence the struggle, hence the almost religious solution to a conflict which was almost religious. The patricians had to recognize the sacrosanctity of the tribunes of the plebs, the plebeian leaders. That was the beginning of the end for the patricians. Slowly the patricians lost "even their religious superiority."[19]

In later days, after the experience of the Franco-Prussian War of 1870 and of the Commune of Paris, Fustel was altogether less interested in the religious aspects of private ownership and more directly concerned with the defense of private property. The cause of private property became in its turn identified in his mind with the defense of Roman law and of the Roman origins of the French nation against the German legal tradition and, more specifically, the theory of the German origins of the French nation. Fustel is not to be confused with his pupil Camille Jullian, who showed by his work to what extreme consequences the anti-German interpretation of French history could lead. All the same, it was observed by the moderate Albert Sorel that the question of the origins of property became "a positive obsession with M. Fustel." For Fustel, after 1871, to fight modern Germans was to fight for private property—and vice versa.

On the eve of his death in 1889, he published that essay on "le problème des origines de la propriété foncière" in which he summed up his attacks on the German interpretations of the origins of private ownership. He had already developed them in three substantial memoirs, one on the right of ownership in Greece and two on the agrarian structures of the Germans. After 1870 he had become well informed about the nonclassical evidence he had previously overlooked in the *Cité antique;* he was far more aware of the German situation and knew some of the materials which had become available about Indians, Slavs, and Celts. He polemized especially with the Belgian Emile de Laveleye — basically a follower of Henry Maine — who had summarized much of the new evidence for the benefit of French readers in *De la propriété et de ses formes primitives* (1874). Fustel stuck to his belief that among Aryans there was no trace of primitive communism but only of family ownership. He reduced the village property to family property: "the property belongs to the ancient body of the family which has become the village."[20] Some of the most characteristic pages of Fustel's mature style try to show that there is no reason for attributing to Tacitus the notion of a primitive agrarian communism among the Germans. The difficult lines of *Germania,* chap. 26, "Agri pro numero cultorum ab universis in vicem [?] occupantur" ("lands, one area after another, in proportion to the number of cultivators, are taken for tillage by the whole body of cultivators"),[21] are made to mean, against von Maurer and Maine, that the Germans cultivate variable proportions of the land they individually possess according to the needs of the whole population. The emphasis is placed on the individuality of ownership — which is not what Tacitus can mean. As for the medieval documents on the German Mark before the twelfth century, in Fustel's opinion they show that *marca* meant either border or estate or forest (whether owned by several owners or exploited collectively by several tenants). What in Fustel's opinion the word *marca* never means is land owned by an agrarian community as such. Fustel died in the belief that he had proved against German scholars that the ancient Germans had never known collective ownership. He never seems to have been aware that there was some contradiction between his dislike of German institutions and his own efforts to prove that original German institutions respected private property.

3

One of the consequences of these theoretical debates was to provoke new research and indeed public investigation into the survivals of communal property in various regions of Europe. Agrarian inquiries were altogether fashionable in Europe in the last decades of the nineteenth century. Max Weber, as is well known, had a leading part in one of them in Prussia. There was a number of these "inchieste" in Italy. Some were organized by the Italian parliament and conducted with remarkable competence; particular attention was invariably given to the survival of common land.

A senator of the Italian Kingdom, A. Cencelli Perti, produced a book *La proprietà collettiva in Italia* (1890) which was still considered worth republishing in 1920. Eminent politicians and eminent academic lawyers (two categories which almost coalesced in Italy between 1870 and the First World War) took part in this research and debate: among them were Antonio Salandra, the future prime minister, Giacomo Venezian, and Silvio Perozzi. The famous inaugural lecture by Giacomo Venezian at the University of Camerino in 1887 reproposed to an Italian academic audience the subject of the debates between Fustel and his opponents in the Institut de France; the title was clear enough, *Reliquie della proprietà collettiva in Italia.* The importance of Italian juridical thought after the unification of 1870 is now recognized and its multiple connections with German, French, and English contemporary legal thought are properly appreciated.[22] What is less easily appreciated is the peculiar mixture of positivist thinking, of Darwinian suggestions, and of frank Catholic conservativism which in various proportions colors Italian juridical thought in the matter of landownership during that period. Marxist influence is not noticeable before the end of the century, but Ilario Alibrandi, who was perhaps the most advanced researcher on Roman law in Italy about 1870, resigned as a professor of Roman law in the University of Rome when Rome was conquered by the Piedmontese. Another great Roman lawyer, Contardo Ferrini, a Pavia professor, was rather soon to become officially beatified by the Church. Even in less complex personalities, such as the four men who had a lasting influence on Italian legal thinking and research—Vittorio Scialoia, Pietro Bonfante, and Vittorio Emanuele Orlando in Rome, Salvatore Riccobono at Palermo—it is not always easy to recognize where the claims of a traditional agrarian society end and the aspirations of a secularized commercial and industrial bourgeoisie begin. This is particularly noticeable in Pietro Bonfante, a pupil and then a colleague of Scialoia in Rome, who from his earliest work showed rare sensitivity to the contemporary sociological and historical thought of Europe and America.

Bonfante's first work in two parts, *Res mancipi et nec mancipi* of 1886–87, made him famous at the age of twenty-four and obscured the rival work by a contemporary professor in the University of Turin, Giuseppe Carle, who in an academic memoir of the same years 1886–87, "Le origini della proprietà quiritaria presso le genti del Lazio," and then in a book of 1888, *Le origini del diritto romano,* had grappled with some of the same problems and still deserves attention.

Bonfante started from the archaic form of *mancipatio,* the solemn sale transaction in the presence of five citizen-witnesses which served to transfer the ownership of land, slaves, and beasts of draught and burden (the *res mancipi*). For Bonfante the *mancipatio* was an act of alienation which only the head of the family community was originally entitled to perform, while the ownership of all the other goods (the *res nec mancipi*) was open to any individual and could therefore be alienated by any individual. Consequently the *mancipatio* made sense, according to Bonfante, only in the preurban context in which the head of the whole patrilinear family or lineage was sovereign in his own territory. In the original text of 1886, Bonfante treated the "famiglia agnatizia" as the collective owners of the land; his extended family was ruled by a chieftain. What he exactly meant by "famiglia agnatizia" is not self-evident. Later, in the reprint of his monograph on "Res mancipi"[23] Bonfante declared that he had now decided to recognize the *gens* as the primitive owner of the land: the "famiglia agnatizia" was now identified with the *gens,* and its head with the head of the *gens.* There was indeed a respectable tradition attributing a chieftain to the *gens,* though one must say that this tradition is more noticeable among modern scholars than among the Roman lawyers and historians living in antiquity. No doubt Bonfante had been persuaded to modify or clarify his ideas by the criticisms of some of his many followers. This was not, however, a great gain. What Bonfante had always intended to convey was the image of a primitive communal organization the head of which was a despotic sovereign. What he had wanted to explain was not so much an archaic form of landownership as the exceptional powers of the *pater familias* in classical Rome. Bonfante had been particularly struck by what any Roman lawyer of course knew: the despotic powers of the head of a household in republican Rome. He thought that they were explicable only in terms of the acceptance by the Roman city of a prior state of affairs. To explain the *pater familias* he postulated a head of a *gens* or of a lineage as the despotic ruler of a precivic little community which owned the land collectively. In other words, for Bonfante the Roman family was the relic of a preurban sovereign community ruled by somebody like the *pater familias.*

Whereas Bonfante and his pupils worried about the precise terms of the transition from the preurban despotic state (whether by a *gens* or by a lineage) to the urban state, there were in Italy critics who simply doubted the value of the whole construction. The discussion, often acrimonious, but never petty, by Gaetano De Sanctis and Vincenzo Arangio-Ruiz of Bonfante's main theories involved the whole evaluation of preurban societies in Greece and Rome.[24]

The main argument by De Sanctis and Arangio-Ruiz against Bonfante was in fact derived from Eduard Meyer, as they were the first to own. It was Eduard Meyer who, since the first edition of the first volume of his *Geschichte des Altertums* in 1884 and then in greater detail in the new anthropological introduction to the second edition in 1907, had denied that the extended family had preceded the state. Eduard Meyer had indeed tried to make superfluous all the discussions about the evolution from family to state: he left no place for evolutive schemes of the kind that Fustel and Engels had proposed and that Bonfante, unknown to him, had refurbished. For Eduard Meyer the family could be understood only within the tribe or other primitive forms of state. De Sanctis and his follower Arangio-Ruiz approvingly quoted Meyer against Bonfante. The notion that the powers of the Roman *pater familias* were the simple continuation of the powers of the head of a lineage or of a *gens* in a preurban stage would not do because the *pater familias* in Rome was different from the head of a lineage or of a *gens:* indeed it was doubtful whether there had ever been a head of a *gens.* Secondly, if anything was characteristic of the Roman state in its infancy, it was that it kept separate the position of a male individual within his family from the position of a male individual within the state itself. A son who was obliged to obey the orders of his father in his private life—and could even be killed by him—might become a consul and as such head an army in which his father was a simple soldier. De Sanctis and Arangio-Ruiz had also no difficulty in showing that Bonfante's idea that the testament was originally the choice of his successor made by the head of a family had no support in the evidence. It seems to me indisputable that Bonfante's theories about family and state, insofar as they were applied to Rome, did not survive De Sanctis's criticisms. Like Fustel, Bonfante had relied too much on the value of the *gens* as evidence for the family structure of preurban Latium.

Here we reach perhaps the crux of the matter, and it is worth considering the point more precisely. It must have struck everyone during my exposition that Fustel de Coulanges managed to have the property structure of the *gens* as the archetype of primitive private property; whereas Mommsen, Maine, and Bonfante, though differing in detail, identified the *gens* with the primitive communist village. How is it possible that the notion of *gens* was used both to characterize private property and collective property in primitive Italy?

The answer is of course that we know extraordinarily little about the structure and the function of the *gens* in early Rome, and therefore opposite interpretations are possible. But there is now one new element, chiefly derived from better linguistic evidence, to be taken into consideration. This element may well become very embarrassing to those theories which take it for granted that the *gens* was a preurban organization preserved as a survival inside the city of Rome.

Linguistic evidence seems to show that in Rome and the rest of central Italy the development of the *gentes* was an urban phenomenon of the eighth, seventh, and sixth centuries B.C. It is characterized by the fact that individuals, instead of being identified by a personal name and the name of their father, carry a personal name (*praenomen*) and a name shared with all the other members of the *gens* (*nomen gentile*): the second name may refer to a distant common ancestor (Claudii from Clausus, Marcii from Marcus), but its real characteristic is that it is transmitted from generation to generation. At least for Rome there is little or no evidence that the *gens* existed before the city. The *gens* looks like an artificial corporation, characterized by the assumption of a common distant ancestor, which developed in central Italy as a result of social conditions we can perceive only dimly. No doubt the existence of military bands with strong leaders, for which we have documentary evidence in central Italy at least for the sixth century (if not before), helped the formation of such groups and gave them something to do, but it is very doubtful that the Italian *gentes* can be explained in such military terms.

All we can say at the moment is that the *gentes* look like early urban structures presupposing developed private property rather than preurban structures involving communal property. What the Latins and the other populations of ancient Italy were before the rise of the city-state remains a mystery. To appreciate the implications of this statement, we must bear in mind the fact that perhaps two-thirds of Italy reached the stage of urban organization as a result of direct Roman intervention, while the other third owed their cities either to the Etruscans or the Phoenicians or, above all, to the Greeks. The ultimate question of what Italy was before it was urbanized by Greeks, Etruscans, Phoenicians, and Romans has not yet been answered. But the *gentes* seem to appear first in central Italy and in urban centers. Future discussions about the relation between private and collective property in Rome will have to start from the curious notion of the *heredium* as the private ownership of two *iugera* rather than from the existence of a clan structure.

The novelty of Max Weber, in comparison with the writers we have so far examined, is that he is much more interested in the relation between private and state landownership in historical times than in the origins of private ownership in Rome.

4

In comparison with the scholars we have been discussing so far, Max Weber seems to lead us into a different world with his *Römische Agrargeschichte*, the book of less than three hundred pages published by him as his *Promotionsschrift* in 1891. Max Weber could boast (if he had ever been inclined to boast) of being the favorite pupil of both Theodor Mommsen, the greatest authority on Rome, and of August Meitzen, the greatest authority on medieval land-tenure. He had a rare combination of trainings, which was, however, rarer among historians than among lawyers. His primary purpose was simple enough. It was to try to see whether the different methods used by Roman public surveyors to measure and map the land corresponded to different kinds of land-tenure. He concluded that centuriation, a rough division into square lots, was reserved to colonial land which was not subject to land-tax, whereas the division *per strigas et scamna* (furrows and

ridges), a more exact measuring of rectangular lots, was used for land assig-
nations which were subject to land-taxation and incidentally required the
recording of the owner's name for each allotment. From these observations
Weber passed to consider the social and economic presuppositions of the
two types of land-assignation. Colonial land was distributed in small lots
which were related (as we know) to the two-*iugera* lots allegedly given by
Romulus to the first Romans. As two *iugera* (half a hectare) are insufficient
to feed a family, Weber agreed that they presupposed the existence of communal land from which the colonists could get additional food for themselves and their animals. In all this Max Weber was following Mommsen, but
he added many particulars from his more detailed knowledge of medieval
economy. The situation was different in the *ager publicus* distributed on condition of the payment of a fee. Though attempts were occasionally made to
limit the amount of land held by an individual (but the limit was never
below five hundred *iugera*), this land was in fact open to exploitation by the
rich who had the cash to pay the fee and the slaves to work the land for
them. It must be added that Weber seems to have implied that in archaic
Rome the patricians acquired their wealth not through exploitation of land
but through trade, even maritime trade—a notion which must have appeared bolder to the contemporary readers of the *Agrargeschichte* than it
appears to us now. As a consequence, Max Weber thought that the exploitation of the *ager publicus* was not so much an early patrician practice as a
trend characteristic of the new patricio-plebeian aristocracy of the Middle
Republic. When the supply of slaves dried up during the empire, the
capitalistic regime was transformed into the so-called colonate, which allowed the landowners to exploit the services of free peasants and slowly to
reduce them to the position of serfs.

What Weber was therefore giving was a rather grandiose view of the
development of landownership in Rome from the archaic stage in which
the relics of clan ownership were still patent to the capitalistic exploitation
of the peasants in the empire. Mommsen was the first to react to his pupil's
juvenile masterpiece. He devoted to Weber's book a fifty-page article.[25] He
had a great deal to criticize, both in the interpretation of the texts of the
Roman *agrimensores* and, above all, in Weber's determination to make a
sharp distinction between the land regime of the Roman *coloniae* and that of
the Roman *municipia* even in imperial times. But clearly Mommsen was
altogether enchanted by his pupil and pleased that the study of Roman
agrarian problems was passing from the hands of philologists into those of
economists and lawyers.

It will not be necessary to go into the details of the later work done by
Max Weber on ancient agrarian history except to remind ourselves that for
Weber the problems were not of prehistory, but of history for which written
evidence existed. As I have already mentioned, he took a leading part in the

survey of agrarian conditions in Germany east of the Elbe which was organized by the *Verein für Sozialpolitik* in 1892, one year after the book on Roman agrarian history. In 1896 he published his famous essay on the social causes of the "Decline of Ancient Culture"[26] which tried to establish a correlation between the spreading of the colonate and the decline of the ancient cities in the fourth and fifth centuries A.D. The great landowners of the Roman Empire, like the Junkers of modern Prussia, had been a negative element in the process of civilization because they insulated the country from the town and consequently weakened the cities both in terms of wealth and of culture. Weber's next undertaking in agrarian history was the article "Agrarverhältnisse im Altertum" (notice the title) for the *Handwörterbuch der Staatswissenschaften,* second supplement, in 1897, later rewritten and enlarged for the 1909 edition of the *Handwörterbuch.*[27] In its new form it became the equivalent of a small book and still showed the typically Weberian interest in the relation between town and country as factors of civilization. But on the whole Weber was now shifting his interest from country to town and giving that shape to his ideas which his later great synthesis on the city was to show most distinctly. One can adduce more than one reason for this shift of interests, but one of the reasons is certainly to be found in the continuous implicit or explicit debate which Max Weber conducted with Eduard Meyer both on questions of historical method and on questions of fact. Eduard Meyer was on the whole insensitive to problems of agrarian history. He was profoundly involved in understanding urban developments insofar as they represented the structure of the state and the centers of religion and secular culture. It is therefore interesting to note that Weber disagreed with Meyer on a hundred points, but yielded to Meyer's influence by renouncing what had perhaps been the most original feature of his early writing—the conviction that civilization develops in towns, but its roots are in the agrarian structure of the country.

It is therefore ironic that this juvenile side of Max Weber should be taken up again by the Russian historian, Michael Rostovtzeff, who later in life was offered and turned down (if I am correctly informed) Eduard Meyer's chair in Berlin. It was from Max Weber's vision of the conflict of interests between country and town in late antiquity that Michael Rostovtzeff took his cue for his own interpretation of the decline of the ancient world. Rostovtzeff had already shown himself to be under the influence of Max Weber when he published his history of the Roman Colonate in 1910. After the First World War, under the impression of his own experience of the Russian Revolution, he gave a new meaning to the conflict between town and country which Max Weber had defined in his essay of 1896. Rostovtzeff now spoke of a Red Army of peasants who were only too glad to attack the cities and destroy civilization in the third century A.D.: it was a civilization in which they had no share.

Mommsen had visualized Roman civilization emerging from primitive farms in the shape of sturdy peasants who wanted to keep their own fields and were prepared to fight for them. Max Weber had directed his attention to the later stage in which the same Romans had degenerated into greedy landowners prepared to separate themselves from the cities they had created. Rostovtzeff went a step further and identified the guilty men not in the landowners, but in the peasant-soldiers who had learned to hate the city life which was not of their own making.

If we go behind Mommsen and return to Niebuhr, from whom I started, the story seems even more dramatic. Niebuhr, who knew little or nothing of Roman primitive collectivism, had placed all the Roman virtues in the Roman archaic peasants. Now Rostovtzeff, like a Roman of the late empire, looked from the battered walls of the Roman towns and recognized peasants in the brigands (let us call them *bagaudae* with a good ancient term) who would drive the empire to its doom. Niebuhr had opposed the Roman peasants to the French sans culottes. Rostovtzeff saw the Roman peasants turning into a Soviet Union.

III: Hermann Usener

1

It may be necessary to explain why I begin with Hermann Usener in my attempt to indicate some of the interesting contributions of the nineteenth century to an interpretation of the religions of the Greco-Roman world and more generally to the methodology of the history of religions. I could easily have started, say, with Karl Otfried Müller—a genius on any account who left his mark on many aspects of the study of the ancient world, from the Dorians to the Etruscans, from the poets to the antiquarians, and who in 1825 published his epoch-making *Prolegomena zu einer wissenschaftlichen Mythologie*. I might, alternatively, have gone nearer to Usener's own university, Bonn, and picked up one of his teachers there, Friedrich Gottlieb Welcker, who in the *Griechische Götterlehre* of his old age (1857–63) gave the first systematic account of Greek religion as a system of beliefs, not of myths. There is a justification for any beginning, and if I have decided for the time being to leave out K. O. Müller and F. G. Welcker and to start with Hermann Usener it is because at the moment I am interested in one aspect of his activity: the use of philology and more specifically of comparative philology for the transformation of the study of religion. K. O. Müller and F. G. Welcker operated in a very different atmosphere from that in which Usener found himself after 1866 and even more in his great creative years, roughly between 1880 and 1900. They lived most of their lives (a short one for Müller, if not for Welcker) in a romantic atmosphere in which myth meant poetic and naive thinking preceding philosophy and theology. Müller explored the myths of the Greeks as if they had been the registration of pre-historic experiences of the Greeks in the time of emigration; the influence of the Brothers Grimm on Müller's work is well known. F. G. Welcker took the myths only as starting points of a polytheistic theology which would ultimately mature into a monotheistic one. It is worth remembering that Martin Buber's celebrated opposition of I and Thou in religious experience is most explicitly at the roots of Welcker's theology. Müller and Welcker's programs were, in terms of the culture to which they belonged, foreseeable and therefore easy to formulate in a systematic way: both Müller and Welcker organized their point of view in powerful structures.

What we have in Hermann Usener is, very differently, a slow realization of certain potentialities of philology which he and others had not grasped before. There is a conscious beginning in Usener. This in itself throws doubt on the conventional opinion that Usener was applying to classical scholarship ideas and methods of his beloved brother-in-law Wilhelm Dilthey. Though the friendship between the two men is an important fact in their biography, we shall see that the evidence speaks in a different direction insofar as Usener's methods and results are concerned. There is no doubt about Usener's awareness of doing something unusual. He was very modest, simple, and extremely likeable. But more than once in his life he gave some indication of knowing exactly where he was going. Before I start discussing him in more detail it may be useful, as an introduction to the man, to translate a few sentences of what primarily, but not ulti-mately, was meant to be a very banal letter of academic thanks. It was pub-lished for the first time in 1980 by Hans-Joachim Mette in his useful bio-bibliographical introduction to Usener in the periodical *Lustrum*. The text of the letter dated 4 December 1888 is in the Staatsbibliothek of Munich. Usener had to thank the president of the Bavarian Academy for having been made a "foreign" member of this academy: as a Prussian subject Usener was still a foreigner for the Bavarian Academy in 1888. But the president of the academy was Ignaz von Doellinger, the Catholic theolo-gian friend of Acton who had not accepted papal infallibility and had been excommunicated. And Usener had just published his book on the origins of Christmas (*Das Weihnachtsfest*). Whether he already knew that Adolf Harnack, the Protestant theologian, was going to attack it in the *Theolo-gische Literaturzeitung* I doubt, but clearly he was expecting unfavorable reactions. So he offered a copy of the book to Doellinger with the words:

> Nobody is in a better position than you are to recognize the weaknesses which must be inherent in the first attempt by a philologist to do theology. But I may hope that you will excuse specific mistakes because of the honesty of my attitude. The ultimate unexpressed aim of my efforts is to help to

prepare the church unity of our nation. On both sides one must realize the inadequacy of the past if in the future a favorable or unfavorable international situation should be really fruitful for our religion and church.

Ambitions by a philologist to contribute to the unity of Christianity were not often expressed in Germany or elsewhere in the nineteenth century. What is even more remarkable is that the man who spoke as an ecumenical Christian in 1888 would probably not have been able to speak in the same sense ten years later.

2

Hermann Usener, it must be readily admitted, is no longer the prestigious name it used to be when he was alive. I doubt whether there is nowadays a scholar in Germany or elsewhere who would still consider himself a disciple of Usener or a continuator. Perhaps Arthur Darby Nock, to whom I alluded in my introduction, was really his last disciple, at least in the sense that he, like Usener, felt himself to be a philologist at heart. But for almost forty years Usener was from Bonn *praeceptor Germaniae*. Partly, but only partly, in collaboration with Franz Buecheler, he attracted more gifted pupils than anybody else in Germany. He was a teacher of Hermann Diels, Georg Kaibel, Ulrich von Wilamowitz-Moellendorff, Ivo Bruns, Ferdinand Dümmler, Friedrich Leo, Eduard Schwartz, Eduard Norden, Alfred Körte, Ludwig Radermacher, Ludwig Deubner. The future founder of the Warburg Institute, Aby Warburg, the neo-Kantian philosopher Paul Natorp, and the Church historian Hans Lietzmann recognized a permanent debt to Usener and were devoted to him. I should probably have to add Franz Cumont, though he was a pupil of Usener's pupil Diels, because his basic interests obviously derived from Usener. Even in the twenties of this century there was still at Hamburg, in direct connection with the Warburg Institute, a philosopher, Ernst Cassirer, who proclaimed his debt to Usener. Now it seems all over. Mette has published his bio-bibliographical contribution on Usener in *Lustrum* with the depressing title: "Nekrolog einer Epoche: Hermann Usener und seine Schule." There are always a hundred concomitant factors for the good or bad reputation of a scholar. But in the case of Usener one paradoxical element is his relation to the greatest of his pupils—Wilamowitz. Their correspondence was published long ago: it is undoubtedly one of the most interesting exchanges between two great scholars. But it is also a correspondence in which all the warmth is really on one side, that of the master, Usener. He had had something to forgive Wilamowitz. Wilamowitz had left the University of Bonn in 1869 after Jahn's death and got his doctorate in Berlin among rather uncongenial teachers because he had offended Usener by a satirical poem. Six or seven years had to pass before the relations between the two men were reestablished, but typically Usener, having forgiven, had also forgotten. Wilamowitz never forgot and never really liked his teacher Usener. Too intelligent not to know his value and too much a man of the world not to know how to behave, he even dedicated to Usener one of his juvenile masterpieces, the *Antigonos von Karystos* of 1881. But in 1875 he could boast to Mommsen, who was not yet his father-in-law, that he had cured Friedrich Leo of his veneration for Usener ("denn von der Verehrung von Usener habe ich ihn geheilt," *Briefwechsel*, p. 22). And after Usener's death he made obvious his dislike in his *Erinnerungen;* in his short Latin autobiography;[28] in the quasi-silence about him in the *History of Classical Scholarship*, where pointedly Bernays has a greater place; and in other scattered judgments. Wilamowitz did not allow his pupils and his pupils' pupils to feel any continuity with Usener.

Here Italian scholars become good witnesses, because there was a school of Wilamowitz in Italy. It was directly represented by Giorgio Pasquali, though he had studied with Leo at Göttingen rather than with Wilamowitz in Berlin, and was reinforced after the Second World War by E. Fraenkel's teaching in Italy. Fraenkel too was a Göttingen pupil of Leo who had transferred his allegiance to Wilamowitz. Pasquali and Fraenkel, as far as I am aware, never cared for Usener (which incidentally also explains why the generation of Oxford scholars educated by Fraenkel does not seem to be interested in Usener). Curiously there were in Italy all the conditions for giving a place to Usener. He had been acquainted with Italian culture far better than any other contemporary German scholar, with the exception of Mommsen or perhaps of Gregorovius. He had been a friend not only of classical scholars like Domenico Comparetti and Giambattista De Rossi, but of the master of Italian folklore, Giuseppe Pitré, and of the remarkable Roman philosopher Giacomo Barzellotti. It was Usener who told Warburg to read an Italian book no Italian read, *Mito e scienza* by Tito Vignoli (1879), the German translation of which he had reviewed. Vignoli's book, as Ernst Gombrich showed, was basic to Warburg's formation. Finally, for reasons too long to discuss here, Epicurus had and has a special importance in Italy. Usener, as an editor of Epicurus, had an essential part in interpreting the Papyri of Herculaneum and was inevitably the man to whom Italian students of Epicurus had to turn. But the formidable succession of Italian Epicurean scholars, from Carlo Giussani and Ettore Bignone to my living friends Marcello Gigante and Graziano Arrighetti, never developed a substantial interest in Usener outside Epicurus's text.

3

Hermann Usener was by birth a typical product of German *Kleinstaaterei*. He was born in 1834 in Weilburg, in the Herzogtum of Nassau where his father was a fairly wealthy minor dignitary—the *Landoberschultheiss* and *Hofrat* Georg Usener—and his mother Charlotte Vogler was the daughter of *Obermedizinalrat* and *Leibarzt* Andreas Vogler. His brother was a Lutheran country parson and his sister married a parson. In the gymnasium of Weilburg Hermann Usener was inspired to a love of the classics by Alfred Fleckeisen, a pupil of Ritschl at Bonn and a scholar in his own right who has given the name *Fleckeisen's Jahrbücher für Philologie und Pädagogik* to the classical journal he edited for many years. Fleckeisen would naturally direct his pupil to Bonn, and in fact at Bonn Usener obtained his doctorate in 1858. But before ending in Bonn he passed through Heidelberg, Munich, and Göttingen. In each place he found something to learn and, what is more uncommon, left his mark. In Heidelberg he liked especially Karl Ludwig Kayser, the editor of Cicero and Philostratus, who had worked much and published little on Homer. Usener collected and published these partly unpublished *Homerische Abhandlungen* in 1881, when Kayser had been dead for several years and he himself was a famous professor. After Heidelberg, Munich, where Usener learned from Leonhard Spengel how to interpret and edit rhetorical texts. His studies on Anaximenes' *Rhetorica ad Alexandrum*, though published when he had left Munich for Göttingen, are a product of Spengel's teaching.

Some of the latest editorial work by Usener, the text of the *Opuscula rhetorica* by Dionysius of Halicarnassus which he published in 1899–1904, partly in collaboration with L. Radermacher, is still in prosecution of these early interests derived from Spengel. And finally, as soon as he arrived at Bonn, still a student, in 1857 he led a team of six fellow students, one of whom was Franz Buecheler, to prepare an edition of the recently discovered and very difficult historical text by Granius Licinianus. The edition became known as that by the Eptas Bonnensis and was the beginning of the friendship between Usener and Buecheler, which matured in a famous teaching collaboration when the two became colleagues in Bonn for the rest of their lives. But then Usener had still to get his doctorate. A pupil of the three great masters of Bonn at that time—Ritschl, Welcker, and Brandis—he wrote his dissertation with Brandis, *Analecta Theophrastea*. The modest title in fact concealed pioneer research in the transmission of philosophic doctrines within Aristotle's school. It provided the model for the great enterprise on these lines, H. Diels's *Doxographi Graeci* of 1879. Diels was Usener's pupil, perhaps the one dearest to his heart.

A series of appointments followed, as one would expect. For a few years he was a classics teacher in the distinguished Joachimsthalsche Gymnasium of Berlin (1858–61), he became professor *extraordinarius* at the University of Bern (1861–63), and rounded off his income by some gymnasial teaching, until he moved as an *ordinarius* to Greifswald in 1863. Three years later he was *ordinarius* in Bonn, from where a pathetic quarrel with O. Jahn had caused the flight of Ritschl, and by implication of Nietzsche, to Leipzig. Jahn himself was fated to die in 1869, while Welcker died in 1868. To fill the gaps, chairs were given to Buecheler as *ordinarius* and to Jacob Bernays as *extraordinarius:* the gradation reflected evaluation not of personal merits, but of religions. The triad Usener, Buecheler, and Bernays collaborated with a reciprocal understanding which made Bonn the center of classical studies. The first to die, prematurely, was Bernays in 1881. It was Usener who, by collecting Bernays's *Gesammelte Abhandlungen* (1885) and writing his memorable introduction (not to speak of the biographical article in *Allgem. Deutsche Biographie,* vol. 46), erected a monument to Bernays which had neither many precedents nor many imitations in the story of German-Jewish relations.

By becoming a professor at Bonn just in 1866, Usener had been absorbed into the Prussian state in a different way from that in which his native land, the Herzogtum of Nassau, was absorbed by Prussia in the same year for having supported the losing side in the Austro-Prussian War. But Usener remained un-Prussian in his basic lack of interest in politics and in his very diluted nationalism. How rooted he was in the little land of Nassau is shown by the fact that in that very year, 1866, he married Lili Dilthey, the daughter of the court preacher of the dying Herzogtum and the sister of Carl and Wilhelm Dilthey, his dearest friends. Carl was later a professor of classics in Göttingen, and Wilhelm ended up in Berlin after vain attempts by Usener to have him installed at Bonn. Usener knew all one was supposed to know about the conflicts in methods inside German classical scholarship. He knew of course that Gottfried Hermann had clashed with August Boeckh and K. O. Müller over the purpose of philology. Hermann centered philology on the interpretation of texts, and especially of poetry. Boeckh claimed for philology the task of reconstructing the whole spiritual and material life of a nation and saw the future in the return to an encyclopedic notion of knowledge, for which it is difficult to say whether he had in mind Aristotle or the eighteenth-century encyclopedists. The conflict must have mattered to Usener because he went into it in 1882, when as rector of the university he gave the famous lecture on "Philologie und Geschichtswissenschaft." But in what sense did the conflict really matter to Usener?

What strikes one in young Usener — or indeed in most of his contemporaries — is the natural attachment to the humanistic notion that the primary task of the philologist is to discover, publish, and emend texts, any sort of texts, provided that the text is new or more complete or better edited. When still a gymnasial teacher in Berlin, Usener had prepared for publication the Neoplatonic commentary to the *Metaphysics* of Aristotle by Syrianus which appeared in 1870 and virtually inaugurated the edition of the commentaries on Aristotle by the Berlin Academy. When he was in Bern he studied the local manuscript of the scholia to Lucan which became the subject of his edition of 1869. We may be inclined to think that a profound interest in the philosophy of Epicurus must have inspired the minute and painstaking work which led to the edition of the Epicurean texts in 1887. The amount of work which this edition implied we can appreciate better than Usener's contemporaries, because it was only in 1977, ninety years later, that Italian money was found to subsidize the publication of that Epicurean vocabulary, *Glossarium Epicureum,* which Usener had prepared, primarily for his own private use, to be certain of Epicurus's Greek. Yet the first to deny that he had a specific interest in Epicurus was Usener himself. What he wanted to do was to produce a clean text of a difficult author. One is reminded of Karl Lachmann, who could pass from Lucretius's poetry to the prose of the Roman land-surveyors (*agrimensores*) when the task was to produce an honest text.

The Humanists had found an impressive literary form for their care of texts in the *Variae lectiones.* The genre perhaps went back to the *Noctes Atticae* by Aulus Gellius, a product of second-century A.D. classicism, but was eminently suited to improve and interpret brief texts or short passages of long texts without committing the writer to general theories. If there was pure philology it was in the miscellaneous, often pedantic *Variae lectiones.* Usener loved them and used and abused the genre. He was not a particularly good emendator of texts, and altogether he appeared in his youth to a sophisticated judge like Otto Jahn to be lacking in the sense of the probable (a motto quoted with pleasure by Wilamowitz in his *Erinnerungen*). But Usener felt deeply that his first duty as a scholar was to know and to understand texts. He knew his risks. In one of his *Variae lectiones* of 1889 he gave himself a motto (*Kleine Schriften,* I, p. 337): "Nonnumquam audendum est scire ut scias" ("Sometimes one must dare to know in order to know"). In 1882 he had already proclaimed in his speech "Philologie und Geschichtswissenschaft," "The true philologist must be a knight without fear" ("Ein rechter Philologe muss ein Ritter ohne Furcht sein"). It has been observed that Warburg's famous dictum "Der liebe Gott steckt im Detail"— for which sources have been sought in hundreds of places from Spinoza to Flaubert — is Warburg's own formulation of Usener's notion of philology.[29]

I shall give two examples of Usener's daring, one which was perhaps a complete failure, the other mingling failure and success. In the rather juvenile *Lectiones Graecae* of 1868–70 Usener interpreted a well-known epigram by Alcaeus of Messene (*Anth.* IX, 518), the poet of the early second century B.C. He argued that the words *Makynou teiche* meant the "walls of the city of Makynos." He then identified the city of Makynos with the city of Mekone which in Hesiod's *Theogony* 1. 536 stays between the world of the gods and the world of men. One can imagine that the epigram was beginning to become interesting. But I shall not go further, because if anything is certain it is that *Makynou* is not the genitive of a nonexistent city Makynos, but the imperative of the verb *makyno:* "raise the walls."

Later, in 1874, Usener reinterpreted an epigram from Knidos which had just been published by the English scholar C. T. Newton.[30] The text

describes some sort of a complex religious structure which includes a place
for the god Pan and a shrine dedicated to Antigonos Epigonos. Usener
thought that Antigonos Epigonos must have been a king. He looked around
and discovered that the king of Macedonia Antigonos Gonatas was a special
devotee of the god Pan. He therefore identified Antigonos Epigonos with
Antigonos Gonatas. This identification was improbable in itself and was later
shown to be wrong by another inscription in which Antigonos Epigonos
appeared to be an eminent citizen of Knidos who was treated as a hero by
his fellow citizens. Usener was again wrong, but he had discovered in the process what had escaped everybody else, the deep devotion of Antigonos
Gonatas to the god Pan.

I have insisted on these *Variae lectiones* because one cannot understand
Usener without understanding his profound commitment to the primary task
of reading and understanding texts. It was the interest in understanding texts
which started him on his more original ways of thinking. Before we get to
them, we may pause to have a quick look at a characteristic example of how
Usener could turn a text into the mirror of an age—and of an age which few
understood. He was asked by Alfred Holder to publish a Latin fragment
which Holder had discovered in a manuscript of Cassiodorus's *Institutiones*
now in the library of Karlsruhe, but earlier in the famous monastic library
of Reichenau. After a long delay, Usener finally published the fragment,
which he called *Anecdoton Holderi,* in 1877 for an academic occasion. He
recognized in it an extract from a family history composed by Cassiodorus
at a certain moment of his life when he wanted to emphasize his family connections with Boethius. Usener also found in this text the decisive proof for
the authenticity of Boethius's theological treatises, which was disputed, and
vice versa ascribed to Marius Victorinus the pamphlet *De definitione* which
went under the name of Boethius.

Usener's readiness to go out of his way in order to edit difficult texts was
duly exploited by Mommsen, who obtained from him and inserted in his
Chronica minora, volume III (1898) for the *Monumenta Germaniae* an exemplary edition of the *Fasti Theonis* and *Fasti Heracliani,* late Roman or Byzantine chronographies. With these editions we are getting very near to
the subject in which Usener made his decisive move from what we would
call the humanistic tradition of the textual critic and interpreter to the
task of the philological—and by implication antitheological—interpreter of
religion.

4

We should know better how this decisive move happened if we were better informed about a mysterious episode in Usener's scientific production which is connected with his relation to Mommsen. It must be added
that Usener's admiration for Mommsen was not entirely reciprocated by

Mommsen; and Wilamowitz, by now Mommsen's son-in-law, cannot have helped. The more surprising it is that, according to several statements by people who were in a position to know, including Eduard Schwartz, one of the many medieval and modern manuscripts which were burned with Mommsen's library on 12 July 1880 was a complete book by Usener relating to the history of astronomy and astrology. Our witnesses are vague, and not in agreement between themselves on details. Perhaps the book was just a first draft of the edition of the texts Usener contributed later to the *Chronica minora*. In any case these texts had something to do with astronomy and astrology. Evidently about 1880 Usener considered ancient astronomy and astrology one of his provinces—or rather one of the fields a student of ancient religion had to master.

It is traditional to connect an essay by Usener published in 1868 under the nontransparent title of *Kallone* with the beginnings of his exploration of religion. Typically he had started from a passage in Aristophanes to get himself landed in lunar myths. Myths in the atmosphere of those years raised questions of Indo-European origins. Max Müller was becoming famous. Usener took the challenge of comparative mythology seriously, polished his Sanskrit, and acquired some Lithuanian in the process of his studies. He was not to become a pupil of Max Müller, but we shall soon see that he followed up Max Müller's intriguing notion that polytheism was a disease of human language, that is, that the ability to produce metaphors led man into the temptation or inclination to reify them into gods.

Before I say something more on this, we have to note the two rather lonely paths along which Usener began to walk in pursuit of comparative philology. The first was prosody. In 1886 he produced a book of *Altgriechischer Versbau* in which Greek meters were given Indo-European ancestors. Usener was not the first on this track. He had been preceded, as he knew, by R. Westphal in a paper in *Kuhn's Zeitschrift für Vergleichende Sprachforschung* (9, 1860). As he was a slow worker, he had also been overtaken by an American scholar, Frederick Allen, who from Westphal's premises had deduced consequences in the same *Kuhn's Zeitschrift* (24, 1879) which were not unlike those which Usener made public seven years later. Both Usener and Allen postulated a basic Indo-European verse of eight syllables, about which Wilamowitz was quick to express private disbelief, later made public. The dubious quest for the original Indo-European prosody later involved the great master Antoine Meillet (1923), who was soon proved wrong by P. Maas, and more recently, for instance, the Oxford don (now London professor) M. L. West.[31] The question of Indo-European prosody is not entirely identical, though C. Watkins would disagree, with that of Indo-European poetics—that is, of the function of bards in early Indo-European society.[32]

Usener was on safer ground in another type of comparative research. He was one of the first to appreciate the dimension which comparative philology could add to folklore research of the type the Brothers Grimm had taught classical scholars since K. O. Müller's days. One of Usener's earliest brilliant essays was that on "Italische Mythen" of 1875, in which he interpreted two minor Roman mythical figures—Anna Perenna and Mamurius Veturius—as impersonations of the year, especially of the dying year. But my favorite Usener paper on such subjects is a much later one,[33] in which he supplemented Mommsen's *Römisches Strafrecht* by showing that Mommsen had overlooked popular forms of justice in ancient Rome. Usener illustrated his thesis by a skillful combination of old literary and juridical texts (beginning with the Twelve Tables) and the modern folklore of Mediterranean countries.

The third line pursued by Usener had been known for centuries, but Usener managed to appear distinctively original in pursuing it. He was soon known as the founder of a new school of research on the lives of saints, a sort of competitor with the Bollandists (who had not yet produced their Père Delehaye). Usener gained his greatest prestige and provoked the greatest controversy on this third line. About 1879 he began to publish carefully prepared studies on lives of Christian saints and on Christian festivals: they were often supported by masterly editions of the relevant texts. Rightly or wrongly he chose saints and festivals in which he thought he had recognized pagan survivals. He was aiming at a definite and systematic examination of pagan elements in Christianity, with the ultimate purpose of preparing their elimination from modern Christianity. The two most famous researches which appeared in his lifetime were perhaps the one on Sancta Pelagia (1877), in whom he saw a transformation of none less than Aphrodite or Venus, and the one on Christmas (1889), where he was the first to pursue rigorously the strange metamorphosis from a pagan festival—the *natalis solis invicti*—into the birthday of Jesus. A third piece of research on Saint Tychon appeared posthumously in 1907. It implied that Tychon—allegedly a bishop of Amathus in Cyprus—had never existed and was in fact the transformation of the fertility god Tychon often identified with Priapos.

Adolf Harnack controverted immediately certain assumptions of Usener's Christmas book in a basic review.[34] He accepted most of what Usener had to say about Christmas as such: namely, that as an official celebration of Jesus' birthday it spread from Rome, where it is first documented in the middle of the fourth century A.D. The difficulties Harnack saw were in the interpretation of the history of Epiphany, which in the fourth century was often connected with the birth and the baptism of Jesus. As the observance of the Epiphany is first attested in the Gnostic sect of the Basilidians by Clement of Alexandria (*Stromateis* 1, 21, 146), Usener had deduced that the festival of the Epiphany had penetrated into the mainstream of Christianity from Gnostic sects. This had for Usener far-reaching consequences for the history of Christianity and even of the Gospels. Harnack accused Usener of confusing Gnosticism with Christianity for the period between A.D. 100 and 160. As far as I know (but I may be wrong), there was never a direct reply by Usener to Harnack. The controversy was echoed immediately in the correspondence between Wilamowitz and Mommsen. Mommsen liked Harnack's review—he altogether liked Harnack —and sent the text to Wilamowitz before publication. But Wilamowitz was for once with Usener, as he was against the theologians: he thought that Usener was still making too many concessions to the theologians.

The conflict about the Epiphany still involved theologians of the stature of K. Holl.[35] It cannot detain us here, but a second edition of Usener's book on Christmas was published in 1911 by the one Usener pupil who was a theologian, Hans Lietzmann. He recommended the book to those "die zu lernen bereit sind" ("who are prepared to learn"). Harnack must have read this.

Far more damaging were the criticisms of the work on the lives of the saints which came from the great Bollandist authority Père Hyppolite Delehaye, beginning with *Les Légendes hagiographiques* (1905; 3d ed., 1927) and then in *Les Origines du culte des martyrs* (1912; 2d ed., 1932) and in various other places, including reviews in *Analecta Bollandiana*. To avoid misapprehension one must immediately say that the Society of the Bollandists, which in Usener's time was presided over by Père Charles De Smedt, fully accepted the strictest criteria of historical analysis: that was made obvious by Père De Smedt's *Principes de la critique historique* which appeared in 1883, and then by the November series of the *Acta Sanctorum* which began to appear under his direction in 1887. Père Delehaye, who became Smedt's successor in 1911 and had already shaped the Bollandist work for some time before, was of course the last to depart from those criteria. What Père Delehaye not unreasonably objected to in Usener was his inability to distinguish between the nucleus of a tradition and its later accretions. He was especially right in emphasizing that the legend of Pelagia was rooted in the Church of Antioch and in the preaching of John Chrysostom. Aphrodite may have colored some of the details of the legend, but did not affect its origins. More complex is the case of Tychon, the bishop of Amathus whose life was written by Johannes Eleemosynarios at the beginning of the seventh century. There is a good chance that the bishop Tychon really existed. But the question whether his biography, of which in any case Usener provided an exemplary edition, was influenced by the homonymous god is another matter. Père Delehaye himself learned something from Usener's editorial technique and, maybe, from Usener's analysis of pagan elements in the cult of the saints.

Though in these pagan-Christian confrontations the Indo-European background was bound to recede, Usener never abandoned his comparative philology. In at least two researches of his last years comparativism is explicit.

In the volume on the legends of the Deluge (*Sintfluthsagen,* 1899; with an appendix of 1901) he went even beyond the Indo-European field in trying to find in a solar myth the common origins of the Babylonian-Hebrew stories of the Flood and of their counterparts in Greek myths, such as the story of Deucalion. More audacious was his long research on *Dreiheit* — or rather Trinity — published in the *Rheinisches Museum* (1903) and collected in a volume only in 1965. Here three points were important: the Christian notion of Trinity had classic and Indo-European antecedents; the combination of three gods was often the development of a previous combination of two gods; and finally, according to Usener, the number three was a number limit for a primitive mentality and as such it indicated perfection.

A volume which appeared in 1896, *Götternamen,* and an essay on "Mythologie" of 1904 (collected in *Vorträge,* pp. 37–66) gave a central meaning and order to all this quite extraordinary activity. In a sleepless night before lecturing on the subject of *Götternamen* Usener lost his faith in the existence of a primitive monotheism which he had received from his Protestant upbringing. He began to admit the priority of polytheism to monotheism. Whether this really implied an abandonment of the Christian faith I doubt. His attitude to the Christian tradition (as the letter to his pastor brother in dedicating to him the book on Christmas shows) had for a long time been determined by a belief in evolution and purification. That he could find artistic satisfaction in himself creating lives of saints according to ancient models was shown by the short story "Die Flucht vor dem Weibe," which he had published under the pseudonym of E. Schaffner as late as 1894. The fact remains that in his article on mythology of 1904 — a sort of testament — he went out of his way to declare that he expected religious struggles in the near future.

Leaving aside these biographical questions which for me have no clear answer, what Usener was trying to do in *Götternamen* was a presentation (mainly on Greek and Roman materials) of a scheme of the religious evolution of mankind before monotheism. The earliest stage would have been of momentary gods (*Augenblicksgötter*), gods who manifested themselves only once on a certain occasion and derive their names from that occasion. Such, in a typical way, was the god Aius Locutius — the voice which revealed the arrival of the Gauls to the Romans and was never heard again. Max Müller's "disease of the language" as the origin of polytheism became for Usener the human power to perceive and register in words the extrarational elements of experience. For his pious soul, the Word was still the *Logos.* The next stage was still in the same direction: the functional gods, the gods who are perceived repeating the same action in different times and circumstances (*Sondergötter*). Usener found the most convincing model for them in the Roman *indigitamenta,* that is in pontifical books which gave lists of gods who acted only for short periods in the life of an individual or in the context of social life. Varro had apparently made the longest collection of such gods, and the Christian writers, such as Tertullian and St. Augustine, depended on him. The meaning of *indigitamenta* and of gods connected with them was, one is bound to say, not very clear when Usener wrote and did not become clearer later. But Usener thought that this category of *Sondergötter* could be found also in other Indo-European societies. With the help of his colleague Felix Solmsen, Usener gave pride of place to Lithuanian examples, which proved to be the weakest link in his demonstration. Lithuanian specialists like A. Brückner showed later that the Lithuanian examples are often either post-Christian developments or in fact inventions of interested reporters.[36] Usener's third stage was the typically Greek notion of personal gods, such as Zeus or Apollo, who have their unforeseeable ways of being present where we would not expect them, not gods with one trick only, but unfathomable gods.

As I have almost anticipated, apart from the Lithuanian troubles, there were various technical objections to Usener's classification. Georg Wissowa, who took it very seriously, was to show in his essay of 1904 (*Gesammelte Abhandlungen*) that the gods mentioned in the *indigitamenta* were by no means coherent, and some of them looked like learned speculations, not primitive notions. Furthermore the Roman gods, such as Jupiter or Mars, never reached, even under Greek influence, the stage of personal gods as defined by Usener: they remained functional gods, *Sondergötter*. The evolution, at least for Rome, worked badly. Wissowa himself, however, did not deny the value of Usener's classification for a morphology of religion. There are other eminent students of Roman religion, such as Kurt Latte, who have essentially made this classification their own. Indeed there were years in which Usener seemed to be the guiding spirit of the study of religion. The *Archiv für Religionswissenschaft* (founded in 1898) owed much to his inspiration; and so did his pupil and son-in-law Albrecht Dieterich, who seemed to be destined to continue his work but died prematurely in 1908. More in general it is to be noted that Warburg (as Gombrich showed) started from Usener in his interpretation of the mythical language of the arts. The artists, too, had their language to express the actions of the gods. On the basis of Usener and Warburg Ernst Cassirer formulated his discussion of *Sprache und Mythos* in 1925. One can go further and ask how much Gershom Scholem—the disappearance of whom we all deeply regret— owed to Usener in his interpretation of cabalistic language as an effort to verbalize the divine presence. Usener is explicitly mentioned in Walter Benjamin's work and can hardly have been bypassed by Scholem, though I do not remember meeting his name in Scholem's works.

5

Now there are three aspects by which one can approach Usener's work on religion. The first is his relation to W. Dilthey's philosophy. It is commonly believed that Usener depended on his great brother-in-law for his philosophic notions on religion. This common point of view can for instance be found in an essay by Klaus Oehler.[37] It is easy to point out that *Götternamen* is dedicated to the brothers Carl and Wilhelm Dilthey. It would perhaps be more relevant to quote a letter by Usener to Wilamowitz, apropos of this book, in which Usener says that next to his two brothers-in-law he had Wilamowitz in mind in writing it. But it is clear that the juxtaposition of the two brothers Dilthey with the addition of the philologist Wilamowitz rather diminishes the probability of a specific philosophic influence of the philosopher Dilthey on the book. The friendship between Usener and his brothers-in-law, as I have already said, is of course beyond doubt. Thanks to the volume *Der junge Dilthey* by his daughter Clara Misch (1933) we know much of the juvenile friendship between the three men. And we know also the text of the report written by Usener on Wilhelm Dilthey to persuade his colleagues in Bonn to take him as a professor: it is worth reading for what Usener found interesting in the mind of his friend. But if one asks specifically what Dilthey gave to Usener or reciprocally got from him, the answer is not equally clear. For the explicit evidence is almost nonexistent, and the implicit references are not easy to evaluate. Usener and Wilhelm Dilthey seldom referred to each other in their printed works, and only on secondary points. Thus, for instance, Dilthey in his *Einleitung* refers to Usener's paper on the date of Plato's *Phaedrus,* hardly a revolutionary piece. In Usener it is not difficult to find some of Dilthey's favorite terminology: *Erlebnis, Verstehen, Leben,* and so on. Yet, as far as I can see, Usener's conception of religion in its three precise stages and Usener's method of understanding religion through comparative philology (including the use and abuse of etymology) seem alien to Dilthey. The act of discovering gods in words—and therefore the confluence of linguistics and science of religion, in Usener—seem to me outside Dilthey's interests, though I could be wrong. It may be significant that the correspondence between Dilthey and Paul Graf Yorck von Wartenburg which went on from 1877 to 1899 and represents, as is well known, a capital document for Dilthey, is far more interesting for what Yorck has to say about Usener than for what Dilthey says. It is Yorck who seems to be really concerned with Usener and frankly disapproves of what he believes to be his lack of understanding of religion. I am also struck by the fact that recent biographers of Dilthey such as R. A. Makkreel (1975) and H. P. Rickman (1979)—the latter with a chapter on the influence of Dilthey—simply do not mention Usener.

I rather suspect that there was in Usener a streak of Kantian thought partly derived from Gottfried Hermann's well-known reinterpretation of philological categories in Kantian terms. It may have stuck to him through life. It would explain not only Ernst Cassirer's interest in him but also the admiration and sense of indebtedness repeatedly expressed by the neo-Kantian *par excellence*, Paul Natorp. Somehow Usener saw in language the instrument for catching the Kantian world of the *Noumenon*. In his rectoral speech of 1882 on "Philologie und Geschichtswissenschaft," which I have repeatedly mentioned, Usener, in discussing Boeckh and his rival Hermann, had indicated his greater sympathy for Hermann and therefore for his Kantian antecedents. While repudiating the encyclopedic notion of Boeckh, he had accepted the Hermannian notion of philology as the art of interpretation. In fact he had extended it by introducing comparative philology into it and by seeing in the new philology a sort of anthropology. Thus I would suggest that it is worth discussing whether the traditional approach to Usener through Dilthey should not be at least partially replaced by an interpretation of Usener in terms of a modified Kantian problematic about the relation between phenomenon and noumenon.

That leads me to the third and last point. As I have tried to make clear, Usener conceived the purpose of his philology, at least as it appeared to him in the last twenty years of his life, to be that of dissolving the primitive elements still lingering in our civilization. How much of Christianity he was prepared, or at least intended, to save after having eliminated the mythical elements of Christianity remains obscure. He never wrote on this, as far as I know, though the five thousand letters to Usener or from Usener preserved in Bonn may in the future give some indication. He had shown by his extraordinarily intelligent and generous attitude toward Jacob Bernays that he could understand, and approve of, a friend's attachment to his persecuted religious tradition. As Bernays was a philologist like him, it is probable that Usener recognized a common ground of religious experience in their common philology. This would confirm that Usener struggled to find in human language the channel toward the *Noumenon*. Now, in a beautiful and deservedly famous essay of 1884, Usener had presented the systematic organization of science in the schools of Plato and Aristotle as a desirable model for the modern, and especially for the German world (*Vorträge*, pp. 67–102). He wanted the universities and indeed the academies to imitate Plato and Aristotle. His pupil Diels remained faithful to that academic ideal throughout his life. But did the master Usener maintain that position? In 1904 Usener ended his essay on mythology by quoting Scaliger's motto: "Non aliunde dissidia in religione pendent quam ab ignoratione grammaticae" ("Religious disagreements derive from ignorance of grammar"). It was an ambiguous motto, and Usener used it ambiguously. The relation between religion and language was assumed, rather than explained, by Usener. It may well be his problematic bequest to us.

IV: Religious History without Frontiers:
J. Wellhausen, U. Wilamowitz, and E. Schwartz

1

I hope certain elementary data of the history of classical scholarship have not yet been forgotten. In 1884 the classical scholar Ulrich von Wilamowitz-Moellendorff dedicated his *Homerische Untersuchungen* to Julius Wellhausen, the theologian or rather ex-theologian who had been his colleague in the University of Greifswald from 1875 to 1882. Wellhausen had to resign his chair and to start again, no longer as a professor *ordinarius*, but as a professor *extraordinarius* of Semitic languages at Halle, because his theological colleagues at Greifswald had disapproved of his Bible criticism. Later, in 1885, he became again professor *ordinarius* at Marburg, but was still forbidden to give lectures on the Old Testament. Only in 1892 when he rejoined his friend Wilamowitz in Göttingen was he left free to return to the Old Testament in his lectures. Wilamowitz's dedication in 1884 had been more than an act of solidarity with his persecuted colleague. It was a declaration of intent with explicit reference to Herder, Wolf, and Goethe about the common purpose of Homeric and Biblical criticism. If Wellhausen was analyzing the Pentateuch, or rather the Hexateuch, in order to write the history of the Hebrews, Homeric criticism was the first step in the writing of the history of the Greeks. Wilamowitz was convinced that with men like Wellhausen Biblical criticism was more advanced than Homeric criticism.

Wellhausen was not the man to answer with a corresponding programmatic declaration, but when he was in Göttingen he dedicated to Wilamowitz his own *Israelitische und Jüdische Geschichte* in 1894. This work had reached the seventh edition when Wellhausen died in 1918. Ten years later in 1928 Wilamowitz reserved no less than three pages of his autobiography (*Erinnerungen*) to evoke his dead friend. He gave a clear image of how Wellhausen in his early thirties (he was born in 1844) had appeared to him in their common years at Greifswald. The son of a Hanoverian country parson, Wellhausen had lost his faith in Göttingen, while he was a student of H. G. A. Ewald, but had preserved the simple piety and habits of a peasant and had stuck to his work during years in which his wife was mentally ill and his colleagues had declared him unwelcome. Wilamowitz prints for the occasion a poem which he had sent to Wellhausen for Christmas, probably in 1879, to accompany a copy of the translation of some *Odi barbare* by Carducci which he, Wilamowitz, and Mommsen had translated into German. At that time Carducci was the anticlerical poet par excellence of the new Italy: his poems tried their best to look pagan. Wilamowitz improved on Carducci in his own poem for Wellhausen: "Wir Atheisten? Monotheismus nur ist Atheismus. . . . Kein Gott lebt ewig," and so on. Wilamowitz must have felt that on that occasion he had not really been speaking for Wellhausen, because he adds that Wellhausen always remained Christian and had invoked Christ at every midday meal. To make the picture even more complex, in the same page Wilamowitz criticized Wellhausen's last period of scholarly activity which, as we know, was dominated by his New Testament studies. Wilamowitz not only disapproves of his friend's analysis of the New Testament but regrets that he had departed from his previous conception of Jesus' personality. "Das kann ich nicht billigen." Wilamowitz even suspects that Wellhausen had become more skeptical about Jesus because he was affected in his judgment by the infirmities of his old age. Though written or at least published in 1928, these pages of the *Erinnerungen* were not Wilamowitz's last words on Wellhausen. In his latest and half-posthumous book *Der Glaube der Hellenen*, Wilamowitz was not to forget Wellhausen. He makes it evident that he still shared Wellhausen's conviction that historical analysis of a religion presupposes a nondogmatic, non-confessional sense of faith, of "Glaube."

The friendship between Wilamowitz and Wellhausen is not an isolated episode. When Wellhausen died, the man whom the Academy of Göttingen chose to speak about him was another classical scholar, Eduard Schwartz, a pupil of Wilamowitz who had long been recognized as his peer. The speech, which we can read in the first volume of Schwartz's *Gesammelte Schriften* (which were published in 1938, when Schwartz was still alive), is rightly esteemed to be the only reliable biographical sketch of Wellhausen, though it is no more than thirty-five pages long. Eduard Schwartz was also the man who said most of what was worth saying about Usener and Wilamowitz. As Schwartz had been a pupil of Wilamowitz in his Greifswald years, some acquaintance between him and Wellhausen may have existed already in that period; but in his speech on Wellhausen, Schwartz emphasizes that he really got to know Wellhausen only when he himself joined the Göttingen faculty for about seven years between 1902 and 1909. Schwartz, typically, wants us to realize also that, notwithstanding all the cordiality of their relations, he was not Wellhausen's Eckermann. The speech is direct evidence for what could bind a classical scholar to an orientalist who had reacted against his own theological background at the end of the last century. Politics was the first motive for such a friendship. Both Wellhausen and Schwartz (born in 1858) were firm supporters of the German empire of Bismarck. Schwartz takes two pages of his brief account to tell how Wellhausen broke with his beloved teacher Ewald because Ewald—a faithful servant of the Hanoverian dynasty—wanted his pupil to agree that the king of Prussia and Bismarck were "Uebeltäter" and "Schurken" ("malfeasants" and "rascals"). Second, there was the attraction which Schwartz felt toward the country boy who trusted God in his way but preferred Arabic poetry to Christian theology. Schwartz was not, like Wilamowitz, a country gentleman who would easily find something in common with the country parson's son. He belonged to the academic intelligentsia and had family connections involving famous names in German universities. All the same, Wellhausen symbolized for him what was sound and honest in Germany. And as he himself was fighting for the abolition of any distinction between ecclesiastical and political history, he felt he had found his model in the historian who (to repeat Schwartz's words) "had pulled down the barrier which already in antiquity Jewish and Christian apologetic had built up between sacred and profane history." Schwartz was in fact toning down Wellhausen's provocative sentence in the *Prolegomena* (1883, p. 256): "Je näher die Geschichtsschreibung ihrem Ursprung ist, desto profaner ist sie" ("The nearer history is to its own origins, the more profane it is"). We shall see later on that this antitheological reaction, in the case of both Wilamowitz and Schwartz, cannot be separated from their analytical approach to the texts. When in Göttingen, Schwartz and Wellhausen worked together on the fourth Gospel and published their results separately. Schwartz applied the same type of analysis to Thucydides ten years later. The fact that evidently Schwartz was far more favorably impressed by Wellhausen's approach to the New Testament than Wilamowitz was has its counterpart in the conflict between Wilamowitz and Schwartz about the proper way of analyzing the *Odyssey*. There were disagreements on details within the basic agreement among the three scholars that source analysis was the foundation of history. Meanwhile theology was exorcised by the formula that there was no difference between analyzing the fourth Gospel and analyzing Thucydides (or the *Odyssey*).

There are perhaps a few remarks more to be made on Wellhausen before we return to Wilamowitz and Schwartz. As I have said, there is no good biography of him, as far as I know, apart from Schwartz's essay. There are, however, two characteristic portraits by the Arabist Carl Heinrich Becker in *Islam* (9, 1918), and by the Jewish philosopher Hermann Cohen, who had been a colleague of Wellhausen in Marburg.[38] But perhaps the most stimulating discussion is a Marburg dissertation of 1938 by a man about whom I know nothing, Fr. Boschwitz, *Julius Wellhausen: Motive und Massstäbe seiner Geschichtsschreibung*.[39]

Taken by themselves, Wellhausen's analytical contributions to the Old Testament are, as we all know, by no means revolutionary: he said with more clarity, precision, and authority what others had said before. But he was an historian of rare power. Having satisfied himself that the priestly source of the Pentateuch was postexilic, he made this date the criterion for separating a preexilic Hebrew or Israelite nation which was free, quarrelsome, aggressive, and almost joyful in the daring of its imagination from the uncreative Jewish temple-state which had given up wars and lived meekly under foreign rule. The country lad, Julius Wellhausen, was also, as we have seen, an admirer of Bismarck. Alas, there had obviously been no Bismarck in the Jerusalem of the fourth or third century B.C. to teach a lesson to the Persians or to the Macedonians. But what splendid warriors the old Hebrews had been! "War is what makes nations," said Wellhausen, and added that war was the chief department of Yahweh's activity, as long as Israel remained a nation (*Isr.-jüd. Gesch.*, p. 26). Wellhausen loved the Book of Judges perhaps more than any other book of the Bible, because it was so fresh, so full of wars and war songs and fanatical generals and even fanatical female generals. What Wellhausen could not quite understand, and therefore had to explain with complicated redactional theories, was that the patriarchs were such a peaceful trio. Herder had already noticed that Abraham was no warrior (many of Wellhausen's remarks have roots in Herder), but he had thought that a "hero of the faith" had to be excused.[40] For Wellhausen there was no such easy consolation. He was even dissatisfied with those prophets who tried to separate the responsibility of the children from those of the fathers. "The most certain of all historical experiences," exclaimed Wellhausen, "is that the children must pay for the sins of the fathers."[41] And he added: "History does not take into account either good will or even persons, but only facts"—which seems to me Hegelian enough.[42] Therefore Wellhausen loved Amos among all the prophets because he had no delusion about individual responsibility: he made all the nation responsible for the sins of the individuals. Amos, the country lad among the prophets, became the ideal prophet among the German professors, to be compared with Hesiod by Wilamowitz. Wellhausen, who had of course little love to spare for the theological prophet Ezekiel, had a soft spot also for Elijah: "Maxime me delectebat a tenera pueritia quod de Elia propheta narrat Scriptura" ("Since my childhood I have found delight in what the Scripture tells about Elijah"); this Wellhausen wrote in a self-presentation in Latin at the age of twenty-four quoted by Schwartz.

More precisely, what Wellhausen liked in the Israel of old was the coexistence with the adventurers themselves of rude harsh prophets who tried to teach morality to a nation of adventurers who enjoyed life, conquered territories, built up harems, and passed into history under the respected names of Saul, Solomon, Achab, and maybe David. What moved Wellhausen toward Arab history, the second field of his exploration, was the feeling that he would find there again what he had liked in old Israel. And indeed he found the conflict between the austerity of the Bedouins and the lust of the city dwellers, and within the Bedouins the mysterious coexistence of the prophet and the warrior. In his book on Wakidi[43] Wellhausen said that he had gone to Islam to see what the Hebrews looked like when they entered history. This is too narrow a definition of what moved Wellhausen. In the decent obscurity of the English language, Wellhausen was perhaps more true to himself when he wrote (in the article on Mohammed for the ninth edition of the *Encyclopedia Britannica*): "The Koran is Mohammed's weakest performance. The weight of his historical performance lies in his work in Medina and not in that at Mecca. . . . The founding of the State upon the feeling of fellowship generated by religion was without question the prophet's greatest achievement" (pp. 561, 554). The combination which attracted Wellhausen was that of religious and political forces, both in their collaboration and in their conflicts. Wellhausen enormously admired the early Ummayads, who were capable of turning the Bedouins "zu räsonablen Staatsbürgern."[44] By the same token, he was full of sympathy for that half-Arab Herod the Great of Judaea who almost managed to turn the Jews into reasonable citizens. But this for Wellhausen was only one aspect of Islamic history. The other aspect equally claimed his sympathy—the side, say, of the Charijites, who opposed what Wellhausen called the "schlechte Katholizität" of official Islam and remained intolerant, utopistic, and unable to accept the dynastic principle. Some of Wellhausen's most forceful pages are those of his description of Bedouin morality. Later he was to declare his sympathy for the Boers of South Africa, notwithstanding his recognition of the advantages of Pax Britannica. He liked prophets and rebels; what he did not like was the triumph of rabbis and priests, the elimination of contrasts between worldly politicians and religious warriors. Above all he did not like, whether in Judaism or early Christianity or modern Germany, the respectability of theologians in control.

If he was glad to be able to prove (or rather to confirm) that Genesis, chapters 2–3 is much older than Genesis, chapter 1, it was because the story of the earthly paradise was delightfully primitive and irrational and showed utter contempt for any cosmological speculation (*Prolegomena*, p. 319). He saw in the older account a healthy pessimism about civilization. It is unnecessary to add that Max Weber, who had great admiration for Wellhausen, made much of Wellhausen's picture his own; but one may well ask how much of Wellhausen passed into Nietzsche, who liked the more primitive Israel better than the later ecclesiastical version leading toward Christianity.

Wellhausen however was not prepared to go as far as Nietzsche, whom he knew well. He felt that he was the heir not of Jewish national ethics, but of Jewish universalism. He had to explain why the late Judaism he disliked as being priestly and unpatriotic had produced the successful rebellion of the Maccabees against the Macedonians and the disastrous, but heroic, rebellions against the Romans. He had also to say in plain words how Jesus stood in relation to late Judaism. These questions had already presented themselves to young Wellhausen when he wrote his book on Sadducees and Pharisees (1874) and interpreted the Psalms of Solomon as a pharisaic text. The problem became more pressing when he wrote his *Israelitische und Jüdische Geschichte* and had to be faced for the third time when in 1906 he found himself in an embarrassing company of theologians, having to write the first chapter of the volume of the *Kultur der Gegenwart* dealing with Christianity. Wellhausen knew the Books on the Maccabees and Flavius Josephus better than anybody else. Even now his account of the political situation in Judaea under Greeks and Romans has few rivals, but he had difficulties in correlating political and religious development. By identifying the Sadducees with the party of the Hasmonaeans and the Pharisees with the supporters of theocracy, he had left himself little to account for the apocalyptic and revolutionary activities of the Pharisees. On the other hand he presented Jesus as a preacher of natural morality, who neither founded a Church nor prepared his disciples for the final judgment. He concluded: "The Gospel preaches the noblest individualism, the liberty of the sons of God." Later his studies on the texts of the Gospels made him skeptical about the possibility of knowing Jesus as a person. He added a note to the sixth edition of his *Israelitische und Jüdische Geschichte* to warn the reader that he was no longer satisfied with his chapter on the origins of Christianity, but he did not modify the text.

The prestige which Wellhausen gained among some of the greatest classical scholars of his time is therefore to be connected with two delicate aspects of the cultural situation in Germany. The first was the conflict which existed between the representatives of dogmatic points of view and the representatives of a secularized culture who understood little, and appreciated even less, confessional orthodoxy. The second aspect is less obvious and perhaps more interesting. Some of the most eminent representatives of the secularized culture were not prepared to forget religion. They were anxious to declare some religious faith. If they were classicists, they were also trying to reevaluate the old religious tenets of the Greeks and Romans, especially of the Greeks, who, as we all know, were the Germans of antiquity. The question of the place of classical education in the modern world had many aspects which cannot be simplified; but one important tendency, which could claim the support of Goethe and Humboldt, was in favor of upgrading Greek religious thought, especially in the tragic poets and in the philosophers. Paganism at its best was not considered to be incompatible with Christianity at its best: in fact it could even help to make Christianity better. Paganism might enrich the sense of the Deity by being many-sided. Apollo, Dionysus, Aphrodite, and even that colonial hero Heracles might exemplify divine manifestations especially to Protestant minds who had no saints to turn to.

I have not the time to deal here with the reaction of the theologians to such a position. But I may perhaps indicate one text which has become accessible only in the last few years and is impressive both for the man who wrote it and for the moment in which he wrote it. Wilhelm Bousset, one of the leaders of the "Religionsgeschichtliche Schule," gave a speech on "Religion und Theologie" in the University of Giessen, in which he was a professor, on 20 June 1919, the very day on which a German government resigned rather than sign the treaty of Versailles (the treaty was signed eight days later by another government).[45] It is dominated by the conviction that a society without a theology divides itself into sects and cannot withstand foreign pressures. There is only one allusion to Wellhausen, to remind us that he used to call New Testament scholars rather contemptuously "homines unius libri." It is obvious that Bousset, who had been in the precarious position of a professor *extraordinarius* in Göttingen for twenty years, from 1896 to 1916, in Wellhausen's days, did not like him﹦

2

It was no accident that Wilamowitz got into trouble with Nietzsche very early. Throughout his long life he was involved in the business of keeping his classicism within an undogmatic, vaguely Christian religious tradition. The man who ended his career at eighty-two with a book on the faith of the Greeks had started to write about Greek religion sixty years before. He was probably no more certain of his own beliefs when he was eighty than he had been when he was twenty-five. He only knew he could not consider himself a Christian in any serious sense. In the strange short Latin autobiography he composed in his last years, he admitted as much: "Christiana cor meum numquam intravere." He had intended to tell us what he thought about the transition from Hellenism to Christianity in his *Glaube der Hellenen,* but he died before he reached that point. Some notes he left may indicate that he would have ended with a Christian Platonism. But we simply do not know enough. If there was a secret, he took it with him to his grave.

Wilamowitz's problems had one aspect in common with those of his teachers Otto Jahn and Usener. He had inherited their openness to all aspects of philology and had to reconcile this unbounded intellectual curiosity for anything Greek with a concentration on specific values. If Usener liked the traditional *Variae lectiones,* Wilamowitz created a German variety of them for himself in his celebrated *Lesefrüchte.* Any new text which was published would be immediately read by him and if necessary commented upon at length. His reaction to the new publication of the British Museum papyrus of Aristotle's *Constitution of Athens* soon amounted to two thick volumes which were ready in less than two years, in 1893. Eduard Fraenkel liked to recall that one day Wilamowitz arrived at his seminar or lecture with the announcement that he would change the subject for the meeting. On the previous day he had received the new text of Menander's *Epitrepontes* and, having spent the night on it, he was now ready to discuss the new find. Much of his paper on the *Epitrepontes* (in *Sitz. Preuss. Akad.,* 1907) was already there. Never more than in Wilamowitz did the art of interpreting any text clash with the requirement of keeping to the essentials.

But Wilamowitz also had another role to play which Usener had been spared—that of the Prussian Junker.

Ulrich Friedrich Wichard von Wilamowitz-Moellendorff was born at Markowitz in Eastern Prussia on 22 December 1848. The estate of Markowitz, which is now in Poland, had been bought by Wilamowitz's father only in 1836, six years after the Polish rebellion of 1830. The purchase had been an episode of the Prussianization of the region, which, acquired in 1772 and lost under Napoleon, was still troublesome in 1848. In his autobiography, Wilamowitz speaks little of his father, more of his mother—a von Calbo, a family closely connected with the court of Friedrich II—and even more of his father's sister Emma von Schwanenfeld, who lived in great style in the neighborhood. Further back there was grandfather von Wilamowitz who had got his *Pour le mérite* on the field of Eylau (1807) and previously gained the friendship of another soldier, the distant relative Field Marshal Wichard Joachim Heinrich von Moellendorff. The field marshal adopted the sons of his friend and left them his glorious name and a fund for their education. Thus not only was the Markowitz estate new, the resounding combination von Wilamowitz-Moellendorff was also fairly recent. The combination obviously helped: a brother of Wilamowitz senior was made a *Graf* and apparently was the first Prussian to win the Derby; an elder brother of our classical scholar was the governor of their region for many years; and ultimately the family came to be associated, through a Swedish marriage, with a different type of warrior, Field Marshal Hermann Göring. The Wilamowitz family was committed to its Prussian mission of keeping the Slavs in order. Wilamowitz's schooling at Schulpforta—an excellent establishment for the ruling class—was a part of this Junker tradition. At Schulpforta there were, however, strange teachers and even stranger pupils. One of the teachers was Wilhelm Corssen, a comparative philologist who would have honored any university but for his drinking habits; and among the pupils there was, four years older, Friedrich Nietzsche.

Wilamowitz came out of the school in 1867 with unorthodox penchants. He cared for philology and (as he proved in the war of 1870–71) he preferred the grenadier corps to the cavalry of his fathers. The father never forgave this; it was worse that in 1876 his son would marry the daughter of a bourgeois professor of dubious political opinions called Theodor Mommsen. There was in fact something like a decade in Wilamowitz's life in which he might appear to have left the Junkers for good. Whoever reads the extremely emotional dedication to Mommsen of Wilamowitz's first book, the *Analecta Euripidaea* (1875), realizes that it was written by a man at a turning point in his life. These were also the years of the polemics with Nietzsche (1872–73) and Nietzsche's friend and ally E. Rohde: Wilamowitz

later extended his attacks to Jacob Burckhardt. Part of our difficulty in
understanding what Wilamowitz had to say against Nietzsche, Rohde, and
Burckhardt is that Wilamowitz himself soon abandoned the premise from
which his polemics derived sense. He attacked Nietzsche and Co. in the
name of bourgeois rationality: he declared himself disgusted by the pessimism, the irrationalism, and the hostility to Euripides and Socrates
expressed by Nietzsche. But he soon returned to the world of aristocratic
values in which he was born and to which Nietzsche was nearer than
Mommsen. In fact he became rather rapidly estranged from Mommsen and
could never quite explain (for instance in his speech of admission to the
Berlin Academy) why he had been so violent against Nietzsche and Rohde.
The inequality of races, the inequality of individuals, the cult of the
aristocratic values of early Greek society are recurring motifs in all the
major works by Wilamowitz, from *Euripides' Herakles* (1889) to the masterpiece of 1910, *Staat und Gesellschaft der Griechen,* and to the extraordinary
series of works of his old age, *Aeschylus-Interpretationen* (1914), *Platon* (1919),
Pindaros (1921), *Glaube der Hellenen.* Although in an earlier academic speech
of the Greifswald days, he had committed himself to some imprudent
comparison between Prussian imperialism and Periclean democracy ("Von
des attischen Reiches Herrlichkeit"), he never went back later to Athenian
democracy. In 1889 Heracles was the incarnation of a Dorian ideal (with
an implicit identification of Dorians and Prussians). Later—more than
once—Pindar was presented as the poet of a warring and refined aristocracy such as Wilamowitz wanted the Prussian aristocracy to be. His Plato
is not a master of metaphysical ideas, but a spiritual leader to his own
nation. Altogether his Greek gods are aristocratic not only because they are
more interested in the select few than in the many, but because their
behavior has the most characteristic feature of aristocratic behavior—
unaccountableness.

This is not enough, of course, to put Wilamowitz on the same level
as Nietzsche, but it raises the question why the two main clashes in
Wilamowitz's intellectual life were first with Nietzsche and then with Stefan
George, with both of whom he had much in common. Wilamowitz did not
like Stefan George and made parodies of his poems. He was repaid by corresponding dislike. One of the members of Stefan George's inner circle,
Kurt Hildebrandt, attacked Wilamowitz violently and at length in the *Jahrbuch für die geistige Bewegung* of 1910. It was generally felt in that circle that
Wilamowitz was still too bourgeois in his tastes, too insensitive to the Middle Ages and to the finer points of Platonic society. The George-Kreis
wanted Plato for themselves (as a book by the same Hildebrandt shows) and
found Wilamowitz's version of Plato too pedestrian. Yet behind the lines
the contacts between the two schools were important and productive.

Wilamowitz's pupil Paul Friedänder, himself a Platonic scholar, was also a disciple of Stefan George. Whether we can call Karl Reinhardt, one of the greatest and most original pupils of Wilamowitz, a member of the George-Kreis is perhaps a question of semantics. The influence of George on him is recognizable and frankly admitted. But even such an apparently prosaic philologist as Eduard Fraenkel never repudiated, indeed gladly confirmed in old age, his juvenile admiration for Friedrich Gundolf. It may well be that what separated Wilamowitz from Nietzsche and Stefan George was the doubts of the latter about the politics of Prussia. After 1919 Nietzsche's disciples, Stefan George's disciples, and Wilamowitz's disciples had in common their dislike of social democracy; but it was perhaps too late, at least for Wilamowitz, if not for his pupils, to make peace with the heirs of Nietzsche and the followers of George.

We are in danger of being unjust to the achievements of Wilamowitz if we give too much attention to those more fashionable aspects of his intellectual activity. He was an exceptionally competent interpreter of texts —and little escaped his notice. He had learned from Usener, Wellhausen, and Mommsen to respect individual situations. His repudiation of theology favored his appreciation of variety and experiment in the Greek world. Whether he studied political institutions or religious cults, he had a keen perception of the structure of such institutions and cults. His program of thinking Greek life in Greek terms gave him the advantage of excluding anachronistic interpretations of political performances or religious rituals. It helped him to recognize that much of what we call the Greek Olympos was not Indo-European by origin. He took Apollo to be a foreign god the Greeks had found in Asia and recognized as being too dangerous not to be worshiped. Wilamowitz smiled at the two opposite suggestions by K. O. Müller that Apollo was a Dorian god and by E. Meyer that he was Ionian. In a preliminary discussion of the development of Greek religion which he wrote in 1904 and published in his *Reden und Vorträge*, he played with the notion that Homer had given his gods the features of a human society and had therefore eliminated their truly divine features. By the time he came to write his final book on the faith of the Greeks, he had abandoned this position, which was indeed impossible to defend, but made extremely shrewd remarks about the power a Greek poet had *not* to tell the truth about anything, including gods (I, p. 333).

No doubt Wilamowitz could never escape the dilemma in which he had placed himself by isolating the Greeks and at the same time pretending that they were the models for modern Europe or at least for modern Germany. But the reader of his books, unless I am grossly mistaken, is far more interested in learning what Apollo *was* in Athens or Sparta than in being told what is the value of Apollo for modern Europe.

3

Less ambitious in his religious rhetoric, Eduard Schwartz had perhaps, as I have already hinted, a more direct purpose in associating himself with Julius Wellhausen. His purpose was to eliminate ecclesiastical history not as a literary genre of the past, but as a valid category for thinking about historical facts in the twentieth century. As an editor of the *Ecclesiastical History* by Eusebius, he knew more than anybody else about ecclesiastical historiography. The knowledge made his feeling that it should be eliminated from twentieth-century historical writing all the more urgent. With Schwartz we have come full circle. He had been a pupil of both Usener and Wilamowitz, and had been the colleague of Wellhausen in Göttingen. He never said a word which was not of love and admiration for his three masters. The only time he came near to alluding to some of the difficulties he must have had with Wilamowitz was in a letter to Otto Kern, who wanted to make himself a biographer of Wilamowitz.[46] He was a faithful man, though capable of devastating criticism. His critique of Fritz Taeger's book on Thucydides in *Gnomon* (1926) may be an example. Perhaps because he was so faithful and so predictable in his reactions, one hears little about him. Wilamowitz was a legend in his own time. Friends of mine who were Schwartz's lifelong friends — such as Giorgio Pasquali, technically his pupil, Plinio Fraccaro, Norman Baynes, and Rudolf Pfeiffer, his colleague in Munich — had nothing to say about him except that they liked him.

As I have already mentioned, Schwartz, who was born in 1858 and died in 1940, belonged to an academic family on both sides: his father was an eminent professor of the medical faculty of Göttingen, his maternal uncle Adolf Michaelis was a famous archaeologist, Otto Jahn and J. G. Droysen were among his relatives. Mommsen was a family friend, and Mommsen was prepared to collaborate with Schwartz in his edition of Eusebius by collating the Latin translation of Rufinus and adding his own edition of Rufinus's supplement to Eusebius. As a true pupil of Usener and Wilamowitz, Schwartz was first and foremost an interpreter and editor of texts. He was perhaps less catholic in his tastes than his teachers, though I am not sure of this. His first great edition was of the scholia on Euripides, to be followed by editions of two Christian apologists, Tatianus's *Oratio ad Graecos* and Athenagoras. Then for many years, until 1909, he was busy with his monumental edition of Eusebius's *Historia ecclesiastica;* however, this was also the period in which he wrote articles in alphabetical order about major Greek historians in Pauly-Wissowa. From *A* to *E* a succession of masterful monographs appeared, including Apollodorus, Appianus, Arrianus, Chronicon Paschale, Diodorus, Dio Cassius, Diogenes Laertius, Dionysius of Halicarnassus, Ephorus, and Eusebius. He added as a bonus a wonderful article on the Latin Curtius Rufus. After the letter *E* he passed on the task to another pupil of Wilamowitz, Felix Jacoby, who less concisely,

but no less originally and competently, reached the end of the letter *K*.
Schwartz had already contributed essays on Xenophon (1889), Callisthenes
(1900), Timaeus (1899), and a basic book on the Greek novel in relation to
Greek historiography (1896). Later, in 1919, he published his famous volume on Thucydides, to be followed by two general papers on Greek historiography in 1920 and 1928. He simply dominated the whole field of ancient
historiography.

Meanwhile he had found something even more difficult to do as an
editor of texts. He began to prepare the edition of the Acts of the Ecumenical Councils. This implied editing Syriac texts, which he translated
into Greek in order to reconstruct the original form and incidentally to
make the texts accessible to more mortal men. For the same work he had
also to master Armenian, and he added Arabic to please both himself and
Wellhausen. Being interested in Homer, he amused himself in the intervals by editing both the *Iliad* and the *Odyssey* (1923; 1924) in luxury editions
with independence of judgment and some original results. It was probably
to get a little extra amusement that in 1933 he made an edition of the poem
Aetna attributed to Virgil, with provocative emendations. Though he edited
less of the Concilia than he had planned, he still managed before dying to
give what is perhaps the first critical edition of Justinian's dogmatic writings
and what is certainly the first critical edition of the sixth-century biographies of Palestinian monks by Kyrillos of Skythopolis. The edition of
Kyrillos alone would be enough for the reputation of another scholar.

In Greek literature he interpreted extensively Homer, Hesiod, Tyrtaeus,
Demosthenes, and Theocritus; he wrote also on the Roman annalists and on
Sallust. Finding pleasure in sketches, he published two volumes of literary
portraits of ancient men (*Charakterköpfe*), while reserving modern portraits
for the first volume of his *Gesammelte Schriften*. He gave lectures on ancient
ethics in 1906 and returned to the subject in 1933–34: the posthumous volume of 1951, *Ethik der Griechen*, is a remarkable collection of these lectures.
I have already mentioned that he was persuaded by Wellhausen to work on
the Gospels, especially on the fourth Gospel. But I have not yet mentioned
the two subjects in which he had no rival: the study of ancient chronology
and of ecclesiastical politics. He continued the best side of Usener in his
work on chronology and reached brilliance in the work in 1905 on the calculation of Easter, which is a capital contribution to the study of the relations between Judaism and Christianity, or rather of their separation. The
research on ecclesiastical politics includes an influential little book on Constantine and the Christian Church first published in 1913 (and modified in
numerous later editions), seven studies on Athanasius, and studies on
Justinian's religious politics.

Schwartz cannot be appreciated without giving due attention to the
difficulty and novelty of the technical tasks he imposed upon himself in his

work. His combination of competence, intelligence, and simple tenacity is exceptional even in a world of scholarship which included patient geniuses like A. von Harnack, Felix Jacoby, and, I would add, Eduard Meyer. A German he was, and he did not want to be anything else. He took cosmopolitanism and individualism into account as historical forces and even lectured about them. They were phenomena of ages of decadence which an historian had to consider. But he liked the aristocratic ethics of archaic Greece. His lectures on ethics are indispensable for the understanding of his character. He was most happy at the University of Strasbourg between 1897 and 1902 and then again between 1913 and 1918 because he was there to represent German culture in what he knew to be an alien environment. He had no illusion about the feelings of the inhabitants of Strasbourg. He wrote a report on Alsace in 1916[47] and gave a public lecture on the same subject in 1929 in a very different situation. He was not to change his mind. In 1916 or 1917 he had proposed the annexation of the Alsace to Prussia as the only remedy for the failure of the politics of assimilation: the idea that one could derive another consequence from that failure never passed through his mind. Consequently he despised the Weimar Republic. He was proud that two of his sons had died in the First World War and that a third had returned maimed. He himself had to run away from Strasbourg in 1918 and found a new place with some difficulty in the University of Munich. But he did not like the look of the Nazis either. Kurt von Fritz, one of the few non-Jews who left Nazi Germany in protest, was his pupil.

As a believer in the notions of honor and courage of archaic Greece, he perhaps disliked Christianity. But his dislike was not conspicuous and cannot have been simple. Religion was to him a political force of the highest order. It organized people with unsurpassed efficiency. Schwartz finally found new territory to explore in the ecclesiastical rivalries of the Roman Empire from the fourth to the sixth century. That gave him a dimension which Wilamowitz had lacked and made him independent of his formidable teacher. On the other hand, he had now a border in common with the theologians, and he enjoyed fighting on that border. His thesis was that ecclesiastical politics was politics. To him ecclesiastical history had ceased being a separate entity. He considered the genre of ecclesiastical history— and its teaching in theological faculties—a survival which was no longer justified.

As one might have expected, it was precisely Harnack, who, having already fought against Usener and Wellhausen, took up the cudgels against Schwartz in defense of theology. In 1908 Harnack tried to prove in a communication to the Berlin Academy that, in publishing a Syriac document of a synod of Antioch of 324, Schwartz had been the victim of a forgery: one of the implications was that Schwartz, as a classical scholar, had no business to meddle with Syriac texts. The answer published in the same year by Schwartz[48] was devastating: the classical scholar had beaten the theologian in the theologian's chosen field. As one of the last pages of the reply shows, Schwartz was in no doubt about what was involved. The rather inept editors of Schwartz's *Gesammelte Schriften* thought it unnecessary to republish this piece because it was only polemical. There is room for an intelligent supplement to Schwartz's *Gesammelte Schriften*.

It was not by chance that Schwartz had chosen to explore Athanasius's fights in the fourth century and Justinian's ideologies in the sixth. Athanasius represented the effort of the Church to fight against state control. Justinian represented state control in full regalia. But the mere fact of treating the Ecumenical Councils as great parliamentary reports on political issues was then, and remains now full of polemical implications. Schwartz had the defects of his own qualities. He was not interested in doctrinal systems as such. Origen, the Cappadocian fathers, and St. Augustine interested him only marginally. What made him such a good historian of the late Roman Empire may have reduced his feeling for primitive Christanity. He himself sensed later that by destroying the unity and coherence of the Fourth Gospel he had not advanced the understanding of the early Church.

A point of method was involved there which no a priori ruling will ever settle. Like Wilamowitz and like Wellhausen, Schwartz relied on a highly sophisticated method of text analysis. The analysis was to indicate contradictions, incongruities, inconsequences, differences of style: it would, in short, provide the means for reconstructing the history of a text and for discovering its sources, if any. It might lead to the conclusion that successive authors had contributed to the formation of a text or it might tell the story of one author drafting and redrafting his own text. Schwartz had had the experience of editing a text, such as Eusebius's *Ecclesiastical History*, which was the classic example of successive editions or drafts by the same author. There are few today who would not accept the theoretical validity of the analytical method, but it is more difficult to agree on its proper use. In practice we observe an extraordinary variety of personal attitudes in using it — and trusting it. Schwartz was perhaps the boldest of the great classical scholars of his time in its use, so bold that even Wilamowitz recoiled. When Schwartz published his book on the *Odyssey* in 1924, Wilamowitz paid him the compliment of replying with another book in 1927. Schwartz was prepared to identify several good poets behind the mediocre compilation of the present *Odyssey*. Old Wilamowitz disliked the whole idea of fabricating poetical individualities by analysis (though he had indulged in that game in his younger years). Schwartz's analysis of Thucydides had similar features. Schwartz thought that analysis would make it possible to recognize where

Thucydides had changed his mind and, even more, where a posthumous editor had intervened to complete the text. Here Wilamowitz was perhaps more sympathetic, but even so had to express disagreement with some of Schwartz's results. It is equally instructive to see how Schwartz and Felix Jacoby disagreed on the analysis both of historical and of poetic texts, though they were in basic agreement about method. The whole of Jacoby's work on historiography is dominated by his suspicion of Schwartz's bold solutions.

Men like Wellhausen, Usener, Wilamowitz, and Schwartz—and we can now add Felix Jacoby—found common presuppositions in a philological method which relied on the instrument of text analysis and avoided any theological or dogmatic interference. Wellhausen became a hero to Wilamowitz and Schwartz because he showed them that the same method was legitimate both on sacred and profane texts. Wellhausen also confirmed them in what they had already learned from Usener: that repudiation of theological presuppositions did not mean absence of religious emotions. But Wellhausen, Wilamowitz, and Schwartz had in common political emotions which were alien to the contemplative Usener.

It is not my intention to take my story beyond this point. Though Schwartz never repeated himself and was active until he died in 1940, he was by then an isolated man. Yet the history of the early Church was never to look the same after his intervention.

Bibliographical Notes

"Niebuhr and the Agrarian Problems of Rome": The main sources for Niebuhr's life are *Lebensnachrichten über B. G. Niebuhr*, 3 vols. (Hamburg, 1838–39), which were edited by D. Hensler. On their reliability, E. Rosenstock, *Hist. Zeitschrift*, 110 (1913), pp. 566–73. The edition of the letters, *Die Briefe Barthold Georg Niebuhrs*, 2 vols. (Berlin, 1926–29), does not go beyond 1816. *Cf.* also Barthold Georg Niebuhr, *Briefe und Schriften*, ed. L. Lorenz (Berlin, 1920); *Politische Schriften*, ed. G. Küntzel (Frankfurt, 1923).

The biography by B. C. Witte, *Der preussische Tacitus* (Düsseldorf, 1979), provides an extensive, but not very reliable, bibliography. *Cf.* especially, among recent works: E. Kornemann, "Niebuhr und der Aufbau der altrömischen Geschichte," *Hist. Zeitschrift*, 145 (1932), pp. 277–300; A. Heuss, "Niebuhr und Mommsen," *Antike und Abendland*, 14 (1968), pp. 1–18; K. Christ, "Römische Geschichte und Universalgeschichte bei B. G. Niebuhr," *Saeculum*, 19 (1968), pp. 172–96; S. Rytkönen, *B. G. Niebuhr als Politiker und Historiker* (Helsinki, 1968); J. Straub, "Barthold Georg Niebuhr," in *Bonner Gelehrte* (Bonn, 1968), pp. 49–78; S. Mazzarino, "Machiavelli, Niebuhr e gli Annali," *De Homine*, 41 (1973), pp. 23–36; K. Christ, *Von Gibbon zu Rostovtzeff* (Darmstadt, 1972), pp. 26–49; Z. Yavetz, "Why Rome? Zeitgeist and Ancient Historians in Early 19th Century Germany," *Am. Journal of Philology*, 97 (1976), pp. 276–96; R. Minuti, "Proprietà della terra e despotismo orientale," *Materiali per una storia della cultura giuridica*, 8, 2 (1978), pp. 29–177; A. Momigliano, "Alle origini dell'interesse su Roma arcaica: Niebuhr e l'India," *Riv. St. It.*, 92 (1980), pp. 561–71; A. Heuss, "Barthold Georg Niebuhrs wissenschaftliche Anfänge," *Abh. Akad. Wiss. Göttingen*, Phil. Hist. Klasse, III, 114 (1981).

"From Mommsen to Max Weber": On H. S. Maine see J. W. Burrow, *Evolution and Society* (Cambridge, 1966), and also his contribution to *Ideas and Institutions of Victorian Britain*, ed. R. Robson (London, 1967), pp. 198–304; L. Capogrossi Colognesi, "Sir Henry S. Maine e l'Ancient Law," in *Quaderni Fiorentini per la storia del pensiero giuridico moderno*, 10 (1981), pp. 83–147.

For Fustel de Coulanges it will be enough to refer to the bibliography of my paper now translated in *Essays on Ancient and Modern Historiography* (Oxford, 1977), pp. 325–44 [chap. 11 of the present volume], and to the introduction by myself and S. C. Humphreys to the Johns Hopkins edition of the English translation of the *Cité antique* (Baltimore, 1980).

On P. Bonfante see the unsigned article in *Dizionario biografico degli Italiani*, XII (1970), pp. 7–10.

On M. Weber see my papers in *Sesto contributo* (Rome, 1980), I, pp. 285–312; my introduction to the Italian translation of *Agrarverhältnisse im Altertum* (Rome, 1981); M. I. Finley, "The Ancient City: From Fustel de Coulanges to Max Weber and Beyond," *Comparative Studies in Society and History*, 19 (1977), pp. 305–24; L. Capogrossi Colognesi, "Modelli Romanistici e Germanistici negli studi di storia agraria romana di Max Weber," *Sociologia del Diritto*, 1 (1981), pp. 107–34. Capogrossi has collected a series of his papers in the volume, *La terra in Roma antica* (Rome, 1981). It is of course essential to read A. Meitzen, *Siedelung und Agrarwesen der Westgermanen und Ostgermanen*, I (Berlin, 1895).

On Laveleye see the bibliography in *Nationaal Biografisch Woordenboek*, 9 (Brussels, 1981), pp. 451–63.

"Hermann Usener": The best biographical introduction is given by H. J. Mette in *Lustrum*, 22 (1980), pp. 5–107. Examples of contemporary obituaries are by L. Deubner in Bursian's *Biographisches Jahrbuch für die Altertumswissenschaft*, 31 [141] (1908), pp. 53–74, and by A. Dieterich, *Kleine Schriften* (Leipzig, 1911), pp. 354–62. But the contemporary evaluation of greatest penetration is by E. Schwartz (1906), now in *Gesammelte Schriften*, I (1938), pp. 301–15. The same Schwartz wrote the best evaluation of the relations between Wilamowitz and Usener, apropos of their correspondence published in 1934 (*Ein Briefwechsel*), ibid., pp. 316–25; *cf.* also A. Körte, *Die Antike*, 11 (1935), pp. 211–35. W. M. Calder III has now magistrally added an important document on these relations by publishing Wilamowitz's Latin autobiography in *Antike und Abendland*, 27 (1981), pp. 34–51. An evaluation of

Usener as student of religion was made by C. Clemen in *Studi e Materiali di Storia delle Religioni*, 11 (1935), pp. 110–24. A general account of his life by H. Herter is in the collective *Bonner Gelehrte* (1968), pp. 165–211. Various texts are put together by W. Schmid in *Wesen und Rang der Philologie: Zum Gedenken an H. U. und F. Buecheler* (Stuttgart, 1969).

On the Epicurean studies by Usener, see the account by W. Schmid in *Würzburger Jahrbücher*, 6a (1980), pp. 19–30. For E. Cassirer's later thought on myth, in which Usener almost disappears behind Max Müller, one has of course to turn to *The Myth of the State* (New Haven, 1946). On the evaluation of Usener's interpretation of Roman religion *cf.* the bibliography given by J. Rufus Fears in *Aufstieg und Niedergang der römischen Welt*, 2, 17, 2 (1981), p. 837. It is interesting that Usener does not appear in the very relevant book by M. Detienne, *L'Invention de la mythologie* (Paris, 1981).

"Religious History without Frontiers": On Wellhausen see the bibliography in L. Perlitt (1965) quoted in the text and in D. A. Knight, *Rediscovering the Traditions of Israel* (Missoula, MT, 1975). The few pages by H. Cohen, *Jüdische Schriften*, II (Berlin, 1924), pp. 463–68, are of special interest. *Cf.* H.-J. Kraus, *Geschichte der historisch-kritischen Erforschung des Alten Testaments* (Neukirchen, 1969), pp. 255–74.

On Wilamowitz see my paper in *Riv. St. Ital.*, 84 (1972), pp. 746–55 (reprinted in *Sesto contributo*, I, 1980). There is a *Wilamowitz-Bibliographie* (Berlin, 1929). The most important collection of letters is Mommsen-Wilamowitz, *Briefwechsel 1872–1903* (Berlin, 1935) (on which, W. Jaeger, *Scripta minora*, II [Rome, 1960], pp. 137–47). But also Usener-Wilamowitz, *Ein Briefwechsel 1870–1905* (Leipzig, 1934), on which, besides Schwartz, *cf.* A. Körte, *Die Antike*, 11 (1935), pp. 211–35. W. M. Calder III is just now publishing most valuable letters and other *inedita* by Wilamowitz in a series of articles too long to be listed here. But I must at least mention specifically the two previously unknown biographical sketches published by Calder: one written by Wilamowitz when he was eighteen (in *Greek, Roman and Byzantine Studies*, 12 [1971], pp. 561–78) and the other composed in Latin in his old age (*Antike und Abendland*, 27 [1981], pp. 34–51). Furthermore compare the Wilamowitz family chronicle published by the same Calder in *Quaderni di Storia*, 10 (1979), pp. 197–211. On Wilamowitz *cf.* Schwartz's fundamental papers in *Gesammelte Schriften*, I (Berlin, 1938), pp. 281–382 (also on Wellhausen). Furthermore, G. Pasquali, *Pagine stravaganti*, I (Florence, 1968), pp. 55–92; E. Fraenkel, *Kleine Beiträge zur klassischen Philologie*, II (Rome, 1964), pp. 555–82; R. Pfeiffer, *Ausgewählte Schriften* (Munich, 1960), pp. 269–76; K. Reinhardt, *Vermächtnis der Antike*, 2d ed. (Göttingen, 1966), pp. 361–68; H. Patzer, "Wilamowitz und die klassische Philologie," *Festschrift F. Dornseiff* (Leipzig, 1953), pp. 244–57; V. Poeschl, *Annali della Scuola Normale Superiore di Pisa*, 3d ser., V (1975), pp. 969–83. For Nietzsche and Wilamowitz, M. S. Silk and J. P. Stern, *Nietzsche on Tragedy* (Cambridge,

1981), and H. Lloyd-Jones, *Blood for the Ghosts* (London, 1982), pp. 165–81. For the relations with the George-Kreis, references in my essay on K. Reinhardt in *Annali della Scuola Normale Superiore di Pisa*, 3d ser., V (1975), pp. 1315–16 (now in *Sesto contributo*, 1980 [chap. 12 of the present volume]). For the political activities of Wilamowitz, *cf.* L. Canfora, *Cultura classica e crisi tedesca* (Bari, 1977); and *Intellettuali in Germania* (Bari, 1979).

On Schwartz *cf.* my paper in *Annali della Scuola Normale Superiore di Pisa*, 3d ser., IX (1979), pp. 999–1011 [chap. 13 of the present volume]. The best account is by A. Rehm, "Eduard Schwartz' wissenschaftliches Lebenswerk," *Sitz. Bayer. Akad.* (1942), no. 4. *Cf.* W. Otto, *Hist. Zeitschrift*, 162 (1940), pp. 442–46; R. Pfeiffer, *Ausgewählte Schriften* (Munich, 1960), pp. 8–25, and *Von der Liebe zu Antike* (Munich, 1969), pp. 87–94.

Notes

1. "Alle origini dell'interesse su Roma arcaica: Niebuhr e l'India," *Riv. St. Ital.*, 92 (1980), pp. 561–71.

2. Transl. B. Perrin (Loeb Classical Library).

3. It will be enough to refer to G. Tibiletti's analysis of Plutarch and Appian in *Athenaeum*, 26 (1948), pp. 192–209 and to E. Gabba's commentary on Appian I (Florence, 1958).

4. *Geschichte der sozialen Fragen and des Sozialismus in der antiken Welt*, 3d ed. (Munich, 1925), II, pp. 328–40.

5. F. Lieber, *Reminiscences of an Intercourse with Mr. Niebuhr the Historian* (Philadelphia, 1835), p. 36.

6. Heyne, *Opuscula academica*, IV (Göttingen, 1796), pp. 350–73.

7. *Lebensnachrichten über B. G. Niebuhr*, ed. D. Hensler (Hamburg, 1838–39), I, pp. 246, 257.

8. A. Heuss, "Barthold Georg Niebuhrs wissenschaftliche Anfänge," *Abh. Akad. Wiss. Göttingen*, Phil. Hist. Klasse, III, 14 (1981), p. 551.

9. Sir Henry Maine, *Ancient Law* (Everyman edition, London, 1917), p. 152.

10. Ibid., p. 158.

11. Ibid., p. 159.

12. Ibid., p. 155.

13. Ibid., p. 138.

14. Ibid., p. 139.

15. Maine, *Lectures on the Early History of Institutions* (London, 1874), p. 84.

16. *The Ancient City*, transl. with introd. by A. Momigliano and S. C. Humphreys (Baltimore, 1980), p. 226.

17. Ibid., p. xv.

18. Ibid., p. 280.

19. Ibid., p. 298.

20. *Nouvelles recherches sur quelques problèmes d'histoire* (Paris, 1891), p. 33.

21. Transl. E. H. Warmington (Loeb Classical Library).

22. See for instance Paolo Grossi, *Un altro modo di possedere* (Milan, 1977) and many papers by Luigi Capogrossi-Colognesi collected in his *La Terra in Roma antica* (Rome, 1981).

23. *Scritti giuridici* (Turin, 1918), II, p. 215.

24. Some of the main texts are the volume by De Sanctis, *Per la scienze dell'antichità* (Turin, 1909) and the inaugural lecture by Vincenzo Arangio-Ruiz, *Le genti e le città* (Messina, 1914). Bonfante's latest reply is in *Scritti giuridici*, I (1916), but De Sanctis was still developing his argument when he died in 1957, as is shown in the posthumous *Storia dei Romani*, IV, 2, 2 (1958). For discussion of Bonfante's theories outside Italy, one may for instance refer to E. Rabel, "Die Erbrechtstheorie Bonfante," *Zeitschr. Savigny-Stiftung*, 50 (1930), pp. 295–332.

25. "Zum römischen Bodenrecht," *Hermes*, 27 (1892), pp. 79–117, reprinted in *Gesammelte Schriften*, V (Berlin, 1908), pp. 85–122.

26. Now in *Aufsätze zur Sozial- und Wirtschaftsgeschichte* (Tübingen, 1924), pp. 289–311.

27. This is the text translated into English by R. I. Frank under the strange title *Agrarian Sociology of Ancient Civilizations* (London, 1976).

28. Recently published by W. M. Calder in *Antike und Abendland*, 27 (1981), pp. 34–51.

29. Dieter Wuttke, "Nachwort," in Aby M. Warburg, *Ausgewählte Schriften und Würdigungen*, 2d ed. (Baden-Baden, 1980), p. 623.

30. It is now Kaibel, *Epigrammata graeca* 731.

31. The bibliography is provided by C. Watkins in the Harvard *Indo-European Studies*, IV (1981), pp. 764–99.

32. On this Enrico Campanile of Pisa has written a book, *Ricerche di cultura poetica indoeuropea* (Pisa, 1977), in which Usener is not mentioned; but Campanile evaluates Usener as a student of Indo-European meters in the volume on Usener edited by me (Giardini: Pisa, 1983).

33. "Italische Mythen" (*Rheinisches Museum*, 1875) and "Italische Volksjustiz" (*Rheinisches Museum*, 1901) are reprinted in *Kleine Schriften* (Leipzig, 1912), IV, pp. 93–143, 356–81.

34. In *Theologische Literaturz.*, 19 (1889), pp. 199–212.

35. *Sitz. Berlin Akad.* (1917), reprinted in *Gesammelte Aufsätze*, II (Tübingen, 1928), pp. 123–54.

36. A. Brückner, "Osteuropäische Götternamen," *Zeitschrift für vergleichende Sprachforschung*, 50 (1920), pp. 161–97.

37. "Dilthey und die klassische Philologie," in *Philologie und Hermeneutik im 19. Jahrhundert* (Göttingen, 1979), pp. 181–200.

38. *Jüdische Schriften* II (1924), pp. 463–68.

39. Reprinted by the Wissenschaftliche Buchgesellschaft of Darmstadt in 1968. A later contribution by L. Perlitt, *Vatke und Wellhausen* (Berlin, 1965), usefully, but perhaps not quite soundly, raises doubts about Hegel's influence on Wellhausen.

40. *Werke*, ed. Suphan, XI, p. 413.

41. *Prolegomena zur Geschichte Israels* (Berlin, 1883), p. 323; *cf. Israelitische und jüdische Geschichte*, 5th ed. (Berlin, 1904), p. 156.

42. *Israelitische und jüdische Geschichte*, p. 118.

43. *Muhammed in Medina* (Berlin, 1882), p. 5.

44. *Das arabische Reich* (Berlin, 1902), p. 83.

45. The speech, which was printed for private circulation in 1919, is now available in the collection of Bousset's *Religionsgeschichtliche Studien* (Leiden, 1979).

46. The letter was published for the first time in *Quaderni di Storia*, 7 (1978), p. 211.

47. Apparently this was published for the first time (in an Italian translation) in *Quaderni di Storia*, 6 (1977), pp. 173-77.

48. *Nachr. Göttingen Akad.* (1908), pp. 305-74.

SEVENTEEN

Introduction to a Discussion
of Georges Dumézil

I

One cannot begin to speak of Georges Dumézil without first paying homage to the scholar who for more than sixty years has pursued a vast and comprehensive program of research in two areas: on one side there is the research that has given him a wider reputation, namely the exploration of Indo-European mythology and social structure; on the other there is the analysis of the non-Indo-European languages of the Caucasus, which he has studied at first hand and often on the spot. His prodigious knowledge of languages, which extends to Chinese and has touched some of the languages of the American Indians, has invariably been accompanied, from the very beginning, by a fine sense of how to organize his material.

Since it is improbable that there will be much discussion of Caucasian languages in this seminar, let it be recorded that Dumézil's most important contributions in that field were aimed at rescuing the unwritten and now dying Ubykh language, which around 1970 was being spoken by only a handful of displaced refugees near the Sea of Marmara. From the book *La Langue des Oubykhs* of 1931 to the memoir of the *Académie des Inscriptions* of 1975 on the Ubykh verb, there has been a whole series of publications of texts, translations, and analyses. In 1932–33 Dumézil also published three works on the comparative grammar of the languages of the northwestern Caucasus, and subsequently between 1960 and 1967 he was the editor of *Documents anatoliens sur les langues et les traditions du Caucase*. These works on the Caucasian languages proper must naturally not be confused with those

"Premesse per una discussione su Georges Dumézil" (introduction to a seminar at the Scuola Normale Superiore in Pisa, January 1983); *Opus: Rivista internazionale per la storia economica e sociale dell'antichità*, 2 (1983), pp. 329–42; *Rivista Storica Italiana*, 95 (1983), pp. 245–61. Translated by T.J. Cornell. (658)

on the Ossetians, the Indo-Europeans of the Caucasus, who have a central role in Dumézil's Indo-European reconstructions and whose heroic legends he has summarized or translated in some interesting volumes: *Les Légendes sur les Nartes* of 1930; *Le Livre des héros* of 1965. These and comparable texts later formed the subject of a volume of research papers, *Romans de Scythie et d'alentour* of 1978.

II

The purpose of these introductory pages is to pose the problem of the relationship between Dumézil's first phase, which extends, broadly speaking, from 1924 to 1938: and what might be termed his mature activity, characterized by the application of a tripartite and trifunctional scheme to the entire Indo-European intellectual legacy. As is well known, Dumézil has repudiated the work he produced before the article "La Préhistoire des flamines majeurs" in the *Rev. Hist. des Relig.* (118, 1938, pp. 188–200), at least in the sense that it represents a period of exploration without, as yet, any precise direction. It is worth noting however an anticipation of this article in a paper in the *Journal Asiatique* of 1930 (pp. 109–30), limited to the Indo-Iranian castes. With the article on the three major *flamines* in Roman cult — the *flamines* of Jupiter, Mars, and Quirinus — Dumézil put forward what from then on he was to claim as his fundamental discovery: the existence of constant basic elements in the Indo-European mentality. Generalizing and in his turn interpreting the elementary structure of the Indian castes — the tripartite division between priests, warriors, and peasants — Dumézil came to conceive of all Indo-Europeans as governed, through the centuries, by a fundamental principle of functional tripartition which was their essential characteristic.

In the long period from 1938 to 1982, however, Dumézil himself recognized a break around 1950, after which he no longer insisted on the necessary existence in fact of three separate social classes in Indo-European societies — priests, warriors, peasants — but was content to recognize a trifunctional mentality, a tendency to organize rituals, myths, and sociopolitical ideas in accordance with three distinct modes of seeing and feeling: the sacral, the military, and the productive. According to Dumézil, even in Indo-European societies in which it is difficult to distinguish precisely the priest from the warrior or from the producer, it is still possible to discern a tendency to distinguish rigorously between the three functions. So if a society, like that of classical Greece, responds negatively or at least only feebly to an investigation of functions, we have no alternative but to acknowledge that it has abandoned its Indo-European heritage. It should be added at once — as Dumézil's most recent volume, of 1982, indicates

(*Apollon sonore*, in part devoted to Homer)—that he has never given up hope of bringing the Greeks back into the Indo-European fold.

Dumézil is of course fully entitled to present his own intellectual development as a direct progress toward what he regards as his greatest discovery. But our primary task is to place in a meaningful context Dumézil's activity in the period before 1938, which in the Indo-European field includes at least five books of major importance: the two theses of 1924, *Le Festin d'immortalité* and *Le Crime des Lemniennes*, then *Le Problème des Centaures* of 1929, and the two memoirs of 1934 and 1935, respectively on *Ouranos-Varuna* and on *Flamen-Brahman*. As we shall see in a moment, this early work implicitly raises the whole problem of the relation of Dumézil to the school of Durkheim and explains why a change in the terms of this relationship serves to characterize the later and more mature activity of Dumézil after 1938: here the name of Marcel Granet becomes essential. But in its turn Dumézil's reversion to a broadly Durkheimian perspective raises the question of whether his post-1938 activity necessarily represents an advance on that of the preceding period.

III

Born in 1898, Georges Dumézil found encouragement and help in his studies from family and school connections. His father, the artillery officer Jean Dumézil, a typical product of the Polytéchnique, ended his career as Inspector General of Artillery in the First World War, in which his son played a part. One of his lycée teachers was Alfred Ernout; and a schoolfriend at the Louis-le-Grand in Paris introduced him to his grandfather, the eighty-year-old Michel Bréal, the predecessor of Antoine Meillet at the Collège de France. In his youth Bréal had combined research in phonetics and in comparative mythology and had been a pioneer of the sociological interpretation of language on eighteenth-century principles, as Hans Aarsleff has recently reminded us. Michel Bréal was the first teacher of Sanskrit to the adolescent Dumézil and could well have determined once and for all the direction of his research. There followed teachers in the narrow academic sense, Meillet among the linguists, Henri Hubert and Marcel Mauss among the anthropologists and sociologists—all three, in one way or another, trained in the Durkheimian sociological tradition. Dumézil took his degree with Meillet. One can discern among the various autobiographical statements of Dumézil that all was not plain sailing in his relations with these men. This can help to explain why he began his career outside France, something which later emerged as a great advantage for a born linguist like Dumézil: *lector* in French at Warsaw in 1920–21, professor of the history of religions at Istanbul from 1925 to 1931, *lector* in French at Uppsala in 1931–33, where presumably he established those contacts with learned Swedes that were later to play an important part not only in his knowledge of Nor-

dic civilizations but also in his interpretation of Indian society (I am thinking here above all of his collaboration with Stig Wikander). He returned to
France in 1933, when with the help of Sylvain Lévi he obtained a post, at
first probationary but later permanent, in the religious sciences section of
the École des Hautes Études. This was the time when he was close to Marcel
Granet, who in the circle of the *Année Sociologique* represented the study of
Chinese civilization. But it is to the immediate postwar period that we must
assign the collaboration with Émile Benveniste. It was Benveniste who spon-
sored the summoning of Dumézil to the Collège de France and was also
his most authoritative companion in his exploration of primitive Indo-
European society.

It is almost certain that from the start an element of political disagreement separated Dumézil from his Durkheimian mentors. Neither Dumézil,
despite his liking for personal reminiscences, nor his French interpreters,
have told us much about the political opinions he held during his youth.
But the dedication of his first book, *Le Festin d'immortalité*, to Pierre Gaxotte
is enough on its own to indicate where he stood politically. Gaxotte, later a
French Academician, was secretary to Maurras and editor-in-chief of *Can-
dide*, the organ of the extreme Right; he was subsequently also one of those
who opposed the resistance against Nazism in 1938–39. Dumézil's book of
1939, *Mythes et dieux des Germains*, bears clear signs of sympathy with Nazi
culture. Politically speaking there was obviously a huge gap between
Dumézil on one side and Mauss and his friends on the other. But Dumézil
almost always kept his politics separate from his scholarly activity, in which
he received indispensable assistance from two Jews, Sylvain Lévi and Benveniste. It is naturally possible that the new commitment, dating precisely
from 1938, to a tripartite and hierarchical picture of Indo-European society,
has some connection with ideas that were then current in Nazi and Fascist
circles of a hierarchical and corporatist society. In addition, a certain nai-
veté in dealing with Indo-European subjects is already discernible in the *Festin d'immortalité* of 1924, where the conquest of the world by the
Indo-Europeans is connected with the springtime drinking of warriors in
their annual celebration of the triumph of life over death (p. 264).

But such speculations on the relation between politics and historical
research in Dumézil are clearly limited by the essential fact that the discovery of the trifunctional Indo-European structure represented in theory, and
even in terms of personal relationships, a rapprochement between Dumézil
and the school of Durkheim.

IV

With the facile wisdom of hindsight we can say today that the undeniable
crisis of Durkheim's school, with the loss of the master and some of his most

brilliant pupils during the First World War, was being transformed in a period of unparalleled creativity immediately after the war. The years around 1924 in which Dumézil published his first books produced a thriving and abundant crop of extraordinary works from the survivors of the *Année Sociologique*. Marcel Mauss published his essay *The Gift* in 1925; the essay on the idea of death dates, I think, from 1926. In Strasbourg Maurice Halbwachs brought out his masterpiece, *Les Cadres sociaux de la mémoire*, in 1925. In 1924–25 Henri Hubert gave that course of lectures on the Germans that was to be published posthumously only in 1952. 1925 was the year of Meillet's lectures on the Gatha of the Avesta, and 1926 saw *Danses et légendes de la Chine ancienne* by Marcel Granet, which, together with the volume of 1919, *Fêtes et chansons anciennes de la Chine*, formed the basis of the work that was so decisive for French historiography between the wars, *La Civilisation chinoise* of 1929. By stretching the chronological limits a little we can add the first volume of Meillet's *Linguistique historique et linguistique générale* (1921); P. Fauconnet, *La Responsabilité* (1920); G. Davy, *La Foi jurée* (1922); J. Vendryes, *Le Langage* (1924).

One only has to skim the first volumes of Dumézil to realize that they would be unthinkable without this surrounding fervor — without, indeed, these very books. The most obvious example is in the book on the centaurs of 1929, which has a long paragraph (pp. 30–32) on the Chinese carnival, with a direct reference to Marcel Granet. However, it is not just academic gossip that Hubert cold-shouldered Dumézil, Granet was unwilling to receive him, and Mauss was kind but distant. The separation of the pupil from the masters is more conspicuous than the points of contact. With Meillet one can perhaps invoke the diffidence of the linguistic expert when faced with a comparative mythology which, in the preceding generation, had accompanied linguistics but had proved itself an untrustworthy companion. With Hubert one could perhaps argue that the anti-German feeling that had built up during the war made him indulgent (as can be seen from his lecture on the Germans of 1924) towards eccentric theories on the Germans as a people not authentically Indo-European, indeed rather imperfectly aryanized, who speak bad Indo-European, "du petit nègre," as he gently hinted (p. 73). To him, a book like Dumézil's on ambrosia, where Germanic facts are continually duplicated by Indian facts, could already be ipso facto irritating. But the most serious reason for the disagreement between Dumézil and his masters is that Dumézil effectively refused in his first books to define a society or to create a framework or background for the myths and religious vocabulary that he was studying. His comparative mythology was Indo-European in the sense that he was pursuing it in an Indo-European field; but fundamentally it was the ambition, which may have been nourished by the Caucasian studies he was engaged in at the time, to do comparative mythology as such — to follow myths and rituals wherever the analogies might lead. This ambition is most clearly evident in the volume of 1924 on *Le Crime des Lemniennes*. Its starting point is the passage of Herodotus (6.138) which attempts to explain why it is that in Greece the worst crimes are called "Lemnian crimes": there follows a story about the Pelasgians of Lemnos, who raped some Athenian women, but then murdered the children the women produced. To Dumézil the Lemnian story presupposes or conceals an annual rite of purification for which analogies can be found in every part of the world. It is unnecessary to say that *The Golden Bough* of James Frazer provides the explanation; and Frazer was the rival of Mauss, Granet, and Hubert in the eyes of the young Dumézil. Frazer expressed the necessity of tracing the evolution of humanity through rituals and myths. He never confronted the problem of reconstructing myths and rituals within a social framework, each time defined in its totality. Dumézil was indubitably attracted by what the undisciplined and imaginative Frazer had to offer, in contrast to his teachers in France. It is worth adding that he gave no sign of having noticed the more serious, but at the same time the more risky, of Frazer's preoccupations: that is, with the relations, or better the succession, of magic, religion, and science. For the moment he was attracted by what at some time has attracted all of us in Frazer: the dying god, the scapegoat, the Saturnalia, the corn spirit, and so on — aspects of the relationship between man and nature. It is not an accident that Loki, one of the characters in the Edda most dear to Frazer, was later, in 1948, to become the subject of a book by Dumézil. Already many years before, in 1899, in their essay on sacrifice (reprinted in *Mélanges d'histoire des religions*, 1909), Hubert and Mauss had challenged Frazer's tendency to group facts genealogically by means of analogy with their own method of analyzing the ritual system of a given group in all its complexity (p. 7).

It is easy to see that Dumézil's other juvenile works also obey, to a greater or lesser extent, the Frazerian demon of analogy. Take his first book, the *Festin d'immortalité*, which remains memorable, such is the freshness, breadth, and originality of its research. In the Indo-European world there exists, widely diffused, the notion that the gods have a special drink — what the Greeks called ambrosia. There also exists, though not so widely diffused, the notion that this drink confers immortality and therefore distinguishes gods in contrast to men, or certain gods in contrast to certain demons. Finally, there exists a tradition of competition for this drink, but it is, once again, asymmetrical compared with the preceding notions. In India ambrosia, or, to use the local term, *amrta*, confers immortality and is contested between gods and demons; in the Germanic Edda the mead of the gods does not give immortality, but it is contested; in Greece, at least in Pindar (*Olymp.* 1.91), there are signs that ambrosia confers immortality, but a specific contest for ambrosia is not documented. Dumézil seeks to create

uniformity where none exists, and he postulates, for example, that Pan-
dora's box is a box of ambrosia, and that the story of Anna Perenna in Ovid
conceals another version of a conflict over ambrosia. Behind the myth, so
constructed, of a conflict over ambrosia there would lie, in Frazerian terms,
an Indo-European festival of ambrosia, which can be reconstructed principally on the basis of Latin and Armenian data. But the fact that Roman
peasants drank abundantly in honor of Anna Perenna, and that Armenian
girls (only girls, be it noted) sipped more discreetly at a spring festival centered around the doll Vicak, does not prove the identity of the two festivals.
Not every drinking session is an ambrosiac ritual. In the end Dumézil is
aware of this, and he makes the witty conjecture that the Greeks and
Romans, having become Mediterranean dwellers, ended up forgetting
ambrosia, that is, a drink made of fermented cereals, for good Mediterranean wine. What matters for us is to observe the operation, with a rare display of learning and acumen, of an attempt to continue Frazer's *Golden
Bough* on the margins of the school of Mauss and Hubert.

We are still in Frazer's territory with the volume on the centaurs of 1929.
Here the defense of the linguistic equivalence between centaurs and
Indian *gandharva* is not as important as the attempt to demonstrate that
centaurs, *gandharva*, Latin *luperci*, and similar monsters from other Indo-
European cultures are all creatures connected with the end of winter or the
start of the new year. In these annual ceremonies symbolic masquerades of
passage are combined with rituals of marriage and of power. The centaurs
would be monster-masks in the new-year ritual. Dumézil succeeds in giving
the centaurs some semblance of new-year monster-masks by accepting the
identification proposed by J. Cuthbert Lawson (*Modern Greek Folklore and
Ancient Greek Religion*, 1910, pp. 190–255) of the centaurs with the *kallikánt-
zaroi*, the demons who in modern Greece control particularly the days
between Christmas and Epiphany. In ancient Greece there is no documen-
tation whatsoever to connect the centaurs with rituals of the new year or
the equinox.

It is not difficult to find in these early works of Dumézil anticipations of
ideas that were later to become dominant. Thus there is already in the book
on ambrosia the observation that at Rome, in contrast to Greece, the myths
about the gods tend to be transformed into the history of the earliest
period of the city (p. 157). And it is in this book too that Latins, Germans,
Celts, and Slavs — not having been exposed to brahmanic mysticism,
Zoroastrian moralism, or the "Greek miracle" — tend to be considered more
genuine custodians of Indo-European ideas: a notion which is otherwise
partly inherited from Meillet. The book on the centaurs, focused on Greece
and India, was to raise doubts about this conclusion in Dumézil himself,
but not for long. On the other hand, it is in the book on the centaurs that

Dumézil for the first time tries to establish a link between archaic confraternities like the Luperci and Roman kingship.

I have the impression that it was only with the slim volume of one hundred pages on *Ouranos-Varuna* of 1934 that Dumézil forged a true rapprochement with the school from which he came; it is less preoccupied with seasonal demons and more interested in problems of sovereignty. Here for the first time Dumézil concerns himself specifically with the royal function, in its blend of moral leadership, magic, and fecundity, which characterizes the sovereign as head of state rather than as commander of the army. It therefore implicitly poses the problem of the opposition between the guardian god who defends the law (in India, Varuna) and the warrior god who massacres demons (in India, Indra). But Dumézil still oscillates between the problem of royalty as such and the problem of whether Varuna and Ouranos should ultimately be considered identical.

The latter preoccupation leads him to a mass of conjectures and subtleties, for instance on the relation between the castration of Uranus and Varuna's momentary loss of virility, or between the earthly king consecrated by him and the act of consecration itself. Uranus, in short, cannot easily be defined in terms of royalty.

The monograph on *Flamen-Brahman* of the following year, 1935, was the first book written by Dumézil after his return to France. It is stated in the preface that Mauss and Granet have read the manuscript, and on page 40 there is an eloquent critical note by Granet. Once again it is the problem of the relation of religious and political authority that emerges from the discussion. For Dumézil, who has in mind the theories of Hubert and Mauss on sacrifice, the brahman is in origin the sacrificer of human victims, and at the same time is himself the human victim sacrificed to preserve and uphold the kingship. The brahman is consubstantial at the sacrifice both as officiant and as victim (pp. 38–39); he is the devourer of sin. Dumézil for his part recalls that in the *Dictionnaire des Antiquités* Camille Jullian, the pupil of Fustel de Coulanges, had defined the Latin *flamen* as "une victime vivante sans cesse parée pour le dieu auquel elle appartient" (p. 2059): a victim that is never immolated.

The coincidence between the functions of the brahman, as they emerge from his own interpretation, and those of the flamen, as they emerge from that of Jullian, constitutes for Dumézil a confirmation of the original identity of the two terms. An etymological link is also sought between these two words and the Greek *pharmakos*, who is certainly a victim or scapegoat but never appears to be endowed with sacerdotal functions.

Whatever may be the value of such speculations, one glimpses a Dumézil ever more committed to his study of what was soon to become the sacerdotal function in its relation to sovereignty within the scheme of the three

Indo-European functions. In addition, Dumézil had made his peace with Granet, was studying Chinese, and was to become for three years the disciple of the great interpreter of the archaic structure of China. It was the decisive moment which Dumézil himself has described in emotional words in the recent preface to a new edition of Granet's *La Religion des Chinois* (Payot, Paris, 1980).

V

According to Dumézil's account, Granet said at their meeting: "Allons, vous n'avez dit jusqu'à maintenant que des bêtises, mais c'étaient des bêtises intelligentes." In Granet's seminar Dumézil glimpsed a new way of interpreting texts. The early Dumézil had not yet discovered mental structure as the ordering principle of a whole society; at most he had seen it as the explanation of individual myths. That was probably what Granet saw as his "bêtise."

The later Dumézil found traces of a common Indo-European mental structure in the whole of society: indeed in the first decade after the discovery he maintained that any society is Indo-European insofar as it can demonstrate a functional tripartition in its institutions, a division into priests, warriors, and producers. It seems beyond doubt that Granet's influence lies behind this interest in society, and still more in the wealth and subtlety of interpretation of texts relating to social life. It is paradoxical that it should have been the sinologist Granet who made the decisive contribution to the mature development of the Indo-Europeanist Dumézil. And that was enough to make Dumézil acceptable to the survivors of Durkheim's school after the war, as is demonstrated for example by two acute and favorable reviews by L. Gernet in *Année Sociologique*, 1952 (vols. 34–36, in fact published in 1955) and 1959, of (respectively) *Les Dieux des Indo-Européens* and *Aspects de la fonction guerrière*.

Dumézil's late adjustment to the requirements of the sociologists around him is striking. From Indo-European myths taken singly he passed to the classes of an Indo-European society that was divided internally but unified by its separation from, and perhaps by its contempt for, classes of other, non-Aryan, races, those whom Firdusi defined as "intent on gain, and proud that they can apply themselves to any trade, their souls always full of resentments."

However, it would be premature to conclude that Dumézil now imitated Granet and accepted his method. Though they had in common the fact of being historians of mentality, the two men remained profoundly different. Granet had defined his method in the theoretical pages of the *Civilisation chinoise* of 1929. At his death in 1940 he does not appear to have changed his position since 1929, to judge from the lectures of 1936 on *La Féodalité chinoise* (published in 1952), and from the fragments of the unfinished work

Le Roi boit, la reine rit, on which there is ample information in the *Année Sociologique* of 1952.

In 1929 Granet had argued that where archaic China is concerned, it is not possible to reconstruct the actual situations, administrative customs, economic practices, and dress. It is curious that Granet cites as an example the fact that in Chinese documents the allotment assigned to a cultivator is five or six times less than would be needed to feed a single man even on more fertile and better cultivated land; to the Roman historian that immediately recalls the difficulty in understanding the purpose of the two *iugera* supposedly allocated by Romulus. As a result of this impossibility of reconstructing political and economic development, Granet set out to do what was feasible, namely to restrict himself to defining the attitudes that characterized the Chinese social system in antiquity. This characterization had to be aimed at two things: social attitudes in the strict sense, and speculative thought. In its turn the method of research had to be stratigraphical and had to determine how village life came to be dominated by an aristocracy with its morality of prestige. It would be a misunderstanding of Granet to expect from him vague mental forms. Songs, proverbs, and festivals were used to define the emotions of the everyday life of periods for which historiography is either lacking or untrustworthy.

By this means one will not be able to reconstruct the agrarian regime, but one will be able to grasp the customs of the peasants, their games, their orgies, their festivals, and their sacred rites: the same applies to the aristocracy. As is well known, the reconstruction of the archaic Chinese family proposed by Granet has provoked dissent, but it is firm and precise. Granet's pessimism about political history is matched by his confident belief that it is possible to enter the daily lives of his Chinese of all classes.

It is enough to read a work by Granet alongside one by the mature Dumézil to be aware of the difference; the former is interested in the minute details of everyday life, whereas the latter shuns any description of the daily life of an Indo-European people, and concentrates exclusively on the discovery of vestiges and survivals of a social order that is in the process of vanishing and no longer has any influence on domestic life or politics.

VI

Three further points can be added that will help towards a clearer definition of Dumézil in the period after 1938.

1. From now on Dumézil assumed—and the assumption has become more evident as his research has progressed—that the most important element to be examined is the relationship between the sacerdotal function and sovereignty. This is not only because the hierarchical relationship between warriors and priests is none too clear, but because sovereignty is

divided between the two elements; and the division is complicated in turn by the double aspect of sovereignty — sovereignty as magical power and sovereignty as juridical, or contractual, power. Dumézil was later pleased to identify this dual aspect of sovereignty with the ambiguous relationship between Varuna and Mithra.

Strictly speaking, then, there are in fact three aspects of sovereignty — the magical, the contractual, and the military — which are uncertainly distributed between the two classes or castes, the sacerdotal and the military. And it does not end there. At least in the essay of 1949 on the *Troisième Souverain*, Dumézil seemed disposed to admit that an element of sovereignty is provided also by the producers, the third class. It is not out of place to ask whether the hierarchical-fascistic phase in the interpretation of the Indo-European social structure was not superseded by a vaguely Marxist phase, in which the producers have a say in sovereignty. But whatever the external influences, there is no doubt in my mind that the internal analysis of aspects of sovereignty represents one of Dumézil's most important contributions.

In the same period, from 1950 onwards, Dumézil began to lose faith (as we have already noticed) in the possibility of fixing the three functions in concrete institutions. Thus, if he had formerly believed that he could identify the three functions with the Romulean tribes (Ramnes = priests; Luceres = warriors; Tities = farmers), as well as with the three major flamines (of Jupiter, Mars, and Quirinus) — he became more uncertain about these identifications, even if he did not renounce them altogether. Dumézil increasingly preferred to speak of mental structures, and in the atmosphere of the 1960s he ran the risk of being identified with the structuralists and of becoming either the master or the pupil of Lévi-Strauss (who later "received" him under the dome).

2. It is in the logic of this functional analysis that one should pass from myth to history, since in practice myth coincides with the organizing principles of a society. One would therefore expect the three functions to appear to operate in real historical events.

Dumézil does not exclude this direct control, but it cannot be said that he writes history (as Granet wrote history) on this basis. Rather he seeks to demonstrate how tripartite mythical motifs are (falsely) transformed into historical events by the historians and chroniclers of antiquity. Thus for example the relation between Romulus and Numa reflects a duality comparable to that of the gods Varuna and Mithra in India; the duel between Horatius and the Curiatii is a pseudo-historical version of an ancient trifunctional mythical conflict of which an Indian model is the struggle between the god Indra and a three-headed monster; and the pair Horatius Cocles–Mucius Scaevola, the former one-eyed and the latter one-armed, is connected with the pair Odin–Tyr in Scandinavian mythology. But important though it is, this transformation of mythical motifs into pseudo-history does not make up, as we shall see better presently, for the scarcity, or indeed the absence, of authentic events based on three functions.

3. Insofar as Dumézil, as has been noted, set himself the task of reconstructing an Indo-European mentality underlying all later cultures, there is no doubt that among these later cultures he has privileged the Roman. That is partly due to the fact that he recognizes Roman culture as one of the most conservative: one thinks for example of his happy comparison between the Vedic myth of the Aurora and the Roman ritual of Mater Matuta. The other reason is that in no other territory does Dumézil find better soil for cultivating the historicization of myth. It follows that it is not our choice, but already that of Dumézil, that the Roman, or, if you will, the Latin, territory is to be considered the best testing ground for Dumézil's theories. To say that is not to diminish his contribution to the study of the mythical heritage of the Indians, Iranians, Germans, Celts, and, to a lesser extent, Greeks, Slavs, and Armenians. It is even conceivable (and in my personal opinion probable) that in recent times Dumézil's contributions on non-Roman topics exceed in importance those on Roman topics. For the moment, however, we must insist on the elementary fact that Dumézil has written a large comprehensive work on archaic Roman religion (1st ed., 1966; 2d ed., 1973) but has not written anything comparable on Germans, Celts, or Indians. Only in the case of Rome does his analysis give the measure of how he conceives the trifunctional scheme within an Indo-European society. It is therefore effectively on the Roman material that, at least for the present, Dumézil's method can best be judged.

There is a corollary to this. As is well known, particularly through the initiative of Jacques Le Goff and Georges Duby, the investigation of the trifunctional mentality has been extended to the Middle Ages. It will suffice to mention the deservedly successful volume by Duby on *Les trois ordres ou l'imaginaire du féodalisme* (1978). Still more specifically, one of Dumézil's direct pupils, Joel H. Grisward, has proposed a Dumézilian reading, which has had the approval of the master, of the *chansons de geste* which go together under the name of the Cycle of the Narbonese, or the Cycle of the Aymers (1981). The volume has the title *Archéologie de l'epopée médiévale*. The fact that the tripartition of social functions is so abundantly documented in the Middle Ages is, however, a problem in itself. It could represent a continuation of Indo-European mentality, or it could be an independent development provoked by Christianity, which accentuated the sacral or sacerdotal element of social life. At the extreme limit, the hypothesis should be considered that Dumézil transferred to ancient and pagan Rome the mentality of Christian Rome. It would be as well in the present context, therefore, to leave out of account the western Middle Ages as a witness to Indo-European mentality.

These three points, if they are acceptable, together with the corollary, can, I believe, shape the questions I should like to ask about Dumézil. It seems to me that it is not a matter of asking if Dumézil's method is valid or false in an absolute sense. It is not a matter, at the beginning of this year 1983, of discussing Dumézil in terms of complete agreement or of total dissent. The real question — for a student of Roman history who, like the present writer, has recently had to write on the origin of Rome — is how far his method and his results have contributed to our understanding of Roman society. In other words:

1. If we suppose that there is a tendency toward functional tripartition in Indo-European societies, what aspects of Roman society are thereby made more easily comprehensible?

2. If the tripartition is not discernible in institutions, as Dumézil tends to acknowledge in his more recent works, where can it in fact be seen?

To respond to these questions it is certainly necessary to have a knowledge of the individual works of Dumézil, of which there are many. But it is equally important not to get lost in details, and to examine above all the fundamental ideas. The Italian reader is relatively fortunate in that Dumézil published in Italian with Einaudi a full and responsible statement of his research between 1941 and 1948 under the title *Juppiter Mars Quirinus* (it appeared in 1955). In 1975 an excellent translation of *Archaic Roman Religion,* in the second edition of 1973, was published, edited by the lamented Furio Jesi.

But there still is not, as far as I know, in Italian — or even in French — a comparable synthesis of the research carried out by Dumézil after this edition, or indeed after the first edition of *Archaic Roman Religion* of 1966. It will suffice here to indicate some of the essential works of the past fifteen years. Especially important are the three large volumes of *Mythe et épopée* (1968–73), of which only the first part of the first volume has so far been published in Italian translation (by Einaudi in 1982). Otherwise: *Idées romaines* (1969); *Fêtes romaines* (1975); *Mariages indo-européens* (1979); *Apollon sonore* (1982). The last-named volume is, as noted above, notable for its application of the trifunctional thesis to the Homeric poems.

VII

The thesis I should like to put forward for discussion is that, even if all Dumézil's suggestions about archaic Rome were accepted (and not all of them can be), his contribution to our understanding of Roman history would remain slight. The Roman historian has four or five vulgar facts to explain in the constitutional evolution of Rome: the rise of the patrician-plebeian dualism; the relation between this dualism and the dualism between patrons and clients; the hierarchical structure of the centuriate organization; the Roman federal structure with its peculiar system of military alliances, of colonies and *municipia,* of citizenship with and without suffrage. All this, and more besides, stands well away from any tripartition. What characterizes Rome is an aristocracy which has cumulative control of religion, war, and production.

Even if we were to confine ourselves to religion (a restriction which I should not consider legitimate), the general system of priests and religious practices is indicative of a society which refuses to separate religion, war, and production. At Rome the struggle for power is not between priests, professional soldiers, and producers, but between privileged groups, or, more rarely, between the privileged and the nonprivileged. In short, none of the important events of Roman history which we can study with any knowledge of the facts—the foundation of the republic, the Twelve Tables, the struggle between patricians and plebeians, the agrarian laws, the municipalization of Italy, imperialism—can be clarified in terms of Indo-European functions.

Dumézil is indisputably a fine interpreter of texts, but of selected texts. A negative list of texts which do not lend themselves to trifunctional analysis has never been compiled by Dumézil. To this must be added—and it is to Dumézil's credit—the fact that several of his better interpretations have only a distant connection, if any, with the three functions. The antithesis Cocles–Scaevola, if it is valid (which I doubt), does not depend on the three functions. The acute interpretation of a detail of the *lapis niger* on the basis of Cicero, *De Divinatione,* II, 36, is in no way trifunctional (*Rev. Ét. Latines,* 36, 1958, p. 109). On the other hand, where the three functions are directly in play (as in the interpretation of the three major flamines or of the three Roman forms of marriage), the argument is often forced and contrived: for the interpretation of Quirinus, to whom Dumézil has repeatedly returned without ever carrying conviction, see now the essay by Daniela Porte in *Aufstieg und Niedergang der römischen Welt* (XVII, 1).

To conclude I should like briefly to discuss, by way of example, the interpretation of the second part of the *Aeneid* that Dumézil offers in a hundred pages of the first volume of *Mythe et épopée.* To my knowledge, this interpretation has not yet been subjected to discussion, although a couple of acute observations on it can be found in the review by J. L. Laugier in *Rev. Ét. Anciennes* (71, 1969, pp. 462–64). Dumézil examines the significance of the alliances formed by Aeneas on his arrival in Latium, and finds that, by associating himself with the Latins, pious Aeneas, the priest, binds himself to the third function of production and agriculture. The alliance with the Etruscans under Tarchon, on the other hand, would bring him into contact with the second function, military force. As one would expect from Dumézil, there is no lack of pegs, acutely chosen, on which to hang the argument. In book XII Aeneas promises that, if he wins the duel against Turnus, he will leave the military command to Latinus and will content himself with "giving the gods and the rites":

Sacra deosque dabo; socer arma Latinus habeto,
imperium sollemne socer; mihi moenia Teucri
constituent.

But the skeptical reader will notice at once that here if anywhere there
is separation between priesthood and military command, whereas *ex
hypothesi* Latinus represents not military command but production. And in
truth it is not obvious why Tarchon should be more of a soldier than
Aeneas: Latinus is less of a soldier only because he is old. In any case the
Virgilian plan is a little more complicated. Virgil naturally does not accept
the view of those who, like Dionysius of Halicarnassus, seek to turn the Trojans into Greeks. The Trojans remain Trojans. But the question of the relationship between Trojans and Greeks — and between Romans and Greeks —
s essential for Virgil. On the other hand, it is even more important for Virgil that the Trojans cannot continue to be Trojans after they have landed in
Latium. They must be amalgamated with the Latins and changed into
natives. Hence the twofold tendency of the *Aeneid,* to present Dardanus,
from whom Aeneas is descended, as originating in Italy, and to present
Jupiter as ready to accept Juno's condition for peace: that the Trojans
should lose their name and become Latins once and for all. In Virgil there
is therefore on one side a preoccupation with reconciling Greeks and Trojans (and for this I should like to refer to my recent article, "How to Reconcile Greeks and Trojans," in *Meded. Kgl. Nederl. Akad.,* n.r., 45, 9, 1982
[reprinted in *Settimo contributo,* pp. 437–62]), and on the other side a preoccupation with fusing Trojans and Latins. We are after Actium, when to be
an Oriental was no longer a recommendation in Italy. At a subordinate
level, there are signs of a third preoccupation: to place the Etruscans in a
favorable light and to rescue them from the bad reputation that had been
perpetuated by the legend of the tyrant Mezentius. Besides, Dumézil himself has noted in another essay that Virgil avoided saying the worst about
Mezentius (*Mélanges J. Heurgon,* I, 1976, pp. 253–63).

Hence the complex solution of the *Aeneid,* which by no means serves the
interests of artistic effectiveness, of attributing much importance to the
Greek Evander, of making Latinus oscillate between the pro-Trojan camp
and the anti-Trojan camp, of opposing the willing Tarchon to the hostile
Mezentius as well as to Turnus. It is out of the question that Virgil wished
to present the Trojans as a priestly group. Aeneas is also a warrior. But in
his offer of a compromise Aeneas must momentarily subordinate himself
to Latinus and acknowledge his supreme command. Latinus is shortly destined to die of old age. The command must then pass to Aeneas, or rather
to his descendants.

The plot of the *Aeneid* does not hinge upon the three Indo-European
functions, but on the threefold and very Roman preoccupation of reconcil-

ing Romans (= Trojans) and Greeks, of not substituting Trojans for Latins, and of rescuing whatever can be salvaged from the Etruscans. From Dido's Carthage, it seems, Virgil found nothing worth saving.

Bibliographical Note

The book by C. S. Littleton, *The New Comparative Mythology*, Berkeley, 1966, (3rd. ed., 1983), can serve as a first introduction. Among the introductory works in French the most important known to me are Alain de Benoist, ed., *Georges Dumézil et les études indo-européennes*, special number of the *Nouvelle École*, 21–22, 1972; J. C. Rivière, ed., *Georges Dumézil à la découverte des Indo-Européens*, Copernic, Paris, 1979; *Georges Dumézil*, various studies, Centre Georges Pompidou, 1981. Rivière has a particularly useful bibliography, to which the reader is referred. There is a whole school of Dumézil in America, on which some information can be found in the book edited by G. J. Larson and others, *Myth in Indo-European Antiquity*, Berkeley, 1974. F. Vian has attempted to use Dumézil's ideas for Boeotian myths in *Les Origines de Thèbes*, Paris, 1963, and elsewhere. *Cf.* most recently D. Briquel, "Initiations grecques et idéologie indo-européenne," *Annales*, 37, 1982, pp. 454–64.

One of the most penetrating critiques of Dumézil is still that of J. Brough in *Bullet. School Oriental African Studies London*, 23, 1959, pp. 69–85. Another notable criticism is that by P. Smith and D. Sperber in *Annales*, 26, 1971, pp. 559–86. Note also the review by Brough in *Times Literary Suppl.*, 3 January 1975.

Still of interest are the criticisms of H. J. Rose, especially in *Journ. Rom. Studies*, 37, 1947, pp. 183–86, and those of J. Gonda, too numerous to mention in particular, but *cf. Mnemosyne*, 4, 13, 1960, pp. 1–15, and the large memoir *Triads in the Veda*, *Verh. Kgl. Nederl. Akad.*, n.r., 91, 1976. Notice also A. Brelich, "Studi Mater," *Storia Religioni*, 28, 1957, pp. 113–23; 29, 1958, pp. 109–12.

The best study of M. Granet known to me is that of M. Freedman, in the introduction to the English translation of *The Religion of the Chinese People*, Oxford, 1975, pp. 1–29. On the situation of sociology in the universities see T. N. Clark, *Prophets and Patrons: The French University and the Emergence of the Social Sciences*, Cambridge, Mass., 1973.

The proceedings of the seminar on Dumézil at the Scuola Normale of Pisa in January 1983 are published in the journal *Opus*, fasc. 2, for 1983.

EIGHTEEN

A Return to Eighteenth-Century "Etruscheria": K. O. Müller

One of the tasks which Franco Venturi's wide-ranging research has imposed on us is that of measuring what the historians of the early nineteenth century adopted, rejected, or forgot from the discoveries or the ideas circulated by their eighteenth-century predecessors, especially Italians. For his part Franco Venturi has already traced some of the main threads of this inheritance, above all for Russia. But the importance of his research is revealed by the simple fact that he has implicitly called in question the more obvious contrasts between the historical thought of the eighteenth century and that of the nineteenth. One of these is the notion that Niebuhr eliminated—so to speak—the "Italian history" that had been pursued in various ways (above all through "Etruscheria") in the eighteenth century, and replaced it with the history of the peasant soldiers of archaic Rome. I am unable here to sketch even in a tentative outline the consequences of the revision that has become indispensable in the field of archaic Italian history as a result of Venturi's studies. But one eminent name, though neglected from this point of view, deserves to be briefly highlighted here in anticipation of further research by myself and others. He was the topic of a seminar at the Scuola Normale Superiore di Pisa in February 1984; and it was precisely when preparing for this seminar that I realized the importance of Karl Otfried Müller for understanding how eighteenth-century "Etruscheria" came to be incorporated in the historiography of the early nineteenth century. I am deliberately omitting the term "romantic," because it can never be applied to a professor at Göttingen between 1819 and 1840 who had access to a library like that of his university, which was

"Un 'Ritorno' alla etruscheria settecentesca: K. O. Müller," *L'Età dei Lumi: Studi storici sul Settecento europeo in onore di Franco Venturi* (1985), vol. II, pp. 653–68; *Ottavo contributo* (1987), pp. 45–58, and see *Nono contributo* (1992), p. 635. Translated by T. J. Cornell. (675)

exceptional in preserving the intellectual heritage of the Enlightenment, including the Italian. The true difficulty in understanding K. O. Müller's importance for Italian history is that Müller published his work on the Etruscans in 1828, more or less coinciding with the appearance of the second volume, and of the third edition of the first volume, of Niebuhr's *History of Rome* (1827–28). As Müller immediately pointed out in his long review of these two volumes in the *Allgemeine Literatur-Zeitung* of July 1829, he in his *Etruscans* and Niebuhr in the second edition of his *History of Rome* had converged in giving more space to the history of pre-Roman Italy than Niebuhr had done in the first edition (1811). There was therefore in Germany a complex growth in the critical understanding of the peoples of ancient Italy between 1810 and 1830; and we should not forget that the reaction to Micali's book *L'Italia avanti il dominio dei Romani* (1810) was slow and contorted, precisely because Micali's book was far from being a simple résumé of eighteenth-century "Etruscheria."

It seemed to me that it would be best to present here in a few pages — in continuation of conversations with Venturi that began in 1927 and have not been interrupted except by greater and sadder events — a simple portrait of K. O. Müller as a whole, and to give the Etruscans no more attention than they receive in the extraordinary activity of the Göttingen scholar who studied them. Mauro Cristofani, *La scoperta degli Etruschi: Archeologia e antiquaria nel 700* (Consiglio Nazionale delle Ricerche, Rome, 1983) gives the best introduction to "Etruscheria"; and Massimo Pallottino's essay of 1976, *Sul concetto di storia italica* (now in *Saggi di antichità*, I, Bretschneider, Rome, 1979, pp. 451–69) confirms that my theme is currently fashionable.

If those whom the gods love die young, no classical philologist was more dear to the gods than Karl Müller, who gave himself the additional name Otfried on the advice of Philip Buttmann, the author of the *Mythologus,* around 1817. Born at Brieg in Silesia on 20 August 1797, he died aged 42, in Athens, as everyone knows, on 1 August 1840, killed by the Apollo whom he had rediscovered at Delphi. He grew up in a family of Lutheran pastors (his father was a noted preacher); evidence of his refined and liberal upbringing is provided by all the wonderful correspondence with his parents that was ended only by his death; as is equally well known, it was published in 1908 in a classic volume by Otto and Else Kern, *C.O.M.: Lebensbild in Briefen an seine Eltern.* In his family surroundings Karl Otfried Müller found the simplicity and resolve of his intellectual personality. His two brothers were his companions: Julius, who became an eminent theologian at the University of Marburg, and Eduard, an able classical philologist with a particular interest in literary theories, who became his elder brother's devoted biographer and editor. Early familiarity with contemporary German writers, which became friendship in the case of Ludwig Tieck; a religious orientation which was curiously little declared for a man of such origin; a provincial outspokenness in dealing with persons of standing; a profound feeling of having roots in the German past—these were all characteristics of the man. Müller wrote poetry in German, of which some examples survive even from the time of his adolescence. His brother tells us in his biography that in those years Karl wrote a "deutsche Heldensage" in three cantos on the Maccabees. And the poet and philosopher Heinrich S. Steffens, who was of Norwegian origin, preserved a memory of the whole Müller family, including the father and the three brothers, in his autobiography, *Was ich erlebte,* shortly after Karl Otfried's death (IX, 1844, pp. 284–88; *cf.* VIII, 1843, pp. 174–75).

Looking forward we may say that it was not an accident that in his maturity he became a friend of the brothers Grimm, whom he had already met at Cassel around 1820, nine years before the Grimms moved to Göttingen. But we can also look forward and conjecture that Karl Otfried Müller would not have gone all the way with his friends the Grimms and the rest of the "Göttingen Seven" in their protest against the abolition of the constitution that led to their banishment from Hanover in 1837. Müller's political interests were limited and timid, for all their basic liberalism.

He was Prussian by birth and in his upbringing: he studied for two years at the University of Breslau between 1814 and 1816. He then became the favorite pupil of August Boeckh at Berlin in 1816–17. At the age of twenty he took his degree in 1817 at Berlin with a dissertation on the history of Aegina, *Aegineticorum liber,* an epoch-making work which became the model for local history. It was the year in which Boeckh dedicated to his friend Niebuhr the first edition of his *Staatshaushaltung der Athener.* It was not an accident that K. O. Müller came to Berlin from Breslau as a student and admirer of Niebuhr.

A mysterious essay on Numa, for which Müller received a prize at the University of Breslau in February 1815, testifies to the young man's interest in the new Roman history. Our friend Andreas Wittenburg has finally succeeded in unearthing a copy of this essay on Numa, and will make reference to it in the proceedings of our seminar in Pisa.

Niebuhr's influence on Müller remained fundamental, alongside that of Boeckh, but unlike that of Boeckh it was not accompanied, as we shall see, by personal sympathy. On the other hand it was Boeckh who rescued Müller from the danger of becoming a follower of Schelling. Müller himself tells us that he dedicated another youthful piece (still unpublished like the one on Numa) to the cults of Samothrace under the influence of Schelling's dissertation on this obscure subject. Boeckh persuaded Müller to put aside the mysteries of Samothrace and to turn his attention to Aegina, then a place of great interest because of the excavations of the temple of Aphaia in 1811 which, after the restorations of Thorwaldsen, had filled the new museum in Munich, the Glyptothek. But curiously, in what has been defined as the first meeting of central European culture with Greek archaism, Schelling reappeared as the author of an appendix to Martin Wagner's published report on the Aphaia sculptures in 1817. Müller's separation from the mysteries of Samothrace was only temporary: he returned to them in the first volume on Greek origins in 1820, but his separation from Schelling's philosophy was clearly revealed, or so it seems to me. In distancing himself from Schelling, Müller could have been influenced by another young Berlin professor, K. W. F. Solger, who himself had moved away from his teacher Schelling. Solger died in 1819, and in 1826 Müller published the notes of his lectures on mythology of 1816–17 (*cf. Briefe*, ed. Reiter, II, p. 48).

After scarcely more than a year as a teacher at the Gymnasium Magdaleneum at Breslau (its director was J. K. F. Manso, the historian of Sparta), the twenty-two-year-old Müller was called to Göttingen as *professor extraordinarius* in succession to Friedrich Gottlieb Welcker, who remained a lifelong friend. Göttingen was then at the height of its international reputation. His post as professor extraordinarius was converted to that of ordinarius four years later, in 1823, and he was made a member of the Göttingen Academy. He fulfilled all the conditions to be able to obtain, in line with the current academic custom, the hand of the daughter of an eminent colleague, the jurist Gustav Hugo, the founder of the historical school of law. Karl Otfried and Pauline were married in 1824. Müller even turned down an appointment at Berlin suggested by Boeckh.

Göttingen had been truly generous in welcoming its new young professor. Even before he took up the appointment he was given the chance to spend two months studying the artistic collections of Dresden, where he formed a lasting friendship with Karl August Böttiger, editor of the journal *Amalthea* (1820), director of the Museum of Antiquities, and future author of the *Kunstmythologie*, and also of the gifted Ludwig Schorn, the art historian and future editor of the *Kunstblatt*. The correspondence with Schorn is among the most important in the Müller collection (published in *Neue Jahrbücher* for 1910). From now on an interest in art, especially the art of antiquity, was to be a constant element of Müller's cultural persona: an element not often found among classical philologists. Later, in 1822, the government of Hanover gave him a period of study leave in which to visit the museums of Holland, France, and England. The Parthenon marbles could be seen in London, and on them and on Phidias in general Müller was later, around 1827, to write some memorable essays. But the letters to his parents which give such a vivid impression of London and Cambridge, and to a lesser extent of Oxford, have little to say about archaeological and epigraphic research as such. Müller established contacts in England which subsequently led to translations of his works and invitations to write others for English-speaking readers. But in his letters he remained irremediably attached to Göttingen: "The masters and bachelors of the Colleges eat infinitely better than we do at Göttingen, but in their conversation and general tone they do not show even a tenth part of the literary life that animates our little societies" (p. 127). Later, in Paris, he was surprised by the authority of the new Germany and by the popularity of German scholars, among them Alexander von Humboldt, whom he found more sympathetic than his brother Wilhelm.

One immediate effect of his journey to England and France in 1822, however, was that it undermined a decision that had been arrived at shortly after 1817, and of which the substantial volume on Orchomenos and the Minyans of 1820 and the equally accurate two volumes of 1824 on the Dorians were only the first expression. Müller himself explains in the preface to the book on Orchomenos and the Minyans that the type of local history which he himself had practiced and refashioned in the work on Aegina now seemed inadequate. A new image of Greek history had now presented itself to him: a coordinated history of the ethnic groups and cities of Greece, *Geschichte Hellenischer Stämme und Städte,* in preparation for a comprehensive history of the Hellenic people in the broadest sense.

The first volume, almost defiantly, took as its subject the most mysterious and obscure corner of Boeotia, centered on the semimythical Orchomenos and its semimythical Minyans—a land of legend more than of history. "Boeotia is like Palestine, a land of caves and grottoes, riddled with desolate mountain crevasses, enclosed marshy basins, and rushing underground streams; it was destined to pour forth oracles from the mysterious deeps of its pitted landscape." It is the land "of many voices of the divine sagas, of the oldest seat of prophecy, and in its assemblage of religious cults of every variety, the home of a Hellenic theogony" (p. 145). Here we find already formulated an axiom that was to remain fundamental for Müller: "Every tribal myth in Greece, and therefore even the Theban, must begin with a tribal and a local god." The gods of Samothrace, whom Boeckh had tried to make his pupil forget, reappear at this point, but in an appendix to the volume Müller coldly announces that the principles Schelling had used to interpret them must be rejected in their entirety. The Samothracian cult of the Cabiri was declared a relic of the religion of the Pelasgians, brought in by the Tyrrhenians, and turned into a mystery cult in the Homeric age (p. 462). Already in this volume, then, a wistful view of Greek history was taking shape, which started from the myths of the individual tribes—Minyans, Dorians, Ionians, etc.—and tried to find in the myths themselves not only the original cults of each tribe, but also the mythical transfiguration of real historical events. One could proceed from myth to history and vice versa. The two volumes on the Dorians circulated independently in the English-speaking world in a translation, revised and enlarged by Müller himself, that had been started and partially completed by a man of the stature of G. Cornewall Lewis (1830). Apollo appeared as the Dorian god *par excellence,* just as Heracles was the Dorian hero. The Dorians, the Prussians of the ancient world, had a message not only for Prussians but for all Germans (including Anglo-Saxons) of the post-Napoleonic era. It was not by chance that for the English edition of the Dorians Müller put together an essay on the original homeland of the Macedonians, thus anticipating J. G. Droysen in inserting the Macedonians into the myth of the new Prussia; the essay was soon published in German also (1825).

It appears from the preparation for the first volume of his historical work in 1820 that at that date Müller still believed that he could do without French scholarship, and make use of the English only in a subordinated capacity, for their archaeological contributions. The journey of 1822 evidently caused Müller himself to rethink this attitude—but not without some moments of embarrassment, as can be seen from an exchange of letters with Raoul-Rochette, whose history of Greek colonization Müller had described as "lacking in judgment" (*Briefe,* ed. Reiter, I, p. 127, of 1829).

The wider international viewpoint of the mature Müller, which is obvious, did not, however, prevent him from remaining substantially faithful for the rest of his life to this image of a history of Greece as the history of individual tribes, each of which reflected in its myths its own most ancient history and its own most deeply rooted moral and religious ideals. Pieces of specialized research and other competing cultural commitments were to hold up the continuation of the work and its extension to the Ionians.

But even during the fatal journey to Italy and Greece in 1839–40 Müller was contemplating the continuation of the history of Greece.

Here it will be sufficient to indicate that among the many detailed articles that Müller contributed to the encyclopedia of Ersch and Gruber are articles on Athenian subjects. But it must be added that Müller's researches dealing specifically with mythology, as well as his historical studies, implied a further stage, of synthesis and psychological reflection, but one that was indefinitely postponed, so that it is not possible to say more than that he looked forward to it.

Nevertheless, the essay of 1833 on the *Eumenides,* truly extraordinary for its beauty and richness, gives a more precise indication of the course Müller would have taken in his mature years in the study of Athens. It offered a securely founded idea of what Greek tragedy was, one that had obviously grown up in the cultural soil of Goethe and Schiller. We know moreover from his brother Eduard that at that time Müller also wrote a tragedy of his own, based on the biblical story of Manoah. The originality of interpretation in the essay on the *Eumenides*—accompanied by a text and translation—gave G. Hermann, a rival of Boeckh, the opportunity to reaffirm, against the latter's pupil, his principles of hermeneutics and textual criticism. This gave rise to a controversy which, insofar as it falls within the wider debate between Hermann's textual philology and Boeckh's "historicizing" philology, has its own paradigmatic value. It had already been prefigured in a review by Müller of Hermann's edition of the *Ion* of Euripides (1828; *Kleine deutsche Schriften,* I, pp. 261–66). Hermann's polemical essays are collected in volumes VI and VII of his *Opuscula;* for Müller, one should take careful note especially of an appendix to his commentary on the *Eumenides* published the following year (1834). Müller went so far as to question Hermann's capacity to understand Aeschylus: and in his view of an Aeschylus who lived in and for the Athens of his time he was not wrong (letter to F. G. Welcker, *Briefe,* I, p. 182).

In addition, between 1824 and 1834 certain studies concerning the history of the Greek tribes had assumed an importance in themselves, and as such were bound to open new paths for the historiography of the nineteenth century. The first result was the theoretical formulation of the principles of mythology. Undertaken as responses to unfavorable reviews of his volumes on the *Hellenische Stämme* by E. R. Lange and F. Chr. Schlosser, the *Prolegomena zu einer wissenschaftlichen Mythologie* of 1825 recalled in its ambitious title two other Prolegomena: those of Wolf to Homer and those of Kant to "Any Future Metaphysic." There was no modesty, then, but there was much simplicity in Müller's essay. In reaffirming more precisely and more elaborately that the Greek myths are an image of the history of Greece in the age of migrations, Müller took a position on all the contemporary theories of myth in German thought from the symbolism of Creuzer to the allegory of Voss, but at the same time he was ready to let it be understood that beyond his affirmations on the Greek myths there lay the possibility of a general theory of myth—a theory that was being left for the future. In concrete terms, Müller reasserted the priority of myth over epic, lyric, and dramatic poetry, and he devalued Homer as the creator of religion among the Greeks.

At almost the same time Müller confronted the theme of Etruscan civilization, which had been proposed as the subject for a prize essay by the Berlin Academy in 1824. Müller's essay won the prize in 1826, and was published in two volumes in 1828.

It was, together with the later essay on the *Eumenides,* one of Müller's two masterpieces, and could still be reissued fifty years later with relatively few changes, apart from the section on the language, by W. Deecke, a professional Etruscologist of the succeeding generation. As for the fact that Boeckh himself was surprised by the essay of his favorite pupil, it must be admitted that the roots of this interest in the Etruscans lay in the work on Numa written while he was a student, and in general in that part of his formation that Müller had always attributed to Niebuhr. The two volumes on the Etruscans combined several strands: these included a further elaboration of Niebuhr's method in dealing with Italic problems, overlaid with the special criteria for analyzing myth and archaic history which Müller himself had formulated, and finally an assessment, of a kind that had not previously been attempted, of the whole legacy of eighteenth-century archaeological research, and particularly of eighteenth-century Italian Etruscheria.

Müller had never been to Italy and had never seen the material that was then available in local museums. But the Göttingen library enabled him to master the greater part of the antiquarian literature that had built up on the subject. The principal significance of Müller's *Die Etrusker* is that it utilized, but at the same time partially demolished, the principles of eighteenth-century Italian Etruscheria. Müller characterizes eighteenth-century Etruscheria with some justification as anti-Greek (I, p. 99); so it was, but it was even more anti-Roman, and this aspect is not explicitly mentioned in Müller's polemic. However, Müller's most original point was precisely to indicate, with all due awareness of the difference between Etruscans and Romans, the immense influence of the Etruscans on the religious and political institutions of the Romans in the archaic period, and indeed subsequently for the whole of the time in which Rome remained pagan. The northern origin of the Etruscans had already been upheld by Niebuhr before Müller. Müller's own contribution, the intermixture, in Etruria, of a northern people, the Rasenna, with an oriental people, the Tyrrhenians, even if today it might appear more modern, does not have much bearing on what Müller had to say about the Etruscans as a specific civilization. But it was in the effort of reconstruction, on the basis of an immense body of both ancient and modern data, of the character of the Etruscans in relation to the Romans, that Müller gave more evidence of originality. Müller was more hesitant than Winckelmann, or even Niebuhr, in attributing the similarity between Greeks and Etruscans to common prehistoric elements; his view in essence was that it was the prestige of archaic Greece that helped the Etruscans to find themselves.

It is not surprising to find it explicitly stated by Müller that Scipione Maffei had been superior to all his contemporaries in his assessment of Etruscan civilization (I, p. 353). Maffei had no anti-Roman prejudices. It is also natural that Müller should have referred explicitly to the essay *Della nazione etrusca e degli Itali primitivi* which Maffei had published in the fourth volume (1739) of that diary-like compilation he called his *Osservazioni letterarie*. By indicating this work in particular Müller was implicitly rejecting the earlier *Ragionamento sopra gli Itali primitivi* which Maffei had appended to his *Istoria diplomatica* of 1727. In fact, there was a huge chasm between the 1727 text and that of 1739. In 1727 Maffei, impatient to have his say after the appearance of Dempster's *De Etruria Regali* (1723, but put into circulation only in 1726, according to Maffei himself), had improvized a theory on the origin of the Etruscans as primitive inhabitants of Italy who had emigrated "from Canaan and Moab, and precisely from that part that was watered by the Arnon" (p. 227). He also made Pythagoras an Etruscan, a point to which Müller took particular exception. Twelve years later Maffei was principally concerned with a different problem—the extension of the Etruscans and their civilization in Italy—in a form which already contained in a nutshell many of the points examined by Müller and which in any case came close to his method of interpreting cultures. The Hebrew contacts were now discreetly limited to a brief appendix to which Maffei himself attached little importance (*Osservazioni*, VI, 1740, pp. 161–78), and which Müller seems to overlook. Naturally, between Maffei and Müller came Passeri, Lanzi, and Micali. What is more, as I have already pointed out, Niebuhr had defined his attitude to Micali and his predecessors already in the first edition of his *History*. In the second edition, as Müller himself noted, his interests in the Etruscans and in the peoples of pre-Roman Italy in general had become much more profound. Only a precise comparison of Niebuhr's two editions and the work of Müller (which Niebuhr, as a member of the Berlin Academy which gave the prize to Müller, could have seen already in manuscript) can permit us a more informed assessment of the relationship between them and their eighteenth-century Italian predecessors. For the present, it is enough to have stated the problem of how much Müller owed to them and how much he, with his greater historical and linguistic experience, rejected.

I purposely leave on one side the more linguistic aspect of Müller's studies, which are very much concerned not only with Etruscan but with Osco-Umbrian. Let it be clear that Müller's two contributions to Latin philology, the edition, perhaps of no great importance save for individual emendations, of Varro's *De lingua Latina* (1833), and the edition of Festus which was, and is, epoch-making (1839), are closely connected with his Etrusco-Roman studies. Varro and Festus were for him, and remain for us, essential sources for the reconstruction of the institutional and linguistic world of archaic Rome. In his own way Müller was comparativist and got to know Fr. Bopp quite well in Göttingen around 1820, and speaks about him already in a letter to Tieck of 1821. However, I do not have the impression that he had a clear idea of the implications of the work done by Bopp on the Sanskrit verb (1816) and of the papers to the Berlin Academy which laid the foundations for the *Vergleichende Grammatik* which Bopp began to publish in 1833. Nor do I know how much significance he attached to W. von Humboldt's research on the Basques of 1821, which he naturally knew well. Müller's linguistic method, as applied to Etruscan, Latin, and Osco-Umbrian, needs to be reexamined.

Already with *Die Etrusker* there are signs of the third path trodden by Müller in those years, that of appreciating Greco-Roman art in its entirety and in relation to other Eastern and Western cultures.

The handbook of ancient art, published twice, in 1830 and 1835, and the collection of reproductions of ancient works of art which Müller started in

1832, have for many years been the constant companions of successive generations of scholars. It is easy to lose the sense of novelty that they represent. Perhaps even more than to Eduard Gerhard (1795–1867) we owe to Müller the close unity of philology and archaeology which subsequently, from O. Jahn to K. Robert, remained for generations a feature of the best German scholarship (*cf.* Müller's letter to Gerhard of 1838, *Briefe*, I, p. 344). The aim was to provide students first of all with bibliographical material and factual data for the understanding of ancient art, all of ancient art, including that of the Near East. But at the same time it offered methodological instruction. This led Müller into a conflict with scholars such as Fr. Thiersch on the originality of Greek art in relation to Egyptian (1826–27), and with E. Gerhard on the question of whether the Greek vases found at Vulci were made in Attica or produced locally by Greek artists (on the latter problem Müller shifted his ground between 1831 and 1832 and recognized the possibility that there may have been some local production). Here one could add the papers on the fortifications of Athens at the time of Demosthenes, on the antiquities of Antioch, on the temple of Apollo at Bassae, and other archaeological pieces, like that on the shield of Achilles, prompted by observations made by himself or others in museums or in literary texts. The two essays of 1834 and 1839 on the antiquities of Antioch, based in part on Malalas's Chronicle, are characteristic in their original choice of subject matter. Müller is here taking an interest in Hellenism in Droysen's sense.

All in all, Müller accumulated an unusual degree of archaeological experience, which would have debouched in the planned works on Greek and Italic history and on the history of Athens.

If an untimely death swept away this whole program, another path, the fourth, was still open to him; that of a history of Greek literature to compare with the work of his Göttingen colleague Gervinus on German literature and in the spirit of the renewed criticism of the brothers Schlegel. The opportunity came with an invitation from England to compose a book on Greek literature, which in fact appeared in English translation in 1840. Other chapters were later published posthumously in an edition of the original German text by his brother Eduard. It was the first Greek literary history designed to illustrate the spirit of Greek literature in all its various manifestations: it ended in the middle of the fourth century, with Isocrates. It seemed to be a revolutionary work comparable to Winckelmann's. But the impression that it was a revolutionary work was, in the case of Müller, stronger in England, France, and Italy than in Germany. This raises the problem that more than any other today needs to be clarified, and which I hope someone else will be better able to handle.

Given the evident uselessness of talk of romantic criticism in general, it remains necessary to place Müller against a precise background. Boeckh is obviously part of this background. Between the teacher and the pupil there was continual correspondence, in this case assembled in an exemplary volume. With Boeckh we can explain Müller's interests in institutions and in interpretation. But already Benedetto Bravo has made it clear that if Boeckh depends on the hermeneutics of Schleiermacher and establishes a parental relationship between philosophy and philology, in Müller there is no philosophy behind the philology; here if anywhere philosophy, or rather a philosophy of culture, is transposed to the future as the possible ultimate result of philology. Nor do Müller's concrete interests, in the history of religion and in archaic Greek history, derive from Boeckh. Still less his interest in the history of art. In short, Müller cannot be explained simply by defining him as a disciple of Boeckh.

On the other hand, it is equally impossible to characterize Müller as a pupil of Niebuhr. There is no doubt that the general interest in the reconstruction of an archaic age, if not of Rome then of Greece, is a Niebuhrian legacy. Furthermore, as we have seen, Müller pursued and elaborated on his own account a picture of archaic Italy, and in particular of the Etruscans, based largely on Niebuhrian premises. But Niebuhr's most clearly defined methodological ideas, on the agrarian history of Rome or on popular ballads, do not seem to count for much with the mature Müller. Moreover, there is the elementary fact that even before the first appearance of Müller's work on the Etruscans in 1828, Niebuhr had expressed reservations about the pupil of his friend Boeckh. In a letter of 1825 to the publisher F. C. Perthes, Niebuhr spoke of Müller as learned and full of talent but too hasty and not without weaknesses. Three years later, in letters to Dahlmann and to W. von Humboldt, the lack of sympathy had become outright antipathy. Müller's book on the Etruscans infuriated Niebuhr. He even said to Dahlmann in December 1829 that Müller was his greatest enemy and that his work on the Etruscans contained a series of vicious attacks on him (*Briefe*, III, 1938, p. 503).

To all appearances, W. von Humboldt would seem to have shared Niebuhr's negative judgment of Müller's Etruscans. It remains to be explained why this work should have offended Niebuhr so deeply, all the more so because Müller explained the points of dissent with profound respect in his review of the second edition of Niebuhr's *Roman History* in the *Allgemeine Literatur-Zeitung* of July 1829. But in general it is evident that one cannot expect to find the key to the personality of K. O. Müller by looking toward either Niebuhr or Humboldt.

But what about the brothers Grimm? The brothers Grimm were already known to him personally from 1820, and in the Göttingen years from 1829 to 1837 they became his intimate friends. It is no objection that at the decisive moment of the protest against the violation of the constitution of Hanover Müller did not join in the public outcry with the Seven—that is, the two brothers Grimm, Gervinus, Dahlmann, Ewald, the jurist Albrecht, and the physicist Weber. Müller's hesitations, which I shall not try to explain, were not a matter of disagreement on principle, since a dissertation he wrote at the time, *De exilio*, indicates with clear allusions his sympathy with the friends who were lost in the reaction.

The true difficulty in assessing the relationship between Müller and the brothers Grimm lies elsewhere. When the brothers Grimm arrived in Göttingen in 1829, Müller was already a well-developed personality. At the most one can note, and connect with the presence of the Grimms, an increasing interest on Müller's part in the history of the Greek language, on which he had for some time planned a book; the history of a single language was certainly an idea of the Grimms.

But it is clear that the question of a possible influence of the Grimms on Müller's formation must be put back to the years preceding their arrival at Göttingen, let us say between 1820 and 1829. For me it is not impossible that an influence of the Grimms on Müller might be discernible precisely at the point that was central for Müller, namely the interpretation of the Greek myths as documents characteristic of an age of emigration and colonization. In general, I am inclined to recognize an analogy between Müller and the Grimms in their respective pursuit of Greeks and Germans in their primitive stages by giving a privileged status to their sagas. Müller's Greeks bear a close resemblance, it seems to me, to the Grimms' Germans. And it was Jacob Grimm, as is well known, who boasted that his philosophy was *from* things, not *into* things—"aus den Sachen, nicht in die Sachen"—which could equally have been the motto of K. O. Müller.

Nevertheless, I have reservations. The *Deutsche Mythologie* of J. Grimm dates from 1835, ten years after Müller's *Prolegomena*. Also, the more strictly juridical work of the Grimms, under the influence of Savigny, does not seem to be very close to the method of Müller. I have already observed that K. O. Müller perhaps counts for more outside Germany than in Germany; he was a German for export. Müller's place in the history of German and European culture between the years 1815 and 1840 still does not seem to me to be clear.

For example, it is curious that J. J. Bachofen, who studied at Göttingen in 1837, during the crisis of the "Seven," and knew Müller personally, reacted negatively to his work in Etruscology and art history, and to his rigorous commentary on the *Eumenides*. And yet Müller had prepared the ground for Bachofen in precisely these areas. It is this kind of obscurity that has inspired our seminar.

Essential Bibliography

The *Kleine deutsche Schriften über Religion, Kunst, Sprache,* etc., collected by E. Müller in 2 vols., Breslau, 1847–48; the archaeological writings in *Kunstarchaeologische Werke,* I–V, Berlin, 1873.

A bio-bibliography in the long study included in the foreword to the French translation of the *Greek Literature* by K. Hillebrand, I, Paris, 1865, pp. xvii–ccclxxx. The *Briefwechsel zwischen A. Boeckh und K. O. Müller* was published first, Leipzig, 1883. It was followed by the letters to his parents, *Lebensbild in Briefen an seine Eltern mit dem Tagebuch seiner italienisch-griechischen Reise,* Berlin, 1908; *Briefwechsel zwischen K. O. Müller und L. Schorn,* ed. S. Reiter in *Neue Jahrbücher,* 26, 1910, in several installments; *Aus dem amtlichen und wissenschaftlichen Briefwechsel von C. O. Müller,* ed. O. Kern, Göttingen, 1936; and finally *Briefe aus einem Gelehrtenleben,* already prepared by S. Reiter in 1940, but whose publication was delayed by the death of Reiter, a Jewish professor at the German University in Prague, at the hands of the Nazis in a death camp in 1942; the book, in two volumes, was finally issued in Berlin in 1950.

Note should be taken of the biographical essay by his brother Eduard prefaced to the *Kleine Schriften,* essential for his youthful formation. Otherwise F. Lücke, *Erinnerungen an K.O.M.,* Göttingen, 1841; F. Ranke, *C.O.M.: Ein Lebensbild,* Berlin, 1870; R. Foerster, *O.M.,* Breslau, 1897; Karl Dilthey, *Otfried Müller-Rede,* Göttingen, 1898. Also A. Baumeister in *Allgem. Deutsche Biographie* XXII, 1885, pp. 656–67.

The best critical essays are B. Bravo, *Philologie, histoire, philosophie de l'histoire: Étude sur J. G. Droysen, historien de l'antiquité,* Warsaw–Cracow, 1968, pp. 105–30; and G. Pflug, "Methodik und Hermeneutik bei K. O. Müller," in H. Flashar, ed., *Philologie und Hermeneutik im 19. Jahrhundert,* Göttingen, 1979, pp. 122–40.

On mythology, O. Gruppe, *Geschichte der klassischen Mythologie und Religionsgeschichte,* Leipzig, 1921 (Suppl. to Roscher's *Ausführliches Lexikon*) is still essential. An essay of mine introducing the *Prolegomena* is published in *Annali della Scuola Normale Superiore di Pisa,* 3d ser., XIII, fasc. 3, 1983 [reprinted in *Settimo contributo,* 1984, pp. 271–86]. The *Annali* of Pisa will publish the proceedings of our 1984 seminar on Müller [3d ser., XIV, fasc. 3, 1984].

On the pre-Müller (1770–1820) atmosphere of Göttingen the starting point is L. Marino, *I maestri della Germania,* Turin, 1975. *Cf.* also H. Thiersch, *Göttingen und die Antike,* Göttingen, 1926.

NINETEEN

From Bachofen to Cumont

I

We may well go back to J. J. Bachofen for a few minutes. In 1869, at the age of 54, he finished his book, *Die Sage von Tanaquil*, which indicated a return to that field of early Roman history with which he was most familiar. His theme was still the sexual power of women and matriarchy. But it was confined mainly to Italian archaic history and was made to serve his long-standing polemic against the methods of source criticism of Niebuhr and Mommsen. In 1869 most scholars, including Mommsen, took for granted the existence of an Indo-European group with its social and religious institutions and looked with suspicion at theories of vaguely oriental influences on early Rome: the Etruscans, after K. O. Müller, had lost prestige and appeared only a minor influence on early Rome. Bachofen, who never adopted the rules of the game of Indo-European linguistics, stuck to his notion that there was a direct and vast influence of oriental or Semitic matriarchal ideas on ancient Italy. The main, but by no means exclusive, intermediary was the Etruscan nation. An Etruscan queen in Rome became for Bachofen the representative, almost the symbol, of such oriental matri-archs: Tanaquil. The wife of King Tarquin, she confirmed her role as an oriental matriarch by presiding over the miraculous birth of Servius Tullius and by helping him to become king of Rome. However, Bachofen also main-tained that Roman legend had toned down the oriental traits of Tanaquil and made her acceptable to a patriarchal society. In its Roman garb, the leg-end of Tanaquil represented the transition from matriarchy to patriarchy: the most offensive allusions to sexual promiscuity, what Bachofen called

"From Bachofen to Cumont," Italian translation, *Saggi di storia della religione romana* (1988), pp. 135–49; English original in *Nono contributo* (1992), pp. 593–607. (725)

the "hetaeric" traits, were suppressed. In this transitional stage Tanaquil's story could be related to the strange duties of the wife of the *flamen dialis,* no less strange than the priestly functions of her husband. Bachofen also found an analogy in the story of Aeneas and Dido. According to his interpretation, the ancestor of the Romans, Aeneas, had to run away from a pure oriental matriarch with "hetaeric" traits like Dido. More than that, the whole struggle between Rome and Carthage became to his eyes a duel between patriarchy and matriarchy. By their victory over Carthage the Romans consolidated the superiority of patriarchy. The next step was the destruction of the Temple of Jerusalem in A.D. 70 which, according to Bachofen, made Rome the center of Western patriarchy and the successor of Jerusalem—an interesting admission for a man of Protestant upbringing. To understand the basic evolution of society from matriarchy to patriarchy was for Bachofen the meaning of philological criticism.

As it happened, Mommsen published his interpretation of the legend of Coriolanus while Bachofen was concluding his book on Tanaquil. Mommsen denied any substance to the tradition that Coriolanus had been stopped by his mother and by his wife in a place which became the Temple of Fortuna Muliebris. Bachofen added a special appendix to his volume on Tanaquil to express his contempt for the rationalistic method of Mommsen, who was insensitive to the matriarchal, Etruscan survivals in the legend of Coriolanus. This attack did not help Bachofen. If few took notice of his book on Tanaquil, the silence on his remarks about Mommsen was even more striking: even later independent scholars, such as Gaetano De Sanctis in his *Storia dei Romani,* ignored them. Yet Bachofen had certainly shown that his contemporaries were not paying enough attention to the female figures of Roman archaic tradition. Only in recent years has research on archaic Rome indicated a sense of debt toward Bachofen. It is, however, interesting to note that Bachofen himself was not satisfied with his own results. As soon as he ended the book on Tanaquil, he conceived the idea of rewriting his *Mutterrecht* on the basis of far wider comparative research. Between 1870 and 1880 Bachofen worked frantically to overcome the limitations of a classical scholar who had specialized in Roman law. He knew by then that what he wanted to reach was a stage of the human past which was far more ancient than any classical civilization—either of the Mediterranean or of the Near East. That remote stage seemed to him important for three reasons, which to him were really one: it was a stage entirely dominated by religion; it was a stage in which the sense of death was identical with the recognition of life; and finally it was a stage in which religion, death, and life were related to women—women as mothers, as determinative elements of the social structure, and as symbols not only of birth but of death. In order to pursue that triadic function of women, Bachofen studied documents of civilization and barbarism which were entirely alien to classical scholars. He read as much as he could of Indian and Chinese texts in translation; above all, he went into what was available to him of ethnological literature. As I have already mentioned, he established relations with English and American ethnographers, but his readings went far beyond them. After his death thousands of pages of notes were found testifying to this search.

Bachofen never managed to rewrite his *Mutterrecht* as he had intended, but in 1880 and in 1886 respectively he published two substantial volumes which he called *Antiquarische Briefe vornehmlich zur Kenntniss der ältesten Verwandtschaftsbegriffe* ("Antiquarian Letters Dealing Chiefly with the Earliest Concepts of Family Relations"). The *Briefe* were characteristically dedicated to three friends who had been helping him: one of them was Lewis H. Morgan, who died in 1881. Bachofen himself died about a year after the publication of the second volume, in 1887.

I do not intend to go here into the details of these antiquarian letters, though they are important and hardly well known. Not one of them is translated in the Bollingen Series volume of 1967 of Bachofen's writings, which in its turn is an adaptation of the German selection made by Rudolf Marx in 1926 for Kröners Taschenausgabe. It will be enough to say that the most important contributions are about the relations between brother and sister and between uncle and nephew in various societies. But there is much about the meaning of number eight in all sorts of cultures from Etruria and Greece to China and Central America: eight being the number of completeness (πάντα ὀκτώ, as the Greek saying goes) and apparently also a symbol of reconciliation between matriarchy and patriarchy.

What is interesting to observe is the internal logic of a research which took Bachofen far away from his classical lands and turned him into a universal comparatist. This development had two aspects. The most obvious one was that in order to understand Greco-Roman classics you have to compare them with other civilizations. This was not surprising nor, even less, alarming. The other aspect was that in order to understand Greek and Roman religion you had to understand what in ordinary parlance is not religion—devious aspects of society, types of family organization, and patterns of cosmology. Bachofen was a Roman lawyer and a historian who discovered that he could not understand Roman law and politics without turning to religion, and yet when he had settled on religion he was compelled to pass from classical religion to comparative religion, from comparative religion to comparative sociology, and finally from comparative sociology to the study of patterns of political and intellectual life. In other words, Bachofen moved between religious history and social history. He tried to explain religion through society and society through religion. In this sense he seems to us an exemplary case, and it would not be difficult to show that other great scholars, who consciously or unconsciously followed in his steps, were involved in the same difficulties.

II

James Frazer is an obvious instance. Like Bachofen, who incidentally did not mean very much to him, Frazer was a classical scholar who turned himself into an ethnologist. From ethnology he returned later to classical scholarship in a modified way. While he had started with a commentary on Pausanias's *Description of Greece,* he ended with Ovid's *Fasti.* His search was for a pattern of beliefs which might be considered universal. He thought he had found it in the notion of the dying god—which returns in Christianity—but somehow the idea did not work. He ultimately produced an enormous amount of comparative material but without the center which Bachofen had found in his *Mutterrecht,* in matriarchy.

The least we can say nowadays is that comparison in religion means less to us than it meant to scholars brought up in the nineteenth-century atmosphere of evolution. What we call religion is in itself a culturally conditioned notion—something which is surely appropriate to the Roman situation and consequently to Christianity, but which is difficult to apply to other civilizations, such as Hellenism, Judaism, and Islam, not to speak of what we find in India or China. In classical Athens one is never allowed to forget that poets, philosophers, and doctors intervened to redefine in public and in private the relations between gods and men. They could influence popular assemblies which decided about gods by majority principle as about anything else. In Jerusalem the priestly class was clearly receding while school masters and interpreters of the law were shaping the new institutions, the synagogue and the rabbinic school. It would make little sense to define the sphere of religion, as perceived in Athens or in Jerusalem, as a separate sphere controlled by priests elected by the political community —which was the Roman situation. Whatever comparative research we intend to do, we have first to understand the relations obtaining between gods and men in a given place and time. After an examination of the development of the historiography of religion from antiquity to the nineteenth century, the first and most elementary conclusion is that priority must be given to the research within individual cultures. It follows that when we come near to our own times we must concentrate our attention on the studies concerning specific religions rather than religion in general. In this redirection from the generic to the specific, the case of Roman religion is exemplary just because Roman religion by itself and through its connections with Christianity has acquired a paradigmatic value and has often been uncritically assumed to be the model religion. How Roman religion was interpreted in, say, the last century and how it should be interpreted now is of more than parochial interest. It provides questions for the whole discipline of the science of religion.

At first sight there is little doubt about what Roman religion is or was. In republican Rome there was a body of priests elected by the Roman community which took charge of the relations of the community with the recognized gods. But the community—through its own assemblies and its own elected magistrates (who were not identical with the elected priests)—intervened directly in the relations with the gods in a hundred ways. It will be enough to remind ourselves of the most important: introduction of new gods, building of new temples, acts of divination to ensure that the will of the gods had been properly understood, acts of purification and expiation when things went badly with one or more gods of the city. There were general assumptions in this politically controlled public cult, one of the assumptions being that there is a difference between proper evaluation and therefore proper cult of the gods (*religio*) and improper evaluation and therefore improper cult of the gods (*superstitio*). There was also a whole chain of regulations defining what was right and proper at given moments—which led to the peculiar Roman obsession with the calendar. The most immediate way of studying Roman religion is to take this model of Roman religion and to define its limits more thoroughly. This is basically what was achieved by Georg Wissowa, a pupil of Mommsen, in the book *Religion und Kultus der Römer* which, in its second edition of 1912, has remained an unsurpassed classic. Wissowa tried to define what was the public cult of the Romans of the republican period. He was of course aware of stages of Roman religion. He described the transition from the monarchic to the republican period and from the republican to the imperial period, but this was only an introduction to his real purpose: the systematic description of the official cult of Rome, as it appeared in the late centuries of the Republic. Wissowa's double task was to systematize the findings and to isolate the sphere of the recognized cults in comparison with arbitrary individual initiatives. What Wissowa tried to reconstruct from the evidence was Roman religion as seen by the Roman pontiffs who organized it and controlled it. It is not impossible to find fault with details of Wissowa's organization of the material. For instance, he treated the distinction between *di indigetes* and *di novensides* as a basic criterion for classification of the Roman gods according to the Roman sacred law: *di indigetes* would have been the oldest gods of the Roman religion, *di novensides* later additions to the Roman official cults. Practically no ancient text—including Livy, 8.9.6, quoted as decisive by Wissowa—makes this distinction, and it is very doubtful that in any case *di novensides* means "new gods." There is, however, no question that most of what Wissowa wrote in his book is still valid now.

The real objections come from the limitations of the approach itself. The analysis of Roman republican religion, as given by Wissowa, leaves out any emotional element, any reference to personal religion, and therefore tends to avoid questions about the penetration of foreign cults into Rome when they are not officially registered by public documents. The situation is bound to become even more unsatisfactory in the imperial period, when the impact of provincial cults is strong on Roman religion, and the general religious atmosphere is characterized by personal search for individual improvement and salvation. Though Wissowa was perfectly aware of these features he could not account for them in his systematic treatment. In his introduction he could in fact claim with some truth that by avoiding questions of beliefs and sticking to sacred law he had proved himself a worthy pupil of Mommsen. No doubt, he had extended to Roman religion the juridical approach which Mommsen had used in his exposition of Roman public law. There was also an obvious reluctance on Wissowa's part to compare Roman religion with other religious systems, but here his defense was easier. When he wrote there was no Dumézil to produce an ambitious program of exploration of Roman religion from the point of view of a preexisting Indo-European society: he, Wissowa, was at most affected by Frazer's *Golden Bough.*

III

The two scholars who came to personify contemporary criticism of Wissowa's approach were an Englishman, W. Warde Fowler, and a Belgian who had studied in Germany, Franz Cumont. Warde Fowler reinterpreted Roman republican religion; Franz Cumont, who was granted a much longer period of intellectual activity, created a new picture of Roman imperial religion.

Warde Fowler, a Fellow of Lincoln College, Oxford at the beginning of this century, had a share in the remarkable modernization of English classical studies in which, together with J. Frazer, Jane Harrison, Lewis Richard Farnell, Robert Ranulph Marett, and Gilbert Murray played leading roles. Religion and literature were almost inseparable concerns for these scholars. Rationalistic undertones were controlled by a firm belief in spiritual evolution. Christianity, even in the reverent agnostic Gilbert Murray, was still the natural term of reference. Behind these scholars there were the masters of Anglo-Saxon anthropology such as Edward Burnett Tylor with his *Primitive Culture* in 1871. More recently men like Edward Alexander Westermark, whose *History of Human Marriage* had appeared in London in 1891, had attracted attention. Max Müller died in 1900, but his opponent Andrew Lang survived him by several years. Education was the business of these men, most of whom were Oxford and Cambridge dons, and one is never allowed to forget that their books were meant to educate. Though Fowler's most important book is indisputably *Religious Experience of the Roman People,* which appeared in 1911, and a great deal can still be learned from his first book, *The Roman Festivals of the Period of the Republic* of 1899, there is something to be said for starting with the later book, *Roman Ideas of Deity in the Last Century before the Christian Era* of 1914. It looks now like the testament of the pre–First World War generation. Warde Fowler did not think that the Roman gods were really alive in the first century B.C., nor did he believe that the philosophic efforts of Cicero had contributed to a valid alternative: to begin with, Cicero had not entirely believed in what he was preaching. But Warde Fowler found vitality and future in four directions of Roman religion. The first was the faith in the almost anonymous spirits of the family, of the house, and of the fields who were called *genii, penates, lares,* etc. The second direction was obviously the most sympathetic to Fowler — the predominance of Jupiter as the supreme god, which offered an anticipation, and promise, of monotheism. The third direction was the formulation of cosmic notions, such as Vesta — fire — and Fortuna — luck — which indicated reflection on mysterious and unexpected sides of human life. The fourth direction was the divinization of an individual such as Caesar. The fourth aspect deserves some comment, because the sympathy with which Fowler greets the divinization of Caesar is unexpected. He says: "There was nothing oriental or meretricious about the conception of Divus Julius; this was not a mystery religion and there was nothing mysterious about it. ... It is possible ... that its contribution to the idea of deity was wholesome rather than the contrary" (p. 123). The assumption, made even more explicit in other pages, is that "in the recognition of a divine element in Man which under certain conditions may claim worship from ordinary men, it may be that we should see rather elevation than degeneracy" (p. 134). We know where Warde Fowler was going — toward the monotheism of Christianity. The Romans had derived little advantage from the arrival of all those Greek gods with their mythology. The Romans had been used to divine forces — to *numina* — which had little individuality. The Romans had no feeling for the plastic beauty of the Greek gods. They did not contemplate them. The only exception (according to Fowler) was Scipio Africanus, who every morning entered the temple of Jupiter Capitolinus to meditate in front of the statue of Jupiter. Virgil was dear to Warde Fowler because he liked the country gods — the *di agrestes* —Tellus, Silvanus, the Manes, the Genii. Fowler liked besides Virgil those other Latin writers who followed Virgil in being rather old-fashioned: say, Livy and Tibullus. He had no use for Horace, Ovid, and Propertius in whom he suspected Hellenistic pretensions. Horace's *Carmen saeculare*, observes Warde Fowler, "had been worked in with such pains as to lose all real effect" (p. 153). About Ovid and Propertius he was near contempt: "Though Propertius seems to me to be the chilliest of the Augustan poets in regard to religion, it is with Ovid that we reach the lowest depths of degeneration" (p. 154). Those practical Italians who

had founded the empire had deserved well of religion when they had preferred their archaic traditions to the imports from Greece. By refusing to
revitalize Greek polytheism they contributed to the preparation of Christianity. It is, however, characteristic of the man and of the place that the Fellow of Lincoln College, Oxford in 1914 was not going to say so in explicit
words.

One feature of this interpretation I have already mentioned—the
importance of the conception of *numen*. To understand its central place in
the thought of Warde Fowler one has to turn to his other book on the *Religious Experience of the Roman People*. It is there that Warde Fowler develops
his opinion that *numen* was the true designation of the oldest Roman gods:
it indicated "functional spirits with will power." Such beings were not personal deities. The turning of Roman *numina* into full-fledged personal deities "could not have been completed without the help of the Greeks" (p.
120). This theory of the *numina* was in agreement with theories of contemporary anthropologists. Indeed *numen* was currently considered an equivalent of *mana*, a term which had been introduced from Polynesia to indicate
vague divine powers. Robert Marett, the rector of Exeter College, had been
the main theorizer of *mana* at Oxford. Exactly in 1911 he summed up his
position in the formula: "whatever has *mana* is *taboo*, and whatever is *taboo*
has *mana*." But later he saw a progression from *taboo* to *mana*, from Lent to
Easter. The emphasis on *numina* had found support in the analysis of classical religions by Hermann Usener, who had isolated and defined a category
of "momentary gods," functional gods who operate only once and then disappear. In this view of a *numen*, the *numen* of a god could be increased by an
offering to him; vice versa, a god could be persuaded to use his *numen* in
favor of a mortal being. In other words, the *numen* of a god became an
almost independent source of power for the god when the god became an
almost human being.

Now it is remarkable that while Warde Fowler put such emphasis on the
notion of *numen*, Wissowa was impervious to it. The word *numen* is not to
be found in the index of his book and very seldom in his text. Certainly
the notion of *numen* plays no important part in Wissowa. He would have
agreed with Warde Fowler that the Romans had simple notions and images
of their gods, before the Greeks interfered. A stone stood for Jupiter, a
spear for Mars. But he avoided speaking of *numina*. Later research has
shown that Wissowa's caution was more than justified. We must now doubt
whether *numen* was ever a word of the old Roman religion. In half a page of
a review in the *Journal of Roman Studies* (38, 1948, p. 166) which became
instantly famous, Stefan Weinstock showed that the word *numen* is not
an archaic term. It is not used in old prayers, in the Arval acts, nor in
other archaic and archaizing texts. It is not in Ennius. When it appears, it
means the power of a divinity: *numen* begins to be used to indicate god *sic*

et simpliciter only in Augustus's time. *Numen* was in fact the transmitter of Greek notions to Rome, such as the notion of the *dynamis* of a god. Professor H. J. Rose, who as a pupil of Warde Fowler had held the opposite opinion (*Harvard Theological Review*, 28, 1935, p. 237), tried to save the theory of his teacher, though recognizing the substantial truth of Weinstock's remarks (*Harvard Theological Review*, 44, 1951, pp. 109–20). Given our evidence for early Latin, we can never be certain that the word *numen* was not an archaic Latin word. But as far as we can go it seems that *numen* was never a key word of archaic Roman religion. It is also doubtful whether we can speak of an aniconic stage of Roman religion. True enough, Varro in his pamphlet on Logistoricus, *Curio de cultu deorum*, thought he knew that the Romans for the first 170 years of their existence worshiped their gods without using human images. Varro even compared the ancient Roman cult with the cult without images of the Jews. But the archaeological evidence is the only one which can decide the issue. And the archaeological evidence is at the moment, to say the least, inviting prudence. The decoration of the archaic temple of S. Omobono, discovered in 1938, includes terracotta statues of gods, probably Hercules and Athena, which have been dated between 550 and 525 b.c. (Anna Sommella Mura, *La Parola del Passato*, 32, 1977, p. 124) and compared with analogous products of other places in Latium. Varro has not yet been proved wrong, but the margins are narrowing. What the next archaeological discovery may reveal is anybody's guess.

The issue about *numen* and the aniconic character of primitive Roman religion, though important, is not, however, decisive for Warde Fowler's position in the study of Roman religion. Fowler had a profound understanding of Romans at work both in politics and in religion. He was, for instance, curious about the Roman attitude to divination and wrote some of the most intelligent pages on it in his *Religious Experience of the Roman People*. He clearly saw the "formalisation and gradual secularisation" (p. 307) of divination in Rome. He had Virgil as his poet, and perceptively touched on the possibility that Virgil had Cleopatra in mind when he wrote on Dido in the fourth book of the *Aeneid* (p. 415). Fowler could understand both formalism and mysticism. He knew that a *pontifex maximus* might hold any opinion he pleased about death (p. 387) and yet share the anxiety of a *pater familias* about the ghosts of his dead relatives (p. 85).

IV

While Warde Fowler was creating a new image of Roman religion in Rome —during the Republic—Franz Cumont was busy changing the image of Roman religion in the imperial age. His interest was permanently turned towards the East, towards oriental religions, though he was deeply rooted in the Celtic land, Belgium, where he was born in 1868 and died in 1947.

There were in fact secret conflicts in his personality which are difficult to assess. Never at ease in the religious and linguistic contrasts of his country, he relinquished his chair in the University of Ghent in 1910 and his position as *conservateur* of the Musée du Cinquantenaire in 1912, and passed the rest of his life as a private gentleman between Rome and Paris. Though a pupil of Usener in Bonn about 1888 and also a student in Berlin and Vienna, he kept himself close to French scholarship. His monumental work on Mithras was basically concluded in 1900 and summarized in the *Mystères de Mithra* first published in that year (3d revised edition, 1913). But Mithras remained in his mind for the rest of his life. Mithras symbolized for him the contact of the oriental and of the Greek mind. According to him, Mithraism was a type of cult developed in Persia from contacts with the teachings of Zarathustra. It was later transformed in Babylonia under the influence of Chaldaean astrology. Later still it was turned into a Greek cult for the benefit of the Romans in the first centuries of the empire. Cumont took the words of Nonnos's *Dionysiaca* almost as his motto: Μίθρης, Ἀσσύριος Φαέθων ἐνὶ Περσίδι, "Mithras, an Assyrian Phaethon in Persia" (21.250–51) because it seemed to define the three elements of Mithraism: the Greek, the Chaldaean, and the Iranian. More precisely, the Persian magi combined their theories about gods and immortality with Chaldaean astrology. In their turn the new astrological theories were reinterpreted on Hellenistic soil according to Stoic philosophy. The final product never became popular in Greece proper, but appealed to Roman soldiers and traders and was eventually received with eagerness by Roman aristocrats in search of an alternative to Christianity.

The research on Mithraism therefore indicated to Cumont three possible lines of development. One was, quite simply, the consideration of other oriental cults (such as those of Isis and Jupiter Dolichenus) which like Mithraism became part of Roman paganism. Another line was the study of astrology among Greeks and Romans, and a third was the examination of Roman views of afterlife and immortality. Each of these lines was pursued in innumerable articles and in some synthetical books. The general book on oriental religion, *Les Religions orientales dans le paganisme romain,* appeared first in 1906 and had its fourth and final edition in 1929. *Astrology and Religion among the Greeks and Romans* appeared first in English in 1912, and equally in English Cumont gave out his preliminary sketch on the subject of *After Life in Roman Paganism* (1922). Excavations at Doura Europos kept him busy in the early twenties, with two famous volumes of *Fouilles de Doura-Europos* published in 1926. And two remarkable collections of texts, which were also original interpretations, appeared in rapid succession in 1937 and 1938, one on *L'Égypte des astrologues* and the other, in collaboration with his lifelong friend Joseph Bidez, on *Les Mages hellénisés.* We can here leave aside Cumont's constant interest in Manichaeism which is already evident in a memoir of 1908 and his direction of the corpus of astrological manuscripts. The last period of his life was devoted to basic research on the subject of *After Life*. His book on *Symbolisme funéraire des Romains* appeared in 1942, while the Second World War was at its worst; the final book *Lux Perpetua* appeared in 1949, two years after his death.

According to Cumont, the magi never quite succeeded in harmonizing their original doctrines with Babylonian astrological lore. They kept for themselves the original Mazdaean doctrines concerning the origin and destiny of man and of the world and fed their ordinary followers with astrological doctrines. Thus astrology, through Mithraic propaganda, spread in the Roman Empire and, as Cumont says, "Mithraism is therefore partly responsible for the triumph in the West of this pseudo-science with its errors and terrors." But Mithraism offered more than that, according to Cumont. It offered purification from guilt, a promise of a better life, and some sort of immortality. It also freed the lonely from isolation and gave scope for fulfillment of modest social ambitions by its elaborate hierarchy of degrees of initiation and of administrative responsibilities. On the other hand Mithraism seems to have been a religion for men only: we do not find a woman initiate nor a priestess among the hundreds of inscriptions concerning followers of Mithras. This kept Mithraism, so to say, outside family life and attracted to it soldiers and civil servants. The male character of the Mithraic cult contributed to make Mithras himself a god for the governing class and ultimately a support of imperial power. But there was more than that. The solar nature of Mithras made him a suitable protector of emperors. Clearly or obscurely, the notion of an emperor by the grace of Mithras came to be linked with the fortune of the emperor; and in its turn the emperor's fortune came to be related to the protection of the sun. Always according to Cumont, the triumph of oriental religions was simultaneously the triumph of astral religion. Indeed a Mithraic priest was proclaimed *"studiosus astrologiae"* (*CIL* V.5893) by his epitaph in Milan. In his poem dedicated to the Emperor Tiberius, Manilius combined trust in the power of reason with credulity in predictions from the stars. That Augustus and Tiberius were believers in astrology is considered by Cumont one of the signs of the new times — that is, of the new structure of beliefs. To turn towards absolute monarchy was also to turn towards the support of oriental clergy. The emperor was destined by the stars to hold power and became the image of the sun on earth. He was the *Sol aeternus et invictus*. The emperors who stressed these autocratic pretensions most loudly were also the ones most favorable to oriental cults. The climax was reached by the so-called Syrian emperors and especially by Elagabalus who considered himself the missionary of his native god of Emesa on the edge of the Syrian desert. In 274

Aurelian was still inspired by the same ideals. Cumont was ready to say that Aurelian proclaimed the dethronement of the old Roman idolatry and the accession of Semitic sun-worship.

Astral beliefs were of course behind Aristotle's First Cause, but somehow the philosophers had not been able to attach reality to the abstraction. A poet like Manilius, however abstruse, had come nearer to overcoming the abstraction. "Thrones have perished, peoples passed from dominion to slavery, from captivity to empire, but the same months of the year have always brought up on the horizon the same stars" (*Astron.* 1.495 ff.). The old gods, being associated with the planets and the stars, acquired a new order and a new influence; they are both in time and above time; they are both subordinate to and independent of the greatest god who is also the most important element in life, the sun. If the sun is the regulator, he is also the Mind of the World, *mens mundi,* as Cicero (*Somnium Scipionis* 4) says. According to Cumont the contemplation of the sky was a source of mystical excitement for many people in the Roman Empire. On the one side there was the astronomer Ptolemy, to whom an epigram is attributed saying something like this (*Anth. Pal.* IX.577): "Mortal as I am, I know that I am born for a day, but when I follow the multitude of the stars, my feet no longer touch the earth; I ascend to Zeus himself." On the other side there were the Syrian soldiers of Vespasian who at the battle of Bedriacum in A.D. 69 greeted the rise of the sun with loud shouts.

The attraction of Cumont's research was that it took the student of the Roman state and religion outside the ordinary categories of Roman thought. He wanted to show that the Roman state had been orientalized not only on the surface but in depth, through new religious ideas which came from the East, such as the notion of king or emperor by the grace of God. At the same time, Cumont believed Mithraism had been an alternative to Christianity: he even said that at the end of the third century A.D. Mithraism might have prevailed and become the successor to the old paganism instead of Christianity. If Diocletian had had his way, there would have been no Constantine. Even after Constantine Julian the Apostate still tried to reassert the claims of Mithras against Christ. Cumont also thought, rather speculatively, that the cult of Magna Mater represented a female equivalent to the cult of Mithras. He noticed that in some places, for instance at Ostia, the sanctuaries of Mithras and of the Magna Mater were neighbors.

Cumont was on safer ground when he conjectured that initiation into certain mysteries, like those of Mithras, gave the devotee a foretaste of the bliss of ascending to the stars after death. The ascent of the soul to the stars and its purification midway by the winds in a sort of purgatory *avant la lettre* were described by Cumont in pages of characteristic power. A whole industry developed to ensure a safe passage for the deceased through the malevolent demons. While the religion of the stars was strongly deterministic in principle, it invited speculations and tricks about the best way to enter that kingdom of order and regularity which was the domain of the stars. Between the earthly banquets of the followers of Mithras and the celestial banquets in the kingdom of the gods—or of the stars—there were intermediate, personal stages, on which Franz Cumont was already eloquent in his *Astrology and Religion among the Greeks and Romans*, the lectures of 1912. But what became clear only gradually in the successive work which culminated in the final *Lux Perpetua* of 1949 is the complex structure of these intermediate stages. First of all, there was never a definite alternative between the more primitive notion of the dead collected under the earth and the more advanced notion of the dead transferred to the sky. Secondly, there was uncertainty about the immateriality of the souls of the individuals. When boats, horses, eagles, even cars were deemed to transfer the deserving souls from the earth to the stars, it could not be immediately obvious that the souls were weightless spiritual beings only anxious to join the superior spheres. Even more acute was the contradiction between astral determinism and individual freedom. If the individual destiny was determined by stars, how could an individual be considered guilty? Astral determinism made it also difficult or impossible to say that an individual had died before his time. Yet parents and lovers went on grieving about premature deaths. We can see something of the mental confusion in a poet who normally was not mentally confused—Virgil—when he classified as dead before their time children, suicides, warriors, and those condemned to death. Deaths of children and suicides of adults were indeed problems. Even Plotinus had no entirely clear ideas about suicide.

One could go on summarizing what Franz Cumont decided to call "les religions orientales dans le paganisme romain." It was a limited picture of a limited sector of the Roman Empire: by definition it left out, as I have said, the peculiar contributions of the Celtic world from which he, Franz Cumont, had come; and he never cared much about Africa. Now it is also easy to see that Cumont relied too much on generic definitions about spiritual weakness and spiritual fortitude. Inevitably he has irritated scholars brought up in a different intellectual climate. Such an able student of paganism in the Roman Empire as Ramsay MacMullen cannot conceal his lack of sympathy, which borders on contempt, for Cumont's studies.

All that needs to be said at this point is that it would be a pity if younger students were discouraged from reading either Warde Fowler or Cumont because these authors brought into their research the concerns of gentlemen educated towards the end of the nineteenth century. Warde Fowler soon found his favorite poet in Virgil. Cumont, more slowly perhaps, but after a good beginning with Philo, retreated into the Neoplatonism of Plotinus and of Julian the Apostate; he may even have returned to his ancestral

Catholicism before he died. Both Warde Fowler and Cumont were trying
to make sense of a stratified world of the past with which they were familiar
from their early school-days and which they felt to be not very different
from their own world. As far as religion went, they recognized the continuity from the Roman religion to the Christian religion, and they were
perhaps not quite sure at which point of this continuity they would place
themselves. This deserves to be emphasized, because historically it was an
advantage. As I said at the beginning of these lectures and repeat at their
conclusion, there is no difficulty in speaking about religion when we talk
about Roman religion or Christian religion. With the Romans there was a
zone of daily life which could be defined as *religio*. This zone was kept well
defined, though differently defined, by Christian religion. Other civilizations, including Greek and Jewish civilizations, are difficult to accommo-
date in terms of religion. European civilization before World War I could
still be accommodated under the notion of religion. This helped Warde
Fowler and Cumont. Whether the world civilization emerging from World
War II can help us in the same task remains to be ascertained.

INDEX

Aarsleff, Hans, 288
Abbagnano, N., 88
Adcock, Frank, vii
Aegina, 304, 306
Aelius Aristides, ix
Aeneas, 241, 299–301, 316
Aeneid, 299–301, 324
Aeschylus, 152–53, 180, 183–85 *passim,* 308
Aetna, 277
Agrarian history, 35, 37, 39, 66, 244–50,
   295; German, 236, 238, 244; Indian,
   232–33; Roman, 35, 37, 224–36, 238,
   243, 245, 248–51, 295, 299, 312
Alcaeus of Messene, 257
Alexander the Great, 18, 39, 109, 147–50
   passim, 152, 216
Alföldi, A., 36
Alibrandi, Ilario, 245
Allen, Frederick, 259
Altheim, F., 36
Amari, M., 207
Ambrosia, 291–92
Androtion, 63
Anthropology, xvi, 66, 213, 215, 216, 265,
   320
Anti-Semitism, xiv, 104, 109, 115–16,
   131–32, 205
Antoni, Carlo, 88
Antonius Julianus, 134
Antony, Mark, 77
Apollonius Rhodius, 148
Apollonius of Tyana, 221
Appian, 189, 227, 228, 231

Arab world, 25, 28, 148, 190, 212, 214,
   269–70. *See also* Islam
Arangio-Ruiz, Vincenzo, 246–47
d'Arbois de Jubainville, H., 167
Archaeology, 25, 26, 35–36, 65, 68, 77, 309,
   311, 323
Archaic history, 65, 106–9, 111, 113, 215,
   303, 308–12, 315–18; Greek, 60, 106–9,
   111, 117, 298, 309; Roman, 65–66, 118,
   214, 224–26, 240, 241, 247–50, 296–99,
   302, 309, 310, 315–16, 323
Architecture, 198–201 *passim*
Ardigò, Roberto, 85
Ariès, Philippe, 243
Aristagoras, 68
Aristocracy, 50, 74–76, 236, 241, 242, 295,
   298. *See also* Patricians
Aristophanes, 152, 153, 259
Aristotle, 28, 59, 60, 125, 128, 129, 131–34,
   162, 181, 256, 265, 272, 326
Arnold, Matthew, 141
Arnold, Thomas, 20, 198–200 *passim*
Arrighetti, Graziano, 254
Art, 8, 305, 310–12; Greek, 25, 27, 35–36,
   38, 49, 50, 110, 153, 305, 311
Aryans, 88, 169, 170, 176, 202–4 *passim,*
   206, 237, 240, 241, 244
Astrology/astronomy, 259, 304–7, 324
Athanasius, 189, 192, 277, 279
Athenagoras, 188, 276
Athens, 17, 21, 23–25, 27, 59–62 *passim,* 68,
   101–2, 109, 118, 136, 137, 148, 153, 163,
   177n.11, 242, 307, 311, 318